W9-BVI-588

Resistance

Resistance

the political autobiography of

GEORGES BIDAULT

Translated from the French by Marianne Sinclair

Weidenfeld and Nicolson
5 Winsley Street London W1

© 1965 by Georges Bidault and Les Presses du Siècle, Paris

English translation © 1967 by George Weidenfeld and Nicolson Ltd

First published in France under the title *D'une résistance à l'autre*

Made and Printed in Great Britain by
Morrison and Gibb Limited, London and Edinburgh

Contents

Appendices

Illustrations

(*All photographs provided by Keystone Press, Paris and London*)

Abbreviations

CED: *Communeauté Européenne de Défense* – a project for a European defence community that would have been an extension of NATO.

CGT: *Confédération Générale de Travail* – French Trade Union Federation, mostly Communist since 1947.

CNR: *Conseil National de la Résistance* – a loose association of all the French home Resistance groups that recognized the authority of de Gaulle.

COMAC: *Comité d'Action Militaire* – military action committee of the CNR.

FFI: *Forces Françaises de l'Intérieur* – French Forces of the Interior.

FLN: *Front de Libération Nationale* – Algerian guerrilla and liberation organization that started the Algerian war of independence against France.

FTP: *Francs-Tireurs et Partisans* – the guerrilla organization of the wartime French Front National.

MRP: *Mouvement Républicain Populaire* – Christian Democratic Party founded after the Liberation by Georges Bidault.

MUR: *Mouvements Unis de la Résistance* – amalgamated Resistance movements, mostly non-Communist, originally in Vichy France.

OAS: *Organisation Armée Secrète* – guerrilla and terrorist organization started by General Salan towards the end of the war in Algeria, directed against the FLN and against the French home government.

OCM: *Organisation Civile et Militaire* – non-Communist Resistance organization.

ORA: *Organisation de Résistance de l'Armée* – Second World War army Resistance movement.

PSU: *Parti Socialiste Unifié* – left-wing militant splinter-group of the Socialist Party, founded by Mendès-France.

RPF: *Rassemblement du Peuple Français* – the 'mass movement' founded by de Gaulle in 1947, which lasted until 1953.

SFIO: *Section Française de l'Internationale Ouvrière* – the French Socialist Party, one of the largest and most powerful parties in France.

UDSR: *Union Démocratique et Socialiste de la Résistance.*

UNR: *Union pour la Nouvelle République* – French party which unites all the various elements once grouped together under de Gaulle's RPF.

URD: *Union Républicaine Démocratique* – French centrist party.

*'Quand je cesserai
de m'indigner
je commencerai
ma vieillesse'*
(André Gide – *Journal*, 3 December 1909)

Preface

This book is my testimony and even if it holds no other interest it will still be the testimony of a man who practises what he preaches at a time when petty conformity is known as 'common sense' or 'sense of history', in a country where politics have degenerated to the level of petty squabbles now that Frenchmen no longer have any faith in their country and refuse to take any risks or to endanger their way of life.

I undertook risks because I wanted to keep certain commitments. I do not care if some people frown on what I did, any more than I care about being slandered by the stupid, contemptible men who attack me for my beliefs although these cannot be altered by anyone or by anything. The insults heaped upon me by countless newspapers and in many a parliament have no effect on me because I am positive that things will change. Although certain attacks were even more odious than I could ever have imagined, I still believe that those right-minded men who have refused to let themselves be corrupted will hear me even from this distance and in spite of my temporary isolation. I know that they will listen to the voice of a man who denounces the forces of reaction and who refuses to cooperate with these forces in their work of destruction.

I intend to talk not only about the past but also about the present and the future. I will go over the recent events which led to the great Algerian tragedy that I was not able to avert, any more than I was able to prevent its author from being praised for destroying what he had sworn to defend. My faith in France's moral and political re-awakening remains as strong as ever; in this book, I hope to discuss France's future without bringing up the trite platitudes and old saws which make up most of today's 'political thought', 'political science', and 'political life' when in fact all genuine thought, science, life and politics have been abolished. I wish to propose an alternative to our present, worn-out system in which action and even thought have lost their place of honour.

France's present situation is inextricably bound up with the fate of the world in general. Right now, hypocrisy and lies reign supreme, while the truth and the genuine rights of men are being abolished in the name of 'realism' and 'democracy'. If this state of affairs goes on much longer, the entire human race will be in danger; but I firmly believe that, before the worst happens, before our most cherished moral and spiritual values are destroyed everywhere, a great wave of reform will sweep the world and will eliminate the old habits of conformity, weakness and cowardice while vigorously reasserting man's eternal need for justice and truth.

I also hope my personal recollections of past events will be of interest to those who enjoy reading books on the last twenty years. Some of these books are honest, but most of them are not. But I must warn my readers that I have not written my memoirs; I had neither the means nor the inclination for such an undertaking. The dangers and hardships of clandestine life and exile made it impossible to travel with all the books and documents I would have needed. Those who, in circumstances similar to mine, were able to take their books and papers with them were protected, unlike me. I am neither boasting nor complaining of the fact that I acted alone and made all my own decisions without any help. On the contrary, as those who owed me a great deal did all they could to forget the fact, I am very glad that it never occurred to me to ask them for anything; yet it is painful to know, even in advance, what small hearts most great men have when actually put to the test and to realize that they are actually proud of despising those who once helped them. But after the way I have been treated, I feel completely free of any obligations, thanks to them, and free of grudges, thanks to myself.

Writing memoirs is a somewhat risky undertaking at the best of times, and the factual accuracy, the disinterestedness, the fairness and integrity of the author are often doubtful. Knowing this, I prefer not to follow in the footsteps of certain well-known contemporaries and predecessors; their main concern was to show their past conduct in the most favourable light in order to further their future careers.

To some extent, this criticism can be levied against the memoirs of both Winston Churchill and General de Gaulle however well-written and important. They *are* important, especially because they tell us so much about their authors, who actually did write most of their memoirs personally, which is unusual.

Sir Winston Churchill wrote two sets of memoirs, one about each

World War. This great man, who wrote for pleasure or from necessity, had already described the role he played during the First
World War; this account would be considered outstanding and the
very best example of its sort if Churchill had not surpassed himself
in his second attempt at writing history and autobiography. Once
again, the *Odyssey* was greater than the *Iliad*. Today, people read
only Churchill's second set of memoirs and they are indeed a mag-
nificently written collection of documents and memories. And yet
they were published just when Churchill was fighting to get back
to power, after being most unjustly discarded during the Potsdam
conference. I suppose this is why there are certain omissions or
hesitations in his otherwise admirable work: the author was writing
about the past, but he also kept in mind his present struggles,
which, as we know, were victorious.

De Gaulle wrote his memoirs during his years of isolation and
exile at Colombey-les-Deux-Eglises, and the first two volumes are
full of bitterness and regrets. But the General was back at the
Elysée as the great 'arbiter' and 'guide' of France by the time the
third and last volume of his memoirs was published. I have often
wondered if an earlier version of this volume exists which de Gaulle
toned down after the events of 1959 because, although he shows
just as much arrogance in this book as in the previous two, he does
speak more leniently of those men he chooses to remember and he
also shows greater restraint. Whether this is so or not, it was the
first time in recorded history that the leader of a nation, in possession of full powers, published a book dealing with contemporary
events. Julius Caesar did write *The Gallic Wars*, but he had not yet
reached the summit and it was in order to do so that he wrote his
work.

Another widespread practice is for civilians or career officers who
are not too well-educated to give a few selected documents and a
general idea of what they want to a trusted aide who has no particular opinions of his own and who writes the book for them. We
have had a remarkable example of this in the United States only
recently; but then everybody knows that a good Chief Commander
does not have to be very learned to win battles, or even much of a
thinker to win elections just as long as he is very popular.

I decided not to use any of the methods I have described above.
I have certainly not yet given up the struggle, and I believe that
a man has to have a certain measure of serenity and even of

renunciation before he can write honestly about himself. Otherwise, his memoirs will only be an ill-disguised attempt at self-justification. Besides, all I have are my memories and the few papers, books and newspapers which I either managed to keep or to recover, or which were given to me by the new friends who have made up to me for the loss of the old, who were not worth regretting anyway. But these few documents cannot take the place of all those I lost in the course of duty or which were mislaid. I have never felt their loss more keenly than now.

I do not have enough papers in my possession today to draw up a detailed picture of so many events or to describe all the men who played various roles in these events. I am not even in a position to criticize my own past conduct wherever I feel that it was open to criticism, although I would rather have enjoyed this novel approach especially now that so many men are writing volumes of self-justification. But I will try to set down certain fundamental truths, to give a general picture of most recent events, to remind some men of what they prefer to forget and to explain what I think ought to be done in the future.

I think that those who read this book will agree that I am in good faith. Anyway, I ask my readers to judge for themselves and to make up their minds and decide whether they find me honest or not. I am not trying to say that I have no strong passions, but I hope that I was able to keep my emotions under control. Whenever I had a doubt and had to choose between two expressions, I always chose the milder one. I have not imitated Tacitus in this, even though we live in an age which cries out for the venom of his pen.

Hypocrisy and deceit reign supreme in this world of ours; lies are only too easy to perpetrate because people want to be deceived. Lies are soothing to hear and the truth often disturbing. So that if a man wants to be heard at all, he has to restrain his language. You would think it was only fair if those who say whatever they please were forced to listen to the other side as well; but we live in an age of accomplices who are recruited even from the ranks of those who claim to be the opposition. For this reason, I have tried to sound as moderate as I could, which is always the best policy. Besides, the facts speak for themselves; I do not need to raise my voice. All I ask my reader to do is to pay attention to the words of a man who is not afraid of speaking the truth and who refuses to grovel.

According to the experts, the present régime in France shows every sign of stability. They point out the fact that the régime has popular support, that it has no critics, that the newspapers sing its praises and that the men who sit in Parliament are so carefully selected and so well paid that they do whatever the government asks them to do. Besides, the majority is always servile and those who pretend to be against the government are cowards. The great political experts claim that, because of all these factors, the situation cannot possibly change. Of course, these experts are afraid of getting into trouble if they say anything else, so that they prefer to go along with the rest. Those same experts used to spend their whole time proclaiming that things would have to change; they now spend their time repeating with equal fervour, 'Let us hope things never change.' For a very long time, the foreign press also voiced this hope, praised the great guide and vilified his only genuine opponents. These journalists said and often genuinely believed that the Gaullists were reasonable and progressive while those who had kept their word were terrible criminals and adventurers, however good their past reputations and however flimsy or absurd the charges which were later brought against them. They considered that any man in his right mind would jump on the splendid Gaullist bandwagon, even if this meant that he would have to go back on his word.

A couple of years ago, even a few months ago, they still said this; but just when the French people seemed to have totally abdicated, those who refused to let the wool be pulled over their eyes began to notice that the régime, far from being stable and good, was in fact precarious and bad.

Time passes quickly. In 1940, de Gaulle was called a lunatic and a criminal and was treated with the greatest suspicion by Roosevelt, Churchill and even Stalin. For a very long time, de Gaulle and his men were dismissed as minor figures, and they were treated accordingly. Later, the lunatic and criminal of 1940 became the wise man of 1962 and even 1965. But we shall see about 1966; things change very fast.

What if the majority was wrong both times? Perhaps the man of 1940 was wise when most Frenchmen called him a madman and most foreigners took him for an adventurer without prospects. And perhaps the man they all admire and fear today actually deserves the reputation they gave him twenty-five years ago. The people of France, their allies and even their enemies are beginning to wonder if they have not been wrong a second time. Of course, when I say Frenchmen I must remember that over half of all those who used to call themselves that now call themselves something else. And when I say allies and enemies, I must not forget that one of our chief problems is to decide which of our allies can still be considered friendly towards us, and which of our enemies hostile, now that France lavishes so much care on alienating its traditional allies and on making overtures to its traditional enemies.

I will also describe my life in exile and the way in which political refugees are treated today; but I want to tell those men who remember our cause that, however painful or long my exile may be, my position remains unaltered. I have continued our work as best I could and I am so far away only because I could do nothing in France or in many another country which celebrated the fifteenth anniversary of the Rights of Man but forgot the rights of the individual.

I have had to come to terms with life in exile and to learn that a sacrifice can be its own reward. Over a century ago, Lamennais wrote a revolutionary book called *Paroles d'un Croyant* in which he said 'the man in exile is always alone'. Lamennais suffered for his beliefs, but he was never forced to go into exile so that he did not know, as I now know, that life in exile has its consolations and that a man in exile makes new friends in foreign lands who console him for the loss of disloyal friends, as well as for the loss of those loyal ones he had to leave behind and who are forced to keep silent.

Besides, when people are kind (and most are; it is usually governments which are unkind), a man in exile does not find it too hard to wait for the day when his countrymen will come to their senses so that he can take up the struggle again where he left off.

But even if exile was nothing but pain, the bitterness of it would still be tempered by certain compensations quite independently of the good effects suffering usually has on the character. Exile gives a man time to think things out, and distance, however disagreeable in other respects, does make him see things more clearly. A man in exile sees everything from a new, unexpected angle, so that his perspectives change. He may suffer from his expatriation, but he also finds it easier to simplify, to clarify his own fundamental position, a task which he may have found almost impossible to do when the daily complications and struggles of his past life interfered with his grasp of essentials. The fact that he is forced to live in a foreign country does not mean that he loses interest in his own, far from it; but it does give him a clearer, more complete picture of the situation.

Life is short, and the man in exile may well be in a hurry to get back to work and to dedicate himself once again to the responsibilities of public life. But then he knows that when this happens he will have so little leisure that he ought to seize this opportunity to think things out clearly and to meditate. He may not be in a position to act and he may find this very frustrating, but he has the future to think of as well as the present. At least he can meditate during those long boring days of solitude which give him ample time to judge the present and to prepare for the future.

In fact, time to think is the one thing politicians never have. They are always too rushed to make plans for the future, except for the very greatest among them who always find time to think out grand designs, however pressing their daily schedules. But nations, governments and individuals deafen the average politician with their demands. He has to keep track of everything, successes, failures, projects, and he has to improvise from day to day. It has always been that way and the perpetual chaos of politics has ruined many a reputation, killed many a hope.

But today, it is even worse. Methods of communication have improved so much and have become so rapid that they have become a positive threat to understanding. In the old days, men did not know very much but now there are so many ways to get information, we have access to such quantities of news that our minds cannot register so many facts. We understand contemporary events not much better than we used to understand them in the past. In those days, we knew too little, and what we learned was often doubtful or out of date so that we had to speculate, to make wild guesses and to stumble about in the dark. Today, we no longer walk in the dark but we are blinded by an excess of light.

A very few men still insist on setting aside some time for meditation and leisure in which to reconsider their past actions and to work out plans for the future; but most of the great and powerful spend all their time watching television, listening to the radio, speaking on the phone and sending or receiving telegrams, without even mentioning the time they spend reading the newspapers. Little did Gutenberg guess that, some day, whole forests would be cut down daily because of his invention. Life for such men is an endless round of getting information, sessions, conversations, interviews, lunches, dinners, cocktails, ballets, military parades, intrigues, secret meetings with people who have nothing to say and who waste their time or with those who do have something to say but who prefer to keep it to themselves. By the time evening comes, these men are so confused by all they have heard and read during the day that everything becomes mixed up in their heads. While they manage to take a brief rest, they know that more telegrams are being sent, more phones ringing, more printing presses operating, more governments meeting to create more problems that will have to be settled tomorrow along with all those left over from yesterday.

After a time, life becomes a sort of continual advance to the rear. Desks become so littered with telephones, so snowed under by papers that only the most energetic or irresponsible of men could get through this work in a day. In the end, politicians give up; they hop on to a plane and try to settle issues through talks and conferences rather than through papers and memoranda. But conferences only add to the volume of all the previous records. Politicians then travel further and further, attend more and more conferences until they no longer have the time to study any of those records which have become so thick that the bravest, most resolute man in the world would be put off by them. As a result, world politics become an incoherent maze of improvisation and contradictions. The only people who have some idea of what is going on are those active but mysterious, almost anonymous, men known as experts. They have a certain understanding of the situation and they can just follow the slender thread of logic which runs through all those vague agreements and baited proposals. They are like navigators on the unchartered seas of diplomacy and they have to try and avoid the reefs although they often have neither maps nor compasses.

Today, the skies are full of planes carrying statesmen from one country to the next. These statesmen are so rarely at home that no one knows when and where they find time to work. Even the stolid Chinese are beginning to adopt the practice of rushing about from country to country. The newest nations with the tiniest populations and practically no administration spend a great deal of their budget on keeping Embassies abroad. Experienced and inexperienced diplomats rub shoulders in a hundred capitals, both ancient and recent, writing out reports which will disappear into the bottomless pit of the bureaucratic machine, destined never to be read until perhaps, in a hundred years' time, some historian uses them to write his thesis. The ambassadors are supposed to do the negotiating and the ministers should come in only right at the end to conclude the deal. But ministers are too impatient to wait that long; they prefer to do the travelling and the talking themselves.

Politicians have many responsibilities; if they are called upon to make genuine decisions which are not merely expedient or dictated by the need to impress or to annoy others, their choices may be of vital importance. But I cannot imagine where they find the time to go over problems, to calculate, to look up the facts.

What they do is to read condensed versions of all the facts they are supposed to know and digests of everything that is going on in the world. Fifty years ago, Marshal Joffre refused to read reports that were longer than one page; he would turn over the page first to make sure there was nothing written on the back. General Eisenhower had much the same views on the virtues of brevity although he is inferior to Joffre in all other respects. I won't mention the names of other famous men who do the same thing but who hide it better; some day, the world will find out their secret. Men like Briand hated reading; there are some who prefer to let others do the reading for them instead of finding out the facts for themselves.

And yet all those men who find no time to read always seem to find the time to talk. They hold press conferences, they make statements the moment they step down from the plane, they start negotiating on arrival and when that is over they leave as fast as they can, announce the results, and immediately set off again for yet another conference.

At least the Communist and authoritarian régimes have kept the right to speak only when they wish to say something precise. The free nations, or those which claim to be free, believe that the more they talk the more important they will sound. It is a dangerous game because a man who never stops talking must sooner or later say things which are both useless and stupid. If you don't believe me, open any newspaper. But I grant you that there are a few men who keep a solemn, majestic silence to hide their bad temper or their total emptiness.

Then when do all those men sit at a table to work, to think things out, to try and understand, to weigh the pros and cons of a given problem? We might well ask. I suppose they have to be in retirement or in exile before they can find the time. I chose exile myself because the situation had made it impossible for me to fight for my beliefs in France. I preferred to leave my country and even to keep silent temporarily rather than to give up my convictions.

I have done my duty and said what I had to say in this book. I would have liked to use the words 'I' and 'me' less often, but this would have been difficult because I talk about my own past so much and because the solutions which I propose to my country-men are all my own. Besides, I have had so many responsibilities in my lifetime which I could not share with anyone that I refuse to hide now behind a screen of vague generalizations, as most politicians like to do. As for using the royal 'we' or the third person when writing about myself, I prefer to leave that sort of solemn nonsense to those who do not find it ridiculous.

Part 1

1940-5

1

The 1940 Defeat /
My Clandestine Life /
Jean Moulin /
The CNR

From the very start the Resistance was a question of outlook, perhaps, even more, of character. It had nothing in common with the
spirit of rebellion against just laws and order that agitates men who
cannot come to terms with society. The Resistance was faithful to
all the great principles for which men have lived and, when necessary, died. The Resistance was a refusal to compromise.

When a man feels this way, he cannot change without going back
on the past and on what he was. His motives for running great
risks become suspect from the day that he decides not to run them
any longer and submit. Disillusioning as it may be for anyone who
wants to admire his fellow men, I must admit that many individuals got mixed up with Resistance movements by accident; they
were young or they fell under somebody's influence. But the fact
that you followed a man once is no excuse for following him again
when he sets off in the opposite direction. The first journey was
full of dangers, the second can be made in the comfort of a government limousine. We Resistance fighters had no such luxuries when
we fought for France; we expected no rewards. We did not have
'ushers', 'telephones', 'gilded mouldings' or any of those worthless
honours valued so highly by some today.

I have never given up struggling over issues I consider vital, and
I feel that my basic position has not altered since the war. Both
then and now, French and Christian civilizations were threatened,

and if they disappeared, life would no longer be worth living. When
Hitler was in Prague, Stalin was not our enemy. Now that Stalin
or his successors are in Prague, the danger is not Fascism or what
remains of it, but Communism.

It would be pleasant if Europe stretched 'from the Atlantic to
the Urals', as I said myself in 1947 when we were making an all-out
effort to bridge the gap between East and West. The men who
attacked me for using that expression then, use it themselves today,
although any hope of bridging the gap has long since vanished,
especially now that France is trying to do the job single-handed.
Such a hope appears even less realistic when it involves on the one
hand welcoming the Communist split, and on the other trying to
drive the *troika* of Russia, Europe, and Peking.

But in that troubled year of 1947, nothing was definite, and I did
all I could to bring about an understanding with Russia; I even
tried to deal with the French Communists during the war, when
the real danger was Hitler and Fascism. Yes, I did cooperate with
the Communists during the war. It was not always easy and there
were many complications. If it was sometimes entertaining it was
never exactly restful. In the second volume of his war memoirs, de
Gaulle blamed me for being too easy-going with the Communists.
He wrote:

Morally it was to de Gaulle that they pledged themselves in the
underground struggle, while practically, in regard to the conditions of
life in the maquis, the raids, the sabotage, the smuggling of arms, the
transmitting of information – operations necessarily carried out on a
small scale – they merely followed their group leaders. On the level of
committees, political influences and slogans, matters were not so simple.
Although the political elements agreed to set aside their ambitions to a
certain extent in the heat of the battle, they did not renounce them
altogether, especially when they glimpsed, as the ordeal neared its end,
the chance of gaining power. The personality of Moulin, who had been
delegated and backed by me directly, enabled him to unite and control
these factions. Now that he was dead, certain individuals would be
inclined to play their own hands more actively.

This was to be the case first of all with the Communists. The
National Council of the Resistance aimed at acquiring a majority and
making it a sovereign body, theoretically pledged to my government but
qualified to act on its own and for its own advantage. It would then be
possible to make use of the Council to carry out those activities, to put
in office those authorities, to formulate those programmes and, perhaps,

to seize those powers thanks to which, in the shake-up of the liberation, the future would be theirs.

. . . the composition of my delegation favoured the Communists in the National Council of the Resistance. They managed to bring it about that, of its fifteen members, five were openly or secretly party members. The Council, on its own authority decided to give itself a president and elected Georges Bidault. As an eminent resistance leader, having in the highest degree the taste and the gift for political life, well known before the war for his talent as a journalist and his influence among the Christian Democrats, and ambitious to see this little group become a great party with himself at its head, he willingly accepted the position he was offered and assumed its risks. One of these, and not the least, was to find himself overpowered at the very heart of this Areopagus by a disciplined group experienced in revolutionary action and excelling in the use of conflict as well as of camaraderie. I soon had indication of this group's encroachments, of the bitterness its pressures involved for Georges Bidault, of the obstacles of its making which I was soon to find in my path. The council made known, in fact, that since its plenary sessions were necessarily exceptional it was delegating its power to a board of four members, of which two were Communists, and instituting an 'Action Committee', dominated by party members, to deal with military questions.

I would have given anything to know the secret of handling Communists, while leading a clandestine existence. I did not have the Compagnies Républicaines de Sécurité at my disposal; but I did have the Gestapo and the *milice* at my heels. The Resistance groups were all infiltrated by Communist agents, who carefully concealed their CP membership. They found it easy to deceive their colleagues, for many were fine men, popular because they were brave and active. When a man is in exile like de Gaulle, even when he is not an outlaw in his own country, he sees men and events only from a distance, so that he makes errors of judgement.

For example, we were not four but five at the CNR bureau, and only one of our members was a Communist. One trade unionist only became a Communist after the Liberation. At the time, he was on such bad terms with the CGT that I got three letters from the organization directed by Benoît Frachon, accusing our member of stealing funds. Emmanuel d'Astier de La Vigerie had much the same political affiliations as this member, and this did not prevent de Gaulle from including him in the Algiers Committee then, or in the Elysée today. Besides, how could the CNR or the COMAC

exclude Communists, or men who later became so, when the
Resistance movements sent them to us as their representatives, and
they themselves carefully hid the fact that they were members of
the CP?

I did have to walk very carefully, watching every step; but the
Communist revolt that everyone was afraid of never took place.
Even de Gaulle had thought it would happen, when he first came
to Paris; he made his fears clear enough during his first government sessions. Everybody was convinced that revolution was imminent. Obviously, the presence of the 'Anglo-Saxon' forces made
the Communists decide not to risk it. But another reason was that
even at that time the odds against were too long. We had done our
work well.

In August 1958, André Malraux and I were both speakers at an
anniversary celebration of the Liberation of Paris. M. Michelet,
who was then my friend, had asked me not to let the Communists
monopolize the occasion. He even told me that de Gaulle would be
present. In fact, the General was in Tananarive that day. With that
charged sombre eloquence of his, Malraux called out to the ex-
Resistance fighters, 'You fought against Hell.' 'Watch out!' I
replied, 'Hell is not always in the same place.'

Some people identify the Resistance with anti-Fascism. But if
there are Fascists in France today, they are de Gaulle's men, who
claim to be the representatives of democracy and of republican
institutions, as they rally around the self-appointed 'Guide of the
Nation'. And what about their 'internment centres', their press-
sanctions, their wiles, their use of force and intimidation and
bribery? For years, only cheers, at first spontaneous and later
forced, have broken the silence. Old Clemenceau, who, God knows,
did not take criticism well himself especially when he was not sure
of victory, used to say, 'Honour to the nation in which men speak
out, and shame on the nation in which men are silent.'

Under de Gaulle, France has become a nation where men keep
silent. I spoke in the General's name when the Vichy government
tried to silence our voices; at that time, it was still possible, although
dangerous, to write for the secret press. There were a lot of clandestine newspapers, although nothing like as many as de Gaulle
claimed in his War Memoirs when he said: '*Franc Tireur*, *Combat*,
Résistance, and *Défense de la France* reached a total of 600,000 a
day.' The surprising thing about this wild exaggeration is that de

Gaulle also gives the lowest estimate I have ever read of Resistance fighters killed (20,000) and deported (50,000). Today, de Gaulle's police, including its unofficial branches, and the terror that reigns everywhere, make it impossible for people to say what they like. When they speak their mind openly, they are punished, and when they write, their newspapers are seized. Publishing clandestine newspapers is harder and just as dangerous now as it ever was. But history will be the judge.

The justice of history has nothing in common with the so-called 'wind of history'.* Fatalists invented the term to justify their cowardice, to worship a man just because he is in power, and to follow his government blindly just because he happens to have created or inherited it. The wind of history also means coming to terms with the century, getting along from day to day, in other words agreeing with Ben Bella and with non-neutral neutralism and with the men who want to turn Angola into a second or a third Congo with more to come. The wind of history means that everything is for the best in the best of all possible worlds, just as long as we adapt ourselves to that world, or fancy ourselves its leaders. The wind of history means being incapable of imagining anything except what is. But Ambrose, Augustine, Gregory, Innocent and all the men who changed mankind and their own times never thought in this fashion. The wind of history is really an ideology of abdication. No wonder that the expression is so much used by the present French régime, which some call a 'monocracy', but which is basically a dictatorship.

I do not intend to write my memoirs; it is too early to do that. When a man writes his memoirs, it means he expects nothing more from the present or the future. Rightly or wrongly, I do not think the time has come for me to say everything, not while I still expect something from this life and still hope to change the course of events. I only want to go over what is important right now and to tell the people of France and of all the free nations how the CNR came to be and what it stood for. There have been two CNRs. I will start by describing the first, of course, and then talk about the second, which I had to revive, twenty years after I became president of the first.

In 1938 I took a strong, even a violent, stand against the Munich

* 'Wind of change' is Macmillan's expression, but de Gaulle called it the 'wind of history'.—*Translator.*

pact. I wrote dozens of articles on the subject in a poor but very respectable and sincere newspaper called *l'Aube*. Since the war, a few people whose facts were weak and bias strong, have tried to put me in the 'pro-Munich' category. They always invariably quote the same four or five lines, lifted out of context from the thousands of lines voicing my fear and indignation. All this was long ago; but I was probably wrong not to publish a collection of my articles immediately after the victory of 1945. I did not want, however, to bring up old quarrels; without disavowing anything, I too wanted to make a fresh start. Perhaps I shall return to the subject only for the record when times are better.

But in 1938, it was a live issue. My articles had just come out and feelings ran high. I was called a warmonger, a *provocateur*, a Soviet sympathizer – in short, every name in the book. Sometimes people even rang me up to warn that I would be shot. Obviously, there is nothing much new under the sun; these details are not important, and I mention them only to remind some would-be innocents that every age has its own terrorism (or threats of terrorism), and one side or the other approves of terrorism at different times. The only safe position is to be on the right side at the right time.

The French political leaders and, even more, the English ones, acted in a tortuous and contradictory way. On the international level, Neville Chamberlain and Lord Halifax, like Daladier and Georges Bonnet, were staunch though undeclared anti-Communists. They had to reconcile this position as best they could with Pierre Laval's Franco-Soviet pact, not yet denounced by us. At the same time, everybody thought either that Hitler could be redirected towards the Russian or Ukrainian plain, or else that the West was not ready and needed time to catch up. Sometimes they thought both these things.

My reasons for disagreeing were simple. First of all, we had to honour our commitments to Czechoslovakia; we could not evade them with blatant ruses of the Runciman variety, while waiting to slip out of them altogether. Second, the grave strategic loss of Czechoslovakia and the possible withdrawal of Russia from the alliance due to a tremendous loss of confidence were too high a price to pay for the gain in time. Lost time cannot be confused with time gained. It was true that France and England were not ready in spite of many warnings; but they would be even less well-prepared without Czechoslovakia and the Soviet Union. When they

had been left to their own devices, they had not even begun to prepare for war, while Hitler's war effort had started long before and
was expanding rapidly. A year of grace meant another year lost for
the Allies. From a standing start, one runner cannot catch up with
another runner going at full speed who is already ahead.

Indeed, right after Munich, that great unnoticed disaster,
Neville Chamberlain announced, among general rejoicing, that he
was bringing 'peace in our time'. He could not, as Disraeli had
done seventy years previously, call it a 'peace with honour'. For
there was neither peace nor honour. Although Daladier was not as
completely deluded, he could do nothing on his own, and he was
soon cast aside by a wave of 'cowardly relief', as Léon Blum called
it with some remorse.

At that time, my connections with men from a wide variety of
backgrounds soon made me realize that one could hope for very
little. I thought we were sliding down a hill; there was war at the
bottom of that hill, and the war would end in terrible trials, probably disaster. But I was wrong about this, not about the consequences of our policy but about the actual course of the war; the
disaster did not come at the end of the conflict but at the very start.

The reason I briefly describe this period of my life is not to start
more quarrels but to show what my situation was at the time. I
already have more than enough quarrels that need settling to last
me a lifetime.

When, for the second time, I put on the uniform of the French
infantry, I soon realized that, as victory was so very certain, no one
was going to take any trouble to win the war. I was stationed in the
exact centre of France, and there, the NCOs at headquarters were
playing at naval battles. In their spare time, they also played un-
enthusiastically at planning for an unlikely land-war. The men who
came there were not youngsters; the young ones were up at the
front where the key word was 'wait'. Anyway, the front line and the
rear had one thing in common during the phoney war, the 'drôle
de guerre' which retrospectively was not droll at all. Of all the
armies the French army was the worst prepared for combat, both
materially and morally; and at the same time, it was the most com-
placent and cocksure about its strength, something which posters
proclaimed on every wall.

Life was totally unwarlike and humdrum, spent in a state of
semi-somnolence, apart from a few exercises that amused us rather

than trained us as soldiers. The French had the best-fed army in
the world. The only incident of any significance that I can recall
had to do with an excess of gastronomic care shown by the local
authorities to the troops. They began giving bars of chocolate to
the soldiers after breakfast, thinking this would impress the defenders of France and show them how much their country cared
for them. But the soldiers were mainly farmers, since the skilled
workers, reinforced by some unskilled workers, had remained
behind in the factories to work on munitions. This was natural,
and every country at war was doing much the same thing, although
other nations controlled qualifications for factory work more strictly.

The mobilized farmers were thinking about their farms, where
their wives were left alone to do the work with occasional help from
the old men in the village. They were also considering their allow-
ance of five sous, the pocket-money given them mainly to buy wine,
which would pass the time and dispel their nostalgia. Much to their
resentment, their wives were very useful here as well; without their
women, they would have been unable to pay for drinks with the
rest. Meanwhile, white-collar workers were on paid leave while
they were in uniform. Factory workers were making several hundred times five sous a day, and were free to go home in the evening,
to stay with the family, or to visit a café or a cinema. This was what
made the chocolate taste bitter to these farmers, who were not
accustomed to the treat, anyway. As might have been expected,
there was a rebellion against chocolate in favour of soup. It was not
an organized protest, but it was better coordinated than the regular
drill. When soup was reinstated, everything returned to the calm,
sleepy routine of useless tasks, until the lightning struck.

The *Moniteur du Puy-de-Dôme*, Pierre Laval's Auvergne newspaper, gave a clear picture of the political leaders' state of mind,
especially after the break-through at Sedan on 14 May 1940. At
about this time, I asked to be transferred to some part of France
where I could be of use. This request astounded everyone, though
not many followed my example. But as I was a sergeant, I was
given a detachment of only fifteen men out of the entire company.
My men were overwhelmed by this adventure; they criss-crossed
the whole of France in those military wagons which still carried
the notice left over from the war of 1870: 'Horses (lengthways): 8
– men: 40'. Those wagons had taken many men on journeys from
which they never came back. My men had one glimpse of the

Eiffel Tower, before they were dumped in the middle of a marshy wood somewhere in the country. They marched at night, and during the day they walked through the forests, because they were afraid of the planes. Finally, they reached a plateau covered with wheat and beetroot, and there they settled down in a large abandoned farm.

To bolster their morale, they went on highly successful hunting expeditions after chickens. The gunfire was still far away, but its rumbling never stopped, and we all knew the fighting was getting nearer. The planes flew overhead, backwards and forwards, gunning down anything that moved, bombarding shelters and buildings at random. All our training could not dispel the atmosphere of terror, for the contingent was undisciplined and it did not have enough time to get accustomed to the situation. We had only been brought to that spot to look good on the maps of the General Staff. The men were asking for pick-axes and shovels, as, theoretically, we were supposed to be a regiment of sappers. Flares lit up the nights, adding to the general uneasiness, especially as there was never an Allied plane in sight. The men were worried and they lacked confidence, because they did not know what was going on: 'We've been betrayed by the Fifth Column.' It would not have taken much to turn that crowd of anxious men into real fighting troops. All they needed was an ideal, a leader, and trained officers. Left in the dark, they stumbled and fell. This happened on every battlefield of 1940, where so few battles were fought, and it happened again during the referenda in the early 1960s, when there was no opposition to the state. 1962 was a spiritual 1940 for France.

My fifteen comrades and I finally arrived on 8 June 1940. There was a command post to the left of us, and beyond that, a ravine. No one, not even the officers, knew or cared about what was going on. That day was a moment of truth. Perhaps someone, with the help of documents, has pieced together the sequence of events and thinks he knows what actually occurred. I established my command post under a flowering elderberry bush. The entire post consisted of my rifle and myself. I soon discovered that the magazine of this rifle, an 1886 Lebel model, altered in 1892, did not work properly, so that it could only fire one shot at a time. In principle, it had a range of 4,000 metres, but the field of fire was only 200 metres anyway. The French side did not have a single light or heavy automatic weapon.

I waited, bitterly reflecting that the Aisne and the Ailette must already be in enemy hands, since we were eighteen kilometres south of Soissons. We had lost the Chemin des Dames, scene of a bloody and heroic struggle during the First World War. I wondered if our line of defence still held, and if there really were reinforcements behind us. There was no geographical barrier to stop the enemy advance. As for the reinforcements, we had seen nothing and no one on our way to the front. The only soldiers we had come across were units which had been dispersed; they were heading towards the rear, not realizing that the rear meant the Loire, the Garonne or the Pyrenees.

There was an infantry regiment ahead of us which was famous for its illustrious deeds. As soon as I heard its number, I felt sure that we would get some advance warning before we were plunged into the fray. And so I stood guard over my ravine and watched the surrounding area. Just one heavy French tank made a brief appearance, and tried out a few manoeuvres although there was no target in sight. It retreated without firing a shot, probably because it had not found the enemy.

The only soldier from the infantry regiment ahead of us who ever came into sight was one officer who later popped up behind me. But we could hear a battery of 75 mm guns firing away, and I listened to the noise without understanding what exactly was happening, except that it seemed to me things were not going too well on our side. As I sat under my elderberry bush, I suddenly heard the battery commander's voice, saying very loudly and clearly, 'Range 900 metres. Fire at will.' A very short time later, I saw their horses galloping by, pulling the artillery and the ammunition wagons. I called out to a sergeant who shouted back, 'The Germans are coming! We're saving the guns.' I turned around and saw that my men were far away, doubtless saving their rifles. It was then that I saw the infantry commander; his chest was covered with medals, testifying to his military valour during the First World War. Without volunteering to go with me, he ordered me to take up position on the edge of a small wood, so as to stop the enemy advance. I had the vague feeling that this was a stupid idea, but I was also convinced that it was more honourable to advance than to retreat. Anyway, I had not lost all my men. One of my soldiers had refused to flee, because we had met before in the Loire Department (which I represented in Parliament until 1962). This soldier, a farmer in civilian life, behaved like a true friend and stayed with me. I saw him again many times after the war, and I am glad to have this opportunity to tell R. that I shall never forget how he paid for his loyalty to me by four and a half years of captivity. Once, during the long exhausting march to the work camps, he admitted a regret to me – he would not have minded eating his dog's dinner. Nothing else, just that.

He and I saw the German soldiers running towards us, not carrying chickens in their haversacks, not even carrying haversacks, but carrying machine-guns, and full of determination to win.

This account will prove, I hope, that I do not only think in abstract terms. I too have memories like everyone's, and now that I have proved the point, I needn't dwell on my experiences in the POW camp. It was while I was a prisoner that I learned about an unknown man called Charles de Gaulle. His name was contemptuously mentioned in the Mecklenburg press, but I was deeply attracted to him from the first, for he was asking all Frenchmen to resist.

I had no books with me, and the camp provided only the most innocuous reading matter. I knew no German, but I remember a poster which was stuck on a barn door. We were all puzzled by it, especially as we had been told it was *nicht gut*. At the bottom of the poster there was a sentence printed in heavy type: FEIND BLEIBT FEIND. After some investigation, I learned that it meant 'The Enemy stays the Enemy'. General de Gaulle and Konrad Adenauer have decided that this is untrue, but I must confess that I often used these words to fight the influence of a French collaborationist paper called *Trait d'Union*. This newspaper, however, was such a disgusting combination of attacks on the losing side and toadying to the winners that I soon stopped discussing it with the prisoners, as its grovelling, servile tone completely defeated its purpose. I have often thought that there was a moral to this story.

My thoughts turned to victory, and I rejected the idea of an armistice. But when I heard the endless lines of prisoners praising the armistice because it gave them visions of going home and eating juicy steaks, it occurred to me that crowds can always be influenced by the right kind of pressure. I don't know if that is a very democratic way of looking at it, but that was how it was, and how I hope it will be again soon; large numbers always contain zeros and you

R.—2

need only one number, sometimes a very low one, even just the number one, to make all the zeros behind it take on a great significance. The fact that de Gaulle was isolated in London did not bother me. There would be misunderstandings, but they could easily be explained away by the fact that there was a war on. One man was talking about victory. He was saying that France was not enslaved, that it had a whole empire which could help to win the war. That was enough for me; although I knew almost nothing about the man, I was on his side. I did not hear his broadcast of 18 June, so that I learnt what he wanted only later and in bits. The worse the situation is, the simpler the solution; de Gaulle taught me that, and it is true. I became a Gaullist because I revolted against defeat and enslavement. I have become an anti-Gaullist because I still revolt against defeat and enslavement. I was not a half-hearted Gaullist, and I am not a half-hearted anti-Gaullist either.

I was a prisoner for thirteen months; at the end of this time, the Germans decided to free the prisoners who had fought during the First World War, in exchange for French workers coming to work in Germany. The only men who did not qualify for release were the career officers, as the Germans obviously did not want to set them free. The men in my age group were classified as First World War veterans because a handful of them had fought at the front for a few days in 1918. The Germans had promised to release 100,000 prisoners, but in fact only 20–25,000 left the camps. I was determined to refuse my freedom if they made me swear never to carry arms against the Third Reich again. But to my surprise the Wehrmacht was so sure of itself after its incredible victories of 1941 that it forgot to make us swear an oath. No one asked me anything, so of course I kept silent. I did not escape from Germany as has sometimes been said; and so, for honesty's sake, I must decline any credit for doing so.

I found myself in Paris once again, weary but determined. The first thing I learned was that policemen had been looking for me everywhere. They had seized an innocuous letter written to me by the ex-Chancellor Wirth, when they had searched my elder sister's apartment. My feelings about the Munich pact were well known and they had decided to investigate me; but it had never occurred to anyone that the Augustin Bidault who was a prisoner in Germany along with two million other Frenchmen, was the same man as Georges Bidault, who had written articles they did not like. This is typical of a police force in an occupied country, and sometimes unfortunately in an unoccupied country as well.

My Clandestine Life

As soon as I got back to Paris, I tried to get in touch with other men who did not accept defeat. They were all of different political opinions, and I never thought that one sort excluded another. Nor do I think so today, now that I am fighting again for the same lofty principles of freedom, honour and true French greatness. When Hitler's troops occupied Paris, I had no scruples about accepting the help of the most extreme radicals. And today I not only accept but I welcome the help of the men with whom I was at odds for twenty or thirty years, if they want to help France to recover its dignity.

I soon realized that Paris, in 1941, was paralysed; it would take a very long time to find men able, or even willing, to risk their lives for the sake of a vague and remote victory. Later I realized that I had not knocked on the right doors; there had been some brave men, but only very few; the risk of being arrested if I made any mistakes, and of compromising others if I succeeded, made it difficult for me to move. Because of this I decided to cross over into the so-called Free Zone. When I got there I was very surprised to discover that there were as many Germans there as in the Occupied Zone. But the Vichy government did not yet cooperate with the enemy as much as it did later on; it had not reached the final stages of '*collaborationisme*', as we were to call it. In 1941 Vichy tolerated, sometimes even helped, people to do things which would have been impossible in the Occupied Zone. Some friends had told me I might be needed in London, so I tried two or three times to get in touch with the Frenchmen who were over there. The Resistance network was terribly intricate, and I did not yet know what was going on; but I never got an answer from London, probably because communications between France and London were so difficult. Later, I learned that the London group was very insulated and exclusive; but it is quite likely that no one ever got my messages. Many of the men who claimed they had transmitters were either lying or else had no official contacts with London. The English capital was being bombed heavily, yet morale there was higher than it was in France. I can understand why so many energetic men preferred to go over to England, where they could do useful work and could enjoy greater freedom. Yet I did not regret staying in France, and I am glad now that I stayed.

As no one ever sent for me, I never had the chance to play the role of an *émigré*. I have left France this time because it was my last chance of leaving, and I believed I would be allowed to do useful work somewhere else in Europe. But in fact, I was not allowed to stay for long in any one place. I had worked hard for Europe, yet its leaders hounded me to please one who pays lip-service to European unity, but who always undermines it in fact.

I did not leave France for a single day. I did not go to Algiers or to London; but I stayed in Lyons first, and later in Paris and several other towns like Toulouse, where I used to visit the Archbishop Mgr Saliège, recently made a cardinal. While I led this secret, difficult existence, my safety depended entirely on the trustworthiness of many people, as everyone knew my real name, including the Germans and the collaborators. No one ever betrayed me. The *concierges*, in spite of their reputations as gossips, never gave my secret away or asked me any questions about the visitors who came to see me at unusual hours. Officially, I was an ordinary *bourgeois* who left his lodgings rather early every morning, and who came back at nightfall. I never received a single letter or postcard, yet the *concierges* held their tongues and never made any inquiries. I owe my life to many circumstances; first of all, to my colleagues, who took every precaution to keep me safe (I do not want to give their names, as they suffered enough during the war). But I also owe my survival to the gratuitous discretion of many a *concierge*, who often realised what was going on. I have never stopped feeling grateful towards all those people, and if any of them read these pages, I want to tell them that I have not forgotten what they did for me.

Clandestine life was like a science; it had to be learned. But this was difficult, for men are not cautious by nature. They usually suspect harmless things, but they take no care about their own appearance; they are careless about what they write, even when they write in code, and about what they tell their friends or their mistresses. They are careless about using the same place twice for an appointment at the same hour. I remember how in Lyons, at the very beginning, absolute orgies of plotting were going on along the

Rue de la République, and in the No. 7 tramway that went between Perrache and Villeurbanne. A young man would be standing like a lamp-post at every corner, waiting for his contact who was late. It was a great mistake to be late and also to stand conspicuously at street-corners. People went about plotting at the top of their voices. Talking about plotting was what made it spicy and pleasurable for many of them.

One day I was in the apartment block where a friend of mine lived. I was going up the stairs, getting familiar with the place, when I overheard my friend on the landing, saying with relish to some visitor who was leaving, 'Well, goodbye, old man. I have to get the apartment ready for the Resistance leaders who are coming over in two hours.' This man was fine and brave; but anybody could have heard him without being seen, and all the leaders who were going there could have been caught.

In Paris and Lyons, towards the end of the Occupation, there were certain areas, usually squares, quays and café terraces where hunted men would congregate. They would sometimes even assemble at a bar that was being watched, or at an apartment which was in danger of being searched, just because they were not used to looking out for traps.

We ourselves had a lot of difficulty learning a few elementary rules of precaution, let alone teaching them to others. Right at the start, we were isolated groups of men lost in a vaguely sympathetic crowd. We had a lot of trouble just finding each other; thus the Resistance was divided into sections, which were really fragments. The leaders of the various groups were inclined to exaggerate their own importance and to refuse to disclose their connections with other Resistance groups. We always had people from every sort of background coming to us and saying, 'I am the Resistance' or 'We are the Resistance'. One man would tell us his group had ten to 20,000 members, sometimes more. The next man would say the same thing. They all knew me by name, but they refused to say who they were and what they represented, so that it was a long, complicated, and often discouraging task to sort them out. They had endless personal quarrels among themselves. Life is always like that, but clandestine life seems to bring it out even more.

It was usually difficult, often impossible, to check their claims, since it was already hard enough to tell the braggart from the serious fighter, and even the *agent provocateur* from the genuine patriot.

The beginnings of the Resistance were badly slowed down by rivalries, which invariably originated in a fundamental difference of principle.

I do not want to discuss these rivalries in detail; but I do want to stress the fact that, in spite of its exhausting and unnecessary squabbles, the men who made up the hard core of the Resistance were outstanding, especially those from the factories. Their courage and daring in overcoming fantastic obstacles to carry out missions, while being tracked down by several varieties of police, all too often ended in their death; these noble men can never be mourned enough. One of France's greater glories is that it had so many heroic men ready to fight for their country although they had not been drafted and had no uniform, pay or prospects of a pension, and who accepted the constant threat of death.

It would be absurd to think that only the present state of affairs makes me say that the relations between the *émigrés* and the fighters who stayed in France were a very real problem. This basic difficulty always exists in similar situations. At first, all the really active men had thought that the only possible solution was to go and join de Gaulle. Others simply felt it would be safer to go to London or to America. Some acted out of wisdom, others out of prudence, and a few sought an opportunity to create dissent among the dissenters. Then, when the Resistance groups became better organized and finally merged, they began asking themselves what authority the Free French had over them, if any.

I don't think that there ever was any serious danger of conflict, rivalry, or even overlapping. The people who made up the nucleus of the early Resistance groups were those who recruited for the Resistance, those who sheltered partisans or Allied airmen (one house in Brittany had eighteen airmen on one occasion), those who were in charge of parachute landings, those who housed the radio operators, the printers, the armed groups and the rest. None of these people made criticisms, drew subtle distinctions, or even asked questions. When a man is involved in serious action and he knows very well that his job is both useful and dangerous, he does not go in for philosophy. It was the leaders who argued. They were running a lot of risks too, and their differences were not illusory. They admired the men in London far less than they hated the men in Vichy.

These difficulties were resolved for a variety of reasons, and they soon became a thing of the past. To start with, the major part of the Resistance was indifferent, even hostile to internecine feuds. In the Resistance groups, and even in the networks, the members were practically interchangeable. When an issue of *Combat* did not arrive, *Libération* was distributed instead, and vice versa. If a local leader was eliminated, and there was no one to step into his place, his men would go over to the nearest organization. The names of top leaders were, for obvious reasons, almost unknown; the cause was what mattered and everyone was welcome. In a great crisis there is solidarity, even among the French, who have had the reputation ever since Caesar's day of being the most divided people alive, which is strange because France also happens to be the most homogeneous and compact country in the world.

The Resistance did not like people to quarrel; it wanted everyone to agree. It had found its myth, its symbol, in General de Gaulle, although no one knew anything about him. The partisans disliked the sound of his voice and the photographs of him that had been parachuted to France; but that did not matter. The priests, teachers, garage mechanics, tobacco-store owners, farmers, postmen, road-menders, landed gentry, workers and students – without forgetting the women of all ages who behaved admirably, these people who made up the Resistance wanted no arguments. They played a major part in eliminating disagreements. Their attitude was that the intellectuals could go right ahead and draw up plans for future constitutions if they felt like it (as indeed they did) but that the first thing was to liberate France. After that, we would see.

There were times when General de Gaulle expected the Home Resistance to declare its independence from him; but he held the purse strings. As soon as the Home Resistance grew large enough, it also began to rely on the money that England gave or lent to de Gaulle, so that it was financially dependent on de Gaulle, at least until the last year of the Occupation. That year, however, one of my dearest friends, André Debray, used his prestige as the admired and respected director of a very large bank, to sign receipts and cheques under a pseudonym, giving the money to us. In all, it came to some ten billion pre-Pinay francs, and it gave us a certain measure of independence.

But de Gaulle devised a very simple method of protecting his 'temporary dictatorship during the storm', as he called it later, and of preventing anyone from challenging his authority. (During the years of 'Free France', no one would have dared to use the word dictatorship, except to say to Roosevelt that the Vichy government was one and Free France was not.) What de Gaulle did was to ask all the key Resistance leaders to come to London. This would put a stop to any uncoordinated efforts, wavering loyalties or outright disobedience. And so, François de Menthon, Henri Frenay and Emmanuel d'Astier de La Vigerie set off on the difficult journey to London. Their enthusiasm varied, but they were all full of curiosity. Of these three potential leaders, only one was ever tempted to usurp de Gaulle's authority in France, and he was the only one who had a strong enough character to try. Not one of those three men returned from London. De Gaulle is an excellent judge of character, except that sometimes he is blinded by his contempt for everyone, regardless of race, colour or creed. He soon discovered which man was whole-heartedly devoted to him, which one was naïvely opportunistic, and which one was deviously ambitious. And so he put François de Menthon in charge of Justice, always a dead end under de Gaulle. Henri Frenay was put in charge of the War Prisoners; without function or staff of supporters, who were all in France, he was soon reduced to wrapping parcels for the POWs. Emmanuel d'Astier was put in charge of the Interior. Obviously, de Gaulle's standard of selection had nothing to do with morality or principle.

The Communists wavered at first; but they finally gave de Gaulle their support after the fall of Giraud. There were twenty-eight Communist deputies in Algiers, kept under lock and key by Pétain at the fortress of Maison-Carrée, where at least they were protected from the Germans. Those deputies had no choice but to back de Gaulle. While Germany and Russia were on the same side, the Communist line was to revile 'Anglo-Saxon Imperialism'. I saw proof of this in a letter that François Billoux wrote to Marshal Pétain in the name of the Communist Party, asking to act as a witness at the trial in Riom, of Daladier, Blum, Gamelin and others; he blamed them for the war and the defeat. When the Soviet Union was forced to change sides because of Hitler's attack, all the Communists became fervent partisans – on the right side this time.

The Communists were a coherent, disciplined group, accustomed to secrecy and fighting on many fronts, with their own hierarchy and administration. The political parties had been disgraced by the defeat and by having a majority of deputies who supported the Vichy régime; they were always split and their jargon was obsolete. The new Resistance groups were inexperienced; they recruited members at random and were sometimes very careless. Whatever double game the Communists were playing when they joined the Algiers government, they effectively put an end to any hope of creating an independent Home Resistance. It would have been impossible. The Communists had ministers and deputies in Algiers; Thorez was in Moscow, and their leaders in France were safely in hiding; the work was done by minor figures, whose lives were not considered as precious. All we had were our fighters, our hostages, our deportees, and our dead.

The British radio, more than anything else, helped to establish de Gaulle's name. The BBC literally made de Gaulle. Even if the English had been tempted to get rid of de Gaulle during one of their many crises with him, it would have done them more harm than good. It would not have hurt de Gaulle's position at all; on the contrary. But without the English radio, de Gaulle would never have been anything more than a minor leader. When the English discovered how inflexible he was, they probably regretted all the publicity they had given him. They even tried to find another military leader, Giraud, or another civilian leader, Herriot. But they overestimated Giraud's intelligence and Herriot's character. Anyway, the harm was done – we believed it was the good. The brand-name de Gaulle had been launched on the market.

Later on, de Gaulle remembered the fantastic advantage of having a radio monopoly. His monopoly of the Free French radio in London explains his monopoly of the French radio today. Now on television, he has perfected his obsessive, Big Brother image as Irreplaceable Guide of the Nation. He chatters, he rants, he roars, until he hypnotizes the French public into voting for him. He does not create a personality cult; he simply projects his own image constantly, and people submit to his authority – at least while he remains in power.

It is absolutely true that the whole French Resistance was Gaullist. General de Gaulle had the dual advantage of being simultaneously unknown and familiar. He was the only man we ever heard about, except for the men in Vichy and Germany, whom we felt honour-bound to disobey. The General was far away; but we talked about him all the time. Distance gave him an aura of mystery, and yet he was in daily communication with us; that was what gave him such prestige. I am not ashamed now of having succumbed to that prestige. If I had my life again in the same circumstances, I would support the man just as staunchly, though I would not have the same illusions about him.

Jean Moulin

I have talked about the assets of the Gaullists; but I have not yet spoken about one of their greatest assets, a man called Jean Moulin. All those who knew and loved him, as I did, remember his appearance, his manner and his voice vividly. It has been twenty years now since we parted, he to die and I to live. These twenty years have gone by like a day. It is a sad fact that France worships the victor and forgets the hero. True merit has nothing to do with success; perhaps later, men will be assessed more justly.

The first time I met Jean Moulin, he was dressed in ski-clothes. I found him charming; but I was rather put off by his costume. There are so many people who love being noticed that I had not given any thought to the art of being unnoticed, although I soon learned.

We met in the house of one of my childhood friends, François de Menthon. That day, his children kept very quiet. Soon afterwards some unwelcome visitors came to the house. They gave no warning, and came unannounced. But it was not yet serious; there were still men in the Vichy police who were well-disposed and even ready to take risks.

My friends told me that their guest was called Rex or Régis, and that he was also known as Max. Names like these could not hide anyone who was active in the Resistance for long. During the Occupation, I used about fifty different names: Bib, Xavier, Constantin, Armand, Renard, Jean-Jacques, etc. . . . I have forgotten most of them. But the Gestapo knew my real name after 1943.

Rex and I talked about the Resistance; but in early 1942, we were still in the difficult early stages, groping in the dark. The French nation had been crushed by the defeat and the panic of 1940, and the majority of Frenchmen, hurt and humiliated, accepted the paternalistic protection of old Marshal Pétain, shrouded in his glory. Under his leadership, a group of practically unknown ministers were running all the risks, dealing with the issues, and selecting the personnel. The ones like Laval and Darlan who became well known were loathed and despised. Most Frenchmen also listened to the London radio and either believed or pretended to believe that Vichy and Free France were secretly in league. The Resistance hated the very idea and refused to admit anything of the sort. Our heroes had to be above reproach and our enemies beyond forgiveness. The world was simple, and we had to sacrifice everything so that good could triumph over evil. Even today I find it hard not to think that way. But angels can fall, and Lucifer was the most beautiful of the angels.

Later, I got to know Jean Moulin well. I think I can even say that I knew him better than anyone else. We met often when we were in the same city, and I cannot recall a single disagreement between us. Moulin's secretary, Alain Cordier, who worshipped his chief, once took me to the little room in Lyons where Jean Moulin lived for a time. He never received any visitors there. It was a dark room furnished in the typical *petit bourgeois* style, with quaint touches, bobbles and old-fashioned curtains; just the right setting for a simple, narrow and active life. There, Jean Moulin would go to sleep every night, thinking over our problems. He was de Gaulle's representative, the Free French ambassador; but at first, many carped at Moulin's leadership and agreed to recognize him only later. Jean Moulin had been sent to us from London and his task was to unify all the different Resistance movements. We had many an exhausting talk on the subject, and I learned that revolutionaries love useless chatter almost more than anything else. But Moulin always stood firm. He was gentle, patient and intelligent; only useless talk and red herrings angered him.

These qualities as well as his many dangerous missions to meet contacts, won him recognition, far more than his promotion as a minister in London, where he was known as Monsieur X. This title was inadequate as a rank and too obvious for a disguise, yet Monsieur X existed and worked hard at his trade.

He had been the head of Pierre Cot's cabinet, and this had won him much prestige. But Pierre Cot went to America, and Jean Moulin stayed in France. He had been a prefect of the Eure-et-Loir department and was at Chartres when the invasion swept over France. The commander of the German occupying troops wanted him to endorse a proclamation that falsely put the blame for certain outrages on the French. Naturally, Jean Moulin refused and was gaoled. On that day, in the aftermath of total disaster, he lost hope, broke a windowpane and slashed his throat. Some have accused this agnostic of being anti-clerical; yet it was a nun, the Mother Superior I think, who nursed him at the hospital and saved his life.

He feared what many others would fear after him: that he would be subjected to the sort of treatment that would make him talk. This was not, alas, his last brush with death; but that particular encounter left only one trace, a rather weak, weary-sounding voice, not unlike Mauriac's. But the similarity ends there; Moulin was a terrorist (as they were called even then), and Mauriac is 'terrorized', or perhaps I should say out of kindness for my fellow-human being, 'hypnotized'.

Jean Moulin later told me that his first encounter with death had taught him a lesson. 'I'll never try again,' he told me. 'I will never seek escape in death.' And he kept his word. He was tortured, his body was broken; but his lips remained sealed and he died on his way to Germany. I am convinced that though he doubted their existence, Saint Stephen, Saint Lawrence and all the martyrs, all those who were tortured for a just cause, all the blessed sufferers, were waiting for him at the gates of heaven, to greet him as their equal and their brother. A horrible death was the price he paid for silence.

But before that sad day we had our moments of gaiety and mutual confidence. He told me the story of how he landed in a swamp the first time he made a parachute jump over France, a very unpleasant moment for an experienced Prefect who was a total novice at jumping out of aeroplanes. When he returned to England, he parachuted again. When he came back to France, in early 1943, he told me confidentially that the Allies would not land in France that year. 'This is only between you and me,' he said. 'Don't repeat it or our men will grow discouraged.' We looked at each other and nodded. I must admit, we were all obsessed by the idea of the landing which would liberate our country. Our losses were heavy. We constantly had to reassemble groups that had been dispersed, look for new men to fill the ranks, new leaders to take the place of old ones. Our path was strewn with tragedies. The endless disappearances, griefs and fears set our nerves on edge, for the front was nowhere and the enemy everywhere.

I remember that we both agreed our chances of survival would be slight if the war went on much longer. Yet I survived, and he, who was usually so careful, died after taking an uncalculated risk. To prevent any leaks, Jean Moulin had not told me about a meeting he wanted to attend at Caluire. I do not want to go over that tragedy; the law courts have studied the particulars of the case twice, but they have not yet found a satisfactory explanation of what in fact took place at Caluire. All I can say is that, if Jean Moulin had consulted me, I would never have allowed him to go there.

Jean Moulin's death is a terrible loss to France. Many people's memories fade; they have new ideas, new friends, new problems to think about. But I will never forget him or stop admiring him.

The French nation has erected three monuments in honour of Jean Moulin, who now lies in the Panthéon. The first is at his birthplace in Béziers, the second at Chartres, where he was a Prefect, and the third at Lyons, where he was most active in the Resistance. But we have yet to build a memorial worthy of him. If I ever get the opportunity, and if men come to their senses and rediscover the meaning of true glory and the greatness of those who died for noble causes, we will make up for that neglect. Perhaps we may at the same time be able to put an end to those long, sometimes pointless, disagreements which began twenty years ago, even though I would not invoke Jean Moulin's name to achieve this purpose, or any other. We owe the dead every respect, and we must spare those men who are no longer with us because of their sacrifices. I would never exploit Moulin's name as a front for some political cause today. There is a Jean Moulin club; but I am not a member of it and I know almost nothing about it except that it sometimes ascribes its ideas to Moulin, knowing that otherwise no one would take the least interest in what it had to say. Personally, I prefer those who rob safes to those who rob the reputation of the dead.

The CNR

Jean Moulin asked me to write an appeal to all Resistance movements in the Free Zone, asking them to accept de Gaulle's authority. They accepted because, largely due to Moulin's efforts, they had already come together and were in the process of merging. Moulin also asked me to write a manifesto definitively proclaiming the CNR to be on de Gaulle's side in his struggle against Giraud. The Communists were reluctant to accept this; they said that we ought not to take sides, but to organize the struggle. But in the end, the manifesto was unanimously approved.

The first meeting of the National Council for the Resistance (CNR), took place on 27 May 1943 in Paris, at the Rue du Four, not far from the Bon Marché department store and the two churches of Saint-Sulpice and Saint-Germain des Prés. Moulin had been the founder of the CNR, and he was its first president. The manifesto we approved during that first meeting is the only one mentioned in de Gaulle's memoirs, although there were many others supporting his cause. I suppose the reason for this is that de Gaulle wants people to know only about the documents which, directly or in- directly emanated from his personal authority, and which show his authority already recognized and established in France. This may be why he just mentions the telegram sent to him by Jean Moulin on the night of 15 May, before the manifesto was even written, and twelve days before it was approved. I had not realized the full sig- nificance of this omission until de Gaulle's recent pronouncements on his legitimacy. At the time, we did not think in those terms; somebody else was doing the thinking. But the fact remains that our endorsement of de Gaulle against Giraud came at just the right time in the muddled situation at Algiers, with its temporary twin rule, as the Gaullists themselves have admitted.

Then, the lightning struck. Jean Moulin and his companions were arrested on 20 June 1943. The following day, I met Moulin's secretary by chance, as no one knew where I lived, not even the *lycée* where I taught (although, as I have already mentioned, there were so many of us in Lyons, and we were so obvious that any really watchful policeman could have arrested the lot of us). Jean Moulin's secretary, A.C., who was utterly devoted to his chief, said to me in a broken voice, 'Our God is dead.' He was a religious man, so that this was only a metaphor; but it gives some idea of his re- action to the catastrophe which ruined his life. We got in touch with Claude Serreulles, an assistant sent from London to help Moulin, whose work had become too much for one man. I am afraid that Serreulles has become one of those old-fashioned Gaul- lists who claim to be left-wingers; but I have never stopped liking the man whom we knew as 'Sophie'. Serreulles had to find a suc- cessor for Moulin in the Southern Zone, while Bingen looked for

one in the Northern Zone. Later, Bingen would also die heroically
for his country: he was caught and shot.

'Sophie' did not feel up to the responsibility of taking on the job
himself, although he could have done so automatically, as the main
CNR group was in Lyons. He thought that the most obvious
solution would be to appoint a man who already knew the CNR
members and the tactics of the Resistance. And so he came to me
and said, 'You were closest to Jean Moulin, and you were in almost
complete agreement with him; therefore, it is you who must take
the job and continue in his footsteps.' Moulin's aides were too
modest about themselves; but there was nothing strange about
their choice. Perhaps when they had made a quick survey of all
possible candidates, they had had to eliminate most of the others –
not particularly flattering for me, but the result is the same. When
I was told about their decision, I was not really surprised. I had
known Moulin well, and I knew we shared the same beliefs, so I
did not refuse the post. When secrecy is vital, strict protocol is not
as important as continuity. It was an added responsibility for me
and, as we had just learned, it would be dangerous; but I went to
work.

I began sending coded telegrams to London in the name of the
General Delegation in France. Naturally, I asked for instructions
on how to deal with political and military problems that had had to
be postponed. It seemed very natural to be continuing in the footsteps of my friend and to be taking up the task where he left off.
And so, I did my best while I waited for my appointment to be
confirmed. We considered ourselves totally under the authority of
London so that it never occurred to us to send a message saying,
'Max disappeared on 20 June. According to his wishes am taking
over his responsibilities, Bip.' No one in France would have been
surprised, even though they might not all have been delighted. Yet
no one thought of doing this, myself least of all. A High Command
existed, and its job was to give us orders and our job was to carry
them out, to suggest, to give information, but first of all to obey.

We did, however, ask ourselves constantly, what was going on in
that remote place called 'Londres', and even those who had gone
there on a visit, even those who had stayed there for a time, found
it difficult to answer clearly. Who was doing what? What was de
Gaulle like? Who had any influence on him? On this last point I
was able to form an opinion and even come to a conclusion, but

only much later, after the war. There are only two ways of having
any influence on de Gaulle. The first is to deal with matters that do
not interest him much, so long as you are clever about it and start
no trouble. The second is to produce arguments in favour of a
course he has already chosen, to read his character and then tell
him what he wants to hear. You *can* influence the man, but only in
the direction he wants to go. If someone has done him great services, he is allowed to express a conflicting opinion, but only once
or twice at the most. And if he persists in trying to impose a different point of view, it won't be long before he is pushed aside
altogether.

And so, we faced a mystery. It is de Gaulle's habit to conceal his
intentions. He has described the principles that made him decide
to adopt this method of command, which is now second nature.
Actually, I am wrong to call it second nature, implying self-train-
ing, an effort of will. It is first nature, the primary one that runs
deepest. Sometimes he tones it down, but he never masters it
altogether.

There was a lot to be said on the subject, but we did not have the
time nor the inclination to think it out. Besides, de Gaulle deliberately covered up his tracks to avoid any attempts at analysing him.
Jean Moulin had been Monsieur X, and he was the most powerful
of all the representatives. Yet we often received unexpected visitors
who also had credentials. They would come to sow seeds of doubt,
undertake actions that were not coordinated with those of the General Delegate in France, and give us other versions of what was
going on in high circles. These versions were not those we heard
from the only man officially invested with the authority to transmit
such information.

Only one of these visitors, Pierre Brossolette, was a man of any
great intellectual and moral worth. He had a clearly defined group
at his disposal, and possessed a natural authority which he borrowed from no one. I don't think that he was in complete agreement with Jean Moulin, although Moulin never complained to me
of any complications that this disagreement might have caused, and
could not help admiring Brossolette. So that even today, this is only
a speculation; but it seems to me that it was a question of differing
temperaments. There are personalities which get along, and others
which clash. Historians construe facts and deduce hypotheses after
the event, but it's much simpler than that. In this particular case,

there was a hidden conflict over who made the decisions, and this was complicated by the fact that some of their duties overlapped. When de Gaulle uses someone who does not belong to his entourage, he arranges to have him controlled, and, when necessary, contradicted by another. He dislikes all the threads being in one hand, when the hand in control is not his own. At that time, de Gaulle had not yet managed to create that mystique of his which would later amaze everyone. He was not yet the Old Man of the Mountain to his mediocre but obsessive and dedicated personnel. And so, a beginner at poker, he preferred to play chess. But Brossolette never did anything in de Gaulle's name that he would not have done in his own.

I saw Brossolette twice during this period, once at Lyons and once in Paris. Yeo Thomas, the English author of *The White Rabbit*, took me to meet him in a street behind the Butte Montmartre, where he was waiting for us. He had a haughty look, with a profile and a complexion somewhat like Gros's painting of the young Bonaparte leading the assault at the Arcole Bridge. We identified him easily. There was a white streak in his black hair. We had known each other, but not well, ever since we had passed our history examinations together. Our political differences, and probably some biting exchanges, kept us apart until Munich. We agreed by telephone to do something if Czechoslovakia put up a resistance after it had been abandoned. If France did nothing at least Frenchmen could do something, however little. I still remember his decided tone as he said to me during our second telephone conversation, 'Very well then, it's arranged. I've spoken to my wife and she's agreed. We'll leave together.' He never had to take that risk, but, as he predicted, the risk soon came in another form. And he took that risk to the bitter end.

After his last mission, he set off for London with some other men who also played an important part in the Resistance, especially Emile Bollaert and Laffon, who is now dead. They left on an old boat from one of the furthermost points of Cape Finistère, an area long dreaded by sailors. There is one bay there called the Bay of the Dead, and the saying goes, 'Whoever sees Ouessant, sees his own blood.' A terrible storm almost wrecked their boat, and the men had to bail out all night to stop sinking. Laffon later told me how he felt about this journey.

'You know how attached I am to life,' he said. 'Well, I was so

exhausted and so sea-sick that on several occasions I hoped we
would sink right away to put an end to it all. Our chief, Bollaert,
made sure his spectacles were safe, and remained perfectly calm.'

Finally, the boat was reduced to a bundle of planks and was
tossed back on the coast. The survivors all set off in different directions to look for shelter. Brossolette had lost his shoes during the
night. He was walking barefoot and his clothes were soaked. The
German police had been alerted and picked him up easily. They
took him to Rennes to interrogate him. Fearing the worst, he
hurled himself down a staircase from the fifth floor. He had a home,
children, and a great future, and he sacrificed them all in three
seconds. He did not believe in life after death; but he did believe
in the honour of France. May the God he did not know but who
knew him keep him from harm, and may his country continue to
respect his memory.

Not all the envoys sent from London were of his mettle. There
was only one Brossolette. No man has filled his place in the Socialist party; he was a member of it, while keeping his freedom of
spirit. No man has since served his country as Brossolette served his.

Other men came. Some disappeared again; others, after doing
their best to confuse matters, survived and had careers. They got
their reward. *Receperunt mercedem suam, vani vanam.* There is
nothing more to be said on the subject.

And so, almost immediately after 20 June 1943, I began sending
coded messages to London regularly, using the transmitters we
had at our disposal. It was quite hard work, covering all political
and military affairs, not to mention the matters dealing with personnel, and the technical information which they needed over there.

I was already quite familiar with this sort of work. Before then
(and I never gave up doing it), I used to send political news and
information to London: I got this news from several sources:
Vichy, the press, the police, and the French Information Services.
This work alone was quite arduous; I had to find the news, check
it, write it out, code it and transmit it, all in Lyons where they had
radio-detectors mounted on lorries which soon picked up the
locations of illegal radio transmitters. These locations had to be
changed often, to prevent search parties from finding us. It was not
easy constantly to find new places for our radio sets, because they
had to be close at hand in case of emergencies, such as parachute
drops of arms and people; we had to reach these as quickly as

possible and we never solved the problem of transportation. The roads were practically deserted and the 'gasogène' cars were always breaking down for one reason or another, which made the authorities suspicious of us. In spite of all these complications, I was able to bring out at least 250 roneotyped issues of the *Bulletin de la France Combattante* for the clandestine press.

This bulletin was produced with the precious and tireless aid of several men, all of whom had different journalistic styles and political tendencies. Pierre Corval was the calm, undaunted king-pin of the enterprise. Rémy Roure, assisted by his wife, worked very hard until a German bullet severed his femoral artery; after an almost miraculous recovery, he was deported. André Sauger, who is a Communist sympathizer now, also worked with us. He used to write in *La Montagne*, a Clermont-Ferrand newspaper, started by Alexandre Varenne, patriotic ex-Governor-General of Indochina, who was later a member of my first government. Roure wrote in the solemn manner of the *Temps*; Sauger in the style of the *Canard Enchaîné*, which created problems. These men later dispersed and some of them no longer agree with me at all. It doesn't matter; I still want to mention their names, even though one of them has a bad memory and has become far too shrill in his opposition. To their names, I also want to add that of the kindly *abbé* Boursier, who worked and hid our roneo press in his parish in a Lyons suburb. One day, men wearing swastika emblems suddenly appeared at his home and shot him down on the spot. He was not one of those who only make for their country sacrifices that cost them nothing.

I still have to mention the secretaries and the coders. One of them died of exhaustion after she was deported, a gentle, sad person of great integrity. Others still survive. I do not want to name those to whom I owe my life and who risked or compromised their own to do so. Circumstances do not allow me to draw up a full list of my helpers. There are no longer any swastikas about today, yet it is no safer than it was then to be known as my friend.

The days passed; I received no acknowledgement of my messages or even of Jean Moulin's arrest. I was patient for a time, as Jean Moulin had told me that he found it very difficult to get the information he kept demanding. Sometimes, he had had the feeling that he was addressing himself to a deaf and distant god. Or was it that the Gaullists were so busy with their troops that they had no time left to deal with the organized Resistance? Perhaps the various

ministers were having a quarrel among themselves over allocations
of powers? Or did they find it difficult to understand the confused
issues they were being asked to solve? Or was it that they felt a
natural indifference to the 'croakings' of distant men who besieged
the Olympian sovereign with their suggestions, their claims and
even their protests, just when that sovereign needed peace and
calm to come to his supreme policy-making decisions? We never
found out, but I must admit that if we did croak like frogs, then
the frogs got a bit fed up with never having even a pebble tossed
into their swamp.

After a time, I had had enough. I did not have the least intention
of imposing myself on anyone, and I let Jean Moulin's lieutenants
do their job while I went on with my bulletin and took part in the
administration of several Resistance organizations. July, then August, went by, and we still heard nothing. The oracle was silent. By
the month of September, Jean Moulin's acting substitutes felt the
need of some leadership, and they turned to the CNR. I knew very
well that the founder and first president of the CNR had only considered it as a symbolic union of the various movements, parties
and trade unions. He never thought of organizing even occasional
meetings. Besides, the CNR had eighteen members; to bring so
many people together in one place would have been very rash; it
would have probably ended in the arrest of everyone. But as we
had been left in a vacuum, we could at least consult each CNR
member individually, so that he could choose who he wanted as
president, since London was in no hurry to appoint a delegate to
France. Thus, we would have a successor to Moulin, not appointed
in the same way, but at least able to act as a responsible adviser.

The trouble with this solution was that Moulin had been both de
Gaulle's delegate and at the same time President of a Council he
had created. We were running the risk of a dual sovereignty and
the CNR might then feel invested with an independent authority.
This was what we had to avoid day after day, for London's neglect
obviously tended to create a separatist atmosphere. This had always
been latent; but we had taken a great deal of trouble to prevent it
and were apparently winning. But how could we act otherwise
now? How could we go on leaving the machine without a motor or
brakes, with the even greater danger of having many hands all
reaching for the steering wheel?

This was how, after three months, I was elected, not appointed, president of the CNR. It is not true that I tried to get the post; on the contrary, I deplored it as an expedient necessity and never asked anyone for anything. All that people knew was that I would not refuse if I were elected, and my chief wish after my election was to bring us all together again as a united body. This I could not wholly do.

As for the three months of silence following Jean Moulin's arrest, I never asked for or received an explanation. De Gaulle described the event in the following terms:

Not that we lacked men of ability and courage at the head of the various movements, despite the continual decimation the Resistance suffered. But each of these men, belonging to a faction, would have been unable to impose his authority upon the rest, so rigorous was the individuality of the leaders and of their groups. Moreover, the day was approaching when France, suddenly emerging from oppression, would find that the life of the nation, law and order, and the judgement of the world would depend on the French administrative structure. To represent me in France and to lead our groups there, and also to prepare, everywhere, the confirmation or the substitution of authorities, I needed someone who was a great administrator, someone who had taken part in our battle and knew its prejudices and tangled roots but was not himself committed to any particular tendency. Furthermore, he must be capable, at the crucial moment, of rallying the kind of administration which the government would soon require. Months were to pass before I chose and established the man who answered all these qualifications.

This is certainly not the right explanation. It is doubtful that any of the men who fought and worked in the Resistance with me believed it then or now. The three 'great administrators' successively appointed by de Gaulle to be his delegates to the Resistance were far more politically committed than I was at the time. Either de Gaulle was extremely well-informed and had legitimate preferences in the choice of the men who were going to represent him, or else he was misinformed by his advisers. I am quite sure it was the first and I do not complain about being told nothing. Probably, had I been de Gaulle's delegate as well, I would no longer be alive to tell the tale.

Frankly, the truth is that de Gaulle was then struggling for power with Giraud and trying to get the French Committee of Liberation recognized by the Allies:

The consolidation of French authority obliged the Allies to depart somewhat from the attitude of doubt and distrust they had hitherto adopted. Official recognition was granted the Committee of Liberation by the United States, Great Britain and Soviet Russia on 26 August. Mexico, Cuba, Norway, Greece, Poland, Chile and Belgium had already taken the necessary steps.

As a matter of fact, the formulas chosen by the other three great powers revealed profound differences. Washington employed the most restricted, announcing that the committee was recognized as administering the overseas territories which recognized its authority. London used the same terms, but added that in the eyes of Great Britain the committee was the body qualified to pursue the conduct of the French war effort. Moscow revealed itself as the most generous. For Soviet Russia, the committee represented 'the interests of state of the French Republic'; it was 'the only executive body and the only qualified representative of all French patriots struggling against Hitlerism'. The example of the Big Three was rapidly followed by others. On 3 September, speaking on the radio on the occasion of the war's fourth anniversary, I was able to say, 'The recognition of the French Committee of National Liberation by twenty-six states furnishes striking proof of our solidarity for victory and for peace.'

It was obviously an exceedingly difficult task. I have quoted this text because it contains a few indications of de Gaulle's future attitude towards the various allied powers. For, as we all know, he has a very long memory.

To understand even better how we fared, I can quote a passage describing how he operated. As can be seen, his methods have not changed:

Around me, interests imposed their claims, rivalries clashed, men became more human every day.

In my office at Les Glycines I kneaded heavy dough. There were papers to read, though my immediate colleagues, Palewski, Billotte and Soustelle, brought me, on my orders, only the most essential. There were decisions to make, even if it was only a question of determining principles. People had to be seen despite the system which I put into effect to limit the audiences to national conmissioners, foreign diplomats, top Allied and French military leaders, a few high civil administrators, messengers from France, those who were to be sent there and certain visitors of note. On principle, I used the telephone only rarely, and no one was ever permitted to ring me up. The confrontation of points of view and the choice of measures to be taken I reserved purposely for the government councils. My own nature warned me and my experience had taught me that, at the summit, one can preserve time and strength only by remaining habitually on the remotest heights.

When de Gaulle says 'remotest' he means it. But his account of the work he accomplished should also be quoted:

It was therefore all the more necessary at crucial moments to make contact with people and affairs. I did so, as much as possible, by going to see them on the spot. During the fifteen months of my stay in Algiers, I spent, independently of the meetings and the ceremonies which took place in the capital, one hundred days travelling. In Algeria, I visited the cities and the countryside, inspected troops, ships and air squadrons. I paid four visits to Morocco, three to Tunisia and one to Libya. In Equatorial Africa, a long tour took me through the entire area. I crossed Corsica three times, made three trips to Italy to spend time among the troops in action. During the Allied landing in Normandy, I went to England and from there to Bayeux in France; shortly afterwards I made my first trip to the United States and to Canada. Such journeys comforted me. Men, so exhausting when manoeuvring for ambition, are so engaging when acting for a great cause.

Let us return to my election as president of the CNR. This new method of selection went through without problems, or so I was told by those who were in charge of the election. I am rather glad to say that the only opposing vote I got was that of Emmanuel d'Astier de La Vigerie.

Emmanuel d'Astier de La Vigerie is an ambiguous figure. Today, he calls himself a progressive, in other words a Communist, yet he occasionally pays the Elysée a visit and runs errands for its occupants. No one ever knows what he really thinks, but whatever he thinks is certain to be complicated and devious. We can, however, be grateful to him for one thing; a little-known book called *Les Grands*, in which he showed that de Gaulle was favourable to Algerian Independence as early as 1957, one whole year before he shouted 'Long Live French Algeria' at Mostaganem. Before the war, this strange and ubiquitous character was first a naval officer, then a minor *littérateur*. He even wrote an amusing article in *Marianne*, angrily comparing the handsome Stavisky vault in the cemetery of Père Lachaise with Drumont's neglected tomb. But it was the style of the piece that mattered; unfortunately I don't possess a copy for obvious reasons. On the other hand, I remember

finding a book by this author at the home of some people who
sheltered me. He had left it there after a visit to them. It was rather
a boring novel about a Franco-American love affair, but the dedica-
tion was interesting. Perhaps he has forgotten it, so I will quote it:
'To myself, an expression of profound sympathy.' Personally, I
feel neither sympathy nor admiration for that type of 'red and pink'
aristocrat, who always remains on the outskirts of every allegiance.

Once the CNR election was over, the London authorities suddenly re-discovered their powers of speech and action, after forgetting them for so long. They appointed Emile Bollaert as their
General Delegate to France. By doing this, they created a dual
authority which duty, wisdom and necessity luckily prevented from
becoming a rivalry and a schism. We had too much to do, and we
were running too many serious dangers to be tempted to quarrel
over precedence and political manoeuvring. Even the idea of insur-
ing our future interests did not tempt us, for our futures were so
precarious. There probably were some who calculated in terms of
the future, but they carefully kept out of the way, and I never met
any of them until after the Liberation.

Besides, Emile Bollaert was less interested in intrigue than anyone I have ever met. He had been a Radical under Herriot and had
a certain way of looking at things which was not really suited to the
discomforts and oddities of clandestine life. Yet he was the most
coolly courageous of men. Perhaps his lack of adaptation to danger
was only due to his contempt for it, as we can remember from his
nautical adventures when he set off for England. He was a calm,
firm man. He luckily came back from the concentration camps,
usually so dangerous for a man of his age and importance. But I
rarely met him after the war, for he was too reserved and dignified
to try and draw any attention to himself. He would be the last who
could be accused of reaping the same harvest twice; when it was
all over, he simply put down his scythe.

After Emile Bollaert, General de Gaulle chose Alexandre Parodi
as his representative on French soil. Parodi was a member of the
Conseil d'État, his father had been one of the leaders of the Third
Republic, and his brother was one of the first Resistance members
to die for his country. The new General Delegate stayed on until
the Liberation, and, throughout those difficult times, we were
never in conflict. It was only afterwards when times were easy
again, that we were completely opposed on every subject from

Europe to Maghreb, although we never fought in the open. But
during the Occupation, I think we helped each other a great deal.
He had a scrupulous and methodical mind, he was cautious in
making decisions, but he was resolute in action and a model
General Delegate.

London – I always call it London because we never knew with
whom we were dealing exactly – could not have chosen a better
delegate, so well adapted to working conditions in an occupied
country. Communications may even have improved while he was
our Delegate, though they were never very good, and we found it
hard to avoid feeling abandoned by men who seemed indifferent to
our fate. When we read the newspapers or listened to the radio, it
was obvious that most of the important work was a matter of top-
level discussion. It was a struggle between Titans: de Gaulle,
Churchill, Roosevelt and Stalin were fighting for the sceptre. We
poor worker-ants often had to carry out contradictory orders and
to obey minor officials, who changed all the time and were hardly
ever systematic. Yet our role was important too, for we served as
good arguments in the battles at the summit.

During those years, I sent not dozens but hundreds of coded
telegrams to the French government in exile. Naturally I did not
count them or keep a record of them. For various reasons, sometimes by instinct, I always acted with the most scrupulous secrecy.
Yet I have always been interested in archives, and once I even presided over an international conference of archivists. But I know
that these two activities are completely incompatible when prac-
tised at the same time. And so I can only say one thing for certain
about my radio messages: there were a great many of them. I
could have been told that my messages were uninteresting, or that
I ought to get information on one or two specific points. But that
was not the answer I got. For I did get one answer and only one.
Remember, only the men who transmit broadcasts run any danger;
they may be caught at any moment, while the men receiving the
broadcast are perfectly safe. This means that too many messages
can bring harm only to those who send them. Yet the only reply
that ever reached me was, 'Reduce traffic'. That was all, but it
certainly said enough.

I was now president of the CNR and this took up all my time.
Soon the CNR acquired an envoy from de Gaulle. We organized
the work as best we could, and I still think we went about it in the

right way. We could not possibly bring together eighteen people, unless it was a really exceptional case. It is a fact that revolutionaries have a tendency to chatter endlessly at least among themselves; they refuse to keep silent and to stop writing letters. The first thing to do was to reduce the flow both of correspondence and of conversation to a minimum. We had to take the most minute precautions and that is what we did. Tragedies occurred, particularly among my friends who dealt with the broadcasts. And 'Lenormand', leader of the movement *'Ceux da la Libération'* and a CNR member, died heroically, gun in hand. But not one of the CNR members ever had any difficulty as a result of our meetings, and there were at least eighty. These took place in a different house nearly every time, except for a few places where we returned because they were safe and convenient. It is hard to imagine all our investigations, our infinite precautions, our continuous vigilance in finding safe meeting-places. Once these were found, we still had to tell our members one by one of the new rendezvous and get them there.

The CNR bureau held its sessions in the presence of the General Delegate. It had a president and four members whose job was to find out the opinions of those who could not attend meetings, to speak in their name, and to inform them afterwards of what had taken place. These contacts were often difficult to establish as some of the members of the CNR were very hard to reach. Whenever I could, I would liaise with the members personally. At that time, the Paris Métro was guarded and the connecting corridors at the stations were often barricaded, so that I did a great deal of walking through the city and the suburbs. It was very good for my health.

Who were the members of the Bureau? There was Maxime Blocq-Mascart, a leader of the OCM (Military and Civilian Organization)', which represented the principal Resistance movements in the Northern Zone, *'Ceux de la Résistance'* and *'Ceux de la Libération'*; although these two organizations were controlled by the same people at the executive level they were completely distinct and the first was open to all. There was also Louis Saillant, who represented Léon Jouhaux's CGT (at that time, not a Communist organization, but including Communists), the Socialist SFIO party, and the Northern Liberation movement, of which he was a member, composed of Socialists and Christian Trade Unionists. Finally, there was a representative of the MUR, in other words, the United Resistance Movements (Southern Zone), *Combat*, *Libération*, and *Franc-Tireur*. The representatives varied depending on the circumstances and especially on the arrests. I cannot possibly list them all. I neither want to cast a shadow of present enmity over the united past, nor to bring up all the various shades of political nuance. But, evidently, the general picture was somewhat vague. Villon knew exactly what he wanted, Saillant not yet. The others were generally undecided (in other words, influenceable), or cautious (in other words, hesitant).

Our life was dangerous, and at the same time monotonous. During the last drab winter of the Occupation, we had to exercise greater caution than ever. Traffic was very sparse and this made the streets easy to control; the police was always on the alert, there were quite a few informers and blabbermouths about, and, of course, there was also the curfew.

On two occasions, when I did not calculate distances well or lost my way, I had to sleep out in the street. Once during the summer, I slept on the Boulevard Raspail not far from Rodin's statue of Balzac. The pavement was hard, but it wasn't too cold. I lay under a bench like an outlaw, not on top of it like a *clochard*. The second time the weather was colder and I spent the night in the corner of a little street in the 17th *arrondissement*; I have forgotten what it was called, but I could probably find it again.

These were minor adventures of no consequence. More often, about every two months, a friend of mine in charge of our security arrived at my door with a determined, anxious look on his face. Before he said a word, I was already packing my suitcase. Twenty minutes later, we would leave, without any elaborate farewells to my hosts, who had been running great risks by hiding me. 'We're going to Dupont's. Its ground plan is like this and like that. Dubois hasn't come back. We've got to cut off every link with him, and cancel everything he knew. We've begun to warn our friends.'

One night I was lying in bed thinking about our problems when the doorbell rang around one or two in the morning. My hostess, a very brave and intelligent woman, opened the door. It was the French police looking none too proud of its role; it had come to take away an old Austrian Jew who had lost all his relatives. His papers were in order and he was wearing the yellow star while he waited hopefully to go abroad. They took him away, and we could do nothing. He never came back. Meanwhile the President of the

CNR listened to everything without being able to go to the poor man's help. The curious thing was that the police had not come to fetch the man of action, the real enemy. I have often thought of the mistake they made that evening. The French police was often on the wrong track, because it lacked the zeal to be efficient. And I must admit that I stayed on longer than usual at the house where this sad event had taken place, because it had already been searched once, and was thus less likely to be searched again. I did not leave until the day one of my comrades set off from it on a dangerous mission and was not back an hour later.

We called a meeting of all available CNR members only twice before the Liberation. On one of these occasions, the meeting lasted all night at a house in the outer suburbs, which we could get to by train. But I did spend a long time every week with several CNR members who were not present at the headquarters of the movement. Auguste Gilliot, now the Communist mayor of Saint-Denis and once a deputy for the Seine district, was the most meticulous and exact of all the members – also the one who took up the most of our time. I met Laurent Casanova once during a conference on military questions. He was then a Communist, and also belonged to the General Staff of the FTP. On that occasion, I took him for a Bulgarian just returning from the International Brigade; in fact he was a Corsican, born at Souk-Arhas (the department of Constantine in French Algeria). But how could I help making a mistake, for he told us only his rank, not his name. On the other hand, General Revers who had succeeded General Frère as chief of the ORA, never concealed his identity from us.

Auguste Gilliot worked like a peasant. He had the perseverance and the untiring capacity for repeating himself that I later found in Molotov; this is a hallmark of the Communists. He would ask me a question and I would reply. He would object and I would reply. Then we would return to the same question again. This went on for a long time. Never did a man carry out his mission more scrupulously and with greater determination not to give in on any point. Gilliot had a remarkable gift for repetition and an exasperating talent for remaining imperturbable, although I discovered later that this was an acquired trait.

What made our encounters even more complicated was the support Gilliot received from a correspondence with an unexpected ally, Jacques Debu-Bridel. My friends were in charge of all the

mail delivery, including printed matter between members of the
CNR – a very dangerous activity. The Communists kept a team of
writers and printers in a safe hiding place, and they were responsible for a lot of the documents that were sent out. They produced
the most, and in certain ways, the best material. Jacques Debu-
Bridel was always the first to back their party line. During our first
meeting at the rue du Four, Debu-Bridel told us that he did not
represent the Republican Federation, although he was a member
of this Right-Wing organization and had run for office under its
aegis. He was the personal representative of Louis Marin who, at
the same time, was openly holding improvised press conferences
at the Aix and Chambéry hotel in Vichy. This was a rather unusual
pedigree but we needed someone from the Right. Therefore, we
took on Debu-Bridel, wrongly thinking that he would cause no
trouble. We had our man from the Right Wing. Or so we thought.

The Communist party regularly submitted questionnaires to the
members of the CNR, usually about issues dealing with Communism, the Soviet Union or similar problems, and demanding
immediate answers. Most of the members either did not reply or
else answered succinctly without going into detail. But Debu-
Bridel, who had no importance except as a representative of the
Right Wing, would hurl himself on these questions, approving the
questionnaires and answering yes to everything. As we were fighting for a common cause at the time I still believe that some of the
questions deserved the answer yes. But Debu-Bridel's total and
immediate endorsement of everything was a bit too zealous, to say
the least. I remember Auguste Gilliot, known to us as Manin,
reading out Debu-Bridel's answers in a quiet little Montrouge
café, and commenting on them with comical solemnity.

'Well, well, I must say, the URD (these were the initials, much
despised on the Left, of the Democratic Republican Union) really
sees things clearly!'

Afterwards Debu-Bridel was the director of the *Front National*,
which became the newspaper for fellow-travellers. Now he is a
fervid Gaullist and presides over a 'peripheral' post in the government. His job may be profitable; but no one who has heard him
can claim he does it brilliantly.

Daniel Mayer was much less conciliatory with Manin, though
there were many conciliators at the time. Mayer is now president
of the *Ligue des Droits de l'Homme*, and a member of the PSU,

probably called the United Socialist Party because it is the most divided in the world. His quarrel with Guy Mollet certainly did Mollet no good at all; but it has left Mayer stranded, which is a pity. In spite of all that has happened since and our total disagreement now, I must do him justice, no matter who objects; I never met a more loyal, liberal and fervent Resistance fighter than Daniel Mayer during the dramatic final year of the Occupation. I won't describe his quarrels with Manin here. The only thing the two men ever had in common was that I had a rendezvous with each of them, the Jew and the atheist, at the church of Saint-Pierre de Montrouge, in the chapel of Saint Rita, patron saint of desperate causes.

Later, we were reproached for not controlling our propaganda and especially our actions better. But, even in normal conditions, centralization is no guarantee against inefficiency. When you lead a clandestine and hunted existence, it is impossible. When your liaison agents get arrested and your leaders move from house to house deliberately leaving no traces, each echelon must work independently and do what it thinks best, as well as jealously guard its own freedom of action. This was how a lot of superfluous or embarrassing matter got printed and distributed. It would have been impossible to run about with a pair of scissors, censoring all the newspapers, tracts, leaflets and broadsheets. The police gave credit for all of it to those men whose names they knew; but in fact even if they could have been traced, the real authors would have been most reluctant to change their style or even a word of what they had written. All this was a pity, and we tried to avoid it whenever possible.

Some unjustifiable acts were certainly committed. But they are a small proportion of those heroic feats that Eisenhower said were worth fifteen divisions during the Allied Landing; they do not compare with the untold number of anonymous sacrifices made to liberate our country. I feel no guilt at all about the acts committed in the name of freedom against informers, torturers and murderers. Of course, there were some excesses and some disorders; that is the way things happen, and the Radio London broadcasts were more full of threats than pleas for moderation. Never once, I insist, did I use the CNR to menace anyone; but no one listened to the few counsels of moderation. It surprises me that the same people who encouraged feelings of anger and violence twenty years ago should condemn them today. There still is a Métro station in Paris named after Fabien, a French army officer who shot a German naval officer in the back on the Métro platform which now bears his name. This painful, not glorious, incident took place shortly after Russia entered the war. Fabien fought bravely in a unit belonging to Salan's division and later died a colonel. I bring up this episode to show that sometimes the same people both praise and condone acts of violence, only to blame them later. Pierre de Gaulle, the General's brother, represented the Municipal Paris Council at the inauguration of the Fabien station.

Some poor people had only spoken foolishly, or else they had inspired jealousy in men who revenged themselves, pretending to be Resistance fighters. These were the saddest cases. There were some butchers, some holders of grudges, and some who got carried away. How could we control people's impulses when we didn't know where they were during that feverish time when regular communications had broken down? We could and did give instructions; but there was no way to enforce them or to prevent disobedience. When it was all over, it was easy enough to reproach the Resistance for its lack of authority. But that same Resistance had been fighting in the dangers of the Occupation; it had seen its groups 'decapitated', its comrades killed. You cannot administer a nation in full rebellion the way you would run the Mortgage Registration Office. I will always regret the abuses of the Liberation, the innocent victims who were sacrificed by mistake to passion or contagious violence. But in all fairness, I believe that we made every effort to limit the damage. The stakes were huge; our limited communications gave us only a very precarious hold over events taking place in scattered parts of the country. And also, the pitiless manhunts after Resistance fighters, *maquisards*, Jews and other rebels, had driven many to paroxysms of hatred after four years of waging a bloody and unequal struggle everywhere.

The rash of summary executions which marked the period right after the Liberation was far more serious, more costly, and less forgiveable. I must insist that the CNR was in no way responsible for them. Voluntarily, it gave up all powers in late August; I no longer belonged to it after that. It continued to exist for a time, then went into hibernation. Who and what could it fight against, now that it had achieved its purpose? Such organizations were only kept on by those who, for a long time, toyed with the idea of setting up an alternative government.

Our means were limited; in fact, they were practically non-existent, particularly in the areas where we were thought to possess vast resources. Does anybody realize what was the French Air Force's actual strength? All I know about it is what Jean Moulin told me on his second and last journey to France: during the worst period, the French Air Force had only fifteen special planes in all, to help every European Resistance movement from Cape Nord to Cape Mataman. They had specially-trained crews for these dangerous and difficult missions; for the pilots had first to get through anti-aircraft defences, before landing as best they could in the middle of fields lit only by flashlights or stable lanterns. The men who found and recommended possible landing-fields were inexperienced, and so the pilots sometimes slewed around in a net which was thought all right. Such mishaps could delay the precious plane and the crew for quite a long time before they could make the perilous journey back to England. In spite of this, the growing number of Frenchmen who listened to the BBC and supported the Resistance only with hearts and ears were firmly convinced that there was a regular air-taxi service functioning perfectly and carrying the top brass off to London or Algiers, where the victory was being prepared.

The reason why one man was taken safely home to port, and the others left to sink or swim, has always been a mystery to me. Did de Gaulle disdainfully leave the choice to those who put their friends first? Why one man and not another? Perhaps de Gaulle thinks that, as no man is worth anything, anyone can take the place of anyone else.

In Algiers, a Consultative Assembly was founded to give the Allies the illusion of symbolic democracy. It was made up of a curious assortment of men, some distinguished and some misfits who had found their niche after seeking it everywhere. This assembly hastily took on all the attributes, institutions and rules of a parliament, and it would discuss every problem with great solemnity. But de Gaulle made all the decisions and remained totally indifferent to their debates. Yet from time to time there would be a slightly more violent tempest in this teacup, and then de Gaulle would make an all-out effort to pour oil on the waters. As everyone knew perfectly that this went against the grain, they were most grateful for his kindly attention and responded to his advances. When the boring duty was over and he had them in the

bag – at least for a time, as professional squabblers are never completely satisfied – de Gaulle would leave again. He would show
what he thought of them either by keeping eloquently silent or by
making one succinct comment. One day there was a meeting of the
Commission for Foreign Affairs, which de Gaulle respected far
more than the rest; he had undertaken the difficult task of explaining his policy in Syria and Lebanon to it. To do this, he displayed his most artful wiles of persuasion, or at least of pacification.
After the meeting he summed up his opinion of the audience in
one phrase: 'Bread for the ducks'.

Many of the ducks, who are either Deputies or Ministers, have
now forgotten the city and the country that helped them. These
men clutched at Algiers the way a drowning man clutches at a raft.
They chose to go and work there under Weygand; later, they
flourished in de Gaulle's entourage. And all of them have forgotten
their haven, how they waved the flag there, how they begged to get
there, and how nice it felt to be on good French soil once again!
Only a very few have remembered faithfully; the others have forgotten their oaths. Many of those who owe Algeria their lives and
their careers merely kept silent or offered their help when de Gaulle
horribly and unforgiveably abandoned that part of France. How
painful it is to see the long list of those dogs who, after eating from
the dish, lifted their leg on it when they had finished!

They whiled away the golden days in Algiers with endless chatter, putting on airs of self-importance because they had nothing to
do, but we who remained in Occupied France continued to count
the days and the dead. Time was deadly, and I mean deadly in the
literal sense of the word; three hundred thousand Frenchmen left
for the darkness and fog of the concentration camps, and the
majority never returned.

2

The Liberation /
The Paris Uprising /
The Parade down the
Champs Elysées

The 'Longest Day' came. We had found all the days and all the years long. But this vast invasion, this fantastic technical victory, this superb assault, galvanized France into hope and activity. Only later did we find out all the risks involved in the landing, and the skill that had been needed to plan it all. At the time, the occupied press and radio only spoke of the cities that were being destroyed, the bombardments that missed their target, the victims who were being sacrificed pointlessly. Even today, it is hard to understand why there were so many bombardments and why so many were off target, sometimes repeating the same error. But the relief at seeing some action, the prospect of liberation and victory at last, seemed more important than the large number of French victims which the Allies could have reduced.

The famous 'Atlantic Wall' crumbled under the assault. Later, I showed a German propaganda film on the Wehrmacht's coastal defences to Duff Cooper, the first English Ambassador to Paris after the war, a courageous man if ever there was one, and a clear-sighted, faithful friend to France in the most difficult times. After seeing the film, he said to me quite simply, 'I'm glad I didn't see it before the landing.'

The *maquis* increased in size and grew more efficient at fighting in France. They had more and more skirmishes with the enemy. Although the Vercors *maquis* finally fell after a heroic defence, and in spite of the hideous Oradour massacre, a scattered army was appearing in every corner of France determined to avenge defeat, to restore honour and not to be left out of victory. The fine Algerian troops, Europeans and Muslims, fought side by side, as can be seen in the large – too large – French military cemetery outside Rome. They played an important and valiant part in the Italian campaign. But the people were ready to rise, and the Resistance, which had begun as a handful of men, was now the entire nation. The railways were torn up and the roads barred to prevent the enemy from withdrawing. Sabotage and bombardment had made all the communications networks useless. The railway employees were threatened from three sides, the enemy, the Allies, and the Resistance. Yet they deliberately created a fourth danger for themselves, that strange, marvellous 'battle of the rails', which, for once, was designed to prevent the trains from working properly. They ran great risks for no other motive than pure patriotism.

After the slow advance and the preparations for the breakthrough, the Normandy front suddenly collapsed. The armoured divisions fanned out for the great mopping-up operation. But Paris, naturally, was the primary objective, the most important symbol of all. For months, the CNR had been repeating de Gaulle's words, 'National Insurrection is inseparable from National Liberation'. Who knows, he may have regretted saying this later, for he does not give it the space in his *Memoirs* that it occupied in our hearts largely because of him. There were uprisings more or less everywhere in France; but we still had to have an insurrection in Paris.

As is usual, the incidents began spontaneously and sporadically. We had to organize the uprising as much as we could and give orders to all parts of the city, including the suburbs. Otherwise, the armed groups which had acted independently might be isolated or wiped out. And, of course, there was one very real danger: one faction might take over and direct the action and the course of events. It was not easy to make decisions amongst all this confusion. We did not know what was taking place, what would take place, or even what had taken place. We had to guess what was happening rather than trust to information, which was often false or doubtful. I went one day to a little street near the Place de la République. I think it was called the rue d'Angoulême. The atmosphere was chaotic, tremendously hopeful, and rather anxious. To get to the street, we had to cross the roads around the Place de la République, which was caught in a crossfire of machine-guns and anti-tank guns. We reached our destination in the end, and I found the little café where Pierre Crénesse had left our radio sets. I cannot understand how Crénesse can reconcile his past views and opinions with his present post in a radio service controlled by the government. I worked with Crénesse on *Combat*, and I was to see him again after the war in memory of past friendship. On the day of the Paris uprising, I made a recording which was broadcast all over the city, urging the Parisians to revolt. I still have a copy of that call to arms somewhere. I find it very moving because it reminds me of those times with the sound of gunfire in the background. This recording was not played again during later anniversary celebrations. It has become even rarer than the record of de Gaulle's speech at Mostaganem.

The Paris Uprising

The insurrection was under way. Paris itself would liberate Paris. The Communists, of course, were the most dynamic group, the best organized and the most skilled at handling crowds. This is always the case. Look at the British and the Australian Trade Unions today, let alone the others. Even in countries where the Communist Party is practically non-existent, there are often still Communists in strategic positions, leading the organized workers' movements in vital sectors. In France, they are even more obvious. This is why the traditional Left Wing and the New Left have to accept Communist domination, whether they realize it or not.

At the time, the Communists did not bother to draw up any plans for a new constitution, unlike so many intellectual members of the Resistance. Texts serve only as instruments for action, according to the Communists. They could compose texts as well as anyone else or better; but they always made everything subordinate to practical results. This was why they had acquired an importance out of proportion to their actual numbers. They had a solid base and a numerous following. Although they always knew where they were going, many of their followers got lost in the intricate labyrinth down which they were being led by the three types of Communist agents, the members, the accomplices and the dupes.

But these Communist realists also made mistakes. There are two fundamental errors to be made in public life; one is to under-estimate the enemy, but there it was not only the Communists who miscalculated; the other is to overestimate one's own strength, and that played tricks on them. They were quite correct in thinking that the section of the Resistance not under their control was scat-tered, inefficient, unrealistic and verbose. But they misjudged the reaction they set off by being over-confident and arrogant. They were so sure of themselves that they helped to persuade the Paris police to change sides. They were far from being the only ones helping to do this; but everything would probably have taken longer without them. That day, patriotic enthusiasm got the better of the Communist leaders' rigid training. They may have been Communists; but that did not stop them from being men first, and they allowed themselves to be carried away by the wave of enthus-iasm like everyone else, without thinking that they would not be able to direct its course.

And so it was the Paris police which captured the Hôtel de Ville and the Préfecture de Police during the uprising, while Paris was still occupied by the Germans. A regular garrison was stationed at these two symbolic buildings in the name of the insurrection. Luizet, a Prefect appointed by de Gaulle, took over the Préfecture de Police, which has always been the servant of the state, the home of law and order, and, when necessary, of repression. Marcel Flouret, Prefect for the Seine, also appointed by de Gaulle or in his name, established his headquarters at the Hôtel de Ville, the citadel of French freedom, which has witnessed so many rebellions against the established order.

I made my way through the barricades to police headquarters almost immediately, accompanied by three or four people. The barricades barred the way, but they opened for me and my com-panions. I made a speech to the garrison which had been joined by volunteers, ex-policemen, veterans and young men, eager to fight. I remember shaking hands with several Algerians, loyal French soldiers who had rushed into the fray. Later, these men, our friends during the Liberation, were shamefully forgotten along with so many of their brothers. I also went to the Hôtel de Ville before settling there myself with the CNR, and I visited the wounded at the Hôtel-Dieu Hospital. From the windows of the two big buildings we had captured, and from the barricades across the bridges and *quais*, our men fired at the German detachments and at the few tanks that were moving about in an effort to clear the main boulevards.

The nurses were running across the deserted Parvis Notre-Dame, sometimes getting caught in the cross-fire, to pick up the wounded. Throughout all the excitement, the fighting and the disorder, they remained wonderfully calm and brave. I went to visit the Frenchmen who had been wounded in the uprising, and also the German wounded – Flouret translated for them my hopes for their recovery and for peace.

The hubbub and the bustle at the Hôtel de Ville betrayed our enthusiasm, our happiness and our exhaustion. Around this time, the Communists began to wonder if they had not made a tactical blunder. Our side now controlled the two most vital buildings in Paris; but the regular authorities were in command. The rebellion was triumphant, yet at the same time under control. Events could very well have gone otherwise, and in that case, the future would have been different. Hesitantly, but with growing insistence, the Communists began trying to convince us that we had made a mistake. The big buildings were too obvious as targets and too vulnerable, they told us; our fighters had to have greater mobility.

Finally, they asked me to evacuate the Hôtel de Ville. If we did, another garrison could be installed to replace the first, although that was obviously not what they told me. One night, they announced that a column of Tiger tanks was coming down the Avenue de l'Opéra to attack us. We would be trapped. They suggested that the CNR should leave the building through the sewers. When I refused to believe this information and pointed out that, at any rate, the tanks were not likely to come through the sewers, some members of the CNR began an argument. Not all the CNR members knew what was going on, for they were scattered, especially at night, in every corner of the gigantic building. One of the members said that the leaders should stay put because they had to share the same risks as the fighters. Another man who was personally very courageous and under nobody's domination then, answered, 'When have you ever seen the General Staff up in the front line?' This argument proved conclusive; we would stay. And so, we stayed. There were no more suggestions of this kind, and no one brought up the subject of non-existent Tiger tanks again.

The significant thing about this attitude of the Communists was that it seemed to contradict their opposition to the idea of a temporary truce in Paris alone. Basically though, it was the same policy: they wanted their guerrillas to continue fighting and to keep their mobility. They were hostile to any notion of obeying the regular army; they wanted freedom of manoeuvre. Parodi had indeed come to an agreement with the German forces; the fighting would stop in Paris if the German convoys were allowed to retreat down specified routes. This truce obviously displeased those who were eager to fight; but, although there were very few Tiger tanks in the Paris area, we had no way of knowing how much damage the artillery and the bombers might do. We had every reason to believe that they might do a very great deal. Monuments, bridges and human lives were all in danger of destruction, if the Germans gave way to a sudden wave of fury and despair.

Parodi, who had almost been shot during the preliminary phases of these negotiations, had asked me to obtain the CNR's approval of this truce, and so we had a meeting at the rue Bellechasse. We held many meetings during this period with all members present. Once we met without Parodi, not knowing that he was being held prisoner. Some of our members were influential and absolutely uncontrollable, so that these meetings were quite a strain on anyone who realized what was at stake and who had no wish to make things uselessly worse. I must admit that when you added the men who didn't care if everything blew up to those who didn't have a clear understanding of the position, you nearly had a sufficient majority to block every decision, leaving the field wide open for those who would be only too glad to take over. Still, the CNR finally, with my approval, gave its support to the idea of a truce. But it was not enough to support the idea; it had to be put in practice. The truce was broken a few hours after it was announced in the streets. We had no way of enforcing it. We had no method of persuading people to observe it. The only thing left for us to do was to admit we had failed and to give up trying. We waited to see the enemy's reaction with some anxiety. Chaban-Delmas, the military delegate for the Northern Zone, did not know what to expect any more than we did. Nor did the men who rejected the idea of any negotiation, but who wanted us to leave via the sewers. Nor did the people who feared for the loss of human lives, the irremediable damage to buildings, and the halting of the Allied advance if the bridges were destroyed. None of us knew.

Fortunately, the commander of the German troops in Paris, General von Choltitz, realized that it would be madness to go ahead with the total destruction of Paris, as he had been ordered. He also knew what we did not: that his means were limited. For both these reasons, he put an end to the fighting. At Montparnasse station, he surrendered to General Leclerc, commander of the Second Armed Division, and to Colonel Rol-Tanguy, the Paris commander of the FFI. To claim that the liberation of Paris was due to General von Choltitz, as some people have said, would be a wild exaggeration. But it would be wrong to deny that he played a humane and important role. I am completely objective when I say this, as I have never met the man in my life.

The first tanks from Leclerc's division arrived at the Hôtel de Ville, before the surrender at Montparnasse. Captain Dronne, a veteran fighter and a Gaullist, was at their head. His flushed face was covered with dust and sweat. We welcomed him triumphantly and I delivered a brief speech for the occasion. He simply answered, 'I come from the Sarthe', and added that the famous Tiger tanks had better mind their manners now – a rather reckless statement, as his tanks were tiny. But those little tanks were led by a brave man, who was courageous in civilian life as well as in war.

I must add a word to this brief account about an episode which has remained etched in my memory for understandable reasons. De Gaulle must be added to the list of those who disapproved of a truce, and this is what he wrote on the subject:

I learned that on the morning of the 20th, the Hôtel de Ville had been occupied by a Parisian police detachment led by Roland-Pré and Léo Hamon. The Prefect of the Seine Department, Flouret, went there to assume his functions. But I was also informed that Parodi and Chaban-Delmas on the one hand, and the majority of the Council of the Resistance on the other – warned by the Americans and British agents that it would be a long time still (weeks, they were told) before Allied troops entered the capital, knowing the weakness of the arms at the partisans' disposal in comparison to the 20,000 men, eighty tanks, sixty cannon and sixty planes of the German garrison, eager to avoid the destruction of the bridges over the Seine (which Hitler had ordered) and to save political and military prisoners – had decided to agree to Mr Nordling the Swedish Consul General's suggestion and, by his mediation, conclude a ceasefire with General von Choltitz, in command of enemy forces in Paris and the suburbs.

This news affected me very disagreeably. The more so since, as I learned of the signing of the ceasefire, Leclerc was preparing to advance. Their arrangement took no account of the military situation. On the morning of the 23rd, as I was leaving Le Mans, I was informed that the ceasefire, opposed by the majority of the combatants, had only been partially observed, although it had permitted Parodi and Roland-Pré, arrested by the Germans on the Boulevard Saint-Germain, to be released after an interview with Choltitz. I learned, furthermore, that hostilities had resumed on the evening of the 21st, that the prefectures, the ministries and the mayors' offices in the *arrondissements* were still in our hands, that the Parisians were throwing up barricades and that the German general, while reinforcing his strongholds, was not engaging in any repressive action. Were these tactics inspired by fear of the future, a desire to spare Paris, or by an agreement with the Allies, whose agents had been in contact with the general staff ever since Oberg and the Gestapo had left the capital? I could not determine which was the principal motive, but I was inclined to believe that, in any case, help would arrive in time.

Neither Parodi nor Chaban-Delmas has ever told us any of this precious information. It is set down by a man who has his own notions of the way history should be written, who finds it easy, ten years after the fact, to present his version in a favourable light. No one ever told us anything while it was going on. When we debated the question at a house in the Montsouris area, Parodi had tears in his eyes on several occasions. I had to force a Communist member of the CNR to apologize for insulting Chaban-Delmas. Chaban-Delmas quickly forgot it, for that is his nature; but I still recall the time, and the pleas and the threats I had to make to force our member to take his words back. I prefer not to repeat what he actually said.

General de Gaulle was certainly better informed than I was, and he had firmer principles. When I later discussed this affair with him, he replied: 'You do not negotiate with the enemy while you are at war with him.' He repeated this rigorous and noble maxim several times on other occasions. Unfortunately, he forgot his words recently, when he continued the struggle to keep Algeria French while secretly negotiating for the exact opposite.

General de Gaulle arrived in Paris and took over. He set up his provisional headquarters at the Préfecture de Police and waited for us to go there. We all acknowledged him as our leader. The CNR had always strictly given its allegiance to the provisional government of the French Republic, and I had certainly contributed to this attitude. We owed the General every consideration; he was then the uncontested leader and the symbol of France. Nonetheless, the Préfecture de Police was not a very suitable place to celebrate the Liberation of Paris. It was better known for putting people in prison than for liberating them. Traditionally great national events were celebrated at the Hôtel de Ville. General de Gaulle made up his mind to come to us; we welcomed him with spontaneous cheering and all the honours we could improvise.

He was cold, and preoccupied with his new world. As usual, he was trying to find answers by closing his eyes and meditating rather than by opening his ears and listening to what was going on. He said three pleasant words to me, not one more, not one less. I had never seen him before, and though he was remote and tense, he seemed no different from the photographs of him I had put up on the walls of my room at Lyons, during the early part of my life in the Resistance. His manner was stiff, just like his voice, before he softened its tone to get away from Colombey. We had waited for this hour for so long that we were overwhelmed. The French flag was flying everywhere over Paris. At last, the dream had come true. In the name of the Paris Committee of Liberation, Georges Maranne and I greeted de Gaulle, who replied. I still have a record of this exchange; that and the record of the rue D'Angoulême are all that I have left of the day I once thought as the high-point of my life.

The record is scratched now, the memory tarnished. If I had known, I would have said Goethe's prayer to that moment: 'Don't go away. You are so beautiful.' But if I had made this prayer on that day of exultation, it would only have been yet another useless invocation to God, asking him to change men and history.

The Parade down the Champs Elysées

The next day, 26 August, the official entry into Paris took place down the Champs Elysées in the famous procession. It was the hour of triumph, and a vast crowd had come for the celebration even though the Germans were still at Le Bourget. The weather was wonderfully beautiful. The enthusiastic crowd roared with joy at being liberated. It saw and heard the victorious leaders only; the past was buried. A vast number of Frenchmen had forgotten that, when they were looking for a protector, they had turned to Marshal Pétain first. They had now turned the page, and with all their hearts and souls they paid homage to the man who had given them back their happiness and pride, the Saviour of France who was walking down the Champs Elysées. Practically no one shouted 'Long Live France', but everyone called out 'Long Live de Gaulle.' In moments of great distress or great joy, the crowd has a natural tendency to turn to one man and make him the symbol of their need to admire or to be protected. The enthusiasm of that first day was so great, so deep and so pure that no later occasions were able to match it even for a single instant.

We had been told to meet at the Arc de Triomphe, and so I took the CNR to the place where we had been told to go, to the left of the monument, going up the Champs Elysées. General de Gaulle passed in front of us, shook hands with a few people and then left again. Actually when I think about it, that wonderful and strange day of public consecration was very risky. The enemy was still extremely close and the capital could easily have been bombarded. It was quite natural that de Gaulle did not want to waste time making introductions. Yet a few of our members were displeased and briefly resented me for their disappointment. But soon everything was swept away again in the emotion of that perfect day.

Afterwards we tried to reach the Tomb of the Unknown Soldier, to pay our respects as de Gaulle had just done together with his companions in exile and those men who had been fighting abroad. But we weren't allowed to get near the tomb; some officials barred the way and they were obviously put off by our tired faces and wrinkled clothing. The ceremony was over before we could convince them to let us through. It did not matter, yet someone might have remembered us. Still, what if protocol is neglected in a popular festivity?

The sun shone in the sky and in our hearts as we went down the Champs Elysées with de Gaulle. Everyone was there, de Gaulle, Juin, Koenig and the CNR members, whose faces and names were unknown. And of course, there were also some of those people who always find a way to be where they don't belong. They follow you through life, and you never get rid of them. It was already like that at the Hôtel de Ville, and it was not going to change. Besides, General de Gaulle quite likes the company of parasites as long as they have the proper attitude. There was a whole group of people surrounding de Gaulle and refusing to let anyone pass ahead. But the central figure, the only one in whom the crowd was interested, kept his eye on the arrangement of his entourage, and knew how to put everyone back in their place – in other words, behind himself. There were hordes of journalists; de Gaulle later said that they were the only Allied representatives there.

No American troops were stationed in Paris, and the units that had passed by the Place d'Italie and the Gare de Lyon the day before had immediately withdrawn. Except for the presence of reporters and photographers, the Allies took no part in the next day's parade. For the entire distance it was to cover there would be only Frenchmen.

At the beginning of the procession, I found myself walking on the right-hand side of de Gaulle; but, by the end of the procession, I was walking to the left of him. Some unpleasant comments were made about this vastly important point in the days when the Gaullists ran very tough electoral campaigns against me; *tempi passati* – not the toughness, the elections. I admit that this switch took place during the procession. De Gaulle had noticed on the way that André Le Troquer, a member of the National Committee, was not correctly placed at his right hand. And so, with great agility (he had such long arms) he switched us around without anyone noticing, and gave back to an official the place usurped by an 'irregular'. As far as I was concerned, I didn't care where I was placed. On that day I felt important enough not to have to be seen in the first row. Anyway, on that particular day, with victory in sight, Paris liberated, all flags flying and our aims achieved, I asked for nothing of any man. I have described this incident not because I was connected with it, but to show de Gaulle's notions of protocol. For him, men do not exist as individuals but only as members of a hierarchy.

I left the procession at the Place de la Concorde, to go and wait for the General at his next stop, the Hôtel de Ville. It was after that point that shots began to be fired. They were not all shots in the air, for a high-ranking civil servant in the treasury was killed as he looked out on to the rue de Rivoli from his window. When I arrived at the Hôtel de Ville, there was a lot of firing going on there as well. But de Gaulle passed on without stopping and went straight to Notre Dame. There again, there were volleys during the *Te Deum*. I only found this out later, for I had not had the time to join up with the General. De Gaulle once told me: 'I am quite a good target. I did not hear the sound of the bullets.' He did believe it was an attempt on his life. Such attempts are dangerous, as was seen then and more recently in Algeria. De Gaulle later hinted that it was a Communist manoeuvre, ordered by the COMAC. There was no enquiry, as he probably had more urgent business, and I don't think the matter was ever satisfactorily resolved.

The day had not finished as well as it had begun; but it would not have mattered if it had been as bad throughout as at the end, or even worse. All those who were present remember that there were moments of happiness during that day which were so poignant and so deep that we felt our dreams had come true.

3

The Provisional
Government /
The Trip to Moscow /
'The Secret of the King'

The parade down the Champs Elysées had been a modern French version of the procession up the Capitol; but it was over now, and we had to begin living again, which meant working. We also had to start fighting again, which meant dying.

There were over two million Frenchmen in Germany, prisoners, deportees, and so-called 'volunteer' workers. As most of them were young men, it was a tremendous loss for France in every respect. The railways were in terrible condition; many of the lines were damaged and others were totally destroyed. The stations had been bombed and the rolling stock was in poor shape. There were not enough locomotives or coal. The bridges below Orléans, Paris and Lyons were in ruins. There was a serious shortage of food throughout the country. The merchant navy was bankrupt and all our big ports had been destroyed, so that we could not consider importing food supplies. Everyone was poverty-stricken, there was rationing everywhere. Our resources and currency were totally inadequate.

While the fighting went on elsewhere, the new régime in Paris was learning to cope with these difficulties from day to day. The complications were sometimes minor, but impossible to overcome all the same. The French administration was suffering from the succession of upheavals it had undergone and from the loss of its trained personnel which had been purged first by the Germans, then by Vichy, and finally by the Liberation committees. To stimulate national effort and state activity under de Gaulle, the Government was reorganized. Now that the London and Algiers Committee was at last set up in Paris as the regular government, it had to undergo some changes. The government would remain provisional; but some new appointments would make it clear to the nation and to the rest of the world that the régime was supported by the entire French community. The General's London supporters would remain, of course, but some less docile individuals would be eliminated, and a few members of the Home Resistance would be asked to join.

General de Gaulle asked me to go and see him at his office in the War Ministry, rue Saint-Dominique. His liking for protocol made him refuse to install himself at the Elysée Palace while his government remained provisional. He also refused to let Herriot use the President of the Chamber's headquarters again for the same reason, apart from the fact that Herriot's claim was unfounded. Herriot was mortally offended by what he considered lack of consideration on the General's part. De Gaulle's office on the first floor at the rue Saint-Dominique was austere with no foretaste of the sumptuous décors of the future.

De Gaulle told me succinctly that he wanted me to work for him. I pointed out to him that I had just started the MRP and that I would have to look after this new party. And indeed, it was I who was responsible for the formation of the MRP, though not for its dissolution. I fear that de Gaulle put an end to his dealings with the MRP only on my account; but at the time he told me that although he had nothing against the projected party he could not do without my help. 'I will give you Justice,' he said, and then, after a pause, he added, 'and Ecclesiastical Affairs.' What a gift! Justice meant purges, and Ecclesiastical Affairs did too. But I did not refuse outright. I had seen so many legal experts make terrible Ministers of Justice that I was almost tempted to see what a layman could do with the job. But then I had not yet seen a layman like my ex-friend Michelet at work, Place Vendôme.

For a few days, I heard nothing at all. Then, the usual photograph was published which announced to the world, and really to myself, that I had been made Minister of Foreign Affairs. This appointment was unexpected and rather improbable, as I had been sealed off from all foreign countries for three years and knew almost nothing about the world in 1944. During the Occupation, the BBC news had been jammed, I had not had the time to listen to it anyway, and nothing in the French occupied press could be taken at face value.

This was not the only paradoxical appointment. For example, Adrien Tixier, an international civil servant, had had nothing to do with French political life for about twenty years and had been totally cut off from his country for four years. Yet he was appointed Minister of the Interior. Tixier was a Socialist; but de Gaulle had worked with him and knew how to handle this gruff yet easy-going man. The General obviously preferred someone like him to a politician who would be too involved with one party. And so, a man who came from the outside world was appointed Minister of the Interior, while a man who had been confined to his native soil for four years was appointed Minister of Foreign Affairs. The least informed man seemed to have been chosen in both cases.

I took over at the Quai d'Orsay and stayed in office there for over five years without counting my periods as head of government, head of State, and head of National Defence, and without even mentioning various other appointments. It has left me a lot of memories, a lot to talk about one day in my retirement. It also made me the target of a great deal of resentment and inaccurate reporting. At the same time, it made me very philosophical. What more can you desire, unless you are after yet another Grand Cross of the *Légion d'Honneur*, or thirst for praise, which grows as stale as insults after a time? De Gaulle once spoke of 'people who need cars, gilded mouldings, ushers and telephones', in an attack on his past cabinets – not his present one. How wrong he was! It is easy to go away, without turning back once, to live in the outlaws' notorious 'comfort' as the Spartans of the *Figaro* have called it. De Gaulle's definition can certainly be applied to his present government and he knows it; but I don't consider myself included in the attack.

I went to the Quai d'Orsay in order to work, and even to live. I did not think it was very decent to requisition someone's apartment or house just because he was a Jew during the Occupation, or an alleged collaborator during the Liberation. I had been staying at the homes of friends who had made room for me, and now I moved to the small apartment set aside for the Minister. With me I took whichever books of mine had not been lost or left behind. My predecessor, René Massigli, was leaving for London, where he was to spend ten years as a hard-working and very influential ambassador. All he left me was some dispiriting advice, his executive secretary and one chauffeur. The rest of the personnel had either remained in Algiers or had belonged to the previous régime, so that it would have been impossible to use them as they would have been forced to go back on everything they had once said. Many people refused to return to France for fear of persecution, so that I had to sack quite a few in order to replace them. The State Council automatically dismissed those men who were absent. Some of these were certainly right to stay away; but a lot of men could have kept their jobs if they had come back. As it was, we had to get diplomats, and I was lucky enough to find some new recruits.

The recent archives had stayed in Algiers and wisely remained there for some time. Some of the earlier archives had been burned during the panic of May-June 1940, and some were seized by the Germans at Charité-sur-Loire and Rochecotte. Others had been destroyed in the fighting during the Liberation; a fire had broken out in one wing of the Quai d'Orsay where there were many offices. To make things worse, General de Gaulle was very secretive about the recent past and about his future intentions, so that only common sense could help me in dealing with everyday problems, some of which I knew nothing about when I began. As Giraudoux once put it, it was rather like approaching the problem of Prometheus, inventor of fire and guardian of the flame, with only a box of matches in my pocket.

The Allies recognized the provisional government when they saw that it had the obvious support of the people. I got in touch with the few ambassadors who were in Paris. They looked at me as though I were some strange animal, lost in the huge, antiquated, deserted palace of the Quai d'Orsay.

I learned all about Russian tact when the Russian *chargé d'affaires* came to see me; he asked to see me immediately and demanded the keys of the Baltic legations as though I were the door-keeper. Not knowing what had been decided in London, I asked for instructions before I surrendered the set of keys. The Anglo-Saxon ambassadors had to handle relations between their troops and the French population and administration. There were some extremely unpleasant incidents. De Gaulle had put François Coulet in charge of these matters, after the landing in Normandy. He would send letters and instructions from his headquarters that

were so disagreeable that people would come and complain to me
about them. This was particularly embarrassing as I never knew
anything about them until people came to me to protest about
their tone, which was, in fact, dictated by de Gaulle in person.
Later, Coulet's style became much milder, and he grew very
understanding. Of course, we were no longer dealing with our war
allies by this time, but with Algerian rebels. Here too, there were
no intermediaries, and de Gaulle's orders to be meek were as
faithfully obeyed as his orders to be insolent.

On 11 November 1944, the French government received
Winston Churchill in Paris. De Gaulle would have preferred
another date, but I managed to arrange it for that particular day.
It is a good thing to honour warriors in their old age. But it is also
a good thing to show them your gratitude right away. There is
nothing falsely sentimental in this idea: good politics has no place
for anger or ingratitude. Churchill, de Gaulle and Anthony Eden
were loudly cheered everywhere they went. I learned later that
some loyal friends of Churchill's had tried to prevent him from
making the trip and going down the Champs Elysées in a crowd
that was still armed, in a country where order had not yet been
completely re-established. One of these friends had even gone so
far as to say, 'If you absolutely insist on this journey, I will come
with you and shield you with my body.' Finally, this would-be
bodyguard who shall be nameless, never made the trip at all. If he
had come, he would have seen that the only bodyguard Churchill
needed was to protect him from the enthusiasm of the crowds. At
the Hôtel de Ville again, a young Communist called Tollet, who
was head of a temporary municipality, gave the English Prime
Minister a swastika emblem which had been captured during the
Liberation. Churchill thanked him for it in that moving French
of his, full of invented words and expressions, yet understood
by all.

I think that swastika emblem was his favourite present except
for one other, the Military Medal, given to simple soldiers as well
as to generals. After de Gaulle had left the provisional government,
Churchill, Chiang Kai-Shek, Stalin, and, of course, de Gaulle
himself, received the medal. Roosevelt was dead, Stalin and de
Gaulle were indifferent, but Churchill was delighted with it. I
don't know who told him this; but he believed that anyone found
drunk in the street wearing the medal had the right to be escorted

home free of charge by the police. This story is unfortunately not true; but he liked it very much and told everyone about it.

De Gaulle's foreign policy, or, I should say, foreign policy under de Gaulle, was difficult to run coherently. I grew more and more to dislike his enigmas and the way he handled everything. Providential decree, temperament, and also, I must admit, the fact that de Gaulle was the only leader in the régime who had the proper authority and who was trusted, meant that he was in charge of all major matters, even though there had been no constitution, no elections and no legislative continuity. We were lucky when we were given some hint, though certainly not an explanation, of de Gaulle's decisions and the courses he intended to take.

De Gaulle is incapable of consulting anyone ('useless chatter and a waste of time'), of describing a situation except in sibylline pronouncements and panoramic glimpses ('never explain any-thing'), or of sharing any authority and responsibility for his actions ('I alone suffice'). I never knew him to let himself be influ-enced, stopped or inspired by anyone except himself. He bases his decisions on reports, gossip, memories – chiefly grudges – and on his own opinions, which can be limited and uncertain. No advice, however good, can modify his ideas, because he does not trust anyone enough. This was my dismal impression before long. Some people have compared the General to Louis XIV; but he isn't like that at all. Louis XIV listened to everyone and drew his own conclusions afterwards. The only thing he and de Gaulle might have had in common was suspiciousness, nothing else. The only people I can think of to compare with de Gaulle are some Spanish monarchs, silent, motionless and secretive; they stood alone, for that was their duty. Someone once passed judgement on such monarchs, a judgement unfortunately true today as well, 'You are great, but the way a ditch is great; the more you take away, the greater it is.'

During the autumn of 1944, we were not on really good terms with anyone. The Resistance had understood and approved de Gaulle's intransigence during the war and had resented the way other nations tried to use Darlan, or the way Giraud intervened, in both cases obviously to get rid of Free France and its leaders. De Gaulle's independent attitude and the way he defended our rights took our breath away during the war, and we considered it a sign of great firmness and loyalty on his part. But even though we had good reasons to worry about England in the Middle East, about the United States in the Caribbean, and about both countries on the Rhine, we did feel a strong sense of solidarity with our two great Allies. The slogans 'Perfidious Albion' and 'American Imperialism' could not make any headway in the Resistance milieu. Now France was no longer in exile; it had helped in its own liberation, but there was no doubt that the Allies had done most of the work. Both the capital and the entire country were almost normal again, and it was time to settle our emotional disagreements with England and the US. The term 'emotional disagreement' was used by a civil servant not long ago to describe our quarrels with men we were fighting in war. But if ever this expression had a meaning or a significance, it was then, after the Liberation.

It was not easy to settle any disagreements with a *prima donna*. The term was used in 1945, and de Gaulle, feeling attacked by the definition, never forgave the man he assumed to be the author of the article. In fact, he made a mistake. It was the wrong man, who lost a much desired ambassador's post which had already been as good as promised to him. Whoever the author, and however badly received the article, it was quite a good definition. Roosevelt, Churchill and de Gaulle had met on the great stage of the world. Owing to circumstances, de Gaulle had been given a less brilliant role to play than the other two men, so that what he remembered most was the pressure, the lack of consideration and the mortification he had had to suffer. Churchill was known as de Gaulle's protector, and he was described as such in the Paris and Vichy press. But de Gaulle never accepted or admitted the part of a protégé, even though he was financed by England. He did not get along well with Churchill, who had one thing in common with him; both men liked to act according to their own ideas rather than anyone else's. In the end, de Gaulle could not bear the sight of Churchill. Churchill had other things to worry about besides de Gaulle, so that his dislike was less intense, and, as I saw myself, was non-existent for long periods of time, although de Gaulle got on his nerves more often than not during the actual period of the war. As for Roosevelt, de Gaulle got on with him like cat and dog. Roosevelt had a feline character and de Gaulle was a dog; I mean that as a compliment. But de Gaulle was a biting dog, and the two men never got along well at any time.

The Trip to Moscow

Quidquid delirant reges, plectuntur Achivi. Not long ago, before the
Church and the State agreed to discourage people from learning
Latin, I would have been ashamed to translate such a well-known
quotation. Today I don't need to apologize for explaining what it
means: it says that arguments between leaders are bad for the
people. De Gaulle's attitude towards the American people today
certainly has something to do with his dislike of Roosevelt's soft
voice and gestures and his covert politics. All the same, de Gaulle
recognized the fact that America was one of the real 'giants'. His
quarrels with the other 'giant' had always been indirect; in Russia,
all power was concentrated in one man, and this may have made
de Gaulle go to Moscow.

I do not propose to describe this vast undertaking in detail. It
came to nothing in the end except for a gradual disappointment,
and it started a lengthy controversy. Enough people have written
on the subject, including Ehrenburg who was not present at the
actual event and who knew nothing about it at the time; but that
only made it easier for him to find literary inspiration after the fact
and to do his duty of kowtowing. It is well known that you only
have to go through all the successive editions of the *Soviet Encyclopedia* to check the variations of Soviet policy.

De Gaulle's basic intention was crystal clear although it remained unstated; he wanted the Kremlin to serve as a counterweight to the Anglo-Saxon powers, who were supposedly hostile
towards us, though we had never seriously tried to reach an agreement with them. We were in Russia from the end of November to
the beginning of December 1944, and I had been in office for three
months. Some ill-intentioned people have since claimed that I persuaded de Gaulle to go through with this scheme out of personal
ambition and that he did it against his will. This idea is so preposterous that I can't understand how it ever got into anybody's
head. I hear that, during the legislative elections of 1962, a film
was shown to a number of UNR representatives brought together
by André Malraux. The press described how the public hissed
when I came on the screen to sign the treaty with Stalin. The
members of the audience must have been blind, for the person
signing with me was Molotov. And behind us, the two central

figures, Stalin and de Gaulle could be seen clearly. The public booed the wrong man. Or at least there were two Frenchmen to hiss at that day; the man in whose name they had come together and myself.

The Moscow negotiations lasted about ten days. We visited the Moscow underground just long enough to take a ride between two stations and then de Gaulle decided he had seen enough. We also went to the Exhibition of Trophies, which housed a collection of objects seized during the war. It was very large and impressive. The many trophies, large and small, were very well exhibited; we stayed there all of half an hour. We also went to visit an aeroplane factory. The director who took us round was the perfect specimen of a Soviet bureaucrat in Stalin's time. It was absolutely impossible to make him say a single interesting thing. If we asked how many planes were constructed, how many workers were employed or anything else, the answer was always a stereotyped tribute to the struggle against Hitler's Fascism.

The negotiations were rather like this and not much easier. I was the one who had to go through the boredom of discussing all the petty details and repeating myself endlessly, for de Gaulle only wanted to state his intentions and to make sweeping descriptions of his visions for the future.

The Russians knew very well that we were after a treaty; what else could we have wanted? There had been an Anglo-Soviet pact since the beginning of the German-Russian war. The United States was sending huge quantities of war materials and transport to the USSR; we had seen the consignments from the aeroplane at first, and later we had passed them when we went on a railway journey that lasted five days, without counting our stay in Stalingrad. What did France have to offer? Nothing except a war-time agreement to fight against the common enemy. And the Russians took that for granted already. France was playing an obvious game, and everyone understood what these endless talks were about; de Gaulle was looking for an ally to help him with his imaginary difficulties with the West. But the Soviet Union did not need any counterweight. What it wanted was France's support, or at least potential support, when the time of reckoning came.

Given the circumstances of the war, there was nothing shocking about a diplomatic agreement between France and Russia. The English had already created a precedent, and American aid was equivalent to a treaty. The Soviet Union also seemed affected by the bloody and terrible warfare, and was apparently going back to traditional values. No one spoke about the Decree No. 1 any more or about the soldier Soviets, although the harshest discipline still prevailed. The campaign against religion had been hushed up. The *Internationale* was no longer the national anthem. If ever there was a time when men could hope to reintegrate the Slavic peoples into a united Europe, it was then.

Yet our conversations with Stalin were not very encouraging. At that period, and later in 1947, I spent about thirty hours working with him. His voice was low, and his speech careless. He was sure of his power and of the fact that he inspired fear. There was something sinister or admirable, depending on one's politics, about this man's total control over such a vast area, such a huge population. General de Gaulle has written an interesting portrait of Stalin in his *Memoirs*, although I think it tells us more about the writer than the subject. I know for a fact that some of the leaders in the Kremlin today were far from delighted by the portrait.

Stalin did not particularly care about a treaty; but what really interested him was the question of spheres of influence. One day de Gaulle, who was present at the negotiations, asked about Greece. 'Ask Churchill,' Stalin replied. He wanted France to agree to the idea of making the Oder-Neisse Germany's Eastern frontier. As everyone knows or ought to know, the other Western Allies later accepted the temporary Russian use of that line for administrative purposes. When I was asked to give my opinion on the subject, I replied that, once the situation was created, it would be 'difficult to reverse it'. This was not a well-put phrase; but it was clear enough. Recently, if I remember right, de Gaulle seemed to go even further, and advised the German Federal Government not to bring up the subject of the Eastern frontier. Some 'Left-Wing Gaullists' have created an 'Oder-Neisse Society', which does not find its funds on trees, or from private pockets, however eager some people are to make donations. But at that time, the French government did not commit itself either way. We did not reject the idea of the Eastern frontier, nor did we accept it. Ours was a perfectly acceptable position, considering that we had nothing to do with that area, and were not consulted by the Americans when their troops retreated a hundred kilometres to the Elbe in the hope that this would improve their relations with the Russians. Although

Stalin was considered a genius by his admirers (still alive, but now discreet about it), he did not know that there were two Neisses, let alone which one he was talking about.

I also had to listen to endless talks about Poland. I did not have to be an expert, after Katyn and Warsaw, to realize that this great unfortunate people was going to be used as a buffer. Long ago, Ernest Lavisse wrote a very clear little textbook for history students; in it, he said 'You do not make a nation out of a piece of plain.' This maxim ought to be a warning to people who care about the truth. Lavisse was talking about so-called 'natural' frontiers; but it so happens that the word Poland means plain. Ever since the beginning, the Poles have switched from East to West and from West to East, depending on which of their two dangerous neighbours was the stronger. They hate both neighbours, Germany and Russia, which seems a contradictory hatred.

This time again it was the Russians who were the stronger and who were planning to push Poland two hundred kilometres farther West in exchange, of course, for taking two hundred kilometres off its Eastern frontier. Finally, our negotiations ended in a formal compromise: we would agree to have a representative of the Lublin Committee (Communist) in Paris, although we would not break off relations with the Polish government in London. We had put our fingers in the works and the entire West would soon follow our example. Later, some attempts were made to amalgamate non-Communist Poles with the Moscow-dominated government in Warsaw; but, like other experiments of this sort, it did not last. When a government contains Communists and anti-Communists, life soon becomes intolerable and one of two things happen. The Communists hunt, gaol and execute the others, as they did in Warsaw, Bucharest, Budapest, Sofia, and Prague, or else the non-Communists get rid of the Communists. If they succeed, they do not imprison the Communists, whether orthodox or revisionist – and these last would be pretty badly off if it weren't for 'imperialism'. Freedom was saved in France by the decision to exclude the Communists, after de Gaulle left power and retired to Colombey. This happened in all the free countries and that is why they are still free.

We still had our treaty to draw up, after losing a great deal of time in endless bargaining, and in brutal and pedantic arguments, for that is how the Russians usually conduct negotiations. When

Molotov finally told Stalin about the compromise we had reached over Poland, Stalin said to him in our presence, 'They've gypped you.' Perhaps he really believed it; but it is unlikely. And as for the Franco-Soviet pact of 10 December 1944, no one could say they had been gypped. There was nothing in it that the Russians could complain about, as it merely made it possible for us to leave honourably in the middle of that sad winter, during those last months of the war which was not yet won. The treaty had been hastily composed and some of the various clauses were vague or even meaningless; they promised little in the way of a serious and prolonged cooperation for the future.

At the end of the meal one evening various diplomats were talking among themselves between toasts. It was customary to have two dinners a night. Later, I was told that Stalin said to someone else, while he watched the diplomats suspiciously: 'Those diplomats are wasting our time. One good round with a machine-gun and it would all be over.' This was his favourite sort of Tartar humour, but those in the line of fire enjoyed it much less. An un-known courtier, who became briefly famous later, replied to his master: 'Would you like me to go and fetch one?' The man who said this was 'Marshal' Bulganin. The press and all the Soviet experts claimed for a time that he would play an important role. In fact, he soon was nothing more than a 'fallen soldier', not much of a soldier, but very much fallen, and without any chance of getting on to his feet again.

When the account of our journey and negotiations was published, it was very well received by everyone, in Paris at least. We had concluded one of those bilateral pacts which authoritarian rulers and régimes love. The newspapers were overwhelmingly favour-able, though they varied in warmth and perception. 'Every word counts', Georges Cogniot wrote in *L'Humanité*, but Vladimir d'Ormesson wrote 'The terms do not matter' in *Le Figaro*. We had not lost prestige as we would have if our long trip had been useless and our request, even implicit, had been refused. We brought a treaty back to France which, like so many other treaties, would find its justification in its application and otherwise would be null. The genuine, historic Franco-Russian alliance began as a military agreement between the two General Staff commanders, Boisdeffre and Obruchev, which was signed in 1892. It was not debated in parliament and the text was not published. It passed almost

unnoticed and yet it changed the face of Europe. That December
in 1944, everyone knew about the pact, yet it changed nothing in
Paris or in the Kremlin.

We had not obtained a guarantee and we had not made any
commitments. Things went on afterwards as they had before.
The photographs of the Yalta conference showed a stereotype
Churchill, Stalin as usual hiding his satisfaction under a benevolent
look, and Roosevelt already showing signs of his approaching end
beneath his hopeful smile. What everybody could see, the doctors
refused to see, perhaps because they knew that they could do
nothing. There was one strange thing about the photographs that
had nothing to do with the three men, one gruff, one rigid, the
third ravaged. France was missing from this conference that would
alter Europe's future for many years to come.

People have said, and no one denies it now, that only Churchill
tried to get France included at the conference, but perhaps he did
it only as a formality for the benefit of his audience. Stalin's reply
was that France had fewer armed divisions in the field than
Yugoslavia. Long before Moscow's unclear and uncertain uni-
lateral denunciation and its absolute refusal to carry out its pact
with France, this sort of attitude showed that our enthusiasm had
been premature and that the later outcries against the pact were
excessive, considering the fact that the pact was dead as a doornail
from the start. The treaty was merely an expedient and not the
cornerstone of a fixed policy. At the time, we did not realize this
clearly; but we have since seen at least one other sensational
agreement in which the spectacle counted more than the agreement
itself.

'The Secret of the King'

We had expected the trip to Moscow to last eight days; in fact, we
stayed there a month. When we came back, the war was coming to
an end. A very few people were not reassured; they worried about
the new arms with which Hitler threatened us. But anyway,
everyone except for the professional fear-mongers was convinced
that the famous, though unwise 'unconditional surrender', would
soon take place. We felt that the spring would bring us victory,
after a winter without coal, but not without cheer. And that is

what occurred after much pain and loss of life, not all unavoidable, though bravely borne.

We took it for granted that peace would soon be declared, although we found out later that the end of the war was not the same thing as peace. Our main political problem was what would happen 'afterwards'. How would we help the world to recover, Europe to rebuild its ruins, and France to heal its scars?

A Consultative Assembly, made up of appointed members, held a meeting in Paris. Except for the Assembly of today, much admired for its silence in session and for its volubility everywhere else, the Assembly of 1945 was certainly the worst we had in twenty years. There was nothing servile about it, even though all its members had been appointed and not elected. (An odd but interesting fact is that the Assembly of 1964, duly elected and representing the entire French nation, abdicated more legislative power than any other Assembly had ever done.) The Consultative Assembly, on the contrary, was always bad-tempered; for four years its members had choked down their words; all their secret resentments had accumulated while the country was occupied; all the self-appointed theoreticians of all the Resistance meetings could not give vent to their bitterness. Their favourite topic was the purges and they outdid themselves on the subject. Even Herriot, whose role during the war had been dubious to say the least, turned what he thought lack of consideration for his dignity into tirades worthy of any 'ultra' or any Gaullist, except that he spoke against de Gaulle.

De Gaulle really did make a tremendous effort to understand this group of strangers and to calm their storms; but their arrogance, their complaints and their mediocrity finished by exasperating him. And indeed, the tone of voice used by some nobody, terribly proud of using the speaker's platform to air his grudges, was absurd and out of place. Every day the crowds made their enthusiasm for de Gaulle evident and the discrepancy between the feelings of the crowd and the feelings of the Assembly must have infuriated him. We know where this led him and what opinion he acquired of the parliamentary régime as opposed to 'direct democracy'.

Yet none of this was very important and it must be said that de Gaulle certainly did put up with it. But the real work was done by others; by de Gaulle first of all; then by his entourage, then by his cabinet; then by his wholehearted supporters, some of whom changed later; by the military leaders he had known for a long time as his friends – at least in those days; then, last but not least, by the 'special services'. These men were initiated into the mystery which was never revealed to the Philistines. The principal Philistines were the Ministers. They were expected to work and to defend their actions; but they did not participate in major decisions and confidential issues. Perhaps, who knows, nobody did. At that time, the Ministers often held long meetings, unlike now, when they only perform a brief ceremony prior to giving their consent. But there were no genuine deliberations. Everyone was called in turn, according to his position in the hierarchy, to give an account of what he was doing. There would then be an exchange of opinions. Then, there would be a conclusion, drawn up like a verdict by the head of the government. At least this is how de Gaulle dealt with the issues he considered important, foreign affairs, war, colonies and public order. Whoever dislikes hearing the word 'dialogue' used everywhere, dialogue of this century, dialogue of the church, will be glad to hear that there was no danger of a dialogue in the French government of 1945. General de Gaulle is well known to be a past master in the art of the monologue.

We usually did not vote on issues, which makes good sense in any government. But on a few occasions, when the General had to deal with a minor question on which he had no fixed opinion, he asked his employees to vote. We voted twice, at intervals of a few months, on the matter of subsidies granted to Catholic schools by the Vichy government. The majority decided to keep them the first time; the second time, it decided to put an end to them; the Communists had changed their mind in the interval. There was no explanation for this sudden *volte-face* except that it had been decided not in France but in Moscow. On another occasion, the cabinet was asked to choose the methods of election. De Gaulle told us that, as a general rule, he preferred elections where the voter voted for one candidate rather than for a slate; but he added that, considering the recent upheaval, perhaps proportional representation was better suited to the needs of the country. Proportional representation was passed, and I was given an acid lecture on the subject by M. Capitant; he must have thought that I was sitting for the bar examinations and that he was already a law expert merely because his father had been one.

Whenever de Gaulle found an issue secondary and could not be bothered to look into it, he would show his lack of interest or his uncertainty by procrastinating for as long as he could before the matter became urgent or before he had reached a decision. He would say, 'We shall see', or 'France will bury us all.' Over matters of detail and technology, the specialists were given a free hand. The civil service was given free rein and sometimes took advantage of this to slow down. For de Gaulle, whatever his ability to understand and to solve economic problems, was not in the least bit interested in this sort of problem. Some people swear that he never said: 'Administration can come later', and 'I did not liberate France to worry about the macaroni ration', yet I heard him say both those things with my own ears. These days, people spend a lot of time denying what they once said; it is the principal characteristic of the present régime.

Everybody, including the teacher, learned his job during frequent and lengthy cabinet sessions. There is no better way to learn than to teach, although of course the master can calculate far ahead of his pupils. I cannot deny that the master is tremendously gifted, even though he has put those gifts to scandalous use. If I am talking about pupils and master, it is because I often had the distinct and rather disagreeable impression at the time that all the Ministers were sitting around their severe teacher just like good little schoolboys. It got to the point when de Gaulle was able to say to us one day, in the most natural way in the world, 'You see, you really *are* learning.'

Although I had been unexpectedly put in charge of Foreign Affairs, no one bothered to explain anything to me, to give me advice or to repeat instructions. I often saw General de Gaulle for long periods of time; he already expressed himself in the style which his speeches and his press conferences have made familiar. He talked entirely in generalizations, lofty observations, and references to history. Every meeting I had with him was an improvised class in political philosophy which taught me nothing about his intentions or even about the facts of the matter we were discussing. His opinions about people varied according to the circumstances, so that I learned never to rely entirely on his judgements. When these opinions happened to be favourable, I found that his choices and preferences were dictated wholly by personal bias. In general, his opinions of people were unflattering.

I will not mention any names, at least not right now; that way a few lickspittles can go on singing his praises until they find out what he really thinks of them.

He already possessed 'the secret of the king', and I think this secretiveness increased with the years. But those who carry out his orders seem to have become thoroughly adjusted and even to have developed a certain knack for explaining the General's intentions when they know nothing about them, and for running things smoothly in spite of constant surprises. The important lesson is to learn the art of self-contradiction, and to go back on what has been said when necessary. In certain very serious cases, the docile body of followers apparently did not think in terms of dishonour, as long as they got by without seeming ridiculous. Luckily, things had not yet reached this point after the war; but that did not make the situation any more comfortable for a man like me who had to cope with lack of information as well as lack of experience.

The idea of confiding completely in anyone never seems to have crossed the General's mind. At least he has never gone so far as to consult or even to warn others about his plans and his betrayals. He is as secretive about little things as about big ones. As he places himself at the centre of the solar system, never stops meditating, and revels in his own hesitations, perhaps he really cannot see the difference between symbolic actions and actions that mean something. For de Gaulle does not follow a policy in the proper sense of the word; he does not have one or even several grand designs which he carries out. His policy consists of symbols, or to put it another way, of a succession of points of departure. His thoughts wander from point to point, so that they startle everyone when he expresses them; this is a good way of keeping his own staff flexible and of inspiring fear or admiration in others. Therefore, questions of protocol like relations with Andorra and Monaco are just as useful as far more important matters in creating disarray and asserting grandeur.

I would like to give just three examples of the difficulty encountered by anyone who got involved in de Gaulle's obscure machinations even if he only wanted to carry out his orders intelligently and selflessly. If I had known de Gaulle better, I might have guessed certain things; but it took me some time to find my way in this labyrinth. Today, I firmly believe that there was nothing mysterious about his intentions, although he kept them hidden deliberately. But at that time, de Gaulle had not yet gone as far along the path of no return. I also did not have the resources that twenty years of public life give to those who know how to look (not that there are many such). The three examples I will give before going on to more serious subjects are the Clipperton incident, the question of the Aosta Valley, and the story of the meeting that never took place between Roosevelt and de Gaulle.

Clipperton is a tiny, uninhabited island in the Pacific which has no fresh water. A passing ship took it over in the name of France during the Second Empire. As no permanent installation was made on this piece of chalky soil, Mexico claimed it; it was nowhere near Mexico, but it was even farther away from France. During the early 1900s, the two countries decided to ask Victor-Emmanuel III to act as arbitrator, and he decided in France's favour. During the Second World War, first the English and afterwards the Americans decided that the little desert island would be useful as a broadcasting station while the Pacific war lasted. And so, a small 'Anglo-Saxon' radio station was set up there without anyone asking Free France's permission. When de Gaulle heard about it, he decided, also without telling anyone, to put an end to this trespassing. He was not wholly wrong, and indeed, the Allies had not shown much tact towards the country they had saved from extinction. That is the way all alliances come to an end; one side is clumsy and inconsiderate, the other is over-sensitive; that has not changed in twenty years.

The General organized a very secret expedition, which was to leave from the Western coast of Mexico, Acapulco, if I remember correctly. A frigate with a 'pirate' crew was to go to Clipperton, take over, and re-establish international right and French sovereignty. I learned about this wild scheme by accident and did my best to prevent it. The Allies were formally in the wrong; but this did not justify an operation which would have unforeseeable consequences, let alone other complications. The plan was dropped. I never found out what made them decide not to go through with it; but the main thing is that they did not commit this folly.

I saw other examples of 'Clippertonism'. As soon as de Gaulle thinks his authority, his prestige and his person have been put in question, he loses all sense of proportion. A personal failure is as tragic to him on a pinhead as on a continent. I need not go on describing these episodes. Very recently, there have been minor incidents demonstrating that nothing is too small for de Gaulle's anger; one midge may challenge the sun's brightness and it does so at its own risk and peril.

De Gaulle does mention the Aosta Valley affair in his war memoirs. When I read them, I found out certain things that no one told me at the time. De Gaulle gives the following account of this incident:

Immediately after the victory a serious incident occurred over the establishment of our Alpine frontier. Our Government had long since declared its intentions in the matter: we intended to extend the boundary of our territory to the very crest of the range, taking in the several Italian enclaves on the French side near the passes; we also intended to incorporate the formerly Savoyard cantons of Tenda and Briga, and perhaps Ventimiglia as well, if it was the wish of the latter's inhabitants. We certainly had every ethnic and linguistic justification to claim Val d'Aosta, particularly when our advancing troops met with an almost unanimous desire to join the French camp. But for eight months of the year the snows of Mont Blanc cut off all communications between France and the Valdôtains. Their existence was consequently linked to Italy's so we decided not to claim possession of the valley; we would be satisfied with Rome's recognition of its autonomy.

. . . The Valdôtains, supported by the liaison officers we had sent them and a militia they had formed themselves, instituted an autonomous government by the intermediary of their 'Committee of Liberation'.

. . . In demanding our retreat [from the Val d'Aosta], the Americans could instance no agreement drawn up with us, nor henceforth allege any military necessities. They merely referred to their own decision not to allow the settlement of any territorial questions affecting prewar boundaries before the signing of the final peace treaties. Of course, Washington formulated the claim with regard to the French alone, and only for the Alpine communes.

The last few lines show how I finally got wind of the affair. I had known nothing about it until the Americans complained to me, accusing France of 'intriguing'. Even though they used this unflattering expression, there is no evidence that they were discriminating against the French in this particular case. The fact that the French troops were almost completely dependent on the Americans for their food supplies, war materials and petrol may have led the Americans to be even more clumsy than usual (one can imagine what that means), and de Gaulle to be even more touchy than usual (one can also see what that means). But I don't see how it can be proved that the American wish to settle no questions before the war was over applied only to the French. Later on, they were just as willing as the English to back our claims on the Saar. It was only the Russians who refused at least fifteen times, and we know the sequel to that.

I have not gone over the Val d'Aosta episode merely to complain about being told nothing, for it no longer matters and could even be rather useful for me to plead ignorance. But I want to show how the chief executive treated the members of his so-called government. He has not changed in this respect except to get even worse; this may well be the only thing that his two régimes have in common.

Anyway, no one had told me of 'our government's intentions', which had been 'long since declared'. The Americans had to get involved in it before I was called in. The cantons of Tenda and Briga in fact belonged to the county of Nice, and they had been made a part of Savoy only by mistake. They had voted and would vote again in favour of joining France. It was only natural that they should be re-incorporated into France, as this was what they wanted. On the other hand, I did not really approve of trying to get Ventimiglia, as I never very much liked the principle of rectifying frontiers at mountain passes – a policy they teach in old-fashioned courses on tactics at the *École de Guerre*. As I have already said, when de Gaulle decides something, he will fight for one acre of land as though it were an entire province. 'Chabertonnism' up in the mountains goes with 'Clippertonism' on the sea.

Naturally the liaison officers at the Val d'Aosta did not receive their orders from the Quai d'Orsay, which had no idea of what they were doing. I first spoke to de Gaulle on the subject when the Americans began protesting about our behaviour. It so happened that I had spent most of my school-days at a Jesuit College near Ivrée, at the mouth of the Aosta valley. I knew what the situation was and what progress Italianization had made there. My argument was short; first I mentioned the difficulty of communication, then the demarcation of boundaries, and finally, I discussed the political aspect. 'Take Piedmont if you want Italy to become your mortal enemy, as it did during the sixteenth century. But you cannot risk getting into a real tragedy just to annex a few cantons, even if they agree, when their existence and their entire future will be decided

R.—4

on the other side of the Alps.' I don't claim that my argument was
the one which convinced de Gaulle. I think he falsely prides himself
on getting Rome to agree that these cantons should become autonomous, when in fact the French government never formulated this
project. For once, circumstances defeated de Gaulle, and he gave in.

The meeting with Roosevelt that never took place, or rather
which was refused by de Gaulle, was a long, tempestuous business.
As everyone knows, de Gaulle is infinitely sensitive on matters of
protocol. Now protocol is, in many ways, a good thing: it eliminates
slovenliness, bad manners and vulgarity, which can all lead to bad
actions. Yet even strict notions of protocol should be kept flexible,
as their function is to make life easier, not impossible.

The American Ambassador to Paris, Jefferson Caffery, came to
see me at the beginning of February 1945. He was, with some
reservations, an admirer of France, and had a strong character. He
was not very fond of de Gaulle and was completely intransigent
and obstinate as far as his country's interests were concerned. He
spoke to me of a possible meeting between Roosevelt and General
de Gaulle. I replied that a meeting would not be enough to settle
all the long-standing quarrels between the two men, aggravated by
the Yalta conference, and by the fact that their characters were
completely incompatible. I did agree, though, that a frank explanation would be a good thing; but I wondered how it could be
arranged. The ambassador interrupted my objections by asking
suddenly, 'And what if President Roosevelt came to France?' I
replied that this, of course, would be quite a different matter, and
that if the American President came, it might be possible to arrange
a meeting. It had not occurred to me that Roosevelt would invite
himself to some part of France, fixing the date and the place
himself.

After seeing me, Jefferson Caffery went to see General de Gaulle,
for the Gaullists' concept of a Foreign Minister's role means that
accredited diplomats had to make useless trips when they had important business, as only one authority has the power to make
decisions, and it was not the one at the Quai d'Orsay. Out of kindness, foreign diplomats would continue to consult the Foreign
Minister, although they knew he was kept out of secret affairs.
General de Gaulle has described how he refused the invitation and
summons in his war memoirs. Being better informed than I was,
he knew Roosevelt intended to meet him in Algiers. He refused to

go there at a date not arranged by both parties in advance. Certainly Roosevelt was wrong to go around making a rendezvous with people in their own home territory without consulting them beforehand, especially as relations between France and the US were far from warm since France had been excluded from the Crimean conference.

This affair caused quite a stir in France, where Roosevelt was much admired. On the whole, people regretted the incident, although de Gaulle was delighted by this opportunity to show his disapproval. He was even more delighted when it was learned that Roosevelt had summoned a number of leading figures aboard the battleship that was taking him back from the Black Sea to the United States; de Gaulle rightly considered that the head of the French government had no business imitating them in their pilgrimage to the battleship. He was amused by those Frenchmen who would have had him follow the Négus, Ibn Saud and a few others aboard. There was nothing wrong with those heads of state; but France would not tolerate a summons.

Even today it seems to me that this was the right attitude to take. But I do want to point out three things. The first is that word 'summons'. I must regretfully state that de Gaulle always uses the word himself when he wishes to see another Frenchman. In this way, M. Michel Debré was summoned to the meeting at which he was informed that he had been appointed Prime Minister. When General de Gaulle came to the Loire Department, which I represented from 1945 to 1962, the Prefect telephoned me to tell me the General's itinerary and to invite me to lunch with the head of state. I was already on bad terms with the government, so the Prefect did not show me the actual programme prepared by de Gaulle's assistants until after the visit was over. When I read the programme, I discovered that I had been 'summoned' to the very department which had elected me as its deputy. Immediately, I told the Prefect my feelings on the subject, although he was not responsible. I also wrote to the Prime Minister, the constitutional head of the government, to make it clear to him in a few words that I would willingly have accepted an invitation to go anywhere, but that I would not have gone had I known I was being 'summoned', and would have made known my reason for refusing. And I must say that Michel Debré answered my letter, agreeing with me and expressing his regrets.

The second thing I want to mention concerns Yalta. It was shocking to leave France out of the conference, and it was also foolish rather than mean. General de Gaulle has repeatedly exploited France's absence in his attacks on the dangerous and unreasonable concessions the Allies made to the Russians. Certainly, France was not responsible for sacrificing free countries to the Communist monolith. Later, this sacrifice was made final at Potsdam, and we were not there either. But de Gaulle's present policies, and the fact that even then he based most of his decisions on his hostility towards the Anglo-Saxon nations, lead one to wonder what role he would have played if he had been present at the conference. I really think he was lucky to have been excluded, for nothing in his attitude suggests that he would have urged the Anglo-Saxons to resist Soviet demands. He would very probably have tried to take advantage of the situation and to turn it to France's sole profit. There would have been nothing wrong in trying to do this; but it is unlikely, looking back on it, that de Gaulle would have backed a policy of Soviet containment. He has turned his absence from the Yalta conference into a political asset. He can pretend that he would have tried to limit Russian expansion, although he was far less disposed to do this than he now claims. France's exclusion from the Yalta conference was certainly scandalous; but I am more and more inclined to think that it soon became nothing more for de Gaulle than a convenient argument.

The last point I want to make is not theory but fact. De Gaulle wrote about Algiers, 'Perhaps for Franklin Roosevelt Algiers was not France, but all the more reason to remind him of the fact.'

These lines were published in 1959, when de Gaulle was back in the Elysée Palace. This man, so arrogant and so pitiless towards those who refuse to submit to him, so quickly changeable yet so oracular in his assertions or his curses, so absent-minded about things he wishes to forget, can make striking phrases: you think they ought to be inscribed in bronze or stone. In fact they are written on sand. The 'wind of history' blows them away. In the Middle Ages, bad kings were already swearing false oaths over the relics of saints.

4

The German Problem /
The Creation of the
United Nations /
Syria and the Lebanon /
General de Gaulle's
Departure

Among all the important issues I had to deal with during de
Gaulle's first administration, I want to discuss the three main ones:
Germany, the creation of the United Nations, and the Syria-
Lebanon affair. I have no dossiers at my disposal or any assistants
and personal documents as de Gaulle had when he was writing his
Memoirs. My memory is all I have left; but it is sharp enough to
help me describe the most significant points and to re-create the
prevailing atmosphere. I also have impartiality and detachment to
help me in my task.

Germany is the centre of Europe. It had been the target of the
war. When France was liberated, the defeat of Germany seemed
certain. The V-1s and V-2s, the counter-offensive in the Ardennes,
could only draw out the final stages of the war. The ultimate
weapon that the Germans had been trying to develop would not be
ready in time to save the country from disaster. Germany had been
on the point of victory. The very ease with which it had won so
many battles, the succession of mistakes it had made out of complacency, had prevented it from triumphing in the end. It had gone
from victory to victory towards disaster and now, caught in a

noose which was getting tighter all the time, it was being worn down by bombing raids and bleeding to death. Things had reached the point where the Germans were calling handfuls of exhausted men 'divisions'. The fate of Germany was the great unknown factor. It had been the great threat during the war, it would become the great difficulty during the peace.

For twenty years now Germany has been the key problem in Europe. And for twenty years, the problem has been insoluble. Germany is facing a long period of crisis without any prospect of relief in sight. Men are not made to walk in the dark towards the unknown without a star, a compass, or a ray of hope to guide them. Europe, cradle of the most advanced civilization and ideas, is now torn asunder, unable to resolve this conflict. Other wars in the past had been inconclusive; but now that we had Germany at our mercy we did not know what we ought to do. The war ended twenty years ago; but there has still been no peace and no treaty. A frontier cuts a nation in half, although the Free World has never accepted this solution. A great Eastern power has declared, 'It's like this because that's how we want it to be.'

The older men in the Kremlin were already in power during the war. They have poignant memories of the German army's advance and this explains their attitude. Hitler, who started the Russian campaign too late, got nearly as far as Moscow, all the way up to the Sparrows' Mount. There, his troops were stopped only just in time by the winter and by the Siberian reinforcements. The Russians remember that the Germans reached Baku; that is why at every conference they refuse to accept the reunification of Germany, even though they have now put one hundred million exploited people between their country and Germany. There are two Germanies, two Koreas, two Vietnams, two or three parts of Laos, without mentioning all the other countries which may be divided like this overnight. Such is the world we live in today, where the Free World, out of love for peace, has had to amputate some countries, when this was their only chance of survival or the only way to limit the damage. The Kremlin keeps Germany divided for the sake of twentieth-century 'Socialist progress'; but in fact this policy goes back to the times of Richelieu.

The Americans are less tough, less suspicious than the Russians, although they are more doctrinaire and more impulsive; they cannot understand these hardened attitudes of hatred and fear.

When the war was over, they helped the Germans, and their generosity was one of the wisest and most moral acts of their usually muddled policy.

The French took some time to recover from their ugly memories; but they ended up by feeling (which is far more important than just understanding) that sometimes hereditary enemies must change, as has sometimes happened, or there must be no such enemies at all. I am talking about the French people today; but in 1944-5, no one was confident about the German problem. Germany was teetering on the brink of defeat, and it soon fell into the abyss.

Bernard Baruch suggested to the Allies that Germany be turned into an agricultural state. This project was about as serious as the idea the Germans had in 1940 of turning the whole of France into a sort of big Luna Park, an alcoholic, frivolous Montmartre that would cater to the entertainment of the new masters of Europe. But Baruch's project was more serious because the possibilities were there staring us in the face: the chancellery of the Third Reich was in ruins, the bunkers were empty, the leaders had committed suicide or were awaiting execution. De Gaulle was not inclined to see the situation in terms of a holocaust, for he is no Romantic. His attitude was not any more realistic, yet it was based on history, which gave it an appearance of solidity. De Gaulle was not haunted by any visions of the Twilight of the Gods, but by memories of Bouvines, Charles v, Frederic ii, Blücher, Moltke, Ludendorff and Hitler. He thought in terms of 'Eternal Germany'.

Every day I had to make up my mind about my own attitude towards Germany. At that time, and for many years afterwards, de Gaulle's ideas about the future of Germany were based on his past reading: Germany had been France's traditional enemy from generation to generation. To get rid of the ever-present danger, to put an end to the nightmare which had always plagued our frontiers, de Gaulle saw only one remedy: to go back to the treaty of Westphalia. I am convinced that he still believes German unification was nothing but an accident, the result of a few victories and of German exaltation. According to him there could be peace only if Germany was weak. His visions of an occupied, divided, patrolled Germany would have suited the Russians perfectly; but they had already got what they wanted. France had nothing to offer except a so-called programme, and it had some difficulty in getting an Occupation Zone in the first place. As Germany was being divided, why not let it be subdivided as well? After the blow it had just received, its inhabitants might be rather glad to return to the peace and quiet of a Weimar in the Goethe style, now that a surfeit of madness had sickened them of heroic exploits. Perhaps they would revert to their own regional folkways. De Gaulle went so far in this train of thought that he did not want the name Rhineland used. I am not talking about what he said to us in private; but about his public speeches which are buried in the *Journal Officiel*.

For obvious reasons, I do not have access to the *Journal Officiel*; those who have this privilege rarely take advantage of it. The *Journal Officiel* is a sort of sepulchre, where speeches and decrees become dust. Sometimes they are resurrected; but only when a leader wants a precedent or a text. The rest is doomed to serve as material for future historians. But I do have some texts by de Gaulle, which I think will serve to illustrate my point and to surprise some people. Nothing is more unexpected than what exists in print; for once things are published, no one thinks about them any more. General de Gaulle, like everyone from his background and like all the students who graduated from Saint-Cyr between 1870 and 1914, was educated to be permanently and irrevocably distrustful of Germany. Charles Maurras, who very much influenced the mentor of the de Gaulle family, Father Du Lac, believed that there was no such thing as a 'good Germany'. General de Gaulle also thought this, until, at the age of seventy, he felt his Baden grandfather awaken in his chromosomes.

I heard him express his hostility towards Germany in private and in public on many occasions and in unequivocal terms. He put it very clearly in London during the war, not in a war message, but in a text defining his doctrine and expressing his view of history, as he so often does:

France also notes that, in the space of one man's lifetime, its soil has been invaded three times, each time more ruinously and horribly than the last, and always by the same enemy. With Germany, which chronically produces Bismarcks, William IIs and Hitlers, there can be no peace without material guarantees, not just words.

These were the ideas behind de Gaulle's entire career as a military officer and as a writer on military subjects. While he was still a Captain, de Gaulle wrote a brilliant book on 'Enemy Discord', a study of the conflicts within the German Army during the First World War and after its defeat.

Throughout his first term in power, and long afterwards, de Gaulle felt that the French and German nations were incompatible. The following extract from a press conference will serve as another illustration of de Gaulle's consistent attitude until his return to power:

QUESTION: Can you tell us how long the German prisoners will remain in France?

ANSWER: Their stay as prisoners will end on the day that a state of peace succeeds a state of war between ourselves and the German nation. Then, the prisoners will no longer be prisoners. But German workers will have to help rebuild France for a long time. As soon as peace is declared, their status will be that of workers under contract, like that of all other foreign workers. Nevertheless, with or without contracts, there will have to be a sufficient number of them to accomplish the work which has to be done.

Of course, I was not asked to give my opinion of that expression 'with or without contracts', which betrays de Gaulle's position in politics and law. But it is true that most Frenchmen would have agreed with the General on this subject, after so much suffering and such a hard struggle. De Gaulle based his policy on this: *adversus hostem aeterna auctoritas.*

That year, 1945, de Gaulle showed me his attitude towards the Germans and Germany in a joke he made during one of the weekly parades in Paris. We usually watched these parades from the Place de la Concorde, where there was a permanent platform on the side of the Tuileries. The foreign diplomats who had to be present had grown a little weary of attending these parades so often. Once, without my asking him, Jefferson Caffery came to tell me that he did not much enjoy having to get up so frequently and so early to 'see *my* tanks passing with *my* petrol in them'. This comment was tactless, and it was not well received; but certainly at the time, France was very fond of military parades. Sometimes, the procession would come from the rue Royale and sometimes from the Pont de la Concorde, with two bands placed on either side of the obelisk to make the men walk in step to the music as they passed the stand. On this particular occasion, the troops were coming

from the direction of the *Chambre des Députés*, not yet known as
the National Assembly. Towards the end of the parade, the
Foreign Legion slowly passed in front of us, following their
traditional sheep mascot. As always, the crowd cheered the
Foreign Legion; it still does today, in spite of all the Legion's
adventures and trials. Then de Gaulle turned to me and said, in
that voice of his which some of my colleagues at the ministry tried
so hard to imitate:

'There goes the future of German youth!'

Those were his very words. I would not have repeated them;
but things have got so bad in France and in the Free World that I
wanted to shed this ray of truth: *et nunc reges inteligite* . . .

Everyone today, including the General himself, has forgotten
that he based his German policy on only one idea. Owing to the
Potsdam decision, Germany had been cut back in the East but not
in the West. Therefore, a special arrangement ought to be made
for the Rhineland and the Ruhr. The Rhineland was not a 'homogeneous territory', and 'the military and political security' of
Western Europe made it essential that the Rhineland and the Ruhr
should be placed under the strategic control of the threatened
nations. These territories had to be separated once and for all
from the rest of Germany 'in such a way that their inhabitants
will realize that their future does not lie with Germany'.

France's solution for Germany is a sincere, practical, humane and
simple one; everybody knows what it consists of. Let the various,
traditional German provinces: Prussia, Saxony, Bavaria, Wurtemberg,
Baden, the Palatinate, the Province of the Rhine and the northwestern
provinces pull themselves together again, administer themselves and
each go its own way. Place the huge arsenal of the Ruhr under international control . . . and finally, fix the Oder and the Rhine as the
security limits for the States bordering on Germany.

I still remember how de Gaulle would stress the plural when he
said 'the Hesses'. His plans for the future were strongly reminiscent of the past, with the idea that Germany was still the old
Germany of provinces, in spite of wars, of unifying victories and
of defeats that would bring them closer together. The wind of
history did not blow in that direction. De Gaulle's old-fashioned
attitudes rooted in the past and unaltered into his fifties, did not
prevent him from changing his mind suddenly. By an effort of will,

he decided that times had altered, and that he needed something new to remain in the limelight.

We did not really know what part of Germany would remain German, now that Russia was cutting a piece out of it in the East and de Gaulle was wanting it broken into fragments in the West. How could Germany survive without the Ruhr and Upper Silesia? But as the Russians had got Upper Silesia without a struggle, why couldn't France have the Ruhr? This unanswerable logic lacked only one thing, the necessary force.

The other question discussed by everyone was reparations. As Germany had destroyed practically everything, reparations were rightly expected. For the second time in one generation, the question was raised, and, for a second time, there was no proper answer.

For Germany was in ruins too. How could a destroyed country be expected to help the countries it had destroyed? It was even more difficult to expect reparations this time, because the Soviet Union would also expect a share. The USSR was already draining the resources of Germany's Eastern Zone; it only remained for it to despoil the rest as well. It would have been madness. The Anglo-Saxons' opposition saved us from committing it, even if we had been tempted to go ahead.

As for the Ruhr, the Russians would probably have been in favour of cutting it off from what remained of the German nation. They already occupied Germany as far down as the Elbe (not the Oder, as de Gaulle has written in his *War Memoirs*) and they asked for nothing better than to get as far down as the Rhine. De Gaulle saw the big Russian hand stretching out to help him; but he did not yield to the temptation of achieving his ambition with such a dangerous ally. This meant that he was forced once again to turn to the Anglo-Saxons. But England and America only saw the ruins and the vast quantities of money Germany would need just to stay alive, now that its population had neither work nor tools. De Gaulle's grand design never got beyond the dream stage. Yet the dream, like all dreams, influenced him so much that he did not wake up from it until long after he left power in 1946.

Little by little, I found out about de Gaulle and Germany. I could have discovered this earlier, if I had read the books by our 'Leading Resistance Member' which had been published before the war. But during the war it was very difficult to get copies of

88 RESISTANCE

the General's books, as they were banned and he himself was condemned to death. Anyway, we did not have the time to look for reference books that were not sold in any bookshops. The de Gaulle of the present interested us then and we were all inclined to remain deliberately ignorant of what de Gaulle had been like before 18 June 1940. So that only in conversations on Tacitus' *Germania*, on the rise and fall of the Romans, and other related subjects, did I learn what de Gaulle's vision of the world had been ever since his youth.

He expressed himself very elegantly and his ideas showed strong traces of Jacques Bainville, a little of Albert Malet and Albert Sorel and the Péguy of later years, and of his studies at the *École de Guerre*.

I knew it was pure romanticism to try applying seventeenth-century politics to a twentieth-century situation. The 'wind of history' had not yet blown away the jargon of another age; the only thing that gave this gibberish some substance was that suffering had stung France into hatred. Our very recent memories of the Occupation, deportations and executions made this old-fashioned doctrine seem up to date. It was even very popular; but politics cannot be based on rancour, punishment, and the illusion of ever-lasting enmity. To keep the German enemy of 1945 helpless and in perpetual subjection was what we had tried to do in 1918 and failed. To plough up the ruins of Carthage, to burn, defile, and curse the land that nourished the enemy is a plan that suffering creates but that reason forbids. Besides, the only way we could be sure that this plan would last would be if public opinion, both in France and abroad, remained unchanging. And this was far from certain.

From the very start, I had fought against the principles of Fascism, and during the Occupation I fought against the enemy who followed this doctrine. But I had also always been convinced that peace in Europe would mean a reconciliation between France and Germany. The hostility and rivalry which made these two nations fight had become more and more absurd. Sedan would avenge Jena, the Marne would avenge Sedan, the 1940 invasion and the second Sedan would avenge the Marne. In this way, from Bouvines to Rosbach to Rethondes, from one armistice to the next, this quarrel would lead one country or the other from victory to disaster in their turn, without any end in sight until the whole West collapsed. Every Franco-German war, whatever the result, was from now on a defeat for both nations. I had always claimed this, and now de Gaulle said the contrary and produced endless historical arguments to justify his position. How was I going to reconcile my position with his?

Germany in 1945 was like a big black hole in the middle of Europe. It was bleeding and crushed, its factories had stopped working and its houses were destroyed. The entire country was still smoking from the bombing raids and everyone was ruined. The East had been raped, and cigarettes were the only currency valid in the West. Germany was facing the biggest economic and moral breakdown of any country in history. The Thirty Years War seemed almost mild by comparison. All those Third Reich triumphs had ended in utter disaster.

The only thing that the great Allied Powers had left in common was their fear of the enemy. After the victory, they would inevitably clash. The only way to postpone the clash was to keep the fear alive, even when it became a fiction, and to believe that Germany was still ready for revenge. Although I did not find this a very convincing proposition, I was forced to make a choice and to decide what my attitude would be while I worked under de Gaulle. Even after he left power, I had to wait for a time before I could admit that I had made an honourable mistake. No one, especially now, will accuse me of choosing between an expedient attitude and an unpopular one. But I had to choose between complicating and interfering with de Gaulle's task, and helping him to get our country back on to its feet when, after all, it also had been ravaged and demoralized. For once France had the opportunity to reconcile personal freedom and public authority. Before then, these two ideas had nearly always been opposed, with one or the other dominant in an endless seesaw of confusion and suffering. I felt that this chance should not be wasted. I did not make the choice out of ignorance; I chose, knowing that I would have to sacrifice one side of the truth. And so I decided rather sadly, to sacrifice the Germans to those who were closer to me, the French people.

The last thing I expected was that the day would come when de Gaulle would abandon his absolute and permanent dislike of the Germans and develop a sudden affection for them. It was a calculated manoeuvre. There was no real emotion in it, although the Germans welcomed the change with genuine warmth. And de Gaulle likes praise and applause so much that he forgets the tricks he plays to win them. They are his elixir of youth. But in 1945, I must admit I never thought the chaos in Europe would grow so bad, so dangerous and so complicated that the cure would come from the very seriousness of the disease, and that old hatreds would go on for so long that they would turn into indifference. I just thought that no excess could go on for ever, and that a wiser and more balanced and realistic attitude would finally prevail. As the world saw, the opportunist who claimed to have permanent doctrines on the subject and who wanted the German State to be abolished altogether, discovered eighteen years later that he liked the German people. I must admit that this change surprised me for two separate reasons: one was the violence of the change, the other was how long he took before he was able to overcome his antipathy.

I thought de Gaulle would be tempted to change his attitude sooner, certainly not out of sentimental reasons, but out of treachery. The trip to Bonn or Berlin would be rather like the trip to Moscow: it would be a way of annoying others. Do not think I say this out of meanness; the idea of annoying, upsetting and disconcerting others is often a strong factor in the General's decisions, and, I must say, in many other great men's decisions as well. God knows how many foolish, unexpected, and often inexplicable actions have been committed for the sole purpose of disconcerting an adversary or an ally. I must also insist that a certain type of secretive, arid, or disappointed man sees almost no difference between an enemy and a friend.

Yet he took a long time, a much longer time than I had hoped or believed. What I did not realize was that basically de Gaulle is impulsive. He thinks things over for ages, leaves them aside, goes back to them, and then decides that there is plenty of time, that 'France will bury us all', and finds any excuse not to make up his mind. Then he comes to an abrupt decision and moves as fast as lightning or the plague when he gets going. At this point, he does not meditate or beat about the bush. He puts his decision into effect immediately. For this sudden mood of his is based on one great life-force, anger. Whenever he is in a calm mood, when there is no wretch around to punish, no fool to humiliate, he takes a long time to make up his mind. The tide goes in and out a thousand times, while men look at the ocean and wonder where the waves come from; but the waves remain static, and all that mass of water only moves up and down.

One morning in January, about twelve years ago, Konrad Adenauer came to see me at the rue Saint-Dominique, when I was Minister of National Defence. We were old acquaintances, although that has nothing to do with my story. After discussing various matters, he said to me, 'I hear that de Gaulle has agreed to come to Aix-la-Chapelle, to make a speech there on 28 January.'

That is the name-day of Saint Charlemagne. I replied that this was excellent news, that General de Gaulle would certainly not be going to Germany to make anti-German speeches when he had made enough in France. Therefore, nothing could be better.

'Yes,' the Chancellor said, 'the Federal Government can only receive him with honours; but what will the French Government think about it?'

'The French Government will be grateful for everything that the Federal Government will do on this occasion to honour one of our most distinguished Frenchmen.'

That was indeed the Fourth Republic's attitude. I cannot help thinking on its gullibility and on de Gaulle's ingratitude. Yet, I do remember saying to the Chancellor, 'Of course, you do realize that he isn't there yet . . .'

And indeed, de Gaulle did not make the Saint Charlemagne speech that year. He gave himself another twelve years before announcing to an admiring world that he'd kept a grandfather from Baden up his sleeve. As for Adenauer, he waited almost as many years to answer a letter from me, which he claims he had not read when he sent his police after me.

The Creation of the United Nations

I went to San Francisco at the end of April 1945, for the founding of the United Nations. I stayed there for about a month, and then left the French delegation to Paul-Boncour, who got useful advice from the members of my delegation who stayed behind. De Gaulle describes this in a way I find rather amusing, though I don't know if everyone will see why.

I instructed our delegation not to give way to high-sounding declarations, as many of our representatives had once done in Geneva, but instead to observe an attitude of restraint. This was done, and done well, under the successive leadership of Georges Bidault, participating for the first time at an international conference, and President Paul-Boncour, whose experience with the League of Nations made him a master of such subjects . . .

As far as instructions were concerned, the only ones I got were that France should not be one of the powers who invited the others to the Conference, as were the United States, England, Russia and China. I have never been able to understand why, unless de Gaulle's intention was for us to make a nuisance of ourselves and to keep at a distance. This did us no harm in the long run; but it was of so little advantage to us that de Gaulle forgot to mention it in his memoirs, although he considered it vitally important at the time.

The conference was run exactly like an American political convention, where, traditionally, the work gets done as if in a club rather than a parliament. This means that every task is complicated and that it is very easy to make mistakes. The newspapers, the publicity, the endless repetitions, the great number of *idola fori* and *idola theatri*, turned the conference into a sort of shambles. Politicians, not diplomats, ran the show. Problems were argued like political debates, so that it was difficult to tell what was important and what was trivial. Ever since then, the UN has used the same method, only it has grown worse. The racket has grown even louder, and it has become a sort of big international circus. Although it is looked upon as a holy institution, it does more harm than good.

De Gaulle had written a piece three years earlier, giving his blessing to this sort of project. Although he had always been sceptical about such an undertaking, his feelings are blameless and his style irreproachable:

. . . France knows very well that it would die without allies. And, as we want France to live, we must maintain the formal or natural alliances that we need. . . .

. . . The only nobility and hope of our time, in other respects so cruel to humanity, is that it will have revealed to our nations not only their material solidarity, but also and especially, their absolute need for moral unity. So that, from one end of the world to the other, above the battlefields and in the factories, among the oppressed peoples and among the free ones, in the minds of the men in the street, as well as in the minds of their leaders, above interests, prejudices and rivalries, a tide of aspiration towards an international ideal is rising.

If the war 'which begets everything', no longer lets nations ignore their solidarity, obviously it will be just as vital when peace returns. To rebuild the world which has become so agitated, so tiny and complex, the nations that were united during the bloody conflict will have to remain united in the effort to do what is right. France has fought in the camp of Freedom since the first hour and will fight until the last; this gives us the right and the duty to participate in the common endeavour to come, which will be very threatened if France abstains. Yes, the organizing of an international solidarity along genuine and practical lines, as well as the inspiration of eternal human ideals, is one of Fighting France's most definite aims. This is why, in practical terms, we welcome the recent alliance between two European powers, Soviet Russia and Great Britain; this alliance, without endangering any country in the Free camp, will play a vital part in the common war effort and in peaceful cooperation afterwards. This is why, on a moral level, we adopt the magnificent programme of the Four Human Free-doms proposed by the President of the United States to the peoples of the world, as a compensation for their suffering and as a reward for their hopes.

By the time the UN was created, these blameless feelings had given way to dark suspicions about Anglo-Saxon deals and un-specified ideologies. Certainly, these suspicions were not altogether unfounded. The United States correctly assumed that its dollars, along with references to Washington, Lincoln, Wilson and Roose-velt, would dominate the assembled nations it had helped to save from Nazi domination or colonialism. The Russians and their satellites were getting recognition as nations separate from the Ukraine and White Russia. They were delighted by the creation of the United Nations, for they saw it could serve as a vast forum in which they would be able to make denunciations and teach the Americans the art of handling crowds.

In fact, a quarrel flared up immediately over Argentina, where Perón was master. The Russians declared that they did not want a Fascist state included in the UN, and the Americans came to the defence of Argentina, although they were not on very good terms with Perón. Their defence of Argentina was embarrassed, as they felt the prickings of their democratic conscience. Later, the Russians were to make a complete *volte face* and to come to terms with Perón as soon as his relations with the US became worse. The difference between the United States and Russia is that America is frank, sometimes to the point of brutality, whereas the USSR is brutal without being frank; the Russians always begin by being righteous before they start to sow the seeds of dissent. The Americans have unfortunately backed many a nationalistic adventurer who was after their dollars, mistaking him for another Bolivar until the so-called liberator has enslaved his country.

Molotov tried the patience of everyone over Argentina. His endless capacity for repetition and his untiring determination gave him a repulsive sort of power. This made the opening sessions of the United Nations rather sinister, and it has gone on from bad to worse ever since. The Americans are absolutely determined to save the principles of the United Nations, though these very principles are thwarted every day. With that blend of naïveté and cynicism which only they possess, they do all they can to ensure the continued existence of a bureaucratic organization where the ideal has nothing to do with the fact.

At that time, we were still at the stage of preparing a charter. Today the theory that the world is changing all the time makes a mockery of that charter, especially as everyone believes institutions should alter with the times. At the beginning we had not yet disowned the importance of treaties. We thought it mattered that promises should be honoured. We were trying to find a *modus vivendi* in the UN between Marxists who had never read a word of Marx and capitalists who were in awe of him.

At first, the result was not as disastrous as might have been expected. But those who were present at the first meeting and who kept their eyes and ears open thought that the painful start and the arguing was a bad omen. There was a Security Council and a General Assembly. In the Security Council, the members had the right of veto, and in the General Assembly, the two-thirds majority rule prevailed. Because Russia abused the right of veto so much, vetoing hundreds of resolutions, John Foster Dulles with his notorious lack of subtlety and foresight got most of the powers of the Security Council transferred to the General Assembly. He assumed that a large number of the underdeveloped countries would be open to American persuasion. But money is no match for subversion; countries torn between the two attractions solve the problem by giving in to both. They take the money and vote against the country which gives it to them. Dulles's naïveté and clumsy slyness brought about the result we see today: American money used to burn American embassies. But in 1945, Dulles was only a secondary adviser under Vandenberg and Stassen. Stettinius, a charming young man with white hair, was the leader of the American delegation. No one could understand why Roosevelt had appointed him Secretary of State, and perhaps that was why Roosevelt had chosen him. Stettinius was an American version of Couve de Murville; but he was more naïve and less talented.

In spite of everything, the United Nations gave some reason for hope in its infancy. I signed the charter for France, and this gives me the right to have my opinion. The child that I helped to carry to the baptismal font has grown up very badly indeed. There seems to be a law that once a building is erected, the purpose of the organization it is meant to house begins to decline. The League of Nations had a magnificent palace in Geneva; but it is extinct. The United Nations has a superb construction of glass and steel on the East River in New York; but the founding spirit of the enterprise is foundering. All those storeys humming with the noise of typewriters already have a hollow ring. There is so little enduring faith about the place that the Secretary-General and his staff must feel the cold wind of defeat blowing through the corridors as they send out yet another expeditionary corps of men in blue helmets. The United Nations is a pauper in the international charity ward, and, as usual, the charity is paid out in dollars. No one knows how long this paradoxical institution will last, when it has made so many mistakes already.

We went to San Francisco Cathedral to celebrate the undertaking and to offer up our hopes and wishes for its success. At the end of the mass, the Archbishop of San Francisco with his mitre on his head, holding his crook in his hand, leaned back against the altar and began to sing the American national anthem. I have often thought about this incident and wondered if the Archbishop was not setting a bad example. But later, I came to regret that our clergy had not done the same; they have forgotten the fourth commandment twice in their lifetimes, once in France and once in Algeria. On both occasions they did not use their crooks to defend their country.

The charter, which was conceived as an instrument for peace, has not yet filled this role. The Secretaries-General, Trygve Lie, Hammarsköld and U Thant spent time and effort on their jobs.

The result is pathetic, nothing but chaos. Personally, I recognize the legitimacy of the United Nations and I approve of it, as it was originally conceived. I do not recognize and I disapprove of what it has become since. Foster Dulles and others knocked down the fragile but reasonable scaffolding. I will go back to this painful subject when I discuss the future.

Throughout the founding conference, the staff I had selected behaved perfectly, although I think I ought to mention that de Gaulle had planted some spies in the delegation. The men in question did not care at all about the structure of power. On one occasion when the French delegation was having a meeting and I was telling it how to act, someone interrupted me to say, 'This is not a criminal Inquiry!' I am glad to say I threw him out. This man, Etienne Burin des Rosiers, has had a particularly brilliant career in the service of the Fifth Republic. The San Francisco conference, like the Luxembourg Peace Conference of 1946, gave me an enduring hatred of international politics, if they are run like political conventions with several hundred politicians always present. The Americans still approve of this method, though, in the long run, it will do them a great deal of harm if they go on with it. Peace can only be achieved by common sense, not by public conferences between nations which do not even speak the same language.

Syria and the Lebanon

The third thing I want to discuss is the important question of Syria and the Lebanon. General de Gaulle, who knew all about the affair, neglected to tell his Foreign Minister how he had dealt with it before and what he planned to do about it in the future. It was one of the most unpleasant and complicated issues I ever had to deal with. General de Gaulle probably had a good reason for keeping it almost a secret, and I must say that he succeeded perfectly. If his *War Memoirs* are compared to General Catroux's important work describing his mission to the Middle East, it is obvious that the two men give completely different versions of the same events. As both writers are clever and cautious, at least in their books, nothing is ever very clear about their accounts. They both sidestep issues, make vague comments without ever being precise. The only certain thing about their books is that de Gaulle and Catroux did not see eye to eye on the question and that they decided to conceal that fact from the public.

The disturbances at Sétif in Algeria were harshly suppressed and given no publicity; but the Syria-Lebanon difficulties were often discussed during lengthy sessions at cabinet meetings. General de Gaulle would speak with great fervour; he was far from laconic on these occasions; but equally, he never made himself very clear. For all his explanations, the story seemed very obscure to all of us. When I say 'for all his explanations', I really ought to say it was *because* of all his explanations that we did not understand. The Middle East was the only part of the world where de Gaulle had served as a young officer outside of France. He had not served in Africa or in Asia and was not a colonial officer; he was only an expert in European strategy. His stay in the Middle East had made a deep impression on him, as it had on all the Frenchmen and Englishmen who had been there.

And indeed, from the very first, France and England had clashed there violently, for religious and political and strategic reasons. I remember making a speech about it at the Consultative Assembly, in mid-July 1945, quoting something said almost exactly a hundred years before by a great Anglophile, Montalembert. England had kept an interest in the route to India even after India had become independent. Like a man who still feels pain in his leg when it has been amputated, so England went on behaving as though it still owned India, although everyone knows that Commonwealth ties are purely theoretical. The French, who protected the Christian community without any thought of playing a double game like the English agents, were also a traditional force in the Middle East. When a French Anglophile goes to the Middle East, he soon becomes an Anglophobe like everyone there. Anything goes in the Middle East, the dirtier the better. From the Egyptian Expedition to Lady Stanhope, from the Sykes-Picot Note to the Hashemite monarchy, from the desert quarrels to the oil drilling, more sordid intrigues go on there than in the *Arabian Nights*. One day, as we stood on the beautiful sea-front in the Lebanon, the Frenchman with me made a sardonic joke that gives some idea of the atmosphere there, 'Have you not read the Third Epistle to the Corinthians? In it, Paul writes that God prefers a blasphemous Frenchman to a praying Englishman.'

The population of the Lebanon and particularly of Syria, the two countries under our mandate, often made trouble. Already under Blum, André Viénot had agreed on independence in principle, but Paris rejected the agreements. Many factors had made the situation far worse. General Spears, a great friend of Churchill's and the former leader of the parliamentary group that was favourable to France, made things worse. So did the fighting between Frenchmen to recapture Beirut, which made us lose a great deal of prestige, especially as the English exploited the situation to the hilt. And we were now at a disadvantage with our Allies, who forgot the Alliance with the greatest of ease. When General de Gaulle dealt with the Middle East, he never thought of decolonization and self-determination. The various religious communities were hotbeds for every form of intrigue; but de Gaulle considered himself an expert on the issue because of his experience as an intelligence officer there. He was convinced that he knew exactly what the English were plotting. He knew all about Beirut University, a stronghold of American influence throughout the Middle East and the rival of the University of Saint-Joseph, run by the French Jesuits and subsidized by the French government even in its worst days of anti-clericalism. De Gaulle had no trouble understanding the Russians either; they were Communists and atheists, but that did not prevent them from exerting a secular influence over the orthodox sects in the Middle East, which they had had since the days of the Czars. De Gaulle had obviously made up his mind about the English, at least in that part of the world, while he was still a young officer in these mandated territories.

This absurd conflict, where the two rivals tried to do each other the maximum harm, ended with the defeat of both. The English chased us out of the Middle East; but, once they had sawn off our branch, the entire tree finally fell on top of their heads. Unfortunately, one thing was sure: France's position in Syria and the Lebanon was badly damaged after the war. These two countries, which had been organized as republics, had been promised independence. But General Catroux described the events very differently from de Gaulle. There was a strongly Oriental, end-of-Empire flavour to the whole affair and the explanations we received were very obscure.

In those countries, every problem is so complex, every deal so subtle, and treachery so widespread, that it would take a great deal of time and documentation to try and explain our difficulties and misfortunes there. I am convinced that there were two different sets of instructions going from Paris to Beirut and Damascus. One set was being issued through approved channels by the minister in charge, who submitted every decision to the head of government and passed them on when these were accepted. The other set of instructions was more important and reached the capitals of Syria and the Lebanon in a less roundabout way; the essential thing about these instructions was that the minister, who was theoretically in charge of the affair, would be the last to know anything about them. No one ever informed me, orally or in writing, about what was going on. De Gaulle preferred to tell no one except his immediate followers. There were two threads of Ariadne, one held by de Gaulle and the other held by Catroux. And they were not even going in the same direction. As we saw later on, during the great Algerian tragedy, the executive and the executing powers were independent of each other.

France had announced and promised independence, and the two countries under French mandate were eager to have that promise carried out. De Gaulle was reluctant to grant them independence except conditionally; he insisted also that the English should get nothing out of it. This independence, first promised and then retracted, finally turned into total independence and hostility towards the French. De Gaulle later accepted the idea of independence for Guinea and Algeria; he even claimed that this was the best of all possible worlds; but his feelings on the subject were very different in 1945. In his *War Memoirs*, he complained that he was misunderstood by the Quai d'Orsay, that it was in a state of total chaos, and that it suffered from chronic Anglophilia. He would have found it easier to deal with these complaints, some of which were not wholly unfounded, if he had made himself clear. But, as we know now, Gaullism is, by definition, confused. This may be deliberate, or else it may be a question of temperament; Gaullism does not reveal its goals, because it does not know what they are, or else because it finds them inadmissible.

De Gaulle thought in terms of the past about Syria and the Lebanon, just as he did about Germany. According to him, Germany had as many states as days in the year. The Orient was like a mosaic or an ant-heap, where the races and religions and hereditary traditions and interests could and ought to be exploited. I often have wondered why he found the Middle East so complex and the Algerian problem so simple, as simple as his certainty that the new nations of black Africa would not revert to tribalism.

The tribal spirit returns as soon as those new nations get their independence; and things stopped being simple the day France left Algeria. De Gaulle's contradictory attitudes are more understandable in the light of one of his basic rules, to retreat forward into the future. The older he gets, the more his philosophy becomes one of *'Après moi le déluge'*. Remember this, to understand his actions of today.

Mass media are always being put to bad use, so that everyone has read or heard a hundred times over that de Gaulle has been the only legitimate ruler in France for twenty years and that he has been a firm advocate of decolonization for twenty years. This propaganda surprised no one; it was accepted without a murmur by everyone except a few courageous men who were immediately called 'ultras'. The French Left, which used to be so vocal, said nothing. An objective foreigner must see a sort of warning in this and find it highly suspicious. For the French public and the individual politicians must really be in a state of submission not to protest against such base lies, such an audacious gamble on people's cowardice, and such utter contempt for the truth.

I will discuss the twenty years of so-called legitimacy another time. But as for the twenty years of decolonization, I can produce facts. I will not just make generalizations or quote his call to 'Algérie Française' in 1958 or talk about the tricolours he gave to the Presidents of the countries belonging to the French community. Those flags which he distributed at the Place de la Concorde on 14 July 1959, had two linked hands printed on them. No one knows what became of them, whether they were abandoned at the customs or hidden in an attic; there were no troops to carry them, no monuments for them to decorate, not even a museum to display them.

France has certainly not always given up her colonies without a struggle, celebrating one Independence after another, always providing the crockery and the cooks for the glorious occasion. The Champs Elysées was not always covered with the unfamiliar flags of new nations. I remember a time when we did not use pop-guns but real cannons. I did not hear much about the Sétif rebellion; but I know it was repressed and that it was a Socialist minister in de Gaulle's cabinet who was in charge of that operation. And the rashness and impulsiveness of the Gaullist policies in the Middle East also gave me a lot of trouble.

The legitimate but insubordinate members of the Syrian and Lebanese governments were suddenly thrown in gaol. In spite of my written instructions to General Beynet, the French High Commissioner to the Middle East, the troops went into action, although de Gaulle had approved my instructions. There was some shooting in Damascus; a few stray bullets found their way into the Umayyad mosque. The trouble with using armed force was that not only our political and legal positions were weak, but also our military situation there was not good. What happened next should have been expected, at least considering our suspicion of England. General Paget gave orders for a British armoured division to intervene, and although the two countries were under French mandate, there were only 4,500 Frenchmen on the spot, along with a few local troops. The intervention of British troops that day, which came after other bad days, dealt a fatal blow to French prestige in the Middle East. Yet, in spite of this, the idea of decolonization never entered de Gaulle's head, although he could have disguised our mistake by putting on a great show of liberalism. Our allies had given us the kiss of death by their intervention. Yet the idea of taking down the flag, leaving the country, denouncing all mandates, calling for self-determination or for any of the General's more recent solutions, did not occur to him. The 'wind of history' was blowing in another direction. I managed with great difficulty to prevent the battle-cruiser *Jeanne d'Arc* from going within shell-shot of Beirut, where it had been directed by de Gaulle to bombard the city.

In fact, de Gaulle did not begin to flirt with the idea of decolonization until he became bored with staying at Colombey and began associating with certain types of people. There was no question of decolonization in 1958, at least not in public. When the subject came up later, there was nothing noble about it, since it was done in an underhand way. It is sheer effrontery to claim that de Gaulle has been in favour of decolonizing for twenty years; but certainly it was our 'First Member of the Resistance' who ordered the rout.

General de Gaulle's Departure

On 20 January 1946, General de Gaulle decided to retire. He was fed up with criticism from parliament and disappointed by the pettiness of the problems which besieged him. The population was cold and hungry. This would bring his adversaries, and even his followers, to their knees. They would have to come and fetch him on his own terms. He would then be able to say what he really thought of the Constitution. By the time the deputies had floundered enough on their own, they would be ready to carry out his wishes, although he had never bothered to reveal what they were. When they asked him to come back to power, he would also be able to change his cabinet and get rid of those who did not suit him.

Basically, neither the French nor their political representatives were fanatical about the sort of constitution they should have. They wanted the basic principles of the Republic to be preserved; but it never occurred to them that this would not be the case. Apart from this vague, yet positive feeling, no one ever believed, even in the worst days of the First Constituent Assembly, that de Gaulle ought to go. He had hardly begun his task. Even though he did not want to use his prestige to fight with the politicians who opposed his wishes, his authority had never seriously been questioned.

He acted alone, without consulting anybody. A very few people were warned at the last minute, when de Gaulle had already made up his mind, but they were not told what to do about it. De Gaulle would probably have felt compromised if he had consulted anyone. He did not want to win a victory, he wanted to vanquish the opposition. He did not want to leave order behind him, but dismay. At least, I can see no other explanation. If his intention had been to get rid of certain men, they would have stepped aside willingly. He would have found support for any constitution he might have wanted to impose. But instead, he left everything unfinished. All he did was to 'summon' his ministers. He did not even ask them to sit down and the only thing he said to them was more or less, 'I'm leaving. Thank you everybody.'

I was at the first United Nations Assembly in London when de Gaulle left office. The day before, on Friday, I had spoken at a foreign policy debate. On Saturday, I made a speech in London before the UN lamenting the fact that Europe as a whole was not represented and asserting that it would play a crucial role in future world affairs. That evening, I received a message from a friend, warning me of what was going to happen and forbidding me to tell anyone. Then we were officially called back to Paris on Sunday for a special cabinet meeting. Vincent Auriol, who was in the French delegation, speculated endlessly about the summons. The fog was so dense that we barely made it to Croydon, and once we reached the airport, the pilot refused to take us to France. He did not mind going without us; but he must have thought our lives were more important than his. We rang up Paris and were told to come. After waiting several hours, we took off and found ourselves in brilliant sunshine a few hundred feet up. By the time we reached Paris, everything was over. On my arrival at the Ministry, I found a message from de Gaulle. When I got to the place where he asked me to go, I learned that he had left several hours earlier; only Gaston Palewski was there, so I left again. Everyone read in the newspapers the next day that de Gaulle had retired; he said his mission was over, now that he had given France back its freedom. De Gaulle left a brief and very strange message, saying that everything was in order and that 'the train was back on the rails'. We all genuinely believed that he felt he had worked hard for France, but that now he had had enough. France could always go to him in an emergency; he would be there if he was needed.

He did not come back to power to help France in its hour of need. When he was called back to save our national heritage, he only squandered it.

Part 2

1945-54

5

Parliament /
The Constitution of 1946

The bees do not make honey for themselves.

(*Virgil, Georgics*)

The Fourth Republic bore no resemblance to the *Georgics*, just as the Fifth Republic bears none to the *Bucolics*; yet I think the story of its decadence can begin with one of Virgil's epigrams. A modern interpretation of this epigram could be that, in spite of many difficulties, the Fourth Republic achieved much, so that the Fifth Republic has often yielded to the temptation of calling those achievements its own. In some southern countries, public works are inaugurated several times over. The satirists make fun of the new governor who takes down his predecessor's plaque and puts up his own. The Americans are wiser; instead of engraving the name of a president or a government on a great public project, they merely write, 'The American people built this dam.'

This was also done in the great days of the Roman Empire. The inscription SPQR, the Senate and People of Rome, was engraved in stone or mortar commemorating the city and its Empire. The Romans started using the names of individuals only when their civilization began to decline. For a long time, historians believed that Rameses II had played a very important part in the history of ancient Egypt, because they did not know then that he had put his name on temples and monuments built before his time, and even on the portraits of previous Pharaohs. But truth will nearly always out. It is unlikely that inscriptions to the greater glory of one president would mislead the archaeologists who survived an atomic holocaust. They would probably not conclude from their studies

that Fallières was the founder of the Gaullist dynasty; it would be
an insult to three successive French Republics. But then, has there
ever been more than one Republic? In spite of a series of republics,
there has never been really more than one, *The* Republic. A
republic does not mean that a country has no authority, it means
that it has no monarch and no privileged groups.

The Fourth Republic may have been a little weak; but it was
active all the same, before it disappeared in a vortex of so-called
glorious institutions under de Gaulle. What an insult to call them
institutions! The only institutions worthy of the name are those
which are lasting and which cannot be interpreted according to one
man's pleasure. When a man can rule a country as he likes, according to his whims, using institutions entirely to suit himself, he is
worse than a monarch, a prince, or even a dictator, in the true
sense of the word; for the Roman dictators were appointed by the
Senate, were responsible to that body, and could stay in power for
only six months. De Gaulle's régime cannot be defined except by
himself, as it changes all the time and is doomed to end with his
death.

Learned professors of law love to construct theories about such
régimes, both favourable and unfavourable. Pay no attention to
them; they are a very fine and respectable breed of men when they
stick to teaching, but not when they try to justify and draw up
constitutions for régimes which are doomed to end in ruin. There
were plenty of law experts during the Weimar Republic, and
before, during and after Hitler and Mussolini and each French
Republic. I am quite certain that there are some right now in the
Arab world and in Africa, writing out constitutions based on the
Magna Carta, the American Constitution, and especially the Russian Constitution. This sort of work is useless nine times out of
ten. The study of law is rarely advanced by these documents, often
prepared illicitly or justified retrospectively, and they can only
harm our respect for legality.

What people call a French republic today does not exist except
in one name, one image, and one past: de Gaulle. But France had
a genuine Republic before he came back to power. From the outside, French political life looked like an endless procession of
people playing musical chairs for the various political posts. There
were meetings, votes, consultations and all the disorderly, useless
apparatus of the Republic fifty years ago, before the age of radio

and television. The public demanded to know everything that was going on, and the only remedy against this plague was discretion, even silence. For only what is certain, what has already been concluded and can no longer be concealed from the public should be reported. To record, discuss, and speculate about the rest is a waste of time and words. But we did not realize this in 1946, and it did a lot of harm to the Fourth Republic's image. The politicians never stopped bickering and hated any final decision which was not a compromise; usually, the more a politician declared himself to be a 'man of the future', the further removed he was from real life, concrete problems and the basic hopes of the people he was meant to represent.

The politicians of the Fourth Republic were usually worthy men, although their policies and their programmes were hopelessly out of date. Their heroes were Pelletan, Jaurès (whom they read in extracts as General de Gaulle did, for he would have liked to imitate such eloquence), Guesde (who by this time was only a symbol), and Marx (who no one read although many recited parts of him they had learned by heart). There were no heroes on the Right Wing except for Albert de Mun, Barrès and Déroulède. Nobody acknowledged Maurras' influence, and few read him. Most of the politicians of the Fourth Republic were just vaguely conservative, although they approved of some reforms.

As for the MRP, there was something definitely new, even novel about it, and its intentions were excellent. The fact that I later left this party can never make me forget the firm, disinterested support it gave me during difficult times, when the nation was in danger, and French soldiers were at war. I think the party's outlook was too narrow, too preoccupied with social problems – an admirable attitude, but one which left the MRP blind to the true perils of Communism for a very long time.

The same thing happened in Italy and in some of the Christian Democratic parties of Latin America. This error of judgement is so universal that no one individual can be blamed for it; there are other, more important reasons. Only the Christian Democrats in Germany out of all the parties in the world affiliated to the MRP seem to have got anywhere. I admit this, in spite of Konrad Adenauer's behaviour towards me; Erhard has done extremely well. Let us hope it lasts. . . .

Times are changing rapidly, and the old-fashioned methods of

R.—5

government will probably have to go. What is strange is that every-one is ready to change their principles, but all cling to the old political ways, the out-of-date rituals and the ridiculous squab-blings of democracy. They still believe that government is the art of compromise and must be done by endless congresses, com-mittees, motions and words, words, words, all gone with the wind.

Some discussions and arguments are useful and necessary because they help to reconcile conflicting interests. What really harmed our system of government was that we allowed anyone entitled to vote and speak to do so. As a result, a flood of useless speeches, orations and old formulae drowned out even the most influential voices, so that de Gaulle's desertion in 1946 seemed almost justified, some-thing which made his return in 1958 more easy.

In our day and age everyone talks so much about the virtues of discussion that they end up by discrediting even what is good about this method of decision. But to begin with, there can be no dialogue with deaf men; and it is useless to hold a discussion with someone who has no intention of reaching an agreement. The parliamentary régime has become obsolete (although its members are the last to admit it) for a number of reasons: one of them is that debates have become too long and too verbose and are not conducted properly. Another reason is that nothing important is ever concluded. The parties are too dependent on their backers, the politicians too dependent on their mandate, the would-be ministers too keen on getting their portfolios.

All these faults made the parliamentary system ring hollow in 1946. A kind of vulgar *camaraderie* existed between politicians, who said, '*tu*' to each other like schoolboys and soldiers. No one really knew what was going on. Everyone would speak about the workers and the farmers; but in fact they were only concerned with defending the group that had got them elected; some were looking after the interests of the metal foundries in the Paris area or the minor civil servants or the 'publicans' or the family organizations. But in the much-needed debates on agriculture, there were always plenty of speakers and practically no audience.

The members of parliament would leave on Fridays to go and canvass in their constituencies. Then, when they came back, they would get together for three or four days at a time in a completely closed world. They lived between the restaurant, the offices, the writing rooms, the library and the corridors. They spent the days together chattering, gossiping, exchanging news, reading and commenting on the newspapers, answering letters and attending to their business, so that, in this hothouse atmosphere, most members of parliament got in the way of the administration, pestering it with their personal problems, their local problems, their group problems, their party problems and their committee problems. They saw their country and the outside world only through the distorting lenses of their own petty interests and concerns.

Human nature being what it is, we believe that when things go badly strong institutions will cure all our little weaknesses. People do, of course, need some institutions. During the Fourth Republic, the lack of strong institutions ended up by corrupting the politicians. De Gaulle came to power and established what seemed to be strong institutions, which in fact he ignored completely. Today we no longer have any institutions, now that the constitution which created them is invalid. We have no good men either; they are all in prison or in exile, or else opposed to the régime.

In 1946, France had to improvise institutions and to look for new men. There had been a long, hard war; the President of the provisional government had been disappointed by the results of the election, so that he left without warning, taking us all by surprise. People forget that when de Gaulle left power in 1946, the country was weak and in danger. De Gaulle may have thought that if he left, he would create such a state of confusion that the parties would have to call him back and allow him to have his way. At the end of 1945, two thirds of the Constituent Assembly and the electorate were either Communists or Socialists or fellow-travellers. What France needed was not long-term planning, but help in the immediate present. The Communists already called themselves 'France's leading party'. Herriot was saying that France ought not to become 'the colony of its colonies', but that did not prevent him from being the president of the *Jeunesses Républicaines de France*, which was a Communist front organization.

The Communist Party attracted veteran Resistance fighters, naïve or ambitious men, and those who wished to protect themselves against the consequences of their past actions under the Occupation. The CP ran a vast assortment of organizations, some of which seemed quite harmless. Theoretically, these organizations were open to one and all and independent of each other; in fact, they were all inter-related, and though some were better at hiding it than others, they were all affiliated to the great 'working-class party', the 'party of the partisans'. This array of clubs and unions included the National Front, the Union of French Women, the General Confederation of Agricultural Labourers, the Patriotic Youth Leagues, the MUR, the Republican and Resistance Union, the Deportees Movement, and many others. Before they got the order to preach 'hatred of the enemy', which did them a lot of harm, they tried to get control of all the various ex-Resistance movements. This was easy enough to do, for the non-Communist Resistance groups were very dispersed and spent their time quarrelling. As for the ex-Free French fighters, de Gaulle's departure had left them feeling lost and abandoned by their chief.

By leaving, de Gaulle recovered the right to criticize the government for everything it did, and the politicians were left with the right of floundering about without him. Only someone as selfish as de Gaulle could have seen France's destiny in terms of a card game, needing three deals. We who were left had a hard time keeping the game going; but we must have managed pretty well, for there was no *coup à la Prague* after the *coup de Gaulle*.

I did not hold a grudge against de Gaulle for leaving, and when the situation got really bad, I did what I could to bring him back. We all know what happened after that.

But France will win in the last deal.

The Constitution of 1946

De Gaulle took three weeks to get his second provisional government together, after the referendum which everyone considered to be a personal triumph for the General. Ninety-five per cent of the voters had agreed to give up the 1875 constitution. Sixty-six per cent had agreed to limit the powers of the Constituent Assembly. Yet there were difficulties, in spite of this victory, and de Gaulle's departure naturally made them worse. We were adrift, and we had to draw up a constitution quickly, now that the pre-war one had been declared obsolete.

Félix Gouin was given the task of making up a cabinet, mainly of Socialists. The Communists were claiming that they ought to be in power, since they had got the most votes. The MRP did not want to be dominated by the Communists and threatened to stay out of the administration. There was the risk that another Popular Front government would have to be created, not that the Socialists wanted it, but they were open to persuasion. In the end, the Socialists were given power, although they were only the third largest party in the Assembly. Félix Gouin had been President of the Consultative Assembly in Algiers and he had kept the same post in Paris after the Liberation. Therefore he could pass for a man above party loyalties. Léon Blum recommended him to de Gaulle, who once said of Gouin, 'He's small, but he's not low.' Still, whatever de Gaulle thought of Gouin, Gouin succeeded him. We cannot choose our predecessors or our successors. History decides chronology, not us.

I will not describe this period in great detail. It would be pointless, and besides, I do not have all the documents I would need. Our chief task in the early months of 1946 was to draw up a constitution. There were some fine men in the committee set up to work out what sort of constitution France needed; but the majority of them were either Communists or Socialists and they decided that practically all authority without any checks and balances would be in the hands of the National Assembly. Pierre Cot, the chairman of the committee, had a lot to do with this particular draft, which was so reminiscent of the first French Revolution, and also of a far more recent revolution. Léopold Sedar Senghor, who was then a Socialist and a French deputy, went through the draft to correct any grammatical errors. Paul Coste-Floret and several others tried to defend rights which had been neglected, such as the public interest and certain points of law, but they were blocked by the majority. Soon after de Gaulle's departure, the Communists and the Socialists had decided to work out together the way the constitution should go, and, as a proof of mutual goodwill, they agreed to celebrate the day of the 'Victory of the Republic'. 12 February 1934 had been the date of the Popular Front 'victory' and it was extremely significant that they should decide to celebrate their solidarity on that day.

The trouble with most of France's constitutions is that they have never been farsighted enough. They were always spoiled by too much concern with the present, even when they claimed to be legislating for centuries to come. The men who draft constitutions are always obsessed with the present and the wish to repudiate the immediate past. The 1814 Charter was written to abolish the

Revolution and the Empire. The reformed Charter of 1830 tried
to go against everything the Bourbons had supported. The 1848
and 1875 Constitutions were both ambiguous, although the second
was very clear on one point: it would do the exact opposite of whatever the Empire had done. This was exactly the state of mind of
our law-makers in 1946, only even more so. They wanted to
abolish everything connected with the spirit of Vichy.

This is not a detailed enough picture of all the French Constitutions for generalization; but I do wish to point out one fact.
Usually constitutions are drawn up to shield a nation from a peril
which has just passed; often they go so far in the opposite direction
that they allow another unconsidered peril to develop. The same is
true in military circles and even in the Catholic Church. People
passionately fight yesterday's enemy, while today's lies in hiding,
already stretching out a hand for the weapon that we ourselves
have just finished forging.

Our legal experts and the French people as a whole do not
realize that there is more to a good government than a good written
document. The way that document is interpreted is what counts.
It can either be diluted or strengthened and sometimes turned into
the exact opposite of what it originally meant. The 1875 Constitution was not particularly weak to start with; it was made weak.
The 1958 Constitution did not decree that the president of the
Republic should be omnipotent, nor did it place all power in his
hands; the weakness of some, and the tyrannical spirit of one man
made it that way.

Pierre Cot, along with the majority of the constitutional commission, had decided that the new constitution would give the
Assembly the most authority. This meant that there would be no
individual authority, that anarchy would prevail, and after that,
God only knows . . . the prospect was frightening. This forgotten
document, if re-read, can be seen to place the emphasis everywhere
on deliberation, delegation of power and the weakness of the executive. It would have rapidly led to government by clubs and by
the National Guard, until the Communists took over. Félix Gouin
made an impromptu speech praising the projected constitution.
Later he insisted that he had only spoken in his own name; but
this very dissociation between the man and his functions was a
dangerous sign of what would happen if we accepted the constitution and that particular mode of 'governing'. François de

Menthon replied in the name of his supporters and of all those who
were opposed to this draft of the constitution. Most were for it and
some were against. The following day, the Constituent Assembly
adopted the constitution by sixty votes, singing the *Marseillaise*
over the din.

Vincent Auriol had replaced Félix Gouin as president of the
Assembly; he made a speech on this occasion, congratulating the
Assembly and thanking both de Gaulle and Léon Blum. This link-
ing of the two names may seem surprising; but in those days,
Jacques Chaban-Delmas had the photographs of his two heroes,
Edouard Herriot and General de Gaulle, together on his election
posters, along with the usual list of personal accomplishments. In
those days, the Gaullists did not mind such links and they only
decided to take offence later.

The French nation still had to ratify the constitution as accepted
by the Constituent Assembly. Félix Gouin, Pierre Cot and many
others announced that they were 'absolutely confident' it would be
ratified. The MRP was the only big party which campaigned
against it, with some support from the Radicals and the Moderates.
In fact, the constitution proposed by the Communists and the
Socialists was rejected by one million votes out of twenty million
cast. General de Gaulle did not campaign against the constitution
and he did not even vote on that day.

He was probably waiting for the second round. The election
had made the MRP the party with the most seats in parliament, so
that I prepared to take over the leadership of the government. But
nothing had changed much. The so-called Marxist parties still held
the majority of seats in the Assembly. The Radicals continued to
sulk, and the Right Wing deliberately kept apart. This made it
very difficult for the MRP to act, since the scars made by the war
had not yet healed.

I became President of the Provisional Government on 19 June
1946. The Communists abstained from voting in my election as
head of state. I noticed that my party and I never got as large a vote
in parliamentary elections as other more easy-going groups, or even
as many votes as the Communists, probably because I do not have
any talent for courting people's ballots. This defect – or quality –
has always harmed me and those who were identified with me. But
I look upon this incapacity to please everyone as an asset now; when
everyone calls himself your friend, you have very few real ones.

Today we must not try to please everybody and to be accommodating. The time has come to be sure of our aims, firm, and determined not to compromise or to lie. I have always tried to act in this fashion and this has earned me a small number of really loyal friends and a host of lukewarm friends or undeclared enemies who prefer the easy-going sort of politician who remains silent when the time to speak has come. Most men like to 'chat', until the day arrives when they decide to keep silent in public and only to whisper in each other's ears.

When I chose my cabinet, the Communists announced that they would cooperate only if I gave one of the key cabinet posts to one of their party members. In November 1945, de Gaulle had already refused to let a Communist become Minister of War, of Foreign Affairs or of the Interior. I also refused and I said that if it was impossible to form a tripartite government, then I would have a government made up entirely of MRP members. Whoever wanted to support them would be welcome. When the Communists were faced with this refusal, they preferred to keep Charles Tillon as Minister of Munitions, which was what de Gaulle had made him. De Gaulle was no longer there, and Tillon, though a Communist, had friends outside the CP, so that I had to keep him. He had been one of the Black Sea mutineers of 1919 and a member of the Home Resistance, which made him slightly more independent in outlook than most Communist politicans.

Before my government was formed and ten days before I was elected Prime Minister, but nearly a month after the referendum on the constitution, General de Gaulle decided to speak. He broke a long, apparently deliberate silence which must have worried his supporters, most of whom by now were ex-Vichyites. The speech which he made at Bayeux, on 16 June, was not a warning or a call to arms, it was an order. He chose that symbolic city and spoke just before the anniversary of the Allied Landing, 'one of the greatest events in history', which he refused to attend on its twentieth anniversary.

De Gaulle was able to talk as freely as he liked in this speech, now that he was no longer expected to carry out the solutions which he prescribed; he was also very stern, like a man who believes that his word is everybody else's command, and that the pressure he applies will be irresistible. As I did not consider his pressure impossible to resist, I regretfully, but not guiltily, decided to ignore him.

De Gaulle once again repeated that he had set the train back on the rails; there was nothing new about this. But the rest of his speech was even more than usually irritating for us to hear. We had not asked him to leave and we had to face up to the consequences of his departure. His speech was full of references, not to France, for which so many men had died, but to the State, which is a cold and abstract concept, that has nothing to do with patriotism, which is a real and warm emotion.

'In this city,' France's so-called leading Resistance member said, 'the State reappeared. The legitimate State because . . . The sovereign State, which . . . The State which has been saved . . . The State which has been preserved . . . The State which is able . . .' and so on.

If you read the speeches that de Gaulle made two years before the Allied landing, you will not find a single reference to the State. He speaks of France, of the Empire and even of the government. But the people of Bayeux did not hear that cold word *l'Etat* until my first government, and on that occasion, they heard it five times in succession. They had been the first Frenchmen to be liberated, the first to see the French flag flying again, and now they heard de Gaulle tell them that what France really needed was a backbone. The inhabitants of Bayeux did not take offence. To them, General de Gaulle had all the prestige of the Resistance, of exile and opposition. They cheered those words of his which heralded the Fifth Republic.

The most clear-sighted and critical political commentators did not grasp the significance of the General's disturbing words, his warnings and his demands, although they were stated clearly enough.

'Now that victory has ensured the salvation of the State, and that national unity has been maintained, the most urgent and essential task is to establish new French institutions.'

We heard him recently proclaim the supreme importance of institutions, not long before he made a mockery of them. He started out with institutions and ended up with a principate.

I will not go on analysing this forgotten speech. What was striking about it then was his timing. Why had he waited several months, leaving without the least fuss and making no previous attempt to explain his departure?

De Gaulle was deliberately placing an obstacle in the path of the new régime. My government may not have been the best, but it was not the worst either. I suppose that de Gaulle objected to it because I was its leader. He did not utter a word against Félix Gouin, not even in private; but I was in the General's bad books just as I had been during the Occupation. I had once been considered unworthy of being Jean Moulin's successor, and now I was considered unworthy of being Félix Gouin's. This conclusion was not pleasant for me to make, but what annoyed me most about it was that I was loaded down with responsibilities, and was trying hard to do the best I could, as I had done once before. I decided to ignore de Gaulle, and to follow the path that I believed was right, without paying any attention to those who sat by the wayside, watching me trudge along and throwing stones at me. Every man in power is a prey to those who consider it their duty to hurl insults at him for having the gall to carry on with the job where they left off. I would not have minded listening to advice; but I never got any, and I was certainly not ready to obey orders from the men sitting on the fence.

My chief reason for not following de Gaulle's advice had nothing to do with vanity or parliamentary considerations. De Gaulle's speech had really been an attempt to reach the people directly over the heads of their elected representatives, whom he looked upon as a parasitic and useless group. Yet there were other reasons for rejecting his suggestions. Certain fools have claimed that de Gaulle's method of government descends from the tradition of Charlemagne and Louis xiv. But Charlemagne had his vassals and Louis xiv accepted the existence of many intermediary groups between himself and his people, even after the *Fronde*. Moses is de Gaulle's only respectable predecessor; but then Moses does not belong outside the context of Sinai. The real reason that I could not accept de Gaulle's proposals, even if they had been good ones, was that at the time the French people would never have consented to a constitution based upon such ideas. De Gaulle obviously did not expect his wishes to be adopted; he was simply expressing his personal views with the intention of putting them into practice himself one day. Gulliver did not care what the Lilliputians thought of his proposals or whether they accepted or refused them. He just wanted to throw his weight around, to make threats and to complicate their existence.

The government was faced with an unruly Assembly and an electorate which had refused Pierre Cot's constitution by one million votes out of twenty million. Crowds are notoriously fickle; but only an irresponsible politician like de Gaulle could have imagined that the French nation would accept the absolute anti-thesis of the constitution which it had almost agreed to a few months earlier. General de Gaulle had abandoned his responsibilities, so that he could afford to make the responsibilities of others even harder. But I was in no position to play his game and answer back. There is such a thing as duty to the State and only totally selfish men and unscrupulous adventurers ignore this fact.

The second Constituent Assembly would never have agreed to the constitution de Gaulle proposed in such harsh terms, so that it could not even have reached the stage where it could be sub-mitted to the people. Even if we had got such a text passed by the Assembly through endless ruses and machinations and miracles, it would certainly have been rejected in a national referendum. General de Gaulle realized this himself. What he wanted was not to succeed but to manoeuvre, not to reach his goal but to prevent others from reaching theirs.

When a man has a violent temper, he likes ordering others to do the impossible. But I do not claim that I can do that; because I know that the man who does make that claim is lying to himself and deceiving his audience. When de Gaulle came back to power after being forgotten for so long, he had become more and more morose as he had received fewer and fewer visitors in his solitude. Thus he did try to achieve the impossible and many people are blind enough to believe him when he says he succeeded.

A constitution is an extremely important document, especially if it lasts; but it is not the only thing that counts in a régime. Anyone who believes that a good government needs nothing more has never studied history which teaches us many lessons about some elaborate and highly-perfected written institutions. England uses only precedent and even the nations under Roman law are very lucky if their written documents suit their national interests and their community life. For twelve years we heard that all our troubles came from not having a decent constitution; this was a demagogic lie, as experience has taught us. As soon as new laws were solemnly proclaimed and written down and passed in 1958, the legislator announced that he was above the law. The author of the constitution decided that he could interpret it exactly as he wished, and that was the end of that sacred document.

Considering what de Gaulle did with the new constitution, there is nothing absurd or evil in suggesting that a constitutional text, however imperfect, can be made more or less flexible and can be adapted according to future needs. The only difference between then and now is that in 1946 de Gaulle was not in power, and tried to prevent the constitution changing for the better, while in 1958 he got to the heart of the constitution and was able to change it for the worse.

The preparation of the new constitution by the assembly was attacked by de Gaulle. The most amateurish psychologist would have seen that his violent pressure and obvious disdain for our petty efforts would only help to confirm the prejudices of those who were determined not to give much power to any one man, and even of those who did not want to abolish authority altogether. Anyway, we began work on the constitution once again, and once again we fell into the same old ruts. I had decided not to involve the members of my cabinet in working out a solution, since they disagreed on the subject. In this way, I would be able to intervene if necessary and veto a really unacceptable second draft. This was not a very grand approach; but you cannot stand on a pedestal and govern. We can see today what happens when a man tries to do both at the same time.

When the second constitution had been drawn up without much enthusiasm, I examined what it contained. I did not go over the minor details; but I studied the more important ones closely. First of all, I looked into the problem of the French Union and only then decided whether to accept or to reject the rest.

The first draft of the constitution had left the question of the French Union open and had simply resolved to call the Union a 'free association'. Even the Communists in those days could not decide whether they approved of the secession or the assimilation of the French colonies. But the first draft had not provided any guarantee for these territories and had left the question open. I decided to intervene when the Commission appointed to draw up the constitution approved a text 'denouncing colonial systems based on domination'. Although the Gaullists now use such terms, de Gaulle had not yet declared his feelings on the subject. With the help of Alexandre Varenne, our Minister of State, and of Marius Moutet, our Colonial Minister, I was able to ward off this threat to our colonies and to prevent any weakening of the French

position in the territories under our care. We accomplished this
with some difficulty. One day, Vincent Auriol showed me a letter
signed by nearly all the native representatives of French colonies
(including Algeria), threatening to resign; but we managed to
avoid this. If you read the articles concerning the French Union in
the constitution of 28 September 1948 (articles 60 to 82 and the
last three paragraphs of the preamble), you can see how falsely we
were accused of trying to decolonize.

On 27 August 1946, at the beginning of the most decisive phase
of the constitutional negotiations, General de Gaulle made a very
long declaration to the press which ought to be quoted just to serve
as a comparison with his later attitude.

France is a great power as long as she remains united with the overseas territories to which she brought civilization. If France loses those
territories, she may cease to be a great power. It is essential for us to
organize our relations with the peoples of different races who are joined
to us in a new but definite way.

On this vital point, the projected constitution only mentions 'free
determination', but considering the actual state of development in our
overseas territories and given the competition of other great powers,
this could only lead to agitation and dislocation among the populations
and finally to foreign domination. The projected constitution offers
nothing constructive on this issue and this is a serious flaw.

The constitution ought, on the contrary, to affirm and to consolidate
the ties between our overseas territories and France. . . .

This was de Gaulle's main criticism although there were many
others. Any man who sees clearly and still has some sense of honour
will, after reading this text, have a clearer picture of just how much
the 'twenty years of decolonization' theory is worth.

On the same day Edouard Herriot made a very successful speech
defending French colonialism; it was then that he spoke of France
being 'the colony of its colonies'. The irony is that the Radicals did
not think we had been firm enough on the subject of the Empire;
that was why they all voted against the 1946 constitution, Mendès-
France included.

In spite of the improvements I obtained in the second draft, I
had no illusion about the difficulties to come. This second constitution was tolerable, as long as we used it properly, but what
made the situation tricky was that de Gaulle had by now launched

a highly successful campaign against the principle of tripartite government. I began wondering whether we would have to reject the second draft of the constitution; but I did not like the idea. We would seem to be yielding, and there was little prospect of reaching a different and better solution.

I talked it over with the Minister of Finance, Robert Schuman. His job was as unpleasant as that of the Minister of Food Supplies. He was surprised when I told him of my doubts, and gave me a straight answer. France's finances, he said, were in very bad shape, and we could not afford any more delays. Our government would have to stop being provisional; even imperfect institutions, as long as they were tolerable and could always be improved, were better than no institutions at all. Robert Schuman spoke in no uncertain terms; he was not touched but shocked by my scruples and seemed to think that they were a kind of weakness on my part. I am certainly not mentioning this conversation to distribute the blame. It was my decision, not Robert Schuman's; but I had to know what the situation was and to take everything into consideration.

I was in this frame of mind when I sent two delegates to see de Gaulle in the hope that he might change his attitude or at least compromise. Although Paul Ramadier and most of the other prime ministers had secret interviews with de Gaulle, I did not think it would be suitable if I went in person considering the nature of the mission and its likely failure, which would lead to grave consequences. How right I was not to go on that pilgrimage! My envoys were received exactly as I had feared, with an inimitable mixture of distant courtesy and scorn. Yet I did not regret having explored every avenue to get a larger vote for a constitution which could still be improved. My trusted envoys may have been badly received; but perhaps they did not make the journey in vain. The two men in question were Jean Marin and Michel Debré. *Sic transit gloria mundi.*

Finally, the second draft of the constitution was accepted by a majority of one million votes. This was a failure for everybody: the MRP had persuaded only a minority of its electors; General de Gaulle's warnings had not been heard by the nation. But the chief victim of all these disagreements was the Fourth Republic and France, which finally chose to lose its freedom rather than to keep it in such inglorious circumstances. The tragedy of 'national unity' is that the man who demanded it never looked upon it as anything more than the duty of obedience to himself. What we did not realize at first was that 'the State' was really one man's pseudonym. I did not know this in 1946. In 1958 I did not think it would matter; indeed, it might even be useful for a time. Those who made the same mistake as me underestimated the capacity for contempt, arrogance and bias of the most sterile leader France has ever had.

Looking back from exile and going over our mistakes and de Gaulle's crimes, I naturally feel angry, but I cannot feel guilty. All our errors began when we first listened to the radio and heard a proud, distant man saying no.

But de Gaulle did not say no only to the defeat. He said no to practically everything except his own morose, repressive ideals. Once during one of those long monologues known as conversations, I quoted Goethe's Mephistopheles to him, 'I am the one who always says no.' De Gaulle only grunted in reply; but I noticed that in a speech he made on television during the early part of his second régime, he used the quotation. The press uses this line out of *Faust* now whenever it wishes to point out the beauties of acceptance and the infernal nature of a refusal.

I am quite certain that the ability to say no is a good thing. I said no once to Pétain and once to de Gaulle. And I did not just say 'maybe' on either occasion. But the reason I said no twice was because I was saying yes to certain unalterable values which I never want to give up. There is a time to accept and a time to refuse. To say yes all the time is to be a coward and a fatalist. To say no all the time is to be arrogant and mean. Ruling, and not only ruling but living, is the art of choosing which cause to defend and which evil to fight. If you automatically reply yes to everything or no to everything, then you have either opted out of the conflict altogether or else you are a bigot.

6

The Peace Conference /
The Spanish Problem

During this time, from the end of July to the beginning of October, the peace conference was on in Paris. The name 'peace conference' was far too ambitious, as the whole enterprise soon came to a standstill after a very poor start. The basic obstacles to a real European settlement were Austria and Germany, and they were not discussed in the conference. A peace conference worthy of the name would not have sidestepped the two fundamental issues and have dealt only with minor matters or petty interests. The chief question apart from Italy was what we ought to do about the states, nations and peoples under the shadow or in the grasp of the USSR. No one openly criticized what the Soviet Union was actually doing. We all remembered the recent tragedy of the war, the United States was still vaguely flirting with the USSR (as it still does periodically), and we all quite reasonably hoped that once the less important problems were solved, we would be able to go over the major ones and even to bring up the question of Germany. I was saying then that Germany was the key problem of Europe. But today, eighteen years later, we still have not found that key.

Only the most ignorant or servile people could pretend that we did not try out every path, even the most unpleasant ones, to try and find the right solution. Little by little, the West grew discouraged; there was still some goodwill on our side and we hoped that the world would be united yet; but the futility of all our attempts began to wear down our patience. By nature and training, the Soviet representatives were indefatigably stubborn. They probably never had the time to think that the Free World might get fed up with spinning a wheel on which there was no thread.

Until now, the West has been too liberal, too deluded, or perhaps too infiltrated to be really tough or even to present a united front. It has got very little out of this attitude, except peace. We are still at peace; but at the cost of a strategic retreat everywhere.

When I look back on that first great public confrontation, when the world was still recovering from its ordeal, I remember clearly what I thought then, although of course I had to be discreet about my opinions at the time. They have all been confirmed; if peace was not the result of that conference, it was because we were not ready to pay the price we would have had to pay – total abdication. The Soviet Union is not interested in offering us any peace which does not involve the capitulation of the Western world.

At the conference, we were supposed to decide on the fate of the non-Germanic belligerent nations. Italy, Rumania, Bulgaria, Hungary and Finland had all fought against Allied countries. There had been a pseudo-juridical argument over France's participation in the discussions and the signing of the treaties at the first conference of the 'Five', then of the 'Four'. The Russian delegates have by now given everyone the bad habit of squabbling over ridiculous minor legal points. Everybody haggles, discusses, gets excited for weeks, months and even years, on some unimportant point of international law. The idea behind those everlasting squabbles is always the same; stop any power which is not too vast and which is not a satellite of yours from taking part in a conference on the pretext that it is not qualified. After a whole lot of incidents both in London and in Paris, some of them quite serious, it was decided that France would be one of the leading participants, although it had not been officially at war with any of the countries mentioned, except Italy.

The Five-Nation conference at the end of 1945 was interrupted by Molotov's sudden decision to exclude France from the discussions and from the signing, although he had seemed perfectly well-disposed towards us at the beginning of the talks. I believe that this was the last conference attended on an equal footing by a representative of Nationalist China. Molotov was so successful at sabotaging the meeting that it was dissolved without even a written report. After a great number of skirmishes and incidents, everyone went away and we had nothing to show for three weeks of negotiations.

France was better treated at the peace conference and it was able to participate fully in the discussions; but the temporary settlement of European and world affairs was totally unsatisfactory.

The conference was held in the Senate Room at the Palais du Luxembourg. The Americans were glad to be running this diplomatic meeting like a session of Congress because it satisfied their tremendously naïve love of show and their belief in the virtues of publicity. The Russians also liked it that way, because this gave them an excellent opportunity to denounce everything and everyone and to provoke incidents as soon as they were at a disadvantage. Not even the Czars could have made such brutal and consistent claims for preferential treatment. A few politicians who wanted to place a speech also approved of the fact that the conference would be run like some minor Congress of Westphalia or Vienna.

Yet in spite of all its inefficiency in solving serious matters and all its preoccupation with minor problems, there was as much difference between this conference and present UN sessions, where nations without a past or a present or a future claim to speak in the name of progress, as there was between the diplomacy of Richelieu and that of Clemenceau.

There is something wrong with an organization where important problems are relegated to second rank, so that people can make speeches merely for their own advancement and give press conferences twice a day. Experience has taught us that no good can come out of contests of eloquence between men from different nations with just about nothing in common, who always contradict each other and who use the same words to mean opposite things. The material resources, the authority and the moral independence of all the different nations in the world vary far too much for them to have a solid base of discussion.

Of course, criminal designs plotted in secrecy are also very dangerous. But the glare of publicity does not eliminate the plotting, far from it. We ought to recognize the fact that letting any ambitious fool air his grievances at any assembly he chooses can only do harm.

Our peace conference was full of the usual complications and foolish, useless talk. None of those conferences are ever free of them. We also had to watch over the safety of Ernest Bevin, who claimed that the Israeli guerrillas wanted to have him murdered, as was indeed true. But Bevin finally died a natural death from an overworked heart that was full of bitterness, and at least he was not assassinated in Paris. As everyone will tell you, I am an expert in assassination plots, so that you can take my word for it when I say that Bevin was never in danger during his stay in France.

We also had to look out for the Communists. Not because their lives were in danger, but because they had a way of turning every complaint into a major affair of state. Whenever the Allies went to any official receptions at the Russian embassy, they always met representatives of the French Communist Party there, including the most famous Resistance members of the Normandy-Niémen area. We were not always on the best of terms with them by the end of the evening.

Not even under the worst Czars was Russian diplomacy as ruthless as during the time the Kremlin was the uncontested capital of world Communism. Molotov was as courteous and as unbearable as a Poincaré from Baikal (in fact, he came from the lesser Muscovite nobility). I had a few really violent quarrels with him, always because of his absolute conviction that the Russian nation and Communism had to come first in everything.

As for the results of these conferences (if they can be called results, as there never were any except on matters the Soviet Union considered trivial) they were always in an inverse ratio to the number of nations that participated in the talks. When everyone got together, there were no results at all. When the conference was held in camera, nothing happened either, but the tone changed slightly. When four countries got together (in other words about sixteen men because of the language difficulties and the Russian suspicions and the American scruples) very little got done either. We were able to get down to real policies and to make progress only when a very small committee met. Between two men, even between eight, which is the minimum you can have in actual practice, you can get down to the basic questions without wasting too much time: 'Who gets what? If we accept that – not that we do – what will you give us in exchange?'

Needless to say, we never expressed ourselves quite as frankly, but basically it all amounted to just that. If Molotov and Vishinsky had cut down their speeches and had come to the point, I would not have spent twelve hundred hours vainly trying to get them to speak clearly. Once Vishinsky was dead and Molotov was in disgrace, things continued exactly as before. That jolly man Gromyko had not the least difficulty fitting into a dead man's shoes or those of one in disgrace. Gromyko is a Russian version of Couve de Murville: without any excess zeal he makes himself as useful as possible to all his leaders in the hope of outlasting them. The Kremlin's foreign policy continues to be a mixture of Communist imperialism and secular Czarism.

This duality can easily be seen in the leaden, pedantic phrases Russian diplomats never tire of repeating. Their basic attitude is that after so many perils, after sidestepping so many traps and losing so many companions struck out of the lists of the Soviet Encyclopedia, there is no point in running any risks, of advocating any definite policy which, once defined, could be fatally compromising. The thing is to be able always to disentangle yourself, and the easiest way to do that is never to entangle yourself in the first place. That is the secret of all those super-subtle, brain-racking circumlocutions; people say they are impossible to understand, but in fact they are very simple indeed. You take everything you can grab, make everybody frightened of you, give up nothing, and if you have to give up anything, never admit it. There's nothing particularly mysterious about that; but your obstinacy and your contempt for everything may end up by making an impression on intellectuals and so-called 'liberals': consciously or unconsciously, they will become your accomplices. The list of more or less knowing accomplices who have been duped by the Communists is a long one, extending from Roosevelt to de Gaulle and from Mauriac to Sartre.

The men at the conference in the Luxembourg belonged to the generation of post-war statesmen. Roosevelt was dead; de Gaulle had gone; Churchill had been overthrown during the Potsdam Conference, and Stalin remained in Russia, as he always did.

Clement Attlee replaced Churchill. He was a Labour politician, although he was no Socialist; only the English, with their fantastic capacity for empiricism, could possibly have admitted a man like Attlee to the Socialist ranks. He was the British representative during the first days of the conference. He was a sort of Churchill in reverse with none of Churchill's qualities or faults. But he was a calm, poised man, with a great deal of common sense. I have never had anything but friendly feelings towards him or his famous rival throughout the years I have known them, and in spite of certain strange silences.

Ernest Bevin was the new Secretary of State at the Foreign

Office, replacing Anthony Eden. The contrast between him and Eden was as striking as the contrast between Attlee and Churchill. Eden had studied at Oxford and knew the Persian language; Bevin was an ex-newspaper vendor who, according to some, could not even speak English properly. He never missed an opportunity to remind everyone of his proletarian background, which was tiring in the long run. Molotov especially, who certainly could not boast any such working-class antecedents, did not like to be reminded of Bevin's. Bevin was the typical clever cockney and a really charming fellow as well; I think I have the right to express myself in this familiar fashion, as for fifteen years I had to live down the fact that he once fondly referred to me as 'that dear little man' in a speech at the House of Commons, a phrase used against me later by some people. Bevin was a worker, a Trade Unionist, and a true Britisher. He was certainly not obsessed by ideological considerations. During the war he kept his party on the sidelines, waiting to take over after the victory. And now in his new job, he was working with all his might for England and for freedom.

When Roosevelt had run for a fourth time in the US, he had thought of making James Byrnes his Vice-President. Byrnes had already left the Supreme Court to supervise wartime industry. But then Roosevelt probably decided that Byrnes was too good to be wasted on the Vice-Presidency. There is a well-known remark by a certain American lady (a remark true for many years, though no longer so) which goes: 'I have two sons. One became the captain of a cargo boat, and the other became Vice-President of the United States, and I haven't heard from either one since.' As everyone would surely have heard of James Byrnes, Roosevelt chose a nonentity. That nonentity turned out to be Truman.

This was how James Byrnes became President Truman's Secretary of State. Byrnes is said to have had a great deal of help in writing his book, *Speaking Frankly*. If that is true, and I don't know whether it is or not, then James Byrnes at least chose his helpers well, which is more than you can say for American statesmen in general. Byrnes believed in the mission of America and he admired any man who had dignity and loyalty. His two assistants came from each of the two big American parties and were both Senators. Senator Connally was a Democrat from Texas and Senator Vandenberg was a Republican from Michigan. Their positions were very different at the start, for Vandenberg had the reputation of being an isolationist; yet they became almost indistinguishable after a time, for their appearance and policies and cigars seemed identical. They were both very pleased with themselves; but I think Vandenberg was the better man. The most difficult thing for Foster Dulles was that not being a Senator, he was entirely dependent on the President. Governor Dewey did try to get him elected Senator from New York; but he only got 900,000 votes, which was the lowest given to a Republican candidate in living memory. Byrnes knew that he could count on his state, South Carolina, and the others also knew that their personal situation was secure, so that they did not have blindly to obey all the wishes of their chief.

During those years, the United States was represented by some fine people. After Cordell Hull, an old hand at the diplomatic game, and Stettinius, Roosevelt's white-haired protégé, the United States sent us Byrnes, Marshall and Acheson one after the other, and all three had a lot of talent and character, though in varying amounts.

For about a decade, Molotov and Vishinsky represented the USSR abroad. Molotov had negotiated with Ribbentrop, Eden, de Gaulle and me, Chiang Kai-Shek, and many others; he had blown both hot and cold, had flirted with Fascism and the Democracies alike. He was strangely colourless for someone who had had such an exciting career. But, apart from Stalin, he was the most reliable man of the régime, as well as the toughest. He ended up by being accused of being the leader of the 'anti-party', whatever that means. Only about twenty people in the world know what 'anti-matter' means, and I doubt whether there are as many as that who know the true meaning of being 'anti-party', the cause of Molotov's disgrace. The materialists also have their mysteries.

Vishinsky was obviously the more brilliant of the two but Molotov was the boss. Anyone could see that Molotov despised Vishinsky, who was indeed utterly despicable. But Molotov used Vishinsky, made him do the work, and exploited his energy, his lack of scruples and his inexhaustible capacity for making speeches. From behind his spectacles Molotov would look on as Vishinsky toiled. One day, at the Embassy in the rue de Grenelle, he said to me, 'You've got Couve de Murville, and I've got Vishinsky.' I don't know how accurate this comparison was, but he also added, 'And Bevin's got Evatt.'

Evatt was the Australian Minister of Foreign Affairs, and Molotov assumed that this made him one of the key figures in the British Empire. For although the Russians were infinitely suspicious of the 'capitalistic nations', they were far more ignorant about them than they would admit. I had heard Bevin complain often enough of Evatt to know what this assumption of a monolithic Commonwealth was worth. Molotov probably thought that Australia was a kind of English Ukraine and could not imagine such a thing as genuine freedom and independence without strings.

Molotov stuttered when he was worried and he never had much of a gift for expressing himself, whereas Vishinsky never stuttered. The Bolsheviks had assured themselves of his loyalty by making him the Public Prosecutor during Stalin's purges, supplying fodder for the firing-squads. He was the sort of man who says and does anything you tell him to do or say, an expert in double-thinking; Stalin had recruited him from the ranks of the bourgeoisie, and every day he made up with his zeal for his unworthy origins.

Alcide de Gasperi was the only really outstanding man among the representatives of the countries which had been defeated by us and with which we had to sign treaties. De Gasperi was head of the Italian government and he had the tremendous task of putting his country back on its feet, after it had been ruined by a régime which he had fought against. When he first entered the old-fashioned and grandiose conference hall, I happened to be chairman of that particular meeting and said a few friendly words of welcome to the representative of the 'new Italy'. But the solution to the problem of Trieste, which I helped to make a neutral zone hoping that the victorious nations would not start arguing about it, was basically unsatisfactory. It was too much like the Danzig solution, which had been so bad. I was extremely relieved when, eighteen months later, I was able to go and see de Gasperi in Turin and tell him that France, England and the US had agreed to give Trieste back to Italy.

As I am not writing a chronicle or a biographical encyclopedia, I probably need not apologize to those whose names I have not mentioned, and I hope they will not think they were unwelcome guests in France during the conference, just because of this omission. We did all we could to give our guests a good time in Paris, and invited them to the Hall of Mirrors at Versailles, where we celebrated well without much lavishness, for times were hard.

There was an atmosphere of peace and glory about the sunshine, the park and the palace. Clemenceau had erased the memories of Bismarck in the Hall of Mirrors, and now we were erasing the memory of Hitler. We had invited a thousand people; but twice that number showed up, not all of them welcome. The crush was so great around the buffet that a slab of marble was broken, so that we tried, as diplomatically as possible, to make some of our guests move on to the terraces and the gardens. As it was a beautiful summer's day, we had no difficulty in persuading them.

The Spanish Problem

At the beginning of 1946, our relations with Spain, which had never been good, became very strained, and this led to a train of unpleasant and rather absurd developments. No one can understand this episode unless they can remember France's state of mind at the time. The Spanish Civil War had had a great many political and emotional repercussions in France. Unlike the Abyssinian War, the tragic conflict in Spain, the atrocities and the strategic calculations had ushered in a new age of international civil war. People can go about today claiming that all ideologies are obsolete and that you must get rid of them altogether. The sort of people who talk like this are secret, though active, accomplices of the very worst ideology of all. Otherwise, it would be easy to dismiss what they say as mere nonsense.

The fact is that there are two conflicting ideologies in the world today – both of them have their variations and both of them are equally determined to win: one ideology is Communism (less united than it used to be about means, but in perfect agreement about ends) and in opposition, the block of nations which is anti-Communist. These nations are in a bad position both for 'peaceful co-existence' and for the Cold War. They disagree among themselves, and contradict each other. They are on the defensive, both intellectually and strategically. That is why the Communists are able to make so many inroads into the nations where freedom and human dignity still prevail, however imperfectly.

A dense mist of abstract emotions, added to some more concrete desires for expansion, floated over the ruins of the Second World War, and there would be more ruins to come. Practically no one could keep a cool head over the subject of Spain, and those who could were weak. Léon Blum's non-intervention during the Spanish Civil War had been a highly personal decision, yet it had given the Socialists, the Communists, and many Radicals passionate regrets, so that they now considered that one of their most important tasks was to get rid of the last dictatorship left in Europe. As for the dictators in Eastern Europe, they were looked upon by some as comrades under Stalin's command and by others as a historical necessity. The MRP members could only remember the help Franco had received from Hitler and the Fascists. Franco had been helped by the Axis powers and he had finally won because of them. When the German attack had forced the Russians to fight on our side, members of the international brigades fought in all the *maquis* of the Resistance, and had become the leaders of the Communist parties after the war. So that we have forgotten, for example, a really violent brochure written by Francisque Gay called *Flames and Blood*, which was a reply to some articles by Jean-Richard Bloch and others, published in *Vu*, a weekly magazine belonging to Lucien Vogel. I noticed that this particular pamphlet was not mentioned by those who spoke at the funeral of Francisque Gay. That is what is called lying by omission, unless the speakers were just so indifferent to the truth that it had finally become a habit to leave out what was awkward.

François Mauriac wrote many a fine article in the *Echo de Paris*, disagreeing with the French bishops who praised Franco's 'crusade' and who sent letters supporting Cardinal Goma y Tomas, Archbishop of Toledo and primate of Spain. Almost nobody has noticed that every single one of these articles has deliberately been excluded from the great writer's collected essays. Mauriac decided to cut out his bolder articles to avoid offending those who had favoured Franco, his 'right-minded' readers, as he calls them today. Bernanos did not do the same when he wrote his *Vast Cemeteries Under the Moon*; but everyone agrees that he never knew how to control himself and to further his career.

In the thirties, I tried to be objective about the giant holocaust in Spain. I did not hush up the massacres, the atrocities on both sides, and the bloodiness of the struggle. On the Republican side, I described how, behind a fragile barrier of legality, the Anarchists and the Communists were fiercely struggling for power, and how the only thing they agreed on was that the chief targets in the zones under their control should be churches and convents, with nuns and priests as the principal victims. But I was also worried by the fact that the Axis powers were using Spain as a testing ground.

I wrote that the Germans had bombed Guernica, which was the truth. No one denies it any more, for it has been proved beyond a doubt; but at the time, I was attacked by the popular weeklies, *Candide*, *Gringoire* and *Je Suis Partout* as well as by *Jour*. The London *Times* defended me. *Tempi passati*.

Even worse, a French prelate became angry with me because he thought that I did not declare myself clearly enough on the side of Franco, who, according to him, was the defender of Christian civilization and the Catholic faith. And so, he officially denounced *l'Aube* and me especially to Rome. I barely escaped the wrath of the Church; in Pius XI's day, the Vatican was not afraid of condemning anybody. Many people would have felt that it was only fair for *l'Aube* to be condemned by the Church, along with *Action Française*. Nothing happened in the end, because Francisque Gay wrote a very long article called 'Catholics first', which calmed the Vatican's wrath.

I now hear that the prelate in question has become a cardinal and that his view of the world has completely altered. Occasionally, I remember his conduct then, and I also think about those who approved of it so highly, and who now indignantly reject the least hint of clericalism in public life and even in the Church, going so far as to take the name of 'Christian' from the old Christian Trade Unions. But history and truth were on my side where Guernica was concerned. What most people do not know is that, until recently, the Chief Commander of the East German naval forces had belonged to the 'Condor Legion' in Spain. I wonder if he still wears his Order of Isabella . . .

But in 1946, I was not sure that I ought to complicate our existence, and even that of our neighbours, by arguing with Spain. It was extremely difficult to avoid this. Everyone remembered that Hitler had met El Caudillo at Hendays, just before Montoire. When the Vichy government had tried to get Germany to guarantee France's colonies, it was refused not only in favour of Italy's claims on Tunisia, but also because El Caudillo had his eye on Morocco, and even on Orania. But what people did not realize was that Spain had done the Allies a tremendous favour by staying out of the war, risking Germany's displeasure by doing so. If General Franco had helped the Germans or even allowed them to get to Gibraltar, we would have lost the Mediterranean and the war would have gone on longer.

There were serious incidents, especially at Chambéry, when the Blue Division returned from the Russian front to be repatriated. Many of the Spanish Republicans who had fled to France after the fall of Barcelona had settled in the South of France, not far from the Pyrenees, particularly in the area of Toulouse, where along with the French Communists they had taken an active part in the Resistance. The situation in that area was rather tense largely because of them; they had acted courageously at times and badly at others. Once France was liberated, they immediately began thinking of liberating Spain. I remember that all the Left-Wing newspapers and some of the others carried editorials promising successful raids, the creation of a Spanish Resistance front, and imminent victory for the Republicans.

The situation was very difficult. France was still in a state of disorder, so that the Spanish *maquisards* could get across the Pyrenees easily. It was on the other side that they ran into difficulty. The Madrid government's reaction to infiltration was very tough. In February, twelve republicans, many of whom had fought in France, were executed, in spite of our diplomatic attempts to save their lives in memory of their French war records. This sad affair unleashed much anger and emotion. Men who had fought against Hitler were being killed by a régime which had been backed by Hitler from the start, and which had later expressed hopes for a German victory and sent volunteers to the Axis powers. The Union of post-office employees and of railway workers acted immediately, and almost the entire Assembly was irate. De Gaulle had left power one month earlier, and, as I have already said, not only the Gouin government but the Palais-Bourbon contained solid Left-Wing majorities. They were backed by the Gaullists over the question of Spain, for many of them had had a taste of Spanish hospitality in the vile Lerida and Miranda camps on their way to Algiers.

At the time, and even today, I was blamed for giving in to CGT pressure, when the CGT was still united, because I closed the Spanish frontier as they wanted me to do. The truth is that a majority of the Ministers asked me to break off diplomatic relations

136

with Spain. I had felt it coming and had formally declared two weeks earlier that France would not break off relations with Spain independently of its Allies. I felt that this was only common sense, but the climate of opinion made it impossible to hold to my declaration unless I accepted some less drastic measure. The only solution or expedient, depending on one's politics, was to close the frontier. I never thought it was a good idea; but it was either that or a complete diplomatic break.

The Republican government in exile, which was still looked upon as a potential and acceptable successor to Franco's régime, began long and involved negotiations with the Allies. The United States published a series of documents proving that Franco's friendship for the Axis powers had not just been platonic. France, England and the United States made a tripartite declaration expressing the wish that Spain would get rid of its dictator without bloodshed and be led by a provisional government made up of patriots and liberals. In that case, there would be no problem about diplomatic relations and Spain would get economic aid as well. But the question of a rupture remained undecided and the three governments refused to intervene in Spain's domestic affairs, hoping that 'the Spanish people will not go through the horrors and bitter experiences of the civil war once again'.

For a time, our only diplomatic relations with Spain were through *chargés d'affaires*. Cardinal Spellman, who stopped in Madrid on his way back from Rome, stayed there for only two hours and did not attend the reception which had been prepared in his honour. The Spanish question was eloquently and passionately discussed in the United Nations; but nothing ever came of it. The sort of debate where a régime is attacked only helps to bring a people closer to its government. In February 1948, when no one had any illusion left about the imminent fall of Franco's government, I was able to have the frontier re-opened and full diplomatic relations were assumed.

There was only one result of the whole affair, and that was the exclusion of Spain from the United Nations. I suppose that Spain is not particularly grateful to us for doing this; but frankly, its government must find it an advantage not to be continuously subjected to the sort of treatment Portugal gets there at the hands of the Afro-Asians.

I have discussed this forgotten problem in some detail out of

love for the truth and out of disgust for hypocrisy. I do not want
to lie to history as so many others have done, even if this means
that I will be criticized by both the Left and the Right. As a matter
of fact, I have never stayed in Spain or been on holiday there,
unlike some anti-Fascists of my acquaintance. I have never been
on good terms with General Franco, who has a long memory. I
think he resents me not so much for closing the frontier as for some
of my articles during the Civil War, particularly the one in which
I described the bombing of Guernica. I noticed this in 1953 over
Morocco. Yet, putting sentiment aside, the world is treating Spain
in an inexplicable and shocking fashion.

The democrats and socialists in France, England, Belgium, Scan-
dinavia, and elsewhere have a kind of allergy to Franco's Spain,
which makes them lose their common sense entirely. Spain has
been officially put in Coventry (though this does not prevent Russia
and Fidel Castro from dealing with it very profitably), while at the
UN an endless procession of nations have hardly passed the tribal
stage and are already well into the stage of quarrelsome anarchy.
We still remember Spain's war and we forget the fact that Sukarno
was a militant collaborator. We pretend not to notice that there
have been and still are some genuine Nazis in top positions in the
governments of Bucharest, Cairo and Algiers, among others. We
never stop calling Franco a murderer, and at the same time we
sing the praises of the great advocate of an 'independent road to
Socialism', Marshal Tito.

When Spain asked to join UNESCO, the official organ of the
SFIO wrote the most extraordinary comment (I quote it from
memory, but I am absolutely sure that the meaning is exact):
'There are three candidates, Nepal, Libya and Spain. It goes without saying that the first two are acceptable, but Spain is a different
matter.' I wonder if it is possible to say something so stupid without being a moron or a practical joker. UNESCO is a cultural,
educational and scientific organization. I suppose that the inacces-
sible valleys of the Himalayas and the burning sands of the most
backward Arab country are well known for their culture, education
and science; but Cervantes, Saint Theresa, Saint John of the Cross,
Lope de Vega, Calderon, Velasquez and Goya have nothing to do
with the history of artistic achievement. It really is too absurd.

Now that we court Peking and seek out the most distant countries, our discrimination over Spain is against our own interest and

certainly unfair. There is an Interparliamentary Union which holds congresses that are supposed to be attended by members of parliament. One of these congresses was recently held in Belgrade, which proves that Communist members elected by 'legislative' bodies are welcome, but not members from Spain. Why? Is this what we call historical materialism? But suppose historical materialism is wrong?

As soon as the main democratic parties start accepting Communist so-called legislative organisms which only have one party, no opposition, and a unanimous vote, only three conclusions can be drawn; the first is that democrats do not really believe in democracy; the second is that men who are elected basically despise the principle of elections; and the third is that these senators and deputies have no sense of fairness or of ridicule. Once you start admitting parliaments whose members have not been freely elected and you include the governments of Eastern Europe, you might as well allow all the authoritarian régimes to join in. Either you have only genuine representatives in the true parliamentary tradition (and there are not that many left today although there were many in the nineteenth century and the beginning of the twentieth), or else you admit everybody. Any other attitude is intellectually dishonest and shows that the representatives of democracy have lost faith in themselves and that they have to use shabby tricks like these to disguise the fact.

During the two years that the Spanish frontier was closed, smuggling flourished and France suffered a lot more from it than Spain. At the United Nations, Léon Jouhaux tried to get economic sanctions applied to Spain; but this was the sort of proposal that never gets beyond the rostrum. Sanctions against Italy for much better reasons and with much more likelihood of success, had failed before the war, so that sanctions against Spain were most unlikely to succeed. I do think that, in the end, France got out of it lightly, although the French economy was harmed.

At least the possibility of another Spanish civil war was averted, and one of the most tragic episodes in the history of civil wars was not repeated. The whole West would have suffered badly if there had been another 'Spanish Question'.

Even Russia, which would have been the only country to benefit from a second civil war, felt that the time had not yet come. The contrast between the way Russia has blocked every solution to the

German problem, and the way it has done nothing about Spain, is striking. In the forties the French Communists had two points of view that were completely contradictory, but excellent for propaganda purposes. At parliamentary meetings and with me, they would demand two things: a complete break with Franco and the liberation or the pardon of the Republicans in his prisons.

Personally, I am no admirer of the heavy-handed tactics used by Franco's régime to prolong its own existence; they are much more repressive than is necessary. But I had to remind our Communist friends that I could not obtain the desired results if I stopped all communication between ourselves and Spain. If we cut off diplomatic relations, we would not be able to help anybody, or even to intervene. You have to know what you want: either you must try to save as many lives as possible, and the only way to do this is to have respectable diplomatic contacts, or else you have to abandon 'the victims of arbitrary justice' to their fate. Needless to say, only Spain has such victims, never Russia or France. Only friends are 'victims of arbitrary justice'; enemies get just what they deserve and we are usually not nearly severe enough with them.

The Left Wing had demanded that the frontier between France and Spain should be closed and it got what it wanted; but this complicated the life of some fervent anti-Fascists. One day, the Communist mayor of a large town in the *Midi* asked me if I could make an exception in his case and allow some Spanish bulls through, because his town needed them for a bullfight. He did not get his bulls; but for me this incident cast new light on the morality of the old maxim that it is the exception that proves the rule.

7

The Treaty of Dunkirk /
The Moscow Conference /
The Marshall Plan

The election of November 1946 gave the Communists the largest
bloc of seats in parliament, because the Gaullist Union candidates
had siphoned off many moderate votes. First Maurice Thorez, and
then I, failed to form a cabinet, and finally it was Léon Blum who
became president of a temporary Socialist administration. Léon
Blum was seventy-four years old, which is not too old for politics
as everybody knows. But he was in bad health, and since his
return from German captivity, he would have preferred to act as
a sort of intellectual and spiritual guide to the Socialist party,
rather than be the active head of government. He was kind enough
to tell me that he would do nothing without asking my advice
during the few weeks that he would be in charge of foreign affairs
as well as head of the cabinet. He did nothing of the sort; but it
was a courteous thing to say.

As soon as Léon Blum was in power, he rushed over to England.
He was not really interested in the obscure circumstances that had
led up to our departure from the Middle East, largely through the
fault of England. Traditionally, the Socialist party is only really
interested in social and economic affairs at home and in Europe.
I am not criticizing Léon Blum for this; although he always
remained true to himself, suffering had made him a better man
and he made a genuine effort to get rid of some of his more old-
fashioned notions. He was not one of those colonialists who, after
fifty years of defending the principle of empire, suddenly become
fanatic anti-colonialists, and want to give away their colonies at all

costs. Blum did not know much about France's overseas possessions, and, like a lot of Socialists, what he knew best about them
was their nationalist rebel leaders. So that our quarrels with
England over distant territories could not alter his strong affection
for the English in general and for the English Labour Party in
particular.

The English Conservatives had been defeated at the time of the
Potsdam Conference. Winston Churchill was replaced by Clement
Attlee and Anthony Eden by Ernest Bevin. The French Socialist
party had certainly always been a firm believer in international
Socialism. In Jaurès' time, the German Social-Democrats had
strongly influenced the French Left. In those days, the Socialist
congresses echoed not only with the names of Marx and Engels,
whom Jaurès did not really like, but with the names of Lasalle,
Betel, and to some extent Liebknecht, and with the great conflict
between Kautsky and Bernstein.

After the First World War, and especially after Hitler came to
power, when German Socialism collapsed and the Jews began to
be persecuted, the English Labour Party became powerful in
England and the leader of world Socialism. The workers and the
trade unions in England were powerful and generous. Although
the continental point of view was foreign to them, they often
helped other Socialist parties in distress.

Léon Blum and Ernest Bevin had almost nothing in common.
Blum was an intellectual and an aesthete turned top-ranking
politician, whereas Bevin was an ex-factory worker, who flaunted
his modest origins and his humble beginnings. Bevin was no
theorist; his policy always remained empirical and thoroughly
nationalistic. But all the same, he and Blum got along because
Blum wanted the alliance and thought that it would help to solve
present and future differences.

I am convinced that this was, to some extent, the right attitude.
I only say 'to some extent' because really good and enduring
alliances have to depend on common interests, principles and aims.
I still had to learn what so many people did not realize during the
war and afterwards: that it is dangerous to assume that an ally is
totally loyal, disinterested and faithful when one's own country
cannot claim to be so.

During the Occupation, we had wholeheartedly and enthusiastically believed that the 'great democracies' could do no wrong,

R.—6

and we took a long time to become more realistic. Today we have gone dangerously far in the other direction, which is doubtless worse. Once Vincent Auriol became President of the Republic, and Léon Blum was replaced by Paul Ramadier, I became Minister of Foreign Affairs once again and continued our negotiations with England, until we reached a satisfactory agreement. We discussed many topics on which we might have disagreed, such as Germany, West Africa, the Far East and Europe. Later, we were somewhat disappointed, for the alliance did not prove to be as durable as we had expected; but at the time, I decided that we had got far enough to conclude an alliance. The French Assembly was surprised when I announced my decision; for some reason, it had thought that I was hostile to the project.

England and France were close enough to justify an alliance; but I had another undeclared reason for wanting it. We still hoped to avoid an absolute breach between East and West; but every exhausting and fruitless conference with the Soviet Union made me less and less certain of success. An Anglo-French alliance would provide an essential basis for other agreements, if the worst came to the worst and we had to organize a system of defence.

Ernest Bevin and I signed the Treaty of Dunkirk on 4 March in the presence of the two ambassadors, Duff Cooper and René Massigli. I had specifically chosen Dunkirk and Bevin accepted enthusiastically. It might have appeared rather paradoxical and provocative to choose that city for signing a treaty of friendship, for it was there that in defeat and under heavy bombardment, the French had competed with the English for space on the evacuation fleet. But that was exactly why I chose it; it would dispel the memory of that tragic defeat and start up our friendship again where it had been interrupted.

Dunkirk was in ruins and the weather was ghastly. We signed the treaty at the Prefecture, one of the few buildings still standing. Few inhabitants had yet returned to Dunkirk: the town had nothing but temporary shacks and an almost useless port. Yet, in spite of the rain from the North Sea, which brought back dismal memories, the inhabitants hailed the treaty joyfully and enthusiastically as a guarantee of future peace. When we had signed, we made a brief speech stressing the special nature of this pact and hailing the cooperation between our two countries. Then I remembered our two war leaders. They had played a great role in the war and both of them had left power. I sent a telegram to Winston Churchill and to General de Gaulle. Winston Churchill replied immediately in the loftiest terms; but General de Gaulle never answered.

A few days after the trip to Dunkirk, I left for Moscow from Le Havre. When I had made the first journey there with General de Gaulle, we had gone by plane around the Mediterranean, through Egypt, Syria, Arabia, Iraq and Iran, and we had then taken a train from Baku to Moscow, stopping at Stalingrad. This time, the French train took us up to Brest-Litovsk and from there a Russian train took us to Moscow. I only remember two simple but significant things about the journey. The first was that, going from West to East, the train went slower and slower with each country we crossed and the second was that people's faces got progressively sadder and more expressionless as we journeyed towards the East. Germany was still in ruins and I wondered how its cities, particularly Berlin, would ever be rebuilt. All that was left of the German factories were a few vast chimney stacks still standing here and there. East Germany was already perceptibly sadder than West Germany. Poland, where Warsaw was not yet rebuilt, was sadder than East Germany. And Russia was saddest of all.

Before leaving, I made a speech to the National Assembly. I want to quote two lines from it, as they show what my feelings were on Germany: 'France must remember, but it must show mercy as well, and it must fear the sight of Germany becoming a pawn before it can choose its own destiny.'

The Moscow Conference

The conference in Moscow lasted from 10 March to 24 April. During the war, there had been celebrations of 'triumphs' on the occasion of victories; there would be long gun salutes followed by firework displays to cheer up the badly-fed population of Moscow, where many of the window-panes had been replaced by wooden planks. The people were better fed now, especially privileged classes like 'academicians', top civil servants, officers and diplomats. It was not too cold, but there was still snow in the streets. So many men had died during the war that the women were working on the roads, wielding pick-axes and climbing on to the roofs to brush away the snow.

The heads of the Western delegations were lodged in the embassies of their countries, so I was the guest of General Catroux and his wife. The French ambassador was a born diplomat and he had no prejudices against Moscow, so that he exercised his functions with great skill and talent.

We were supposed to be four at the conference table but, in fact, there was a crowd of us. I already knew Molotov and Bevin, but it was my first meeting with General Marshall. I met a great many Americans during that period of my life and they were all amiable, especially Foster Dulles, although he used to make up for his friendliness in person by being vicious in print. The Americans were usually talkative and they loved telling the journalists from their country all about confidential and important matters; this was a great nuisance and often a real threat to security. But of all the Americans I ever met, I put General Marshall in a category all by himself. Perhaps he, too, wrote some harsh things about me according to a diplomatic law of compensation; but that does not stop me from agreeing with Truman's judgement when he said that Marshall was 'the greatest American alive'. No other man since 1945 approaches him in uprightness and stature. Compared to Truman's Foreign Secretary, the most brilliant reputations seem shabby. He was not vain; he spoke with great simplicity and humour about his career. One day, he told me quite naturally, 'When I was ambassador to China, I tried to please everyone. The result was that by the time I left, nobody trusted me.'

He was unaffected and did not pretend to be infallible. He would ask others for advice and could be unsure, even hesitant. But once he had made up his mind, nothing could have made him change it, not even the President of the United States in person. He was quite cautious and sure enough of himself not to strike up rash poses or to speak off the cuff in public.

I have good reasons for believing that what they say about Marshall is true: he had been at the very summit of the military hierarchy and the only authority above him had been the Commander-in-Chief, in other words, Roosevelt. Therefore, logic required that he should have been chosen to command the Allied landing. But although Marshall had no leanings at all towards politics, in the vulgar sense of the word, he belonged to a traditionally Democratic family. His home state, Pennsylvania, was Republican then, and Marshall himself told me how he had not been able to enter West Point because he could not get a Senator from his state to recommend him.

But he did not tell me what others have said. The fact is that Roosevelt decided that Marshall, being a Democrat, would become a formidable political rival if he won a great victory. Thus, although Marshall was not at all the ambitious type, the American President decided to choose a distinguished officer who came from a Republican family with pacifist leanings. This was how General Eisenhower won fame and the White House as well, while Marshall continued to do his duty without complaint.

The lengthy Moscow conference was drawn out by endless festivities, frozen 'amusements', formal parties and sumptuous banquets where most of the time was taken up in toasts. These utterly boring occasions marked the end of an era, in spite of all our attempts to postpone that end. Disraeli once said, 'Life would be just about bearable if only it weren't for the amusements.' I have often thought of those words when I attended yet another festive event during some international conference. Each time they became harder to bear and more futile; but the politeness also became more elaborate. Yet it was a purely verbal politeness and it did not spring from the heart.

In Moscow, the French were well treated by everyone, but there was nothing pleasant about the conference all the same; on the contrary, the situation was most complicated. If we had had any success at all, it would have justified the discomforts, but that was not the case. The Eastern block stopped being well-disposed towards us soon after the conference for three reasons. The first was that Soviet policy made it impossible to keep the balance between East and West. The second was that the Russians always wanted more than what they gave in exchange. And the third was that Paul Ramadier had got rid of all the Communist ministers in his government when he came to power.

The Russians were both suspicious and ambitious. Russian diplomacy under the Czars had never been famous for its flexibility or its moderation, and shortly after the October Revolution, the Bolsheviks continued in the footsteps of Peter the Great and Ivan the Terrible, those two great Russian heroes who were the precursors of contemporary Russia's expansionism and style of government. There had been a brief period of radical enthusiasm and liberalism right after the Revolution; but Russian Communism soon proved to be the spiritual heir of Czarist ambitions.

Living side by side with a brutal giant was never easy; but once the giant decided to be fanatically anti-religious as well, co-existence became a day-to-day miracle.

Stalin received the head of the French delegation first of all. In the USSR, the least nuance of protocol is full of significance, and sympathy for each of the countries present could be mathematically calculated by the number of lines given them in the Moscow newspapers. Therefore, this priority gave rise to many a comment and much speculation. I was received by Stalin at midnight, for in those days the Russians began work at bizarre hours. I found Stalin heavily guarded and always the same with his low voice, his lack of expression and his dominating air. I saw him again on another occasion and I think the atmosphere of the conference can be summarized in two conversations I had with him.

I was explaining to the all-powerful master of Russia (Stalin himself always called it Russia; it was Molotov who called it the Soviet Union) what the French wanted out of the Saar. I pointed out to him that Saarbrucken had been a French city until the end of the First Empire, and that it was only fifteen kilometres away from the Lorraine frontier. And after all, Russia, which had not yet backed France's claims in that area, had annexed Königsberg without hesitation, although the first king of Prussia had been crowned there as early as 1701.

'I'm sorry,' I said, 'but I cannot remember what you call Königsberg now.'

Stalin turned to Molotov and said to him, without lowering or raising his voice,

'Well, what *do* you call it?'

'Kaliningrad,' Molotov replied.

Kalinin had just died; he had been President of the USSR, in other words, a mere figurehead. That had been his reward for being an old harmless Bolshevik. Stalin revealed his utter contempt for constitutional appearances by bursting out laughing when he heard this.

'Kaliningrad! That's a good one!'

He was very ignorant and cared nothing about the history of the Bolsheviks or geography.

Another thing he said to me showed clearly what the Russian policy was; it still is like that today after three changes of leaders. 'It is better to be two against two than three against one,' he told me. In spite of all their principles, the doctrines and claims, about Socialism, Communism and progress, the Russians basically believe in nothing except tough cynical bargaining, as I saw on many occasions.

Will this change? I do not know. In spite of several upheavals, the Kremlin has not altered much. No one knows if it has altered at all. Probably only the surface has changed, but the basic attitudes remain the same.

The chief issues we discussed at the Moscow conference were war reparations, the status of Germany, the Saar, and German coal for France. As nothing got done, there is no point in my listing all the various discussions we held; nothing ever came of them. The only thing which France did get was more coal from Germany, but this was not recorded in the agreement, although Molotov seemed well-disposed on that issue. But he refused to let us decide anything about the Ruhr unless Russia was included in its administration and control. In other words, he wanted a share in the parts of Germany that were under Western occupation. The only reason France got more coal, which was very useful though we did not get very much, was that the three Western powers came to a separate agreement without Russia. However hard France tried to keep East and West together, the two seemed destined to disagree and finally to split, particularly over Germany.

France also wanted war reparations very badly; but it did not get these either. There was no way of getting around the fact that Germany was still in ruins and was only surviving because of Allied handouts. The Russians had looted their zone, although the loss to Germany was greater than the gains to Russia; German equipment went rusty because the Russians did not know how to use it. And now, the Russians wanted reparations from the whole of Germany to make up for the huge stretches of their land which had been laid waste. What this meant was that the parts of Germany under Western occupation would have to contribute too, even though they had practically no means of production. The Germans would have been unemployed and starved without the Anglo-Saxons. If they were made to give up a percentage of their production, which was already very low and far below minimum standards, the United

States would have to increase its aid and its subsidies to West Germany, so that Soviet Russia could get from the Germans war reparations that were really provided by the Americans.

Although France had the support of the English and the Americans over the Saar, it was not able to get what it wanted from the Moscow conference. Stalin made me understand that he would not agree to our demands unless we gave him far more. His attitude was that if France wanted war reparations, it had to back Russia's claims as well. France wanted the Ruhr to be placed under international control, therefore Russia would also have to benefit from this. Needless to say, he did not mention the nationalization of the Silesian mineral deposits, which had been given to Poland.

The Russians would accept the French solution to the problem of the Saar on condition that they got the reparations they were asking for and a share in the control of the Ruhr. Obviously, although the Western nations avoided putting it that way, they could not accept Russia's presence on the Rhine. This was the weakness of France's position over the internationalization of the Ruhr. It had been de Gaulle's idea and I had to go on defending it until it became impossible because Russia could use it as an argument for getting even further west into Germany, even though it had already got as far as the Elbe. It is clear from what happened to Berlin as soon as it was placed under the control of four nations, and the way it was split into two like Korea and Vietnam, what the Ruhr would have become if it had been similarly internationalized. The Russians would have looted their section; they would have tried to make the workers revolt; production would have come to a standstill; France would not have got the coal it needed so desperately, and America would have continued to subsidize the entire area.

We could not come to any agreement on the questions we discussed at the conference. Gradually, we saw that nothing would come of it; Germany would continue to be the Allies' stumbling-block and the biggest obstacle to a genuine European peace. I defended de Gaulle's German policy to the bitter end and tried hard to get the Ruhr placed under international control, while respecting the rights of the occupying power (England in this case). I wanted the Ruhr to be politically independent of Germany with the aid of the Big Four, Belgium, the Netherlands and Luxembourg. And I wanted the Rhineland to become autonomous and detached from the rest of Germany.

I persisted in this policy, although I did not really believe that it was practicable or likely to further the cause of peace. But finally, I had to face the fact that all our partners rejected the French solution for varying reasons, as we might have expected. Russia was indifferent to everything except the prospect of getting some control over the Ruhr. England and America did not want to have anything to do with what seemed to them nothing but an ambitious pipe-dream. France would not get what it wanted, therefore the only reasonable thing to do was to give up. But it took us a long time to forget our bad memories of the war and to accept a different and more realistic policy.

After the Moscow conference, I gradually started making steps in the right direction, basing my decision on a concept of the future which was bitterly contested by the far Left and even by the Gaullists, until the day de Gaulle changed his mind, stopped reviling this view of the future and began to take credit for originating it.

If, to satisfy public opinion, I had persisted in our policy towards Germany and had tried to maintain France in a situation of 'non-alignment' between East and West, the French nation would soon have become isolated, powerless and weak. It would have had to witness the re-emergence of a strong Germany, without being able to do anything to prevent this. Germany would have been hostile to the French and there could not have been even a semblance of reconciliation between the two countries. There would have been no Marshall Plan and no Atlantic Pact, and there would certainly have been a revolution in France, for which General de Gaulle would have blamed me. The conference in Moscow proved that the only future for us lay in a Free Europe.

The Marshall Plan

One and a half months after the Moscow conference, General Marshall made a speech at Harvard which turned out to be the most important post-war event. He called on all the nations of Europe to work out a plan for their own economic redevelopment with American aid. He explained that the success of the programme would depend on Europe and that 'the consent of a certain number of European countries, if not all', would be necessary. Bevin and I immediately let Washington know that our two countries accepted

150 RESISTANCE

and that we would get together to make arrangements for the
application of the Marshall Plan.

Bevin came to Paris shortly afterwards and we agreed that a
European economic commission would have to be created. My
comments on Marshall's speech were published at the time. In
them I said, 'France has always known that its own economic reconstruction would be bound up with that of all Europe.' France
and England agreed to ask Molotov to attend an urgent meeting
of our three countries. General Marshall had specified that Russia
was included in his proposal.

This invitation created problems, as it came right after the
Moscow conference, which had given us some idea of what behaviour to expect from the Russians. If the USSR accepted Marshall's
offer, everything would become more difficult. Besides, America
was rich, but its wealth was not unlimited, and if the Communist
countries of Europe joined in, then obviously there would be that
much less to go round. The American Congress would also be far
less well-disposed or even interested if the Communist countries
were included. But all the same, I insisted that they should be
asked and Bevin allowed himself to be persuaded. I believed that,
whatever the drawbacks, we could not miss this opportunity of
achieving a genuine *détente* in Europe if the Russians accepted, or
assessing the Communist position if they refused, as General
Marshall's offer would be harder to refuse than anything offered
up till that time.

Molotov came to Paris and we started on talks between our three
nations towards the end of June at the Quai d'Orsay in the hall on
the first floor called the *Salon des Perroquets* because of its decora-
tion. I suggested that all of Europe – allied, neutral, and ex-enemy
countries – should participate in the Marshall plan. The only exception would 'provisionally' be Spain, for reasons I have already
given. Molotov obstinately refused everything. He rejected any
programme covering the whole of Europe because, he said, such a
programme would undermine the sovereignty of each individual
nation. I took infinite pains to settle our differences, to propose
clauses that would reassure everyone, to discard all plans that
might have compromised the sovereignty of any nation; but
Molotov continued to repeat the same objections, droning out his
set speech. His determination to refuse was unshakeable.

After this failure, I wrote out a declaration which was a kind of swansong to our hopes for European unity 'all the way to the Urals'. We had hoped for this against all hope, and now it was at an end. 'France solemnly declines any responsibility for the consequences of a decision which it has done everything it could to prevent.' I also added that France naturally continued to adhere to the Marshall Plan and expressed the hope that it would help as many European nations as possible.

Bevin and I then decided to send out invitations to all the other European countries and to create an organization that would decide what was to be done. Within ten days, we held a conference and created a committee of cooperation and four technical committees. Sixteen European nations attended this conference; but none of the Eastern countries was able to come, even those we knew would have liked to be present. Finland wanted to participate, but did not dare to declare this officially. Czechoslovakia, which was not yet totally under Communist domination, formally accepted, but had to retract its agreement after an order from Moscow; that was how the USSR saw national sovereignty.

We spent about a year drafting a general report and working out the best ways to apply American aid in each country; the American Congress took about as long to accept. France was one of the countries which benefited most from the Marshall Plan; thanks to it, we were able to rebuild our economy far more quickly than would have been possible otherwise. In fact, American aid prevented the French economy from coming to a standstill. There has never been a finer, more far-sighted gesture in history than the Marshall Plan. When France was prosperous with stable finances and a lot of surplus capital, the French also invested a lot of money here and there and lost a great deal too, because their investments were often bad; fifteen billion gold-francs lent to Russia never came back. But these funds were always loans, invested with the hope that they would bring back a high rate of interest. They had nothing to do with charity, even though some of them finally turned out to be no more than that.

The Marshall Plan was completely different. It was a gift and there were no strings attached. The United States was paying for the goods and the tools needed by the European economy, and this helped Europe to recover; our economic condition improved rapidly, the cornerstone of future European cooperation had been laid, and the peoples of the Western nations were saved from

152

RESISTANCE

hunger, poverty and despair. Needless to say, the Communist parties followed the Kremlin line in denouncing the Plan; the fact that the working classes would now have work and would not revolt was called a menace to peace, slavery to American capitalism and an abdication of national identity.

Agitation started again with renewed violence during the autumn of 1947, coinciding with Marshall Aid and the departure of the Communists from the government. Robert Schuman, who had just succeeded Paul Ramadier as head of the administration, remained calm and was able to put an end to one revolutionary strike, which had specific political aims. All over France, slogans mysteriously began to appear on the walls and continued to do so for the next ten years. My little house was often decorated with these slogans, painted in tar; but these crude tactics did the Communist cause more harm than good and CP membership remained static over the years.

Meanwhile, the RPF party created by de Gaulle was growing in France. Its tone was 'colonialistic' as we say now, violently anti-Communist, and utterly contemptuous of the other parties, although these same parties were doing all the work. As for the Americans, de Gaulle never said a word about the Marshall Plan, but accused the Americans of being opportunists, ignoramuses and exploiters; that may well have been his one consistent attitude over the years, for he has changed his mind over nearly everything else.

The French people may have some legitimate grudges against the Americans, but nothing can do justice to General Marshall and to the generosity of the American people. I criticize the Americans enough in this book to appreciate this opportunity to praise them.

We voted on the status of Algeria in August 1947; this status had already been generally accepted during my first government. We had debated it during the second Constituent Assembly, and I still recall the final words of a speech made by Edouard Depreux, who was Minister of the Interior then and is president of the PSU today. I agreed with him at the time and still do now, of course, when he said, 'The Algerian flag is the flag of France, red, white and blue.' During Guy Mollet's government, Algeria's status changed, and then changed again under de Gaulle in a series of declarations and events which are only too well known. I will discuss all that later, but I would like to quote a speech made by de Gaulle in August 1947. Algeria's status no longer matters, unfortunately, but the author of this speech still does:

What will happen to Algeria in the modern world is of vital interest to the future of the whole of France. Therefore, a new status for Algeria will be a very important event for the nation. France must be fully acquainted with the terms and the extent of this new status, so that the men who will be responsible for carrying it out will know exactly what is expected of them.

The French conquest saved Algeria from a state of anarchy which had lasted for a thousand years. The population of European descent, along with the Moslem population which includes a wide variety of ethnic groups, have made Algeria what it is today by working and living together under French sovereignty. We can be proud of the work that we have accomplished, although the task, like all human endeavours, is neither perfect nor complete . . .

Whatever happens, France will not abandon Algeria. Certain excesses or agitation by separatists of various allegiances, whether on the French mainland or in Algeria itself, as well as various attempts by foreign interests, may one of these days provoke some discontent. In this day and age, it is easy enough to stir people's emotions by exploiting the difficulties that France is going through at the moment, and the inconsistency of the régime which now rules our country.

But in spite of these difficulties and the inconsistency – which are both temporary – those who deliberately try to sow the seeds of disorder will fail. Because, in spite of attempts by a few defeatists and illusionists, France, of which Algeria is an integral part, is basically very determined to help all its citizens and to remain the master.

8

The Prague Coup / The Brussels Pact / German Affairs

In February 1948, there was a revolution in Czechoslovakia; it had been secretly organized by the Communists and was all over in a few hours. Russia did not even try to hide the fact that it had taken part in the coup: it had lost any interest it ever had in an alliance of victors and had decided that infiltration into the Western countries would no longer yield any important results, now that the Communists were gradually eliminated from the governments of France, Belgium and Italy. And so, the Russians decided to use force in order to obtain another sphere of influence, or rather of domination. Their new acquisition extended further to the West than the Elbe in Germany, placed them in the heart of Bohemia, cut Austria into two, and gave them access to the Adriatic as far as Trieste.

And yet Benes had always been a Slavophile like most Czechs. I met him in London when his country was putting together a coalition government made up of Socialists, Partisans, Fierlinger's Socialists, Mgr Shramek's Catholics, and Communists. On that occasion, Benes told me that he was not worried about the government being taken over by his dangerous Communist allies, although they had the support of the liberating Russian army. He seemed most serene and confident; but what he did not realize was that Moscow's strategic considerations, now that it was preparing for a cold war, placed his country in immediate danger. Benes died not long after the coup.

A few months before the coup, the Prague government awarded me the Czechoslovakian Cross in gratitude for my opposition to the Munich pact before the war. Just to maintain the balance, they also gave the medal to Charles Tillon, ex-leader of the FTP, who had taken a part in the French government after the Liberation. Czechoslovakia sent two ministers as delegates to the embassy in Paris for the ceremony. As one of the men who was getting the medal was a Communist, one of the ministers had to be a Communist as well. Clementis, the Communist minister, came to keep an eye on his colleague, Jan Masaryk, Minister of Foreign Affairs. I knew that Masaryk did not have his father's inflexible nature and that he hated being kept on such a short leash by the Soviets, although he only complained discreetly and never protested openly. One day, after a rather rough session at the founding UN conference in San Francisco, I told him as we left the hall together that I was surprised by the docile way he accepted Russian measures which he could not possibly approve. He answered with some bitterness, shrugging his shoulders, 'What can I do? Molotov has just threatened to break off the alliance if I don't go along with him. What do you expect me to do?'

Occasionally, I think of the fate that befell the four men who gathered at the Embassy on that day. Masaryk threw himself out of a window in the tragic tradition of Prague, although the circumstances of his death have never been clarified. Clementis was hanged when Moscow suddenly noticed that its trusted servant had been opposed to the German-Soviet Pact. Charles Tillon, an ex-Black Sea mutineer and thus a friend of André Marty, was disgraced by Marty's fall. And as for me, I was the last to go; but here I am in Brazil, waiting for justice to be re-established.

The Prague coup came as a surprise to a lot of people, who, in spite of everything, did not expect to see an entire nation lose its freedom overnight. I do not claim any merit for having foreseen that this would happen once the union of the 'Big Four' had broken down because Russia refused to compromise on any subject. This alone should have served as a warning that we could expect the Soviet Union to act brutally and to loom as a terrifying menace.

I cannot recall the exact date, but some time during the early part of 1948 I wrote twice to General Marshall to point out to him that the Soviet menace now threatened the whole of Western Europe. The Russian armies were only 200 kilometres from the Rhine, so that it was absolutely necessary for us to have a formal agreement with America to provide a force to help us re-establish our threatened security. I also pointed out to him that if the Americans helped the Germans too fast and too much this would have disastrous consequences on their relations with France, as French public opinion was still extremely sensitive after four years of recent occupation.

General Marshall replied that the American public would not accept any more aid to Europe unless Europe itself made some effort to unite and to organize its own defence. He was not the sort of man to try and force the French into a change of heart towards the Germans nor to hint at blackmail of any kind. Everyone realized that it was impossible for the time being to conclude an alliance with our ex-enemies; an alliance with the Benelux countries to reinforce the alliance that already existed with England would be a fine symbolic gesture, which is why I proposed such an extension right after the Dunkirk treaty. It would not be enough in the long run, but an alliance with Germany or Italy right then would have been unthinkable.

In London, we held a conference *in camera* to prepare for a union of the Western nations, or at least of as many of them as we could get together. While this was going on, there was the Prague coup which led to the Communist takeover. The three great powers invited the Benelux countries to attend the conference and the Eastern European governments reacted immediately with a great show of indignation, very alarmed by the fact that the meeting was taking place in secret. I suppose they believed that only they had a right to secrecy, as there had been a Communist conference at Prague just before the *coup d'état*.

The Brussels Pact

A Summit meeting was held in Brussels in March for the purpose of organizing a union of Western nations, although unfortunately not all Western nations could participate. The French National Assembly approved the scheme while the meeting was taking place, after a debate in which the only opposition came from the Communists. I made a speech in which I said:

As for those who bring up the fact that a Western bloc might seem directed against other countries, I should like to remind them that fifteen pacts exist between the countries of Eastern and Central Europe.

For the sake of freedom, Western Europe has the right to do at least as much as others have already done, not against others, but like others . . . The time has come for us to do all we can as quickly as possible to persuade what remains of Europe to get together.

The Brussels treaty was signed on 17 March, by Paul-Henri Spaak, Van Boetglaer van Oosterhout, Joseph Beck, Ernest Bevin and myself. The treaty stipulated that a consultative council of five ministers should be established which would meet at regular intervals, while one permanent organ would guarantee regular contact between the nations. In case of armed aggression in Europe, all the countries would automatically be expected to help, and if aggression occurred on another continent, the countries would have to be consulted. I tried to explain what this agreement meant to our countries by saying, 'What we are doing today represents the cornerstone of European unity . . . in terms of both economics and security.'

These were the modest but resolute beginnings of the Atlantic Pact and the construction of a new Europe. We had not been able to let Italy join in the Union because its status as an ex-enemy country would have endangered our enterprise which was hardly beyond the planning stage. Moreover, it probably would not have been good for Italy. Yet the previous autumn I had had a study made of a project for a customs union with Italy, as this seemed to me a good way to begin bringing Italy back on to the side of the Free World; after all, Fascism had been an anomaly in Italy, a yearning for prestige and power. I also thought that if one day Germany found its way back into a united Europe, this would be a good start.

The idea of a customs union was easily accepted at first. The opposition, both political and economic, took a certain time to get organized. But when negotiations progressed and it became obvious that the idea of the customs union was serious and that we really intended to put it into practice, the strength of inertia and the opposition of certain business interests confronted with the prospect of foreign competition began to make themselves felt. We needed a great deal of perseverance to overcome their objections. But after I stopped being Minister of Foreign Affairs in the middle of 1948, Robert Schuman did not display enough energy to carry the project through; he was interested in slanting European policy towards the North rather than the South.

Due to Count Sforza's indifference, a motion to put Italy's ex-colonies from pre-Fascist days under Italian trusteeship again failed by just one vote in the UN, partly because there was a revolution in Haiti that day. The project of a customs union was also gradually abandoned. Later someone told me that he had met de Gasperi at Sorrento, and that de Gasperi had spoken with tears in his eyes about the project for the customs union that he had worked so hard to bring about and which had now been given up.

Italy's hour of hope came in the spring of 1948. Three days after signing the Brussels pact, I went to Turin to sign a document with Count Sforza declaring our intention of establishing a customs union. After signing, I made a speech which caused a great stir and which surprised many people. For several weeks, the United States, Great Britain and France had been negotiating secretly on a certain subject and had finally reached a decision which I now announced, speaking for the three countries at a public ceremony before an astonished audience.

In 1946, Trieste had been turned into an independent zone; but the spirit of conciliation in which this had been decided was no longer justified by the present atmosphere in Europe, so that the three Western powers had decided to give Trieste back to Italy. This in fact took place in a less satisfactory fashion six and a half years later, when Yugoslavia and Italy agreed to share the territory and to give the city of Trieste back to Italy. We had put an end to the long argument at last; there was no longer a risk of the ambiguous situation leading to a Danzig on the Adriatic.

Even though Fanfani got me chased out of Italy when I fled to his country, I never felt sorry for playing a major role in the return of Trieste. Forgetfulness, ingratitude and stupidity rule life, particularly political life, and Fanfani's action is not the first example of this.

German Affairs

Meanwhile, German affairs were evolving much too fast for French public opinion. Most of the French political parties seemed to believe that we could do something to influence US policy, at least in certain sensitive spots like Germany. The members of the French Assembly were extremely displeased because they felt they were not being told enough; they wanted to be informed of every step taken by the Americans in Germany. In fact, we had to conduct talks with the Americans secretly, because any brake we might put on their policy depended on the discretion of the negotiators, as in the Trieste affair.

Around this time, I came under heavy fire from the Foreign Affairs Commission which decided its dignity was being insulted because it was not being told enough, forgetting that the fourteen Communists in that Commission would have put any information to good use. Now practically no one protests against any of de Gaulle's policies, although even the men who carry them out do not know about them until the last minute; as for those who are supposed to control these policies, they accept that they will never know anything until they hear all about it on television even if they are meant to ratify the policies by a vote. This has made me very cynical about the relativity of courage and opinions.

I had to spend many hours trying to persuade the government about Germany, for René Mayer was totally opposed to the idea of a German Federal Republic and Jules Moch was against any agreements which might bring about a split between East and West. In fact, the split already existed. There were endless hours of debate before the Commission, where, for once, the Communists and the Right Wing agreed not only to oppose me but also on the reasons for this opposition. I cannot quote the actual agreement, because the documents are no longer in my possession. But basically it provided for the creation of an inter-allied organization to control the Ruhr, which was obviously not at all the same thing as internationalizing the territory or the economy of that area.

The United States was keeping Germany alive, and for that reason it was eager that the economy of the western part of Germany should recuperate. America wanted to stop subsidizing Germany so extensively just when the Marshall plan was temporarily making America financially responsible for the whole of Europe. This was why the French negotiators had to fight tooth and nail against what I had already warned Marshall about: that our security would be sacrificed for economic considerations, and that the economic advantages of Germany's prosperity would endanger our hopes for war reparations as well as our notions of security. A lot of Frenchmen, Socialists, ex-members of the Resistance, and nationalists had the vague feeling that France would not be

160   RESISTANCE

safe if the German Zones of Occupation were given up and a
West German state created, and if Germany became a powerful
industrial nation once again.

Considering the recent painful past and de Gaulle's opinion on
relations between 'Gauls and Germans', this suspicious attitude
was perfectly natural. The impatience of the Americans and the
bleakness of the German people's existence made it impossible to
move slowly enough to give public opinion in France time to
evolve. The French could not see, only three years after the war,
that this was the only logical course of action.

Parliament hounded me over this question and I finally lost
the little credit I had by defending this point of view. Yet my
arguments must have been valid since all the people except the
Communists who attacked me then use the same arguments now,
including General de Gaulle. Many of the men who opposed me
then, or who were very reluctant to accept my plans, are professional 'Europeans' today, assiduously attending Franco-German
meetings without showing the least trace of guilt or even of
memory. The only ones who helped me and who stood by me
throughout were the members of the MRP.

All men ever remember are their grudges. Their capacity for
forgetting may be the only explanation of the spontaneous, almost
childish friendship, that suddenly made de Gaulle and Adenauer
fall into each other's arms. Those two cold hearts began to beat as
one in the twilight of their long, loveless existences, but not even
this can stop me from claiming that, knowing what the cost would
be, I was the one who made it possible for Germany to join the
Free World Camp; I knew that this was inevitable in spite of all
the slogans to the contrary.

I deliberately helped to accomplish a monetary reform in
Germany which saved the German nation from bankruptcy. While
this reform was being organized, Pleven began a very unpleasant
campaign against me, questioning me personally on the subject.
After this debate, Daladier was able to make a sanctimonious speech
to the Assembly, voicing his fears and his indignation without
taking any risks. Now that the risks exist, everyone only whispers
his indignation. The monetary reform was passed during the second
half of June 1948. I left the Quai d'Orsay two weeks later.

I made a speech on 11 June 1948 at a very tough session of the
National Assembly, answering my opponents, de Moustiers,

Billoux, Pierre Cot, Terrenoire and Capitant. Honest speeches are often forgotten, but I would like to quote a few words out of my speech, for I think that it deserves to be remembered.

I reminded the Assembly of what I had said in July 1947, a speech approved by 415 votes.

If we have to talk, then it is our duty to have talks with three if not four sides, rather than with only two . . .

And so, we have had talks with three. Not that we were at all eager to let Germany be divided, especially into two parts, nor did we want the Western part of Germany to be re-organized; but we cannot just leave the ruins of the former Reich as a black hole right in the centre of Europe, if we want to reconstruct this continent.

. . . First of all, Germany has to become a peaceful member of the European community in the world of today.

. . . France has taken the firm position that it will back a constructive policy for Europe, and it has shown that this is what it wants irrevocably, I think, by its adherence to the Brussels pact and by its participation in the programme of European reconstruction.

We are living in difficult times, so that we can only speak in terms of Western Europe and West Germany for the moment. Nevertheless, we must build up Europe, and we must find some place in it for Germany.

We will do all we can to create a united Europe, for this is the only way we can reconcile the countries of Europe. I wish to say that France would be wise to reconcile itself eventually with the presence of Germany in Europe and in the Free World, for no other reconciliation would be genuine.

Any man who cares for the truth can look up these words in the *Journal Officiel*. They may seem trite today, but people found them very hard to swallow in 1948. What I said is not important, but the replies of my opponents are. I have told you their names, and I dare them to look up the speeches they made then. Practically every word of what they said has been demonstrated as false and ridiculous, and of course many of those speakers have recanted since. But the obvious and negative comments got the loudest applause on that day, as usual.

The motion was passed by fourteen votes at the end of the session. The Gaullists, the Communists, the UDSR, the RRL and other small Right-Wing groups voted against it. As I have already said, the debate had been very stormy and our task was made even more complicated by two different people. One was Couve de

Murville, then Director of Political Affairs and Government Commissioner. He decided that it was his duty to campaign openly against the motion, although his function was supposedly to help me obtain votes. Later, when many had changed their minds yet again, he told me personally that he regretted his action.

When he heard about this, Ambassador Jean Chauvel, Secretary-General of the Quai d'Orsay, came to offer me his help to win votes. Given the atmosphere which prevailed, this unprecedented offer was an unusually courageous gesture, and Chauvel was under no obligation to do this. I want to thank this remarkable man for his gesture, especially since I doubt that my later actions have kept his support. The late Paul Giacobbi was another of my opponents, and this very clever political operator influenced the votes of many hesitant deputies, including some absentees. Later, he came to visit me from time to time to try and persuade me to join the RPF, until the day when he came to see me for the last time, shortly before his death, and with clenched fists and flashing eyes, begged me in no uncertain terms to forgive him for having given me such bad advice.

General de Gaulle had officially decided to oppose the motion and he attacked it in characteristic terms:

Under the guise of a few formal clauses, the '*communiqué*' postulates that the three German Zones occupied by the United States, England and France should very soon form a 'constituent assembly', from which a 'German government' will emerge, to 'piece the fragments of Germany together', in other words, to create a Reich in Frankfort.

After that nothing will stop the Soviets from creating a second German state either in Berlin or in Leipzig, with a government run along Soviet lines, in other words, totalitarian and entirely dependent on theirs. This means that only one question will preoccupy Germany and Europe: which of the two Reichs will absorb the other, as it has been decided and announced that 'the Future of Germany is unity'.

The nationalistic rivalry between Berlin and Frankfort caused by such a situation can easily be imagined, as can the resultant international atmosphere. Even if the conflicts between Germans and between other countries caused by this rivalry do not start a war very soon, we can at least guess which of the two German Reichs will be tough enough and have enough outside support to win the contest in the end. One can go beyond that and imagine a German nation once again concentrated around Prussia, but a totalitarian Prussia this time, linked body and soul to Soviet Russia and to the 'popular governments of Central and Balkan Europe', accepted by the Anglo-Saxons out of weariness, insularity and blindness: a solution of appeasement. But if there is another great Reich, especially one created in those conditions under such an influence and with such allies, what chance will France have?

The diplomatic activity conducted by France from our original position to the present *communiqué* agreed to in London, has been a continuous succession of retreats until the final capitulation. For some reason, the course of events which led up to this proposal has been kept a secret, although we were officially reassured many times that French policy would remain consistent. We see now how empty those promises were. We are being asked to accept this just when the baseness of the present régime is becoming apparent. Public authorities have allowed this régime to do what it has wanted for two years, without ever interfering except to make hollow declarations. Even today, certain 'officious' persons who pretend to be rather surprised and disappointed now that the pathetic results have been made public, do not seem to think that they can reject the propositions of the present government. Who will ever know the full extent of the harm done to our foreign policy by the weakness and the inconsistency of the present régime? It has consumed or neutralized all our efforts and it would have endangered our national defences too, if it could have done so.

Who could have believed after reading this contemptuous attack that de Gaulle would some day exhume a long-forgotten grandfather from Baden? In those days no one mentioned that embarrassing ancestor. De Gaulle once demanded the partitioning of Germany into several scattered fragments and ended up by proclaiming 'Es lebe Deutschland' several times in a loud clear voice during his memorable journey to Germany. The general was not able to break up Germany into fragments and so he decided very late in the day to turn it into an ally.

When Michel Debré testified at the trial of Salan, he tried to justify his changed attitude by saying that the entire world had turned against French Algeria. The world had already turned against French Algeria when Debré savagely attacked all the governments before his because, in his opinion, they were incapable of defending Algeria. But if you believe that world opinion is against you when you are trying to hold on to what you have, then surely world opinion should make you stop trying to obtain the impossible. I suppose that was de Gaulle's tardy conclusion.

Anyway, de Gaulle's predictions on the subject of Germany turned out to be wrong, and that day he was the bad, false prophet, not I.

The moral of the story is that Chancellor Adenauer had me arrested by his police fifteen years later. After that, he went off to Paris to sign a treaty with de Gaulle and to let himself be kissed by the General.

I knew that my days in the government were almost over and so I spent my last weeks at the Quai d'Orsay settling questions which remained unfinished and breaking the ground for a genuine and solid European policy.

On the evening of 28 June, the American ambassador, Jefferson Caffery, and I signed the final agreements between France and the US concerning the application of the Marshall Plan. At least that was done. It had taken time, patience and lengthy negotiations before France obtained the means to recover and even to survive. The French economy would have been paralysed without the Marshall Plan. This urgent and vital agreement was opposed by the Communists and about another hundred deputies abstained from voting. People who always hesitate over every step are un-lucky because they can never be satisfied. Because of their desire for perfection, they prefer to let the country be saved without their help if the measures for saving it do not correspond exactly to their requirements. But while the abstentionists accused those who voted of dirtying their hands, the others were doing the work and saving France. Bakers get covered with flour and chimney-sweeps with soot; but that is the way bread gets cooked and chimneys smoke.

On 19 and 20 July, there was a conference at the Hague attended by all the countries which had signed the Brussels pact, and it was there that the Western nations really mapped out the future course of Europe. This was the last thing I was able to do: Robert Schuman's cabinet resigned on 19 June, and I set out for the Hague with a clear conscience, knowing that I had done my duty and my initiative could no longer be undone by my successor, whoever he might be.

At the end of the session of 20 July, after all the routine ques-tions had been settled, I stopped discussing details and asked the conference to think in more far-reaching terms: 'We are perhaps at a unique moment in history, when Europe's future can still be changed. The governments must support this movement and realize our hopes.'

I then made two proposals which amazed everyone. I can still see Paul-Henri Spaak's startled look, although he has the reputation of being difficult to surprise. I proposed that the six nations should create an economic and customs union, which could be joined by any other European nation that wished to do so. On the political level, I suggested the creation of a European assembly, made up of representatives from all our parliaments and from the parliaments of any nation which decided to send delegates. That speech eventually led to the economic creation of the Common Market and to the political creation of the European Consultative Assembly at Strasbourg. In spite of all the later obstacles and the violent opposition to those two ideas, both of them have flourished.

The French National Assembly ratified the creation of a European Council one year later. If I remember correctly, the debate was quite routine, except for one speech made by René Capitant. Anyone who is not afraid of overpowering emotion can look up this remarkable speech in the July 1949 number of the *Journal Officiel*. René Capitant blamed the text of the European agreement for being too weak. He claimed that we had not been bold enough and that only total integration including the rearmament of Germany could have solved the problems of Europe.

In the light of later developments, this was a really incredible speech. I have often wondered why it did not receive more attention and why no one replied to it as it deserved. Later, Capitant along with the other Gaullists blasted away against European unity at every opportunity; but no one ever produced his own speech for arguments against him. Why in fact did Capitant make a speech like that so unexpectedly? I think the explanation is quite simple, although not particularly flattering. I could find a hundred other examples of the same sort: what any government apart from General de Gaulle's suggests is bad and should be attacked with any available weapon. But what had to be opposed because it came from others, becomes good, even excellent, when de Gaulle decides to adopt it. When you use this simple technique, you can say anything and you can contradict everything you have said before.

When I came back from the Hague, André Marie, who was forming a new cabinet, offered Léon Blum and me joint posts as Vice-Presidents of the Council. Our job would be to discuss financial and economic affairs with Paul Reynaud, who would be

Minister-in-Chief. This triumvirate did not appeal to me in the least, and I soon realized that I had been right to decline the post. That particular ministry lasted only a month. But the new head of Foreign Affairs, Robert Schuman, stayed in that post for four years, in spite of many government upheavals. I had known him for twenty-five years and I liked him. Some of his loyal supporters at the Ministry of Finance, where I had put him originally, had followed him when he became Prime Minister, and they had tried hard to put him in the Quai d'Orsay. This may seem paradoxical; but it was only because I accepted the beginnings of the German Federal Republic that I had to leave the government and that Robert Schuman took my place. Schuman had many fine qualities and he had practically no enemies. He had acted calmly and firmly when there had been a revolutionary general strike in France. He had a pleasant character and was both discreet and modest. I must also add that he made a speech at Poitiers on 18 April 1948 which doubtless reassured those who wanted our foreign policy to remain static:

Germany has to have a status which will be based on democratic principles but which will not exclude effective precautions. Any plan which would allow for the establishment of a centralized power would be a permanent and growing threat to us and would be for Germany a temptation first of all to avenge itself and also to have aggressive, imperialistic designs. We do not want to be responsible for any catastrophe that might befall future generations. If we allowed the Germans to build up another empire, we would be all the more guilty as there is no such thing as a homogeneous Germany. There are several Germanys which we ought to allow to disengage themselves and to become autonomous states. Later, these states could join in a federation for common but limited aims. That is the way we see it, and we will not give up the hope that our allies will agree with this view.

There was nothing about this traditional attitude which could make us anticipate the paradoxical transformation that would come about through a change of governments.

9

The Atlantic Pact / Economic Affairs / The Schuman Plan

I left the Quai d'Orsay as soon as I had handed over power to Robert Schuman. I had lived there for four years, ever since September 1944, as I was homeless after the Occupation and had refused to requisition an apartment for my personal use, as was the custom at the time. There were enough Catos and Brutuses who took a fancy to Marshal Pétain's furniture and to the possessions of many a Vichy notable who had left his home to go and live in the prisons of la Santé and Fresnes. I am not giving any names; those men will know to whom I am referring. But before I left the Quai d'Orsay, I had bought a charming house in a suburb of Paris. I left all the gilded mouldings, the telephones and even the ushers without looking back twice and went on holiday to the Antibes.

During that trip I was present at a most amusing event, the inauguration of the Picasso Museum. This great painter and prankster had given a large collection of his paintings to the Grimaldi Palace; but he had not signed any of the canvases, which was a clever way of keeping some control over the people to whom he had made this gift, as they would always hope that he might sign them one day. The one museum guard who, until then, had guarded a small collection of Napoleonic relics, was in despair at seeing his modest treasures relegated to one or two dark rooms. But he changed his mind about the paintings when the Palace was flooded by generous American tourists. The inauguration was a poem of eloquence. Communist politicians, enthusiastic critics and one Dominican friar all sang the praises of the occasion in chorus; the Dominican won the contest of eloquence, however, when he announced that the day of the inauguration 'was the finest since the Liberation'.

Shortly afterwards, Robert Schuman asked me to preside over the French delegation at a session of UNESCO in Beirut. Both Edouard Herriot and Léon Blum thought that they were entitled to this honorific post and I heard that they were not pleased when I was chosen.

While I was in the Lebanon, I visited the schools which France had founded, encouraged and often helped for long periods of time. There was something very moving about hearing the children of that delightful people singing First World War songs like '*C'est un oiseau qui vient de France*', and '*Vous n'aurez pas l'Alsace et la Lorraine*' in their schools up in the mountains. I also studied the various religious communities there and met a minister who was no longer a friend of France, but who spoke perfect French; in fact, when he tried to read a text in Arabic, he got mixed up and had to admit that he could not understand it. I have a great many memories of that trip; but they are mainly personal ones and cannot be of any interest except to myself.

The principal object of this particular UNESCO conference was to appoint Torres Bodet, a Mexican who had spent most of his career fighting illiteracy, in the place of Julian Huxley, who was retiring. Apart from choosing a successor to Huxley, there was very little to do at these sessions which dragged on and on. The assembly was rather small; but the galleries were always full. Teachers would conscientiously bring their pupils to the sessions, although I cannot imagine what they must have thought of an assembly where delegates discussed in a bored but methodical way if 'a quorum was necessary in the sub-committees'. Paul Rivet, Louis Massignon, Jean Gueheno, Lucien Febvre, Francis Perrin and Marcel Abraham were all members of my delegation, and they pursued their own activities separately. Only two of them are alive today. I remained on good terms with all of them apart from Massignon.

When I was flying to the Middle East with some members of the delegation, our small plane went south to avoid the bad weather and found itself in the middle of the worst storm I have ever known. This turned out to be a bad omen for some of the other men aboard as well as for myself.

I went to Damascus to try and improve relations between Syria

and France, which had been bad since the events which led up to
our departure in 1945. There I saw the President of the Republic
and had dinner with the President of the Council, Djemil Mardam,
who had been France's friend and debtor until the war when he
became friendly with the English and his feelings towards us
changed completely.

We left the following day at about twelve o'clock. Curtains were
lowered in all the squares, and there was some shooting going on
in the streets. Soon afterwards, my host of the previous evening
fled to exile and safety in Beirut. On my journey back, I stopped
briefly in Cairo where Farouk, who was still King, spoke to me in
an intelligent but cynical way. The ambassador, Arvengas, invited
me to meet the President of the Council, Nokrachi Pasha. I left
on the following day, the very day on which Nokrachi Pasha was
assassinated.

These events were of minor importance except to the victims.
French foreign policy was evolving along the lines which had
already been mapped out, although Robert Schuman paid less
attention to Italy than I had done. The Atlantic Pact which I had
prepared with Marshall was concluded by Acheson and Robert
Schuman. The French Assembly ratified it by a large majority on
26 July 1949.

Since then it has become fashionable in certain circles to say
that NATO is obsolete and that it should be altered, brought
up to date or abolished altogether. One argument put forward is
that atomic weapons have made NATO meaningless. In fact,
what all those objectors really want is to join the neutralist camp,
to hold the scale which they pretend is equally balanced between Washington and Moscow, and to retire into an inglorious
isolationism, while secretly waiting to abolish the alliance
altogether.

Today the French government is withdrawing both its navy and
land forces from the Atlantic alliance as fast as it can, claiming
that NATO is obsolete, but that the actual alliance still holds good.
This subtle distinction takes no one in, even when great care is
taken to foster the illusion. In spite of recent erosion, NATO has
been and remains the cornerstone of French security. Without it,
France would probably have been swallowed up, European freedom would have been destroyed and world peace would have been
in much greater danger than it has been so far. There have been

many bad moments and some serious failures, but at least the worst has not happened.

For years, I was president of the French Association for the Atlantic Community. This meant that all the American commanders-in-chief came to see me, as well as all the French prime ministers from Guy Mollet to Michel Debré. When they were the guests of the Association, all the French government leaders sang the praises of the alliance and swore eternal fidelity to the spirit of the organization. During one of those dinners, I was sitting between Guy Mollet and General Gruenther, who was retiring from the post. To our surprise, Mollet disappeared for an hour. He had just learned that Ben Bella and his followers had been arrested in Algiers. When he came back, he did not look very pleased, but he immediately told me that he would stand by the decision of Robert Lacoste.

I am not claiming that our allies, particularly the United States, behaved perfectly in the application of the Atlantic Pact. Foster Dulles was so rabidly anti-colonialist and pro-Arab that he often forgot that the Atlantic Pact also applied to the 'French departments of Algiers'. I never missed an opportunity to remind him publicly of the fact; but he listened to himself far too much ever to listen to others.

Although France was caught between the cross-fire of the Communists and the Gaullist RPF, the French economic situation was improving all the time, despite a succession of precarious governments which were supposed to protect the nation's interests abroad and to help economic growth at home. But the governments were unstable. There were endless rivalries between the parties and the most determined efforts to maintain some sort of political equilibrium were fruitless. The French public was weary and discouraged; it finally despaired of the party system and this ultimately led to the destruction of government by parties. But at the time there seemed to be no way around the problem: one parliamentary régime followed another just as in Italy today.

Each party had its own parliament, and it could not even always be sure of obtaining a clear-cut majority within its ranks, as happened when the Socialists had to decide over the European Defence Community. After each party's parliament had come to a decision and often a complicated and confused decision at that, the real Parliament had to try and find a solution to every problem, and to get it accepted by a majority. If the nation was in danger, as it was when the Communists began using extremist tactics, or if the Republic was threatened, as many thought it was by the RPF, parliament did not have too many difficulties. But as soon as the danger had abated and the short-term future seemed assured, the usual quarrels flared up again and intrigue was rife. Dusty moth-eaten documents about French history would be produced to fan the flames of old quarrels. You could always be sure of getting votes or of baiting your opponents if you took an anti-clerical line, for example. Nothing could be more useful and less compromising than bringing up that old spectre, because everyone had heard the arguments before and the clergy had neither the money nor the trade unions to defend itself.

All this gave public life, especially electoral campaigns, an artificial, archaic and often sordid character. But in spite of it all, France was gradually becoming prosperous again. Behind the petty and disorderly façade, order was being re-established, production was increasing, employers and salaried workers were slowly beginning to have confidence in the future. These concrete results got very little publicity; only the hordes of detractors were heard. One reason for the improvement was the stability of the French civil service. Our institutions were perhaps flimsy; but at least they existed. Administration was good, the State Council was respected, and our law courts were respectable. Our army was discontented, but it had been modernized. When I see the situation in France today which we are told is so glorious, I see no institutions: the 1958 constitution is worthless. Administration has disappeared along with the administrators. I am not praising the old Republic, but all I can say is that today more than ever we live in an age of false appearances and disappointed hopes.

Once again, in October 1949, I had to form a new government, after a long and exhausting parliamentary crisis. René Mayer, and afterwards Jules Moch, had been asked by the National Assembly to form a government, but both of them were buried under an avalanche of complications and soon had to give up trying to accomplish anything in that depressing atmosphere. The members of parliament were weary and the French public was angry. Nearly everyone agreed more or less over the more urgent problems that we had to meet. Daniel Mayer, the head of the Ministry of Labour, had lost interest. These factors allowed me to make up an excellent cabinet very quickly.

When I read through the list of ministers I had then, apart from two or three exceptions whom I shall not name, I see that if talent had been enough I would have governed for a long time, for my ministers were extremely gifted and capable men. Some of them were outstanding; but I found out that brilliance is not enough when you have neither homogeneity nor determination to work in common for any length of time. I don't think it was my fault and I did all I could as head of that government to take over responsibilities and to establish a line of conduct. I will not give you a detailed account of this government, because, after all this time, it could be of interest only to historians and specialists.

Most of my efforts were concentrated on two vital questions. One was the financial administration of France, the other was the creation of a European Iron and Steel Community.

Economic Affairs

Maurice Petsche, the excellent and conscientious director of the Budget and the Treasury, helped me a great deal over our financial policy. His advice was always useful, but it was sometimes rather inconvenient as well. He was already in bad health and he was suspicious by nature. Because I knew this, I did all I could not to upset him and to show him how much I really liked him. Basically he was not a happy man, and if he was sometimes brutal and intransigent, it was because he was shy and at the same time convinced that he was always right.

While we were both responsible for France's finances and economy, our efforts were very successful, as the price of gold, the Stock Exchange and the budget sheets of that period prove, although the going was not always easy. Unfortunately, the system we established was changed after my departure, so that it lasted only a brief time. But even while it lasted, I had had quite a few difficulties. Pierre Pflimlin resigned his post because he disagreed with me over the fixing of the price of beetroot, and Paul Ribeyre left after him. I happened to think their calculations were wrong and that there was no cause for worry. I must have been right, for in spite of the price at which I had fixed the sale of beetroot and

September 1944. Men of the *maquis* on the march near Dinan, Brittany

August 1945. General de Gaulle leading the singing of the Marseillaise in Paris after the announcement of the end of the war in Europe

July 1946. Bidault, then Prime
Minister, receiving Ho-Chi-Minh,
President of Vietnam, in Paris

August 1946. Bidault during a
session of the Paris Peace Conference
held at the Luxembourg Palace

October 1946. Bidault giving an
official radio address to the French
people

March 1947. Bidault, then Foreign Minister, and Ernest Bevin signing the fifty-year Anglo-French Treaty of Alliance, at Dunkirk

February 1953. Bidault (*second from right*) at the European Defence Community Conference in Rome, with (*from left to right*) de Gasperi, Van Zeeland and Dr Adenauer

October 1953. The 'big three' foreign ministers (*from left to right*) Anthony Eden, Bidault and John Foster Dulles with Sir Winston Churchill after a luncheon at No. 10 Downing Street

December 1953. Bidault with Dr Adenauer during the opening session of the Committee of European Council Ministers at the Château de la Muette, Paris

5 March 1963. The controversial interview with Bidault on the BBC television programme 'Panorama'. This interview greatly displeased de Gaulle

December 1960. Unrest in Algiers. *Opposite above:* Moslem demonstrators carrying FLN banners. *Opposite below:* Rioters, emerging from the casbah, clashing with security police

March 1963. Bidault, in Steinebach, Bavaria, after being refused political asylum in West Germany

which they thought too low, there was a marked increase in the cultivation of beetroot the following year. The trouble with the policy of a severe budget is that, as with all austerity measures, you may approve of them in principle, but arguments against the measures can always be found for every individual case.

My government's brief existence was threatened daily. One day I asked for a vote of confidence. The votes for and against me were evenly divided. The Assembly ruling is that in such cases the measure is rejected. Afterwards, the ministers held a cabinet meeting and Henri Queuille got up and began making the customary complimentary speech before a government breaks up. I hastily declined his compliments and reminded him that although the Assembly had not adopted our measure, the government had not been given a minority vote.

There were other times when things were hardly any better and I sometimes received a majority of only three or four votes. Worse than that, there were occasions when some of the deputies did not vote according to their conviction. One day I asked all the members of the Assembly to vote according to Kant's famous maxim, as though each vote would be the decisive one. After the voting, in which I received a majority of only three votes, a veteran politician, Joseph Denais, said to me with great relief: 'Congratulations. You can understand that I had to vote against you in my position. But I was praying for you.'

The work got done. When people write today about the disadvantages of government instability and of the omnipotence of the Assembly, I don't bother reading the arguments. I don't have to be told because I know about it only too well by experience.

Daladier's arch-enemy, Edouard Herriot, did all he could to help me. He was a Radical and the President of the Assembly; by this time, he had lost all his fondness for the Communists and no longer even tolerated them, especially as the extreme Left had started shouting insults and making a racket during the Assembly sessions. But he also heartily disapproved of the RPF. One day, as he had done on one occasion twenty-five years earlier, and as Gambetta had done before him, he left his presidential chair to vote in favour of the government. We had never been on very close terms, and we had even been on bad terms, as we were to be once again over the European Defence Community, but that will never make me forget how he helped me then.

R.—7

The Communists were violently against us and they showed it by organizing a succession of strikes, most of which failed, and by systematically doing all they could to obstruct parliamentary proceedings. They insulted us and even assaulted us physically on a few occasions. Certain deputies, among them François de Menthon, and several members of the Assembly personnel were seriously hurt during one of these fights. The turmoil lasted for some time and blows were freely exchanged before Herriot decided to call in the guards to put an end to the fracas. This had almost never happened before, especially not several times in succession. Before then we had had to suffer the Communists' shouts, insults and threats in silence.

Some Communist deputies would come over to where I sat with the other ministers and wave their fists at me, shouting the most sinister threats. One session lasted for nearly three days without a break. The 'fighters for peace' could not have been exactly pacific, as the desk in front of me was split in half and the microphone was twisted out of all recognition.

I remember one fine and honest man, Louis Cordonnier, Socialist Mayor of Lille, putting himself between the Communists and the ministers. I also remember the way Pierre Montel, a moderate man from the Rhône, removed his spectacles before joining the fray. When I recall all these events, I am amazed at the way politicians change; those Communists, who were so aggressive then, have become meek as lambs now.

The Schuman Plan

On 9 May 1950, my government agreed to the creation of what was then called the Iron and Steel Pool, and is now known as the European Iron and Steel Community. This organization included France, the Benelux countries, Germany and Italy. As Germany could no longer act as a common link between all those who had fought against Hitler, we had begun to deal with Germany in the same way as we did with our war allies. This was inevitable and, anyway, it was the most reasonable course of action. The common factor between Germany and France was, of course, Europe.

General de Gaulle once said to me, 'The worse the situation, the simpler the solution.' He always did have a gift for coining phrases, if only his worshippers had not ruined his reputation by quoting and commenting on every platitude that has ever fallen from the general's lips.

The situation was serious, and, indeed, the solution was simple. But the methods of achieving this particular solution were far from simple. The French, and not only the French but many Americans and some Englishmen, had only recently been advocating a policy of permanent German weakness and of prolonged control over Germany. Baruch had proposed a German nation that would be nothing but fields, forests and prairies, and which bore about as much resemblance to the reality as Siegfried to Krupp or Schiller to Erhard. The English had refused to let Konrad Adenauer become President of the Rhineland and Westphalia, because they found him 'incompetent'. This 'incompetent' had to wait until he was seventy-two before he was elected Chancellor of the Federal Republic of Germany by 172 votes to 171, with the deciding vote his own.

The Americans were the first to give up their dream of a pastoral Germany. The English admitted that they had perhaps under-estimated Adenauer. As for the French, I have already described how I undertook to reach a solution in their name. From 1944 to 1954, France's foreign policy was in the hands of only two men, Robert Schuman and myself. Apart from certain variations in style and judgement, we shared substantially the same views on the subject of foreign policy, and these views were not dictated either by a party or by a leader.

Right from the start, I had worked very hard for European unity, although very few appreciated my efforts at the time. Later, everyone, even de Gaulle, became a 'European', though difficulties arise as soon as you start to define the term. Some men are what Adenauer calls European 'perfectionists', who want to go through all the successive stages as quickly as possible. They want Europe to get together very soon, even right away. There is only one thing missing from such an ambition and that is the lack of a revolution-ary spirit among the peoples of Europe. Experience has taught us that this spirit is non-existent. The people will agree to a change, but they remain passive. The European revolution depends on the governments, and the enthusiasm of these governments varies according to the countries, the governments, the parties, the individual leaders and the circumstances. The Gaullist approach to Europe for example is in the spirit of the Holy Alliance: it is all there – the ancient recipe of coalitions, the monarchic tendency, the misconceptions, and the idea that refusal to integrate is sacrilegious. The Gaullists think only in terms of symbols and vague ideals. Their first attitude, which rejected the concept of European unity altogether, at least had the merit of being more clear-cut; but it was really no different. In both cases, they wanted no change of any kind in the *status quo*.

For a very long time, Robert Schuman had been a moderate in parliament. He was hard-working, learned, conciliatory and obstinate. Everyone liked and respected him. Between the wars, he had acted as a kind of legislator for the special problems of the three Departments of Alsace and Lorraine which we had won back from the Germans. He had acted as Under-Secretary of State in Marshal Pétain's government for a few days, until the Germans arrested him and sent him to prison, then placed him under house arrest in the Spire district. He came back from there in 1942 and led a life of studious retirement until the Liberation. Jean Moulin once told me that London very much wanted Schuman to become a member of the Free French; but nothing came of it. They also wanted Herriot to join their group and they asked him to at about this time; but there again nothing happened. It was a shame; but both men, though of very different character, had strong scruples against joining the Free French.

Robert Schuman was elected to the First Constituent Assembly, at the head of a Republican and Democrat ticket which contained candidates of various political shades. He then joined the MRP, became President of the Financial Commission, and later, during my first government, Minister of Finance. He was not a party man although he always remained loyal to his own. In an interview he once had with de Gaulle, he defined himself as a 'Catholic and a native of Moselle'. He was born in Luxembourg, but his family came from Lorraine and he had studied in Germany. This dual culture made him eager to bring about a reconciliation between Germany and France, especially as after all the two nations had only been 'hereditary enemies' since 1870. His way of achieving a *rapprochement* between France and Germany was to find them interests in common.

I would like to talk about the Schuman plan with all the respect and the affection I felt for its originator, but that does not mean I can make it sound like an illuminated broadsheet on the lives of the saints. Jean Monnet was the true intellectual author of the Iron and Steel plan and Robert Schuman only its political godfather. Monnet had submitted the project to me when I was at the Hôtel Matignon, and later people would say that I did not grasp its full significance. The truth is that I felt the plan could be improved by making certain changes and omissions which would not have altered its basic structure. But the prevailing atmosphere of agitation, the constant strikes, the hesitations of the Trade Unions, and what came to be known as the *'affaire des généraux'*, made the few corrections I felt were necessary for the success of this vast enterprise difficult to work out and to incorporate into the plan.

Jean Monnet does not like waiting when he has a great idea in mind. He rushed to the Quai d'Orsay, although he had a long-standing quarrel with Schuman, which had started back in the days when Schuman was at the Ministry of Finance. Just as I had done, Robert Schuman was beginning to feel the effects of the Assembly's resentment, now that he had been Minister of Foreign Affairs for over twenty months, always adhering to a policy of European unity. Germany had been invited to the Strasbourg Assembly in April and this had created a lot of ill-feeling, aggravated by Chancellor Adenauer's somewhat premature proposal for an English-French-German alliance.

On 16 April, while I was opening a fair at Lyons, I proposed the creation of a High Atlantic Command which would be an extension of NATO and would increase the cooperation between Europe and the United States over matters of economics and defence. But the Americans were still a long way from the famous 'Kennedy Round' and my suggestion was coldly received. Perhaps the idea was too ambitious or too premature, but anyway, nothing came of it.

I don't believe that this is the last we have heard of my suggestion and I think that, in a modern form, it could still be used at some time in the more or less distant future. But when I actually made the proposal, it got a very poor welcome. It was sometimes even deliberately misinterpreted by some people. One of the men who had encouraged me to take the initiative, Jean-Jacques Servan-Schreiber, actually turned against the idea when he saw it was a failure.

People imagine retrospectively that the government and Parliament enthusiastically welcomed the idea of an Iron and Steel Pool; but this is far from true, although some of the men who opposed it then later became supporters of the plan. I have read accounts of discussions between Ministers over the Schuman Plan in books and newspaper articles on the Plan and on its founder. These accounts are a tribute to their authors' imaginations or to the deliberate inaccuracy of their sources. After Robert Schuman died, exhausted and abandoned by almost everyone, I read an account of his life which said that he had been at school with Konrad Adenauer and Alcide de Gasperi. And indeed, de Gasperi was born an Austrian citizen in the Trentino, although his native tongue was Italian. And Robert Schuman did study in Germany, as of course did Adenauer. But the story-tellers must have reasoned in the same way as children who think that anyone over thirty is just old; the three men could not possibly have known each other then as de Gasperi stayed in Vienna, and the other two, although they did both study in the Rhineland, would not have met since there was a difference of eleven years in their ages. Schuman did not encounter his 'childhood friends' until 1948; there was no need to exchange views before the First World War to support a united Europe after the Second.

The governmental debates on the Iron and Steel project were not at all easy, and in spite of what people say now, the project would have got nowhere without my help. I am very glad I helped the 'Father of Europe', who won the label partly because of me. If anyone wants proof of the fact that the Plan ran into trouble, all they have to do is to recall that the Schuman Plan, which was adopted by my government on 9 May 1950, was not ratified by the National Assembly until 13 December 1951. My government had ceased to exist during that interval and had been replaced first by a Pleven government and then by a Queuille government, not to mention all the unsuccessful attempts that were made to form new governments. The third government (Pleven's again) decided to revive the Plan more than a year and a half after the general election of 1951. Two out of the five parliamentary committees set up to examine the Plan decided against it. The Right Wing, the extreme Left and the Gaullists were either lukewarm or openly hostile to the idea. A minority of about 230 to 240 votes (the Communists had lost many of their seats after the vote-pairing system was

introduced) went against the Iron and Steel Plan. There was
bound to be some opposition, as there always is when a government makes a decision of great importance. Some were concerned
about their personal interests, others disapproved of the European
Community in principle, and there were some who just found any
change suspect. They made many speeches against the Plan, some
of which were very clever, others merely emotional.

Oddly enough, parliamentary jargon being what it is, the people
who were against change of any kind often accused all the others of
only wanting to maintain the *status quo*. But just because nearly
everyone today is for one form of united Europe or another, people
must not think that the idea was easy to put across at the beginning
or that the pioneers of European unity always found their task
simple.

In fact, attacks on plans for a European Defence Community
were often violent and sometimes highly successful. The scheme
for a united Europe was not abortive; but its birth was difficult and
its growth was slow and sometimes stunted. Although Robert
Schuman fought a long, patient battle, for which he was honoured
during his lifetime, he died before his hopes and dreams were fully
realized.

The reason for my departure was that Maurice Petsche insisted
on making me defend his budget by asking for a vote of confidence
over the question of alterations in the civil service. But for obvious
reasons the Socialists had always attacked us on that particular
subject. The previous winter, nine Socialist Ministers, Jules Moch,
Christian Pineau, Robert Lacoste, Pierre Segelle, Eugène Thomas,
Jean Biondi, Max Lejeune, Jean Meunier and Georges Gorse had
already sent in their resignations to me. Léon Blum wrote an
article making the customary Socialist distinction between participation, support and opposition; he advocated, now the Socialists
had stopped participating in my government, that they should give
me their support. But in spite of this, the Socialists abstained from
voting when I proposed a government which no longer included
any of their members.

Petsche's intransigence brought about the fall of my government, which was voted down by a majority made up of various
parties already looking ahead to the election. This happened on
24 June 1950. I vainly appealed to the deputies' sense of duty,
pointing out the danger of a power vacuum and the need for a

180 RESISTANCE

rigorous budget. The Korean war began on the following day,
25 June. There had been a government crisis before the Second
World War on the day of the Austrian Anschluss. This time I had
to abandon my responsibilities against my will on the eve of a great
international crisis. Internal politics never take foreign politics into
consideration except in cases of total disaster and sometimes not
even then.

10

The European Defence Community /
Morocco and the Two Sultans /
The Berlin Conference /
Indo-China and the Geneva Conference

After I left the government where I had agreed to let Maurice Petsche remain to limit the damage, the US proposed a scheme for Atlantic rearmament to the members of Pleven's cabinet. This proposal involved the presence of German contingents in Europe. President Truman needed all the men he could get to settle the Korean war both promptly and energetically, for in spite of the help of various contingents from the Free World, the Korean war remained essentially an American effort.

Besides, the armies of the various nations which had signed the Atlantic Pact, even with the help of a large American force, would be no match for the Eastern bloc if the worst came to the worst. And so the United States, where public opinion had shifted rapidly, decided to bring up the question of German rearmament, claiming that it was necessary for the defence of Western Europe. The Americans were very insistent on this point and their attitude could not fail to surprise and upset a great many Frenchmen, coming so soon after a conflict from which France had not yet recovered physically or morally. One of the current slogans during the period when Europe was gradually uniting was 'Germany in a United Europe, yes; Germany in the Atlantic Pact, never!'

The Prime Minister, René Pleven, and the Minister of National Defence, Jules Moch, negotiated the issue for France. What they wanted to prevent at all costs was the creation of an autonomous German army; to do this, they proposed the creation of a 'European Army', which would be composed of integrated units from various countries broken into the maximum number of fragments, so that each unit from a given nation would be tiny. They suggested a 'combat team' unit, which was half-way between a battalion and a regiment. This breakdown of units into the smallest possible fractions probably left much to be desired from the military and tactical point of view. And we could expect a great deal of opposition at home, not all of it for traditional or sentimental reasons, if we had to give the European Army most of our forces in order to prevent the creation of a German national army.

Between 1950 and 1954, this project was widely debated in France. Ultimately it failed and this led to the reconstruction of a Bundeswehr, which was allied but autonomous. When I discuss the failure of this project, I will also describe my own feelings, and what I did to make this great and complex scheme more acceptable to the French nation and to the rest of the world.

I was Minister for National Defence during Pleven's second government and during Edgar Faure's first. During this period, I also made a proposal, which was accepted by the government, to make the dying General de Lattre de Tassigny a Marshal.

I came back to the Quai d'Orsay in January 1953 and left once again in July 1954. During this time, two successive governments maintained a policy of European unity and French colonialism, although in both cases they were unable to guarantee the duration of their policies so that their authority was soon nullified. The great disaster in Indo-China was used to justify France's retreat in all its overseas territories and to put an end to the scheme for a European Defence Community. Three months after Mendès-France had signed the Geneva agreements over Indo-China, the Algerian uprising began.

Morocco and the Two Sultans

In 1953, I suggested to the Laniel government that Sultan Sidi Mohammed ben Yussef, who had been the ruler of Morocco for twenty-five years, should be deposed. The stir that this created in France, the political opposition it aroused, the show of false or real emotion, all revealed the strong influence that Arab nationalism already exerted in certain political and journalistic circles in France. It was not the first incident of this type, but the violence of the campaign which it started was unprecedented. This was not the last we were to hear of it either. Ever since that time, the representatives of Arab and Asian and African nationalism have found ready champions in the press and advocates in parliament as well as in public opinion. The daily and weekly progressive newspapers and the liberal journalists who specialize in this sort of propaganda are now notorious, and there are a great many of them. Far from appeasing their wrath, the progress made by decolonization has fanned the flames of their fury, and I know for a fact that some of them are bought.

You really have to go back a few years to understand what happened in Morocco during the early fifties. Sidi Mohammed ben Yussef had been chosen as Sultan by the Resident General, Théodore Steeg, because he was unknown and young and poor and presumably easy to handle. All four qualities disappeared with time. Until 1940 and during the first few months of the Phoney War, the Sultan remained loyal to France. When France was defeated, he stopped thinking of France as a great power and turned first to the Germans, then to the Americans when they landed in North Africa. From that moment, he began, very cautiously at first, to think along the lines of independence, while General Noguès was in Morocco and de Gaulle was head of the government in Algiers.

During all the time that Morocco was under our protection, I said nothing and even refused to admit the fact that the archives found at the German Consulate in Tangiers were most compromising. Even today, I would not consider the fullest reports by National Socialist agents as sufficient proofs for establishing guilt. I want to tell the so-called historians and even the so-called Catholics who throw themselves on documents of this sort to tarnish the memory of Pius XII that the Moroccan dossier I have just mentioned is far more incriminating than the papers they are making such a fuss about. General de Gaulle knew all about it, although this did not prevent him, during his second reign, from exchanging promises of friendship at Aurillac with the Sultan,

who had returned to the throne. Part of the General's contempt
for the validity of the Nazi archives must be attributed to the way
his 'friend' the Sultan had cautiously eluded Roosevelt's offer to
help Morocco win its independence during the Anfa conference,
attended by Roosevelt, Churchill, de Gaulle and Giraud.

I was not unfavourably disposed towards the Sultan and his
policies until the day he declared his intentions in unequivocal
terms at Tangiers in April 1947. After refusing to go to the International Zone aboard a French warship, the Sultan made a speech
before an assembly composed mainly of nationalists who had been
warned beforehand. He had sent the text of the speech to the Resi-
dency in advance, as was the custom; but the speech he delivered
was completely different. A reference to the role that France would
play in Morocco's future had been deleted, while the following
paragraph about the Arab League had been inserted:

This League has tightened the bonds between all Arabs, wherever
they are, and has allowed their kings and their rulers, both in the West
and in the East, to unite their voices and to march towards moral
progress, the greatness of Islam and the glory of the Arab people.

This was bad enough, but the Sultan also announced during a
press conference that:

Morocco ardently desires to obtain all its rights.

If he felt this way, he should have addressed this request to the
French government, not to a gang of journalists. He also added:

It goes without saying that Morocco is an Arab country, that it has
solid ties with the Arab nations of the East, and that it wishes those ties
to become stronger and stronger, especially now that the Arab League
has become an institution which plays an important part in world
politics.

Many men in the Sultan's immediate entourage and some members of his family said much the same thing, so that after this
incident, which reminded me of Moulay Hafid's past conduct except that it was more serious, we had to give the Sultan a moderate
but clear warning. Much to my regret, I had to call back our
Resident-General, whom the Sultan had insulted by his behaviour.
Our ambassador, Erik Labonne, had already got a mining project

under way which he was later able to extend over the whole of North Africa. I sent General Juin to Morocco and he put an end to manifestations of solidarity with the Arab League, which was openly hostile to France.

For some time Sidi Mohammed ben Yussef acted with the utmost discretion and avoided any sort of conflict with the Resident-General; but at the same time he was secretly encouraging the nationalistic elements in his country. When General Juin had to leave Morocco against his will because Eisenhower had persuaded him to take over the control of NATO, General Guillaume, who knew Moroccan affairs well, replaced Juin. Gradually, the Sultan made his views so obvious that the traditionalist elements in Morocco, those who had been our companions in arms since Lyautey and who were loyal to France, got together and began opposing the Sultan. This hostility was aggravated by the methods of taxation introduced by the Sultan, which discriminated against the leaders and the rich.

The French government and the Minister of Foreign Affairs did not want the Sultan to be deposed; but I did tell the Resident-General to keep a close watch over him and over his immediate entourage, to prevent them from creating any more disturbances. But the Moroccans themselves had become so hostile to the Sultan that we soon realized something would have to be done.

Of course, I am not denying that there were some French civil servants in Tangiers who approved of the way things were going and who encouraged those developments. A top-ranking civil servant whom I trusted implicitly conducted an enquiry on the spot, and when he told me what he had seen, I realized that we would unfortunately have to use force. Did this mean that we would have to repress a bloody uprising of the very leaders who had been our companions in war and our supporters in peace? If we did this, we would lose our friends without changing the Sultan's opinions about France. In fact, we would probably make the situation worse, because we would have lost our most loyal supporters.

Whatever the French advocates of Arab nationalism said in their newspapers, I felt no pleasure at all at what I had to do: I personally asked the government, then headed by Laniel, to have the Sultan deposed, according to our traditional and legal right, and to ask the Moroccan leaders and the Moslem religious powers to choose another Sultan.

On 20 August 1953, I announced this decision to the press in the following terms:

M. Georges Bidault has transmitted to the Council the following news, which he received this morning from General Guillaume.

According to the general, the mission of conciliation with which he was entrusted has encountered difficulties which can only be surmounted by armed force. The government hesitates to have recourse to this just before a great Moslem festival and against men who have been faithful to France.

The Resident-General has been instructed to take all the necessary steps to ensure the maintenance of general security and the future of the throne in conditions which cannot be challenged and which conform to traditional procedures, according to the rights and the duties of the protecting power.

There was some opposition to the decision we reached during a second cabinet meeting the same day. Vincent Auriol, the President of the Republic, did not conceal his dissatisfaction with the course of events; but he made no attempt to act outside the bounds of his constitutional role. Edgar Faure protested vehemently, but stayed in the government. François Mitterand protested even more vehemently and asked for sanctions against the French civil servants in Morocco. I told him that certain men would be replaced, but only after the new Sultan had begun to rule; we did not want him to start his reign under conditions which might seem to show hesitation or remorse on our part. As for the Resident-General, there could be no question of calling him back just when the principle of French continuity was being asserted. And so it was Mitterand who left instead.

The deposed Sultan left Morocco without protest. He did not abdicate, although he was very worried. First, he went to Corsica, and later, after complaining about the climate and the inadequate facilities 'for his family', he was allowed to go to a spa in Madagascar called Antsirabé. He wrote me two letters from there, written in a very flowery French style which I easily recognized as that of the present King Hassan II. In one of the letters, Mohammed ben Yussef supplied details about his fortune, which I had not confiscated to give to the new sovereign, as was the custom. The ex-Sultan insisted on telling me how he had acquired his wealth. In the other letter, which he sent first, he thanked me for saving his life.

And I had indeed saved his life. If the French authorities had made any slip-up, Sidi Mohammed ben Yussef could have fallen into the hands of a mob, as often happens in the Arab world. If the French had not intervened, the tribesmen would certainly have stormed the palace. Later, Edgar Faure brought the Sultan back from Antsirabé under the escort of General Catroux and he became King Mohammed v of Morocco. Many Frenchmen were massacred in his name by people who now have streets named after them in all the cities of Morocco; but all the same I am not sorry our soldiers were able to save the life of a monarch, even though he was hostile towards us and had been deposed in a country which was under our protection.

The pashas, the caïds, the notables, the members of the ex-Sultan's family, the Moslem University of Fez, and the Ulemas chose Sidi Mohammed ben Arafa to be their Sultan in the most traditional and regular fashion. In spite of Robert Schuman's hesitations, I had decided to break up the nationalistic conspiracy for several reasons. It was based on retrogressive fanaticism and revolutionary Communism, and I had not forgotten what Lenin had said about the three phases of Bolshevism in former colonies – nationalism – chaos – Communism. I also knew what the Third Republic had known – that if another power got control of Tunisia and Morocco, 'our Algeria' would be in danger. I turned a collection of articles that I had written for *Carrefour* into a book on the subject, which I called, *Algeria, the Bird with the Clipped Wings*. The prophecy contained in this title was only too easy to make, and, of course, it turned out to be correct.

François Mauriac, who had always been well-disposed towards me before then and had even sometimes shown signs of great friendliness, attacked me violently over this episode, and passionately endorsed the Sultan's cause. In fact, I now know that he sent Sidi Mohammed ben Yussef the most incredible protestations of adulation and adoration; his reasons for doing so are unknown or perhaps I should say that they bypass reason and fall into a category I prefer not to explore. Mauriac was under the influence of Louis Massignon, a great scholar, whose bizarre career had often brought him to the brink of disaster. Massignon went around hinting that I had an interest in the white-slave trade and that this was the reason for my actions.

Mauriac and Massignon had completely forgotten that around

1937, when they had signed and got others to sign a petition demanding humane treatment for Allal el Fassi, they had asked me to present this petition to the Popular Front cabinet, without asking me to sign it or showing me its contents. In those days, François Mauriac was writing for the *Echo de Paris* and Louis Massignon was a follower of Colonel de la Roque, so it was not surprising that they thought I was better qualified than they to make the request. I presented the petition to Albert Sarraut and asked him to mitigate Allal el Fassi's punishment by transferring him from Gabon to the West Indies.

Albert Sarraut obviously found me a nuisance and did not lavish any fine words on me, as he did later when our positions had changed. But all the same, I think my mission achieved something. Allal el Fassi is still alive and healthy, although I was told then that he was at death's door. I very much doubt that he will be at all grateful to me or to the two other 'infidels' if he ever learns what we did for him. For the Istiqlal calls all Westerners 'infidels'.

During Sultan Mohammed ben Arafa's brief reign, the French government behaved very badly towards him and finally got rid of him by treachery. When Edgar Faure became head of the government again, he persuaded Antoine Pinay, the Minister of Foreign Affairs, to bring the ex-Sultan back to the Moroccan throne. Edgar Faure's theories of Islamic legitimacy are a mystery to me. Gilbert Granval has written a book about his mission to Morocco, which ended in massacres that could have been prevented if the French troops in the area had been given the order to intervene. In different circumstances and with better instructions Granval could have made a very able Resident-General and he would not have had to play a double game.

The Istiqlal acted in the most ruthless way and the humiliated El Glaoui soon died after the deposition of his protégé. He was one of the first of our many loyal friends and companions-in-arms to be sacrificed and systematically abandoned during the Fourth and Fifth Republics. We get rid of our friends and then put our enemies in their place. Ingratitude is one of the first laws of politics. This has been proved over and over again, first in Tunisia and Morocco and later in Algeria: those who helped France must be punished for the crime of not realizing that they should have fought against us according to the 'wind of history'.

All of North Africa was upset by the Moroccan affair and

Algeria's future was threatened from the day that Mendès-France and Edgar Faure began to put their policies into practice. Did they realize this, and, if not what were their aims?

The Franco-African community began to crumble in an atmosphere of deceit and self-delusion. It was razed in an atmosphere of deceit and vanity.

The Berlin Conference

At the beginning of 1954, a four-nation conference in Berlin discussed once again the problem of Germany, the treaty of Austria, and Molotov's so-called 'European security': it also prepared for another conference which would deal with the question of Korea and Indo-China. We debated for three weeks, but it was hopeless. In spite of all our efforts at conciliation, all our subtle arguments, our policies remained fundamentally incompatible. The only outcome of these talks was the agreement to hold another conference in Geneva during April, where we would deal with the problem of peace in Asia.

The conference held alternate sessions in a West Berlin building and in a palatial mansion built by Stalin in East Berlin to house the Russian Embassy. In this building, apart from all the concealed microphones, someone had tactfully left red and blue pencils on the tables for the delegates, which were stamped, 'Made in the Sacco and Vanzetti factory'.

Yet the atmosphere was less tense than it had been seven years before in Moscow or even in Paris when Vishinsky had displayed all his polemic skills to the Western Ministers who had come there full of hopes and who had left empty-handed. Whatever the international press may have said, I felt a tremendous loathing for Vishinsky, who still looked and acted like an ex-prosecutor and who had so many dead men on his conscience. But journalists only see external appearances and forget about past actions. Compared to Vishinsky, even Molotov seemed quite sympathetic; he was a narrow-minded man, who always made life difficult for others, but at least he had not committed any crimes like his assistant. The old Bolshevik was far less horrible than the bourgeois who had paid his way to power with blood, after others had won the Revolution.

In Berlin Molotov once again tried to draw France into the

Soviet camp. He even treated us to an allegorical ballet at the theatre of the Soviet Embassy, in which one dancer, wearing the white gown and the phrygian cap of the French Republic, evoked the early days of the Paris Commune. Molotov made himself much clearer in his speeches explaining that a European Defence Community would make the reunification of Germany impossible and would be a threat to French security. 'No wonder the number of Frenchmen opposed to a European Army is growing,' he said. I told him politely that I could look after France's internal politics, but I saw that he had a point: what would happen to the EDC if Germany were reunified? This question later aroused a great deal of speculation and controversy in France. I want to quote what I said on the subject:

The German government itself will have to decide whether or not it wants to undertake the international obligations previously contracted by the Federal Republic or the German Democratic Republic. I wish we could be certain that the government of a united Germany would not question the need for European unity. I also can understand that Mr Molotov would like to be certain of the opposite. I must, however, point out that the only way we can agree on this subject is by leaving the decision up to the German people. In other words, France will not make a reunited Germany's entry into the European Community a condition for that reunification. But we must obviously continue to insist that we cannot possibly allow Soviet Russia to impose a different condition on the German people, in other words, forbidding a united Germany to participate in such a Community.

Ten years have passed; the European Defence Community is nothing more than a memory and Germany has not yet been re-unified. I now wonder if the arguments which claimed that the EDC would prevent the reunification of Germany were in any way sincere. I think that this particular objection was merely used as a good excuse during sessions, but that did not prevent either Robert Schuman in Paris or M. Rollin in Brussels from disagreeing with me. Schuman was for the principle of EDC and Rollin was violently against it, but I can not see why either could reproach me; my attitude was simply based on common sense. A French journalist summed up the situation accurately when he said, 'Whatever M. Bidault gains in Berlin, he loses in Paris.' Things have changed a lot in France since then; but obviously I ought not to have been right so far in advance.

While we discussed the problem of German reunification and the treaty which would decide Austria's status, Foster Dulles behaved in a very friendly way towards me. He obviously thought he could show no greater sign of trust than by complaining about Anthony Eden to me. I have somewhere a whole sheaf of complimentary requests which he sent me or had sent to me. I mention this because he soon turned against me during the Geneva Conference; you can make anything out of bronze, even weathercocks.

The United States objected to the presence of Communist China at the Geneva Conference. But as Communist China had intervened even more than Soviet Russia in the Korean and Indo-Chinese wars, we would obviously have to include it if we were to achieve any results. Later, I read in General Navarre's book on his mission to Indo-China as Commander-in-Chief of the French armed forces, that the morale of his troops had been affected by the announcement of the Geneva conference and that the enemy had been much encouraged. I don't think that the terrible defeat of Dien Bien Phu was a question of morale; but I suppose the prospect of a conference may have made the Viet Minh decide to attack and to win some good bargaining counter in time for the negotiations. If they had such intentions, then obviously the conference was a very urgent matter, which could not be delayed. But no one ever told me about Viet Minh reactions and all I was ever told was that we could hold out for ever. If I had known that our installations were in danger, I could have put an end to the long delays, which were mainly due to the reluctance felt by England and America at negotiating over Indo-China; our two allies were obviously afraid that embarrassing requests which they were determined to refuse would be made during the conference.

Yet we had to have this conference. France was fighting alone and was only being given financial aid. We were fighting seven thousand miles away from home and the war was costly in human lives. The war came under heavy criticism in France and in the United States. Acts of treason and sabotage were committed in France. Notebooks were found in Jacques Duclos' car giving advice on how to work for the defeat of the French army; but in spite of this, the National Assembly did not force him to stand trial. He had not, of course, taken the side of those who wanted to preserve the territories which France was defending. If he had, his parliamentary immunity would have been lifted soon enough, as mine was. Léo Figuères, who was prosecuted, is now free to go wherever he likes, although he collaborated outright with Ho-Chi-Minh. He never even needed an amnesty, for the Fifth Republic declared his case closed.

The magazine *Life* first applied the term 'dirty war' to our efforts in Indo-China. International Communism immediately seized on the expression and put it to good use in its massive propaganda drives. President Eisenhower begged me to send all the men we had to Indo-China and made his Secretary of State declare that Communism was not to be tolerated a moment longer in South-east Asia; but Ike also remembered that he had promised the Americans that the GIs would be home for Christmas, and he accepted an armistice in Korea on 27 July 1953.

This meant that all the men and the material which the Communists had concentrated against the American troops would go South and be used against the French, which is why I asked for and obtained the conference at Geneva. It may have come late; but I had been misled into thinking that it would come in time.

Indo-China and the Geneva Conference

I have often been accused of showing blind obstinacy over the long and painful issue of Indo-China. But I was accused of the opposite at first. In 1946 I had received Ho-Chi-Minh in Paris and had even let him be officially present at a parade on 14 July. For years the Gaullists bitterly reproached me for having done this; they looked upon it as a sign of weakness and of tolerance towards international Communism. After the failure of tripartite rule when the French Communists had left the government, they also blamed me for the failure of the Fontainebleau conference and claimed that it had come to nothing because the delegation had been composed entirely of capitalists. Both these accusations are absurd, although the second one was repeated for years. Finally, under Mendès-France, the two contradictory accusations merged and became one.

As a matter of fact, Marius Moutet (who was at one time I believe Ho-Chi-Minh's lawyer), Alexandre Varenne (who had been Governor-General in Indo-China, although he was not much loved by the Right) and I all agreed at the Fontainebleau conference on one point: that the Viet Minh did not have the slightest intention of coming to an agreement with us and were merely killing time before the rupture. The Viet Minh were already sending out instructions for an insurrection during their negotiations with us in Paris. I no longer have the proof of this, but I did have it once.

The only people who still believe that it was our fault that the negotiations broke down are either those who always assume the adversary is in the right or those who are so blind that they still believe, after eighteen years of endless conferences, that you can negotiate with the Communists. The words used by the Communists and by us do not even have the same meaning. We cannot possibly have anything in common when they believe that the only ultimate goal is the total triumph of Communism all over the world. You can make concessions to their hypocrisy but you can come to no lasting agreement with them. To them, war and peace are only means to an end, and if peace proves ineffective, they prepare for war. This happened in Indo-China throughout the entire conflict from 1946 to the present day. If you do not believe the evidence, you are either a fellow-traveller or you are deliberately refusing to admit the truth.

After the failure at Fontainebleau the war in Indo-China, which had been going on openly since the end of 1946, could no longer be kept under control just by increased military efforts or by political measures. When I saw Eisenhower during these years, he complained to me about what he called France's subordination to the Bao-Dai government. At the same time, with that frankness which makes Americans so nice, he complained about Syngman Rhee's indocility in Korea. Once or twice, I proposed to swap with him, but he did not have much sense of humour, so that this joke annoyed him and I don't think he saw the moral at all.

In the first volume of Eisenhower's *Mandate for Change* you can easily see how reluctant the Americans were to let the Geneva conference deal with Indo-China, where a war was being fought. They obviously wanted to limit the talks to the Korean problem, where an armistice had already put an end to the fighting.

. . . Molotov was fully aware of the political pressures on the French Foreign Minister Bidault to achieve a settlement in Indo-China. Bidault, in fact, felt that if the Laniel government was to survive, he had to bring back at least a tentative pledge to discuss Indo-China at a meeting scheduled later for Geneva.

The life of the Laniel government was important to United States policies. We were convinced that no succeeding government would take a stronger position than his on the defense of Indo-China, or in support of the European Defense Community. We had to be sympathetic to the French desire. But there was danger in the attitude developing among the Western allies, which to us, seemed to put too much faith in the validity of negotiations with the Soviets and Chinese Communists. Secretary Dulles attempted to discourage Bidault from overanxiety to negotiate, pointing out that this could lead to further deterioration of morale in Indo-China and France itself.

Bidault persisted. On 9 February Foster notified me from Berlin that French pressure for a conference on Indo-China at Geneva was mounting. He held little hope of being able to withstand it, and said that if the United States was held responsible for blocking such a conference, the moral obligation to carry on the war in Indo-China might be shifted from French shoulders to ours. . . .

Before I go any further, I would like to point out three things: (1) When he wrote this Eisenhower had all the documents and several assistants at his disposal, so that he finds it easy to give his version of the facts after the event. (2) I do not remember Foster Dulles's warnings that a conference on Indo-China would harm French or Indo-Chinese morale. He did say to me several times that we ought to negotiate only from a strong position, as America had done in Korea. I pointed out to him that the Korean war had ended in an armistice and that the Indo-Chinese war had already lasted twice as long. I also challenged the assertion that America had been in a strong position when it began negotiating; in fact, the Americans were neither the winners nor the losers. (3) In any case, if the Americans had their reasons for turning the Korean armistice into a permanent agreement, the French nation, with its position endangered by the armistice, could not allow its soldiers to fight on alone without the help of the United Nations and without any end to the war in sight, even though the US was aiding us financially.

On 9 March 1954, Mendès-France made a speech attacking the government, as he had done so often before, and blaming it for addressing itself to the Soviet Union and to China instead of trying to negotiate directly with Ho-Chi-Minh. He declared, freely interpreting our intentions as he always did:

There is one basic thought in the back of your minds which you refuse to admit: you hope that the Americans will intervene. The conference is nothing but a diplomatic trick to enable you to continue with the war, after pretending to seek peace and giving yourselves an alibi.

He added that if America intervened China would too, and that this would lead to a World War. He also said that we had to end the war in Indo-China before Europe could become united and our financial position could stabilize. In fact, none of these statements turned out to be true. I refused to discuss my intentions, especially with Mendès-France; but I am amazed that he never made a reference to the significant fact that he had made this speech only four days before the attack on Dien Bien Phu. I cannot believe that he was warned about the attack in advance; but I am sorry that he never showed any regret at having made such an ill-timed intervention.

Almost immediately we discovered that the stronghold of Dien Bien Phu was a deadly trap. We had counted on our superior artillery and our air force; but the Viet-Minh artillery turned out to be lethal and invulnerable to our counter-attacks because it was hidden underground or sheltered by slopes. The Viet Minh anti-aircraft guns made it very difficult for our planes to cover our troops during land operations. We had counted on maintaining a regular supply service to Dien Bien Phu, but the air strip soon became almost unusable. The size of the fortress got smaller and smaller, as more and more outposts were captured, and we soon could do nothing to help except parachute arms, food and medical supplies. We would have had to bomb the area extensively to check the pitiless assaults of the soldiers under Giap's command.

Before the attack Eisenhower had told the United States that, now the Korean war was over, he had no intention of letting himself be dragged into the Indo-China conflict. Years later, the United States did let themselves be dragged into it long after they had refused to send us some provisional military help and thus had forced the French to leave that part of the world. During the American election campaign the previous year, the Republicans had promised to change the shilly-shallying Democratic policy of Communist containment into a more aggressive one of making the Communists 'step backwards'. But now that the soldiers had come back from Korea, Eisenhower's government, which was always very sensitive to public opinion, was having second thoughts about helping France even in a limited way.

Eisenhower was quite determined to take no risks. This meant that his successors have had to take those risks for him, and begin fighting alone in a country where they are as unpopular now as they claimed we were then. They are experiencing all that we once lived through and they have learned nothing from our example. They have not even bothered to reread all the friendly warnings they used to address us in those days.

Right at the beginning, Foster Dulles's conscience troubled him a little. In early April, he said to one of the Congressional Committees for Foreign Affairs, 'The participation of the Chinese Communists in the battle of Dien Bien Phu looks very much like direct intervention. . . . The fact that American power exists and that the US is ready to use that power constitutes a safeguard for the Free World against Communist blackmail.' When Gaston Defferre learned about this speech, he immediately warned the French National Assembly of how dangerous American intervention would be. But after the American Secretary of State went to see Anthony Eden, he became much more reticent. He came to Paris after his trip to London and I told him how anxious the French government felt about Dien Bien Phu. In spite of all our efforts, the fighting, which had been going on for a month, was making our defences more and more costly and dangerous to maintain.

I did not hide my fears from Foster Dulles and I made some urgent requests, pointing out to him that a powerful US Fleet was in the Gulf of Tonkin, and that he had told me and the rest of the world that the US would not tolerate the advance of Communism in South-east Asia; if he wanted, he could reconcile theory with practice by helping us in Dien Bien Phu. If the Americans bombarded the surrounding area extensively, this would save the garrison and boost the morale of all our troops. Foster Dulles obviously realized how difficult it would be to make the President and Congress accept this, so that he merely looked glum and did not even promise to back my request in Washington.

What he did do, however, was to ask me if we would like the US to give us two atomic bombs. I think that he spoke to others about this project, for he always liked to ask different people's advice, however unseemly or embarrassing. But it was I who answered without having to do much thinking on the subject,

'If those bombs are dropped near Dien Bien Phu, our side will suffer as much as the enemy. If we drop them on the supply line from China, we will be risking a world war. In either case, far from being helped, the Dien Bien Phu garrison would be worse off than before.'

When 'the curtain fell on Dien Bien Phu', Eisenhower wrote a very revealing letter to General Gruenther, which he quotes in his memoirs:

As you know, you and I started more than three years ago trying to convince the French that they could *not* win the Indo-China war and particularly could not get real American support in that region unless they would unequivocally pledge independence to the Associated States upon the achievement of a military victory.

Eisenhower added that the Western nations could only send military aid to Asia if they agreed between themselves and if they consulted the 'local Asian populations':

To contemplate anything else is to lay ourselves open to the charge of imperialism and colonialism or – at the very least – of objectionable paternalism. Even, therefore, if we could by some sudden stroke assure the saving of the Dien Bien Phu garrison, I think that under the conditions proposed by the French the free world would lose more than it would gain. . . . Consequently, we have had to stand by while the tactical situation has grown worse and worse. Now, unless there should be a sudden development of discouragement on the part of the enemy, it looks as if Dien Bien Phu could scarcely survive . . .

In any event, I do believe as follows:

(a) That the loss of Dien Bien Phu does not necessarily mean the loss of the Indo-China war.

(b) The heroic exploits of the French garrison (which are all the more wonderful in view of the weak support thcy have had from Paris) should be glorified and extolled as indicative of the French character and determination.

(c) We should all (United States, France, Thailand, United Kingdom, Australia, New Zealand, *et al*) begin conferring at once on means of successfully stopping the Communist advances in South-east Asia.

(d) The plan should include the use of the bulk of the French Army in Indo-China.

(e) The plan should assure freedom of political action to Indo-China promptly upon attainment of victory.

(f) Additional ground forces should come from Asiatic and European troops already in the region . . .

This idea was completely and tragically false. It made conditions and encouraged others to get involved in Indo-China (knowing very well in advance that the others would not get involved). Only then did it suggest that the United States might consider sending aid, though not before a conference at an unspecified time was arranged by nations which had not yet made any promises. Meanwhile, the French would continue to fight for the goal dictated by the Americans. We were left by our allies to struggle on alone. The Americans refused to help us and by doing so they were preparing for an ordeal which grows more difficult and less likely to succeed every day.

Of course, I did not know about the letter which I have just quoted until its recent publication. But I could see the contrast between the vigorous-sounding declarations for public consumption and the actual refusals to give aid which did not even have the merit of being clearly formulated. Foster Dulles once defined his policy as one of 'calculated risk'. Over Indo-China he certainly made a lot of calculations and circumlocutions, but he took very few risks indeed. It is only since then that the US has been forced to take the risks and make up for their carelessness.

On 29 April Eisenhower went one step further and began discussing the possibility of reaching a *modus vivendi* in Asia as well as in Europe. This eventually made him accept the Geneva conference and invite Khrushchev to the United States, although both these gestures contradicted his election platform and did not further the cause of the US or of peace. Another step in the same direction by Eisenhower was to declare that the Americans would not join us in fighting the war unless Congress approved. The Communists, who can always read between the lines, immediately understood what this meant: they could relax; the United States would do nothing.

Foster Dulles made a declaration on 7 May which sounded a little stronger, but which, in fact, said much the same thing:

France has shown that it wants an honourable armistice with adequate guarantees. If France could conclude an agreement and obtain conditions that did not endanger the freedom of the Vietnamese people, this would be a genuine contribution to the cause of peace in South-east Asia. But we would be seriously alarmed if an armistice were to be concluded in Geneva which would lead to a Communist take-over or to new hostilities. If this took place or if the fighting continued, the need to unite in defending that part of the world would become even more urgent.

Dulles may have been sounding the alarm, but this was no call to arms. He was postponing every decision until Dien Bien Phu fell. We could hold conferences then. We would be ever so brave in the face of adversity and make many a moving speech and funeral oration.

The more evasive the Americans became, the more aggressive the opposition at home showed itself. On 11 May, a brilliant Gaullist speaker called Christian Fouchet demanded the immediate departure of the government in the name of the French national interest, claiming that this was France's last chance for a victory. M. Fouchet later showed us what sort of victory he meant: 'You are unsuccessfully trying to defend our heritage. Go away. When we get to power, we will surrender it successfully.'

At the end of this debate, the government received a majority of only two votes. Le Figaro and Le Monde were sounding the knell. Every hesitation by the Americans made the opposition in France worse, and each time the opposition got stronger in France, the Americans hesitated even more. The position of the negotiator was literally intolerable. He was constantly stabbed in the back, criticized in the name of patriotism on the Right, in the name of pacifism on the Left and of Communist solidarity on the extreme Left; he had to make endless journeys between Paris and Geneva. I had been plagued with interminable letters from the Communists during the Berlin conference, but during the Geneva conference it was even worse, for there I received flesh and blood delegations. They would come and bang on the doors of the official French delegation, and when they were turned away, they would rush off to the Communist delegations, especially the Viet-Minh one, where reporters from l'Observateur were working round the clock.

I was accused of every outrageous deed during this period, although I hardly think my proposals at the conference deserved such attacks. During the first session specifically dealing with Indo-China, two days after the fall of Dien Bien Phu, I made the following proposal in the name of France:

First of all, we want the conference to declare that it accepts the principle of a general truce with the usual security guarantees. These guarantees are intended to protect the troops on both sides and to shield

the civilian population from the consequences of an over-hasty ceasefire. There should be two sorts of guarantees: first of all, while the
conscripted forces should be disarmed, the regular units on both sides
must be regrouped into clearly-defined zones. Secondly, the agreement
must be carried out under the supervision of International Committees.

I added that, in spite of the civil war, the unity and the territorial
integrity of Vietnam had to be recognized, and that the best way
to re-establish that unity would be to hold free national elections.
I also pointed out that the war in Laos or Cambodia was not a civil
war but an invasion by forces from the exterior, so that the problem
there was different and could only be settled after the withdrawal
of the invading troops. I still consider that these proposals were
both reasonable and realistic. The Viet-Minh made a counter-
proposal which was phrased in the well-known terminology of
International Communism and which would in fact mean a total
and immediate Communist take-over of Indo-China.

On the day the French government got an Assembly majority of
only two votes, Foster Dulles made a declaration in the United
States, which I was given to read in Geneva by General Bedell
Smith, who was replacing Dulles at the conference. Dulles obviously
preferred to be some distance away, as his policy now consisted of
waiting until a new government took over in Paris before deciding
what course of action the Americans would take:

Some people have said that I believed South-east Asia could perhaps
be saved without Vietnam, Laos or Cambodia. I do not wish to under-
estimate the importance of these countries, nor do I wish to give the
impression for a single moment that we think these countries are going
to be lost or that we have given up trying to prevent the problem in
South-east Asia from becoming even more difficult to resolve if these
countries are to be lost. But I don't want to give the impression either,
that if events which we can do nothing to prevent and which we do not
expect lead to their being lost, we would consider the situation hopeless
and would abandon other countries to their fate.

This declaration proved to be the kiss of death to our efforts. I
was not even surprised by the fact that the speech did not make a
single reference to the Communist menace: Dulles had already
explained to me that we would have to win over England, the Commonwealth, Siam, the Philippines and others, before America
would agree to intervene on our side. But I had seen Anthony Eden

not long before, when he had come to Paris, and he had told me to expect nothing from the English. He added in that good-natured way of his, 'I don't like the job I have to do.' Meanwhile, Dien Bien Phu had fallen, our prisoners were brain-washed, and the Viet-Minh troops were able to fan out over the entire delta.

After such a terrible defeat on such a distant battlefield, France could not continue to fight alone. The Vietnamese government was no match for the coalition between Russia, which supplied the war material, China, which supplied instructors, and the Viet-Minh, which was tyrannical but obeyed. I had warned Foster Dulles that France would soon have to pull out of Vietnam because it had not been given adequate support from its allies. He had answered, 'Losing a battle is not the same thing as losing a war.' I had replied that the Americans were wrong to pose as the winners in Korea and that his maxim might be correct during the first year of a war, but that it was certainly false when applied to a war that had already been going on for eight years. But Dulles had obviously given up the French presence in the East as a lost cause and he may well have believed that the 'colonialist' countries were harming whatever ideal he felt the Americans were defending there.

What he did not realize was that his policy of many tough words and little action would, in the end, force the Americans to fight on the same battlefield and to be accused of colonialism and neo-colonialism not only by those they were fighting, but by those who they were supposed to be helping defend themselves. Two maps published in Eisenhower's *Mandate for Change* show how blind the Americans were and how many prejudices they had against 'French colonialism'. The first map shows the Communists nearly all over Vietnam while the French were fighting there. The second map shows how, after the country was partitioned, all the Communists were cleverly contained in their part of the North and how all the rest of Vietnam was free. General Maxwell Taylor would be a very happy man right now if such were the case.

However powerful a nation is, when it makes selfish mistakes it has to pay the bitter price. The state of mind in Washington right now, particularly among those Americans who so admired Mendès-France back in the fifties, reminds me a lot of the atmosphere in Paris during our misfortunes. I want to add the final touch to the tragic misunderstanding between France and the US by quoting Eisenhower once again. In one chapter entitled 'Chaos in

Indo-China' he made two remarks that give some idea of his shrewdness and his far-sightedness:

During this period I often expressed a thought in conversation with Secretary Dulles. 'France ought to recall General de Gaulle,' I said.

I wonder if President Eisenhower and his present successor are so delighted now that he has his wish.

On the 12th of June the Laniel government failed to gain a vote of confidence in the French Assembly by a vote of 306 to 293. France was without a leader and without a government.

We decided that it was best for the United States to break off major participation in the Geneva Conference. The days of keeping the Western powers bound to inaction by creating divisions of policy among them in a dragged-out conference were coming to an end.

Around this time, I made yet another quick trip to Paris to celebrate, in the most dismal atmosphere, the fiftieth anniversary of the Entente Cordiale, just when there was neither 'entente' nor even 'cordiality'.

On 29 May, the nine delegates at the Indo-China conference unanimously passed a resolution deciding that the military representatives from both sides should meet in Geneva. Their task would be to work out zones of control, which meant that perhaps all was not lost. For this very reason, the opposition, which contained some elements that wanted us to lose everything, quickly set to work to try and overthrow a government which was trying so hard to keep something. There is no doubt that the enemies of France abroad and the enemies of the government at home worked hand in hand. The proof of this is that the Viet-Minh line became much tougher on 8 June in Geneva, and on the very same day the opposition launched an all-out attack on the government in the National Assembly in Paris.

On 9 June, I made a speech in which I defended the government's policy. I don't want to quote this long speech; but it invoked things like human dignity, patriotism and plain common sense, and it gave an up-to-date account of what we had been doing in Geneva, what our losses were, and also what chances there were of saving something, if we did not become too impatient or discouraged. For impatience and discouragement would play into the hands of the enemy, and that was just what the home opposition was expecting.

I made a great effort to speak with moderation both on that day and during the next few days, doing all I could until the last to save what could still be saved by avoiding controversy and not denouncing the hypocrisy and the betrayal of others.

Mendès-France never tried to imitate my moderation. He attacked the government untiringly, displaying much stubbornness, shrewdness and treachery; he could afford to be righteous, as he had not been a member of the government for some time, and he made full use of his skills to hit out at us. Although he had long been absent from the government, he had not given up his various international financial and economic posts, to which he had been appointed by the successive governments he now reviled. His rival, the Prince de Broglie, who has sunk even lower than him since then, always did accuse him of ingratitude. Mendès-France made one significant speech on 9 June, from which I quote the following passage:

We find ourselves faced with a government whose lack of foresight has been obvious for years. This cabinet has been noted, more recently, for its impulsiveness, its irrationality and continual contradictions.
Georges Bidault: Thank you.
Pierre Mendès-France: That thank you was long overdue. France has not deserved this. France will not let this go on much longer. All you who speak in her name, you representatives of the people, you must hear her voice at last, her anguish, her will, her demand for redress!
. . . There is only one solution, and you will come around to it. It is a difficult solution, a painful solution, a cruel solution, and, in some respects, an unjust one. The solution is to open direct negotiations.
Show the Vietnamese people that they can have peace and independence, that they can receive it from us and not from Moscow and Peking. That is the very best investment we can make.

This passage is very reminiscent of the words Clemenceau used when he spoke to Jules Ferry after Langson, although that is the only thing Mendès-France and Clemenceau could ever have in common.

The Laniel government was overthrown by thirteen votes. Forty-four Gaullists voted for the precursor of decolonization, who advocated total retreat by falsely promising that everything would be marvellous if we negotiated directly with Ho-Chi-Minh. We saw where this policy led us: after we had given up Asia, we lost

Africa. Edgar Faure and General de Gaulle felled the century-old tree, but Mendès-France's axe struck the first blow. All his reassuring promises about the wonders his policy would accomplish turned out to be false, as we realized only a few months later. He was so resentful and so emotional that I can almost believe he meant what he said. But he was wrong nonetheless. He bought the Gaullists' votes by making them promises on EDC and I am certain that this was part of a bargain.

On 17 June, Mendès-France became head of the government and announced that he was giving himself until 20 July to reach a 'satisfactory solution'. This seemed a stroke of genius: at last, people said, here is a man who faces up to reality, who gives dates, and refuses to remain static.

It did not take much thinking to realize that Mendès-France, who by his opposition to the French policy in Indo-China had made himself the accomplice of our enemies, was putting an end to any possibility of successful negotiations by doing this. If we were to obtain something at Geneva, we would have to show that we were not ready to accept just anything. But by setting himself a time-limit to end the negotiations – perhaps because he felt, like General Ely, that we were the only ones who had a vested interest in ending the war – Mendès-France was throwing himself on the mercy of the Communists. All our enemies had to do was to wait for the day before the time-limit expired or for the day itself, to force the French negotiator to accept everything they wanted. They would merely have to take certain precautions to help save the face of a government which was so understanding. This brilliant manoeuvre was just like an engineer's decision to remove the rails beyond a certain point in order to guarantee that a train will stop exactly there.

When parliament was told about the Geneva agreements, I still had enough faith in Mendès-France's good intentions to express myself with moderation, which was in complete contrast with the way I had been treated. I did not fully realize then that Mendès-France's policies were quite so woolly and insincere, but we have all had ample proof of it since. Yet there was no doubt that the Assembly felt relieved when France withdrew from Indo-China. The Assembly no longer wanted to have anything to do with that distant war and our defeat was a good argument for pulling out altogether.

Later, history repeated itself in Algeria. We had lost Indo-China after suffering many setbacks there, and we gave up Algeria, even though we were winning all the military victories there. These events and the defeatist attitude which they betray serve as a poignant lesson. For ten years, however much they have tried to conceal it, the French government has been proclaiming, 'At last! We have lost!' I have tried to show a spirit of resistance to this coward's credo and to show that there are still some men left who do not favour abdication or retreat.

I will not discuss the details of the Geneva agreements. They have not been honoured any more than the ones concluded at Evian have been. No free elections were held within two years. The French were not able to remain and their military commitments did not decrease. Vietnam was not united and the 'end of the nightmare' did not come either for the Vietnamese or for the French soldiers, who had to go and fight in Algeria only three months later.

As for a European policy, Mendès-France said on 22 July 1954, 'The Government of the United States does not regret having allowed itself to be convinced; the war in Indo-China was a heavy liability for the European defence policy which, after Geneva, is no longer weighed down by outside obligations: there had never been any question of letting it stay that way.' This declaration may have sounded definitive; but EDC was rejected only six weeks later on 30 August. The assembly voted against it after Edouard Herriot made probably the last and the worst speech of his career. He generalized about national independence and made inept comparisons between EDC and the League of Nations. He declared that he was against the treaty, about which he knew very little, and argued against the political unification of Europe, although EDC had nothing to do with that.

Mendès-France refused to let the government vote on this subject, claiming the Assembly was too divided. This was how he carried out his promise that 'European policy . . . after Geneva is no longer weighed down . . .' On 11 December de Gaulle made a speech at an RPF congress, praising Mendès-France's 'feelings, values and vigour' and making his satisfaction quite clear over the rejection of EDC. The general added a few words which were to take on genuine significance some years later, 'France is historically, geographically and politically qualified to make the attempt to try

R.—8

and bridge the gap between the Eastern and the Western blocs. . . .
It is up to her to begin negotiations in this direction.'

Throughout the war in Indo-China, 'our Indo-China', as de
Gaulle used to call it, the general did not say a single favourable
word about any government with a policy of holding Vietnam.
But he did praise Mendès-France, who had always attacked this
policy. I don't know why, but Jules Favre's words after Sedan
suddenly come to my mind, 'The armies of the Empire have been
beaten.'

The United States began making attempts to contain Communist expansion, and, to do this, they found a new government
leader who had the reputation of liking Americans and disliking
the French. That man was Ngo Dinh Diem and we all know his
tragic end. On 19 October 1954, Eisenhower wrote a letter to Diem
which marked the beginnings of American policy in South-east
Asia. Anyone can see for himself what the results of this policy
have been; but I do feel that neither Mendès-France nor de Gaulle
has the right to make any comments on the situation in Vietnam
today, considering the fact that one helped to create the situation
and the other did nothing to prevent it.

Part 3

1954-64

11

From Mendès-France to Pflimlin / *The Return of de Gaulle* / *Michel Debré's Word* / *From Integration to Self-Determination* / *The Rebellion*

I must now talk about Algeria, try and explain Algeria, although it has become a subject which everyone refuses to discuss, both in France and abroad. Some because their political ideology obliges them to accept at any price an event which they refuse to recognize as shameful, others because the only way they can avoid a painful truth is by trying to forget it, though these may have occasional bursts of anger that they do not explain.

On 13 May 1958, the French population in Algeria gave vent to its resentment and its fears of being betrayed by a shady government deal. On the night of the 13th, the National Assembly accepted the cabinet which Pflimlin proposed, and on 14 May, I wrote to General de Gaulle, asking him to save France. M. Michelet came to fetch the letter at my house and delivered it personally to Olivier Guichard, who took it to Colombey. I asked General de Gaulle to take over the government so that the people of France would remain united and France itself would not be divided. This letter was published in *Carrefour* on 21 May at the General's request, for, I have been told, he wanted it to be printed.

Later I will explain why I thought that de Gaulle was the only man who could save Algeria and France's other overseas possessions. Although this turned out to be a colossal error, the reasons for that error are quite simple. I must confess that I was somewhat uneasy about the prospect of de Gaulle's return, for I did not have a very clear idea of where he stood on the question of Algeria. He had said nothing about the subject for a long time, and he was on good terms with men I thought were very suspect, and whose ideas the General had never once denounced. Frankly, no one knew what to expect; but Pflimlin's government, which did not commit any follies during its short term, might at any moment have allowed itself to be persuaded by its Left-Wing allies in the Republican Front to make some irrevocable mistake. Everyone knew that Pflimlin planned to negotiate with the Algerian rebels, so that French Algeria was in serious danger as long as Pflimlin and his government remained in power. Also, it was perfectly clear that the army, which was worried and dissatisfied, was looking for a national leader to guide its action and to revive its will to fight. The army was on the point of turning to de Gaulle, who was available and whose reputation had not yet been compromised by defeats, and of asking him to take over the leadership of the nation.

As I was positive that the army would soon recall de Gaulle and that his return was thus inevitable, the best course was to avoid all delays, all the *ifs* and *whens* and *buts* which would have looked like political quibbling on the eve of national salvation. I was not trying to cash in on these developments; but I merely hoped that de Gaulle would listen to the arguments of those who had actually brought him back to power, especially as no one had even thought of his return until a few days before.

The French nation flocked to de Gaulle. The Radical and the Socialist opposition came to nothing, and everyone accepted the Fifth Republic. As soon as he was able to play the role of arbitrator, de Gaulle made it quite clear to those who had brought him back to power that he no longer needed their support. In fact, it was partly *because* the military and civilian partisans of an *Algérie Française* had played such an important role in the creation of the Fifth Republic, that they were eliminated, persecuted and attacked.

Not only did they clash with the General's theories about the 'wind of history', but also they could have said to him: 'We put you there.' And de Gaulle much prefers an opponent whom he has crushed and rendered helpless, to a supporter who may want something from him in return, even if that something is an ideal.

The Algerian rebellion had started on 1 November 1954, in the mountainous Aurès district. It was followed by a whole rash of isolated incidents in various areas. Recently, Ben Bella's government issued a stamp to commemorate those murders. The stamps were printed on French printing presses and were even sold to collectors at post offices in Paris.

In 1954, the commemorations were still a long way off and public opinion in France reacted indignantly. Mendès-France was then head of government, and François Mitterand was his Minister of the Interior. The Prime Minister had already concluded a peace treaty over Indo-China. He had said that if we concentrated French troops in our African territories, which were much closer both geographically and spiritually, all would be well. We would be following the advice of a geographer he much admired, the Anarchist, Onésime Reclus, who had said, 'Let Asia go and we shall take over Africa.'

This turned out to be completely false; if you take away one stone from under a building, the whole edifice falls down. Now that de Gaulle has done just that, although his followers once promised us he would do the opposite, we can witness the total collapse of that vast structure, under which so many victims lie buried. That entire undertaking, that magnificent heritage is all lost, and it is no use to our heirs. They did not know what to do with it, so they resorted to the simplest course – its destruction.

Mendès-France's government had based its reputation and had come to power by widely advertising its love of peace. When I quoted its past words on various occasions, the newspaper Le Monde, which dislikes repetitiousness, merely said that I had made the usual use of quotations. And indeed, the best thing is never to bring up the subject of promises which were not meant to be kept. Le Monde and many people would like politics to be the science of forgetfulness: memory comes in useful only if there are grudges to remember. But as promises are meant to be kept, programmes to be carried out, and policies to remain consistent, then I must

suppose that the main reason for the Algerian tragedy was that the
defeatists in Parliament, the cowardly parties, the unprincipled
journalists and the men of no nationality never meant to carry out
their promises, and looked upon them only as tranquillizers to
pacify the country.

No wonder, then, that the brave and upright men who still love
France and still have a sense of duty and honour (values considered
obsolete by the advocates of the 'wind of history') revolted
against the way these words were prostituted. A lie is a betrayal.
Perjury is an act of treachery which has been plotted in advance
and later carried out.

On 3 June 1953, Mendès-France had tried to put a government
together and had failed. On this occasion he made a statement:

France does not stop at the Mediterranean coastline. Beyond it, the
people wait for the 1946 Constitution confirming – though it was
hardly necessary – their *integration* in the French Republic.

This was perfectly correct. And even after he became head of
government, and once the rebellion had started, Mendès-France
continued to voice the same principles. On 12 November 1954,
he said to the National Assembly:

You can in any case be sure that the Government will not hesitate or
tolerate half measures and delays. . . . It will stop at nothing to put
down the rebellion and will make no compromises; everybody in France
and in Algeria must know that.

You have to act firmly when the internal peace of the nation, the unity
and the integrity of the Republic are at stake. The departments of
Algeria make up a portion of the French nation. They have been French
for a long time and will remain so irrevocably . . . There can be no
secession on the part of the Algerian population from the French
mainland.

This must be made clear once and for all, in Algeria, in France, and
abroad.

No French government, no French parliament, whatever its particular
leanings, will give in on this basic point.

Ladies and Gentlemen, several deputies have made comparisons
between our policy in Algeria and our policy in Tunisia. I insist that
this comparison is completely false and extremely dangerous.

In the first case, the country in question is a part of France; in the
second case we are talking about a foreign country which has close ties
with us. . . .

During this Assembly session, François Mitterand defined his point of view and made several promises:

... Algeria is France because the departments of Algeria are departments of the French Republic.

The same French law extends from Flanders to the Congo, even if the application of that law varies a little, because it is the law supported by our votes and there is only one Parliament and one nation for our overseas territories, the departments of Algeria and metropolitan France.

This is our rule, not just because our Constitution says so, but also because we want it that way. . . .

All those who try, by one method or another, to create disorder and to encourage secession will be punished with all the means given to us by the law. We shall also strike down all those who give their help in this undertaking even indirectly. . . .

Algeria is a part of France, and who among you, Ladies and Gentlemen, would hesitate to use every means to safeguard France?

The major concern of the government of the Republic is again, and once and for all, to defend the Algerian people, who are an integral part of the French people, against their enemies. All those who want to dissociate the Algerian people from the French people, those who want to destroy Algeria, to abandon it and to leave it to its own resources, will be condemned and punished. What can you expect of me? . . . A firm policy, believe me, and the determination to remain in Algeria.

These words were well received, yet I must admit that, although they were firm, they were only half-believed. Mendès-France realized how hostile so many people were towards him and his followers, and this may be why, at the time of his downfall, he said to the National Assembly on 3 February 1955, 'This evening I will not talk about politics. I am asking you to believe me, and there is no reason to smile or to snigger. This evening I am thinking only of maintaining French presence in North Africa, and the symbol of this continuity is the opening of a new school of Saint-Cyr in Algeria tomorrow.'

The disaster seemed a long way off. The words I have just quoted do not date from the Middle Ages or even from the war of 1870. They were spoken ten years ago and they began the long string of lies that finally strangled the French nation.

I am not denying that politicians and even statesmen can make mistakes; things can change so that men have to go back on what they said. There is nothing shameful about honestly explaining a mistake and asking one's followers to adopt a different line. But what is outrageous and unforgiveable is to change without giving any reasons or even admitting that one has changed at all. A man who says 'I was wrong', and gives the reason why can be trusted. A man who changes his mind half-way and refuses to admit that he has made promises which he has not kept deserves only anger and contempt, especially when men have died because of lies.

Mendès-France has gone back to political economy and Mitterand at least has enough guts to attack the present régime now. Neither of these two men could have made France give up Algeria willingly; their words show why the army was growing more sceptical and suspicious all the time. But it would take a more important figure to allay the doubts of the nation and to undertake the task which someone who was merely a clever demagogue could not have accomplished. France had to wait for the Liberator before it would surrender totally.

Edgar Faure succeeded Mendès-France largely due to me, although I am not particularly proud of the fact. His oratorical style was to drown everything under a flood of words. Yet he did say in the National Assembly, on 23 February 1955, 'Algeria is the flesh and blood of France.' And on 13 October 1955, he added, 'We therefore reject the idea of secession. . . . Algeria . . . is France.' But Edgar Faure had already done his bit to demolish our national heritage before the day he made that speech.

Mendès-France had gone to Tunisia with Marshal Juin to watch over him and had made a speech in Carthage; that was the second axe-blow which he struck against our overseas possessions. We had somehow expected Edgar Faure to do the opposite of what Mendès-France had done, if only because the two men disliked each other, but in fact, Faure continued in Mendès-France's footsteps and went even further along the same road than his predecessor. Before he made the speech in which he said 'Algeria . . . is France', Edgar Faure had discussed Tunisia on 8 July 1955. He spoke about the Franco-Tunisian agreements which Mendès-France had made before Bourguiba rose to power. These agreements were supposed to guarantee France's economic and military presence in Tunisia, or so we were told. Edgar Faure made a memorable declaration about those agreements which might have worked if France had adhered to them firmly:

The French government solemnly declares that the agreements which it is asking you to ratify will in no way harm France's position in Tunisia, for that remains sacrosanct. The rights and the guarantees which we have given the French residents of Tunisia must not be questioned or reduced for any reason whatsoever.

What fine words: 'solemnly', 'sacrosanct', 'in no way', 'for any reason whatsoever'. Within eight months, it all went wrong. After that, Faure stopped making speeches and waited until he was needed as go-between in the liquidation of Tunisia. But before that, he gave Morocco the coup-de-grâce, by bringing Mohammed v back to the throne. The most shameful action had already been accomplished: our friends and compatriots had been sacrificed, our strategic positions had been badly weakened, and our honour had been declared obsolete except in speeches, so that the stage was set for France to give up all the good it had done to the African continent, which was a great loss not only to France but to Africa.

Since our departure, Black Africa and White Africa have not got beyond the speech-making stage, for all their claims of unity. The only point on which they have agreed so far is to make the ex-colonialists admit their past sins by giving more money.

Edgar Faure had also dismissed the whole idea of 'independence within interdependence', and had even made fun of the slogan. Yet it was not such a bad idea if only the members of the Assembly had not finally made the term meaningless by using it too often and too glibly. And it might well have acted as a link between old-fashioned colonial principles and a true independence which would have had nothing in common with the pathetic sort of 'emancipation' ex-colonies possess today.

After Edgar Faure, we had a Socialist government which lasted quite a long time, although its record was poor. Whatever Robert Lacoste got done in Algiers was undone again in Paris and in the places where the enemies of French Algeria were allowed to speak. Guy Mollet tried not to contradict himself publicly and merely repeated what he had always said, leaving out only his speeches on Suez, of course. On that occasion, Guy Mollet had hurled himself into the fray along with Anthony Eden, and the United States and Russia had ganged up together to complicate everything. I don't want to start a controversy by bringing up the subject of that abortive excursion, which was almost France's last show of force,

although the main reason we went in was that most of the French
Socialist party was very well-disposed towards England, as were
many other politicians who were not in power at the time.

Our official policy in Black Africa, North Africa, and particularly
Algeria was notoriously inconsistent, because we were continually
trying to do impossible things. On 6 February 1956, the Algerians
made their discontent so clear that for a time the government,
which had lost a good deal of prestige, acted a bit more sensibly.
But basically, the situation was being handled on two different
levels. We were officially at war with the rebels, and secretly
we were negotiating with them. The negotiations made the war
drag on and the fighting was called a barrier to negotiations.
The government walked the tightrope between fighting and
negotiating for some time, and indeed it managed to give away
almost nothing.

The Prime Minister, Guy Mollet, probably wanted to do his
duty, or at least to make speeches to that effect, although he grew
silent during later governments. No one has yet tried to find out
about his feelings on the subject and I suppose no one will for a
long time; but I personally believe that the Socialist leader had no
preconceived ambition to abandon Algeria. Only his feelings were
as usual very complex, and he gave up trying to do anything after
others took on the responsibility. Guy Mollet did not denounce
the machinations of subsequent governments and he approved the
final result.

After Mollet, there were two Radical governments which each
lasted about three months. Bourgès-Maunoury was patriotic and
he remained so. During his premiership, barriers were built along
the Algerian frontier, particularly on the Tunisian border. These
were very effective, until another French Prime Minister had them
removed. Félix Gaillard, who succeeded Bourgès-Maunoury, was
a talented young man who had few convictions and thus was not
very dogmatic about anything. He began the 'good offices' mission
to Tunisia after the Sakiet incident, during which FLN contingents had been bombarded on Tunisian soil; the very fact that they
were training there constituted an act of aggression on Tunisia's
part.

The Gaullists attacked Gaillard savagely, not because of Tunisia,
the aerodromes or Bizerta, but because they had a personal grudge
against Robert Murphy, the American diplomat who had been put

in charge of the 'good offices' mission. This very clever, too clever diplomat had been de Gaulle's bugbear ever since the general's quarrel with Giraud in Algiers during the war. Murphy had no business being sent on a mission of this sort, especially as he never seems to have cultivated the art of making friends; but de Gaulle need not have taken so much trouble ranting against everything Murphy did when he himself gave up everything at the first opportunity. The world soon learned that 'good offices' were completely unnecessary, if everything was to be thrown away in the most majestic fashion possible.

Finally, the worn-out party régime, that was so popular with second-rate politicians who waited eagerly for each cabinet crisis in the hope that they would be made ministers, ended with Pflimlin's cabinet. Pierre Pflimlin was a dedicated worker and a good speaker. He was well-qualified for the post which he had longed to get, but which he got at a bad moment. He had persuaded my MRP colleagues not to help me when I tried to form a cabinet, so that I had failed to get a majority in the Assembly by only one or two votes, thus losing the last opportunity to save French Algeria and the Fourth Republic. Pflimlin blamed me for asking Jacques Soustelle to work with me, although he himself later became a colleague of Soustelle in de Gaulle's government – which I never joined, thank God! Afterwards, Soustelle and I met on the true path of honour which is a thorny one, not the path of official honours which are meaningless, especially now that belonging to the government does not mean governing.

Pierre Pflimlin's cabinet lasted about two weeks. Pflimlin had the reputation of being tough, but he had one fault; he attached too much importance to getting ahead. In fact, although this may seem strange, it was his timidity and his modesty which made him feel the need to prove his worth by being successful. When he became head of government, he was rash enough to state his intentions publicly, while he was still choosing his cabinet. He made it clear that he wanted to put an end to the Algerian war by asking Tunisia and Morocco to act as middle men. This would have been sheer folly on his part, and it was a very dangerous thing to say. When he realized it, he tried to go back on his words and to explain that the sort of armistice he had in mind was one like the victorious Armistice of 11 November 1918; but no one believed him and anyway it was already too late.

The Return of de Gaulle

The immediate reaction to Pierre Pflimlin's investiture was the *putsch* of 13 May 1958. Unlike Michel Debré, Roger Frey, Lucien Neuwirth and many other defenders of so-called Republican legality, who waited until they were our lawfully appointed leaders before abdicating all power, I had nothing to do with any of the famous 'thirteen plots of 13 May'. But the situation was so bad that, on 14 May, I wrote to General de Gaulle asking him to prevent a civil war and to save French Algeria by coming back to power.

I had hesitated a great deal before undertaking this step, as I had always refused until that time to get involved in any campaign to bring de Gaulle back. But once Pflimlin was made Prime Minister, I became convinced that Algiers would soon try to call back de Gaulle, although I had no inside information on the subject. Besides, I still trusted Michel Debré in those days; we had attended quite a few meetings on French Algeria together and I had tried in vain to control his ardour on the subject. If ever there was an *ultra*, Michel Debré was that man. At his father's house not long before, Debré had said to me, after a passionate tirade on the subject, 'I give you my word of honour that de Gaulle will have no other policy than that of French Algeria.' I soon learned how much that word of honour was worth.

I must admit to Pflimlin's credit that he did not make the situation worse, after to some extent provoking it, by not being careful enough. He gave General Salan plenary powers in Algeria. Although he refused to face up to the situation and the stakes he had enough integrity to take the first opportunity to step down without unleashing a crisis. If he had clung to power, he might not have caused a civil war, as there would have been no one to fight in it; but he might well have created some unnecessary complications and a few violent incidents. I am sure enough people tried to make him stay on and play the role of a Brutus or a Cato; but he chose to go away instead.

The Socialists voted unanimously, minus three votes, to prevent the 'Fascist' de Gaulle from coming back to power. They were calling him a Fascist a little early in the day, and by the time they had some justification for using the term they completely stopped doing so.

Towards the end of May, the Communists organized a vast
demonstration which was supposed to be a protest against the
'Fascist' take-over. They were joined by a few naïve liberals and
some stooges. But the buses refused to go on strike and the country
felt it needed the general's help.

Soon afterwards the General Assembly gave de Gaulle plenary
powers, although it had disgraced itself once before by giving
them to Marshal Pétain in 1940. De Gaulle's cabinet contained
Guy Mollet, who had changed his mind about the general's
Fascism, and Pierre Pflimlin, who did not bear the president a
grudge. Those who had brought the general back by crying
'Algérie Française!' began drinking the cup of bitterness that they
would drain to the dregs as soon as they heard the names of
de Gaulle's ministers.

His first speeches on Algeria were, however, extremely reassuring. I think that I ought to quote a few of them to give some
idea of the instructions received by the French army around this
time. People prefer not to remember those well-known words and
a vast coalition of interests, emotions and cowardice is linked in a
conspiracy of silence. But nothing is ever completely forgotten,
and those who are guilty are ultimately punished for their deeds.

Michel Debré's Word

Those who brought de Gaulle back to power did not yet know
that they had committed one vital mistake; a great man does not
admit to debts. If he has creditors, he gets rid of them. Everyone
must know by now that this is the reason why ever since 1958, he
has been eliminating all those who could say 'Who made you
king?' when he claims that he has been the legitimate ruler of
France for twenty years.

I have challenged the government at least a dozen times, in
writing and in Parliamentary speeches, to publish a collection of
the Fifth Republic's official declarations on French Algeria. The
Fifth Republic is not that stupid. It wants to abolish both precedent and memory. The press remains silent and the deputies
don't say a word; they are too well paid and too well selected to
make any demands.

Besides, who cares about written documents? The general is

the living incarnation of the law. He has no predecessor and he is reluctant even to think about a successor; he is the symbol of France. What he says is the gospel truth, and what he wants can only be good for the people. When he changes his mind, so does the nature of the public's welfare. The only hope anyone has of salvation is to follow him down whatever path he chooses, to change direction when he does, and to turn back if that is what he orders. Keeping a record of his inconsistencies is not advisable. The proof that his régime is no good is that it refuses to publish its archives, because it cannot justify its needs by its past words. If those words were published, they alone would be enough to condemn the régime. The people want to be told one thing on Saturday and a different thing on Monday, so that the 'realists' of the régime have only one rule: say every day of the week what the public opinion polls tell you to say, what the general tells you to say, and always be in tune with your century by letting the latest mass survey dictate your attitude. This way of looking at things is the ultimate servility, the ultimate baseness and decadence.

Yet we had been promised great things. Michel Debré, the ex-Senator and former Minister of Justice who drafted the Constitution and who became the Prime Minister of the new régime, had filled page after page of the *Journal Officiel* with his imprecations against the previous government. He had accused everyone who was not a Gaullist of being a traitor, and he was the most vehement partisan of French Algeria. I even had to calm him down a few times and to tell him that his rantings were a bit too much, even for those who agreed with him. That strong, uncompromising man, one of those rare politicians who actually went too far rather than not far enough, was now the Prime Minister. He was in charge of the government and of the nation's policy, according to articles 20 and 21 of the new Constitution, which was ratified on 4 October 1958.

Not long ago, a collection of speeches on Algeria was published. Although it is incomplete, it is about 412 pages long and more than 100 of those pages deal with Michel Debré's speeches; they show only too well that violent words are not always, if ever, a proof of firm convictions or of strong character.

Today, Debré does not seem to feel any shame, despair, or even remorse about what he once said. He makes speeches, he rants away amidst roars of applause, he talks about the future as if nothing had ever happened. Of course, his vision of the future is different now from what it was a few years ago; but old speeches can always be torn up and thrown into the dustbin.

I must admit that, before Michel Debré began doing all the dirty work of the new régime, his words were rather reassuring, although a little bit extreme. Those who read and heard him were foolish enough to think that he would at least make some attempts to keep his promises.

I will try, in the following extracts, to give a brief survey of Debré's opinions on Algeria. His sermons, his accusations, his curses, and his warnings made him the number one defender of *Algérie Française*. No words were too strong for him to use and he considered no one above suspicion. I hope these few quotations will make the reader want to look up the rest for himself. Most of them were published in *Carrefour*. On 4 April 1956, Debré wrote:

Let us not forget . . . that if Algeria were no longer French, it would become a stronghold of anti-French feelings. . . . Are some of our leaders not already on the point of capitulation? . . . If France ceases to be present in North Africa, there will be a total upheaval in which thousands of Frenchmen will be destroyed, particularly those who have a share in the responsibility for the disaster!

The Michel Debré of yesterday was giving the Michel Debré of today a clear warning.

On 27 June 1956:

What the men who are playing with France's future in the name of government do not want to understand is that the crusade which has been declared against us will never cease of its own accord. Crusades cannot be ended with conciliatory words and agreements. The conciliatory words are looked upon as a sign of capitulation and the agreements are violated before the ink is dry on the paper.

On 18 July 1956:

Men who have been entrusted with authority, and who are making such rash use of that privilege, do not have the right to dispose of French territories, French citizens, treaties and laws which guarantee French possessions and French rights.

And on 24 October 1956:

Some men want to negotiate the surrender of the rebels – the only possible negotiation – they want to work out a new status – the only acceptable status. . . .

On 4 September 1957:

On 26 August our national pride received a bitter blow. On that day, the newspapers published a statement by the members of the cabinet . . . which reminded me of La Celle Saint-Cloud. A so-called government team which is not competent to deal with the nation's future is liquidating our heritage. Algeria is being sold down the river the way so many other glorious possessions and interests have been before. Frenchmen are dying, the French Army is fighting, and meanwhile, Algeria is being stabbed in the back.

On 31 October 1956:

France is delighted to hear about the arrests of all five leaders of the Algerian rebellion at the airport of Maison Blanche in Algiers. All Frenchmen feel as though the weakness and the shame of the last few years had vanished in one instant.

What does Michel Debré think about the shame and the weakness for which he is personally responsible, after pretending to fight against the rebels and to hate them, now that Ben Bella comes to pay de Gaulle a visit at the Château des Champs? If he has any opinions on the new developments which he, more than anyone, helped to bring about, he certainly keeps them to himself. He used to be voluble enough once; but he is silent now. But it is too late for him to undo his words. He should have followed one expert's advice: 'Never write anything down.'

Before he became Prime Minister, Michel Debré wrote hundreds of pages cursing, reviling and denouncing any man who spoke about giving up Algeria, only to start blindly following the very man who did so and to obey when he was asked to go back on all his past words.

On 29 May, he was cheered by the Gaullists when he declared: 'I will repeat the words which I think sum up the situation; we must not be afraid of victory, for we can win.' In this speech, Debré spoke disparagingly of the United Nations, France's allies, Switzerland and the Communist Party. He claimed that the only solution was to call back de Gaulle. If he sincerely believed in this solution at the time, it was his duty afterwards to choose between the victory he wanted and General de Gaulle. He chose de Gaulle and defeat.

But he went even further on the other occasions. On 9 October 1957, the man who accepted Evian said:

If Bizerta, Algiers and Mers-El-Kébir stop being French, France will have a Mediterranean frontier to defend in twenty years as in ancient times, only it will be even more difficult then.

He even started a newspaper called *Courrier de la Colère* to have a mouthpiece. In it he wrote on 20 December 1957:

The Algerians must learn that to abandon French sovereignty in Algeria is to commit an illegal action, in other words such an action places all those who take a part in it in the category of outlaws, and all those who oppose those outlaws by whatever means are acting out of legitimate defence.

This statement justifies every deed committed by the partisans of *Algérie Française*. I once quoted it in print and it was read in public during the famous *Affaire des Barricades* in Algiers. When the Barricades trial took place, the prosecution repeatedly stated that I had written these words myself. The Minister of Public Affairs did not apologize to me for this and never even admitted that Michel Debré was the author of words which actually cleared those who were standing trial. Michel Debré was Prime Minister by this time and he was punishing as traitors those who had obeyed his words. His master had already taught him quite a few lessons. The very pragmatic moral of this story is that in this case, as in so many others, we were told, 'What I say is fine when I say it; but if others repeat it, and I have changed my mind in the interval, then it is a crime.'

Men in power do not have to obey the same rules of conduct as their subjects. All arbitrary dictatorships have behaved like this; but some tyrants are more despicable and more odious than others. Michel Debré ought to have some of his fine words tattooed on his forehead; in 1957 we had thought he was a wolf, but in fact, he was only a dog waiting for a master.

In the few books I still have in my possession, I cannot find the words he addressed to the victims of the parliamentary system: 'Do what your ancestors did, revolt.' His advice did not fall on deaf ears; but those who followed it were brutally put down by the man who had incited them to armed rebellion, silently adding, 'Do what I do, not what I say.' But the past, which teaches us that all liars must be found out in the end, also teaches us that the easiest way to end in prison is to gaol those whose only crime was to believe what they were told.

On 25 December 1957, Debré wrote in *Carrefour*:

I will write until the pen falls from my fingers. I will speak until I can no longer utter a word. The politicians and the administrators in the Ministry of Foreign Affairs and in the Ministry of Finance are writing the ugliest, the saddest and the most dishonourable pages in the history of France. Our régime is one of permanent capitulation, our policy is one of continuous surrender and our absurd concept of negotiation only furthers the interests of others; we do not insist on taking necessary precautions although we know that the documents we sign will never be respected – how sad it all is! How unworthy! And how much easier it would be not to know any of those who are responsible for this situation, so that I would not have to blush for them!

This is a very grim and very accurate picture of the 'régime of capitulation' that France accepts today. When he painted it, the author did not realize it was his own portrait. He later committed all the stupid blunders which he so rightly attacked and many worse ones. 'I will write until . . .' 'I will speak until . . .' until I become Prime Minister, and after that I will do the opposite of what I now advocate, I will commit all the follies I now attack. A noble ambition!

In a speech on 16 January 1958, Debré asked why Ben Bella had not yet been tried, and he shed a tear over the fate of the friends in Morocco whom we had abandoned. But once the man who wanted Ben Bella sentenced and gloated over his arrest became Prime Minister under the new constitution, once he was asked to 'determine and carry out' the nation's policy, he helped to make Ben Bella first a privileged prisoner, later a partner at the conference table, then – after Paris decided that Algeria should secede – the leader of the new Moslem-Marxist state. Debré has never, as far as anyone knows, voiced a single regret, and Ben Bella, whom he helped so conscientiously, has nothing to fear from his ex-adversary.

As for the Moroccan pashas who are now working on road gangs in their own country, Debré and others like him have long since given up worrying about their fate. Colonel Bourgoin received several hundred thousand postcards when he asked everyone to help him save the unfortunate Captain Moureau; but he has long since stopped cluttering the mails and he no longer even speaks about Captain Moureau. That officer was sacrificed in the name of decolonization as were so many others who disappeared during the evacuation or who were treated as 'a dead loss' when they opposed our withdrawal. The majority of those victims were the *harkis*, who were tortured and murdered by the thousands, probably by the tens of thousands, because they remained loyal to an ungrateful France.

In the *Courrier de la Colère*, of 24 January 1958, Debré made it quite clear that he knew the consequences of the policy which he later adopted. He does not have the excuse of ignorance. He may not have foreseen that he would commit the very acts which he blamed; but he certainly knew where they would lead. This makes him even more guilty, because it proves that he already knew those acts were wrong before committing them; by first denouncing them, he was able to mislead others even more easily. He was able to betray us only because he had denounced betrayal so often. De Gaulle, who is a cynic, used Michel Debré as a screen to hide his true intentions. He needed a pseudo Algerian die-hard for that. Afterwards Michel Debré employed the same tone to revile and condemn those who had been his followers and who had trusted him. This is known in another milieu as 'double-crossing the customer'.

On 21 February 1958, Debré wrote:

Shame on the régime, shame on the so-called government . . . Pontius Pilate. . . .
Shame on all those liars. . . .
Shame on all those cowards. . . .
Shame on all those bad servants of the state. . . .
Shame on all those who want to abdicate. . . .
Shame and shame again, etc. etc.

On 27 March 1958, Debré wrote again in the *Courrier de la Colère*:

Young men are dying for France: the government does not care, but the bereaved families are swelling the ranks of those who accept sacrifices as long as those sacrifices are made in the name of France. They would revolt if those sacrifices turned out to be in vain. The only way to justify those deaths is by refusing to capitulate, to humiliate ourselves, to give up. But the government does not care, it does not feel any emotion, it capitulates, gives up, humiliates itself and us.

Debré was still talking in a prophetic vein and was accurately describing what would happen a few years later, when he did the very things which he had attacked and became the same sort of man he had contemptuously accused. The prosecutor did not realize that he was standing trial. Michel Debré was the accuser and the accused. He has passed judgement on himself. We not only have his full confession, we also have his definition of his crime, his verdict and his sentence. Michel Debré has dropped those who sought to imitate him, but that does not matter. Even if he decided to repent, all his tears could not put out the fire which he himself started.

On 16 May 1958, during a cabinet meeting, the following scene took place:

M. Pierre Pflimlin, Prime Minister: 'We have gone over the many problems which concern us, but the most vital issue is the defence of Algeria. . . .'

M. Michel Debré: 'French Algeria!'

M. Pierre Pflimlin: 'The defence of *French* Algeria.'

I don't think one could find a better example anywhere of the insincerity shown by those two ambitious men. There is something utterly crushing about rereading Debré's speeches on Algeria. He tried to pass himself off as a Jeremiah or a Cato; but today we realize that the man was nothing but a ridiculous puppet basking in false glory.

From Integration to Self-Determination

During his first trip to Algeria, de Gaulle made many speeches which did not quite live up to the hopes of those who looked upon him as their saviour. A perceptive listener could have already caught a certain note of hesitation in the general's words; but on the whole, they were satisfactory and reassuring. That too was 'bread for the ducks', but we could not yet believe that anyone could hide such deceit under so much solemnity. Even so, we would have done well to reread *Fil de l'Epée*; for in it, de Gaulle makes his philosophy of utter contempt for the common herd very clear.

Not long before the Fifth Republic was born, de Gaulle stated his intentions and showed quite clearly that he favoured the principle of French Algeria during a press conference on 19 May 1958:

Now the Algerians shout *Vive de Gaulle*, just as the French also do in moments of acute anguish, and are yet carried on the wings of hope. They are, right now, making a wonderful show of fraternization, and this will provide a psychological and moral base for the agreements and the discussions to come, a much better base than fights and ambushes.

They are also giving the best proof that the French people of Algeria do not want to be separated from the rest of France at any cost. For people do not shout *Vive de Gaulle* unless they are for France.

Therefore, I can understand the military command's feelings and deeds in Algeria extremely well and I hope that, in the national interest, the army will remain coherent and united, and that it will set a good example just when we need coherence and unity.

QUESTION: Don't you think that the rebellion, the Algerian mutiny, was beginning to die down until you launched your appeal? You have given the mutineers new courage. Your press conference will help them even more.

ANSWER: I want to give courage and strength to all Frenchmen who want national unity on both sides of the Mediterranean. For that is the central issue! The rest does not concern me. We shall worry about it later. Today there is only one issue. There are some who treat as rebels the Army leaders who have not been punished by the government and who, indeed have been delegated governmental authority in Algeria! Now, I am *not* the government: so why should anybody expect *me* to treat these Army leaders as rebels? You see, in this crisis, we must be serious. I am trying to be serious. That's all!

The general's words did, of course, contain certain evasions and loopholes; but those could be explained away and interpreted as a wish to get back to power in the least dangerous way. Anyway, national unity on both sides of the Mediterranean was exactly what I had asked for in my letter to de Gaulle. The Communists, the Socialists and quite a few other demagogues interpreted the general's words as such, and began screaming and making demonstrations against Fascism.

On 4 June 1958, accompanied by two ministers who were kept under lock and key during the trip and by some journalists whom I did not think were trustworthy, as I had told Olivier Guichard, General de Gaulle made his famous '*Je vous ai compris*' speech.

After discussing the updating of French institutions (a great issue in those days) and paying tribute to the spirit of solidarity between Frenchmen and Moslems, the general said:

. . . I acknowledge all this in France's name and I declare that from now on, France considers that only one category of citizen exists throughout Algeria, Frenchmen, all Frenchmen who have the same rights and the same duties. . . .

The French Army which has remained orderly, determined and disciplined and which obeys its leaders, the army which has been through so much, yet which has done such a wonderful job of understanding and pacification, the French army which began this movement is my witness, and it will vouch for these developments.

The army has been able to contain the torrent and to use its energy. I acknowledge this, and I wish to express my trust in its actions. I am counting on the army both today and tomorrow.

Frenchmen who all belong to one single category, we will show that we are all Frenchmen in just three months' time, on the solemn occasion when all Frenchmen, including Algeria's ten million Frenchmen, will have to decide their own future.

The votes of the ten million Frenchmen here will count just as much as the votes of all other Frenchmen.

As I have already said, all the Frenchmen here will have to select the men they want to be their representatives in the new government, as all Frenchmen will do everywhere else.

With the representatives that you elect, we will work out the rest. . . .

I have never realized more fully than here tonight the greatness, the goodness and the generosity of France.

The Fifth Republic had defined the role that it wanted the province of Algeria to play. Algeria had given birth to the Fifth Republic and it was the cornerstone of the entire régime. De Gaulle had made his promises and had stated his conditions. What he said was published, then torn up, then contradicted, and finally denied. Nothing remains of the basic pact on which the legitimacy of de Gaulle's régime rested. When such a pact is violated, the Constitution is null and void, even if its investiture was regular. Nothing remains of the régime except the use and the abuse of force, and it has therefore lost its right to rule.

I say this now; but at the time everyone in France breathed a sigh of relief. The word integration had not been mentioned; but everyone believed that it would be the *mot d'ordre*. No one yet knew what was in store, what one man was plotting in secret. If being an impostor, concealing your intentions from those who cheer you and promising to do what you in fact intend to undo, is not treason, then what is treason?

De Gaulle made the same promises in Oran on 6 June 1958, only this time he made himself even clearer and was even more eloquent. This speech is important because it is a categorical statement of intention, which cannot be suspected of any *double entendre* or ambiguity in spite of certain hesitations and repetitions:

France is present here in you men and women of Algeria from every community, category and religion. France is present here in its Army which is doing a magnificent job of security with a determination that will go down in the history of France.

France is present in me, the man she has chosen as her leader.

If only you knew what an honour and a responsibility it is for me!

Yes, yes, France is present, and she has a mission. She is here to stay and to accomplish her vocation of a thousand years. Today, that vocation can be summed up in three words: liberty, equality and fraternity.

The government of the Republic must pay attention to what has happened in Algeria in the hope that the movement which has started will include all Frenchmen, wherever they are. The government must also do something about the great movement which, as we have seen in Oran and everywhere, has taken such a fine and hopeful direction.

All the barriers and the special privileges which now exist in Algeria between and within communities must disappear. There must only be ten million Frenchmen and Frenchwomen all having the same rights and duties. That is in itself a lot to accomplish. In three months, when all French citizens will be given this great opportunity to show that their country is a part of France now and for ever, the whole of Algeria with its ten million citizens must participate with all its heart and soul like other Frenchmen everywhere.

I am here to guarantee that new institutions will emerge from that national consultation. Algeria, with the other parts of France, will have its representatives, and those representatives will decide what steps to take to make Algeria into a country of ten million equal Frenchmen.

Oran has left me with an unforgettable memory of the faith and strength that must be the basis for all that we have undertaken to do here and elsewhere.

. . . Long live Oran, a city I love and hail as good French soil.

On the same day, de Gaulle made his most famous speech at Mostaganem. In it he did not just talk about the Algerian crisis, but also about some of his favourite topics, the failings of the previous régime and improvements to the constitution:

The movement which has started in this wonderful country will serve as an example of renewal and fraternity. From this land which has suffered and has been through so much, the repercussions of that great movement have spread to the whole of France and remind her of her vocation both here and elsewhere.

Because of this movement, France has given up a system which did not suit her vocation, her duty or her greatness. Because of this, and, first of all because of you, I have been given a mandate for changing our institutions and pulling us away from the abyss into which we were about to fall and leading us towards the summits of the world.

After what you have done for France, France must do her duty here, in other words, must realize that from one end of Algeria to the other, all the categories and communities contain only one kind of citizen. In France's name I give you my word that there will be only Frenchmen here, only citizens and brothers who, from now on, will walk through life hand in hand.

Thank you, Mostaganem. Thank you from the bottom of my heart, which is the heart of a man who knows that he is carrying one of the heaviest burdens of history.

Thank you for your aid to me and therefore to France.

Long live Mostaganem!

Long live French Algeria!

What can one think of the man after reading this and knowing what happened later, especially when we are told that his greatness lies in his ideas? Words cannot express what one feels.

General de Gaulle chose Bône, the city of Saint Augustine, to tell the Moslems: 'Come to France, she will not betray you.'

At least one hundred thousand faithful Moslems were massacred after Algeria got its independence; and the two hundred thousand French soldiers who were still there did not fire a single shot to save the men who had been their comrades in arms nor did they lift a finger to keep the general's promise to the Moslems. Not only were the soldiers never asked to keep that promise, they were specifically told to ignore it.

As Michel Debré said on 4 December 1957, 'The worst humiliation, the worst shame, the worst cowardice is to abandon those who have trusted us.' France and its army had to accept that humiliation, that shame and that cowardice, and the man who had said those words was the one who ordered them to accept it.

What is even more awful is something de Gaulle added on the same day, addressing himself to the army this time:

I am saying in Bône, as I said yesterday in Algiers, and a few hours ago in Constantine, that I look upon the loyal, honest and disciplined French army as the guarantee that France will keep her word.

With those words, de Gaulle took the army as his witness and made it the executor of his promises.

Have any of the brilliant journalists who have been mouthing the Gaullist line for years ever considered the effect that those words were bound to have? Fervent young men heard an appeal to defend the principle of French Algeria whatever happened. They were being asked to fight and to make sacrifices and they accepted enthusiastically. Later, when all was lost, the memory of this appeal would be enough to provoke storms of fury, dismay and resentment. When a proud man agrees to risk his life for a noble cause which would give meaning to his death, only to find out later that his noble leader has made a complete fool of him, it either breaks his spirit or else it makes him a rebel for life. Only the most cynical and indifferent cannot understand that.

Hypocrites, particularly old ones, who become more hypocritical each year, actually imagine that they will be allowed to go on exploiting the sincerity and the faith of their followers without ever having to face up to the consequences of their deeds. They ruin the lives of young men and they end by changing the love and admiration they once inspired into hatred. General de Gaulle has promoted all the mediocre career officers who remained docile under his command, and has either gaoled or threatened the rest. He forced the army to choose between apostasy and open rebellion.

I have given only a small sample of de Gaulle's false promises and soon nuances began to appear in his speeches.

On 14 July 1958, he went to Toulon because he could not bear the idea that René Coty, then President of the Republic, would take precedence over him during the Paris celebrations of the National festival. At Toulon, de Gaulle was greeted by a huge crowd, for there still were crowds who admired him in those days; now he has to go all the way to Teheran and Mexico to draw crowds. He made a speech declaring that Algeria would enjoy 'a

privileged place in the Community'. This was the first indication
we had that the tide was beginning to turn, for he had never used
such an evasive term before when he had spoken about the future
of Algeria. His words always have a ring of finality and he can be
utterly ruthless; but in fact de Gaulle is basically inconsistent.
People have called him a military expert, although he has never
put any of his written military theories into practice, and they have
also praised his political integrity, which shows that many intellectuals are as naïve as illiterates. De Gaulle is indeed a past master,
but only of one art: equivocation.

The first referendum was a success. The French nation was supposed to be voting for a new constitution; but this was only a
pretext, as practically nobody, whether for or against, had actually
read the draft. The constitution was an excuse for making the
nation approve one well-known figure, not an unknown document.
Already, people had stopped seeing the difference between accepting a particular form of government and accepting one man's rule.
The Gaullists got around to discussing the actual contents of the
draft constitution only a few weeks before the referendum, and
only in order to get even more votes. De Gaulle made the following
speech in Algiers on 29 August 1958:

On 28 September, every Algerian will vote 'yes' or 'no' on a perfectly
equal footing, and by doing so, he will directly influence the future of
France. For it will depend on the French voters whether we will renew
our national institutions or return to the old shortcomings which almost
brought about the downfall of the Republic.
. . . Everyone who answers 'yes' in the present circumstances will be
showing that he wants to be a fully-fledged Frenchman and that he
believes Algeria must evolve within the context of France.
Through their votes, the Algerians will be settling the question of
their own future. However painful the civil war has been, whatever
individual Algerians feel on the question of their future status, when the
fighting is over and peace returns, their ballots will be a clear and
important indication of what they want.

There is a great difference between these rather vague and
ambiguous words and the clear-cut speeches of the early days.

In September 1958, I went to Algeria with the feeling that all
would work out all right in the end. I had had to break away from
the MRP, which vacillated too much and which was opposed to
certain policies I considered essential for France's welfare. And so

I created a Christian Democratic party, which won a lot of support and sympathy and got several members elected to parliament. But the Gaullists blocked all our efforts and the circumstances, which had seemed hopeful at first, soon began to seem much less so. Yet on the whole, the experiment was a success. I wanted to go to Algeria to talk about my new party and to tell the Moslems about our plans for integration, as I considered that this was vitally important.

I met de Gaulle only on two more occasions after the letter I had sent him in May 1958.

My first meeting with him took place on 1 June 1958, at 11 o'clock in the morning. I had read the list of the men he planned to appoint as his ministers, and when I saw that his cabinet would contain Pierre Le Brun of the CGT, a brilliant and dangerous Minister of Labour, I immediately asked for an interview. Olivier Guichard arranged a meeting, and although I said that 1 June would be too late, I was not allowed to see de Gaulle before that day. Naturally, de Gaulle and his newly-appointed personnel all thought that I had come to ask for a cabinet post. As I know from experience, most politicians do not put themselves out except when they are seeking an important post and have to solicit it personally. When I arrived at the rendezvous, the first thing de Gaulle said to me was, 'Let us talk about you.'

I answered, 'I have not come for that, and I do not want to talk about myself.' 'But we must,' he replied, 'you've been so helpful recently.' And, getting straight to the point as usual, he added, 'In spite of our serious disagreements in the past, etc. . . .'

I changed the subject and began talking about the Unions and Le Brun. De Gaulle interrupted me and said in a rather unfriendly tone of voice, 'Well, you see, I took on Bacon. The poor man won't make any trouble.' After that, he added, 'The ones who began this great national movement, Soustelle, Morice and yourself, will have to be in my government, not right away, but a little later. . . . Goodbye, *cher président.*'

As the saying goes, a good fisherman has to use a very fine line and a very small hook. And of course, the fish have to be biting.

I did not go to Matignon again, until I was about to leave for Algeria. Everything seemed to be going well and the French people were satisfied. Georges Pompidou had sent me an extremely courteous letter apologizing for not asking me to be in the committee which was drafting the constitution. I replied that I could

234 RESISTANCE

not care less. Whether he had left me out by accident or on purpose, he spared me at least a few hours of all the useless boredom politicians have to endure.

As I was leaving for Algeria, I went to see General de Gaulle to tell him what I was planning to do. His reaction was neither approving nor disapproving. Later, he forbade Soustelle to sign a very similar appeal to the one that had brought the Gaullists back to power. In May 1958, we had asked for the creation of an emergency government without giving any names. The second time, Roger Duchet, André Morice and I made the same appeal; but not to the same man. In the early days before we knew what the general was like, we all stepped aside willingly to make room for him and for his henchmen.

De Gaulle accepted my project to go to Algeria and preach the old gospel which was still fashionable, though not for much longer. I had already been sent away once before by a government which was only too pleased to get rid of me; Schuman had politely sent me off to UNESCO three months after taking my place in the Quai d'Orsay. General de Gaulle probably thought that I would not be much trouble in Algeria, as he was already firmly in control. His arrogance even then ought to have served as a warning to all of us; but we only lost faith in de Gaulle individually and by degrees.

The general was very lukewarm with me. He advised me to see different Arabs from the ones General Salan would produce, and when I asked him what Arabs he had in mind, he replied, 'Jacques Chevalier could show you a few.' I hope that by now Jacques Chevalier has got over some of the theories he then had. Events proved that those theories were wrong. He wrote a book called *Nous Autres Algériens* that he must find saddening to read: he must even feel guilty about having written it now that he is just another Frenchman living on French soil.

De Gaulle's words were not encouraging, yet they made me feel even more strongly the need for a referendum which would make all Algerians become equal Frenchmen in the eyes of the law. I realized that if the Algerian vote was inconclusive, this would play into the hands of those who wanted Algeria's independence. And so I travelled all over Algeria in a plane which General Salan had put at my disposal. I went all the way to the Tunisian and Moroccan borders and went as far South as Mzab and the oilfields of Hassi Messaoud. A crowd of about 30,000 people greeted me enthusiastically in Oran, and I don't know how many thousands came to see me in Sidi-Bel-Abbès, Tlemcen, Constantine, Tiaret, Ouargla and other cities. Everyone from the Mzab area came over to Chardahia to see me. The Algerians were anxious but full of hope, although I already had the vague and uncomfortable feeling that the Arabs were whispering to each other that perhaps de Gaulle wasn't *that* keen on keeping a French Algeria. There was something rather nervous about the excitement of the crowds who chanted *Algérie Française*, as though somehow they wanted to be reassured.

The words '*Ici, la France*' had been written on every wall and every roof, and it was true. I told my audiences that it would go on being true if they decided that equality between citizens and communities could have only one meaning: equality not just in theory but in practice. Integration meant equal rights for everyone, equal jobs and equal social status. Although de Gaulle's speeches were still in the spirit of 13 May, I felt that some people were beginning to doubt his sincerity, so that I added, 'The river does not disown its source.' I was never forgiven for saying this; it was my one attempt to force the government to keep its word.

I was wrong. The river did disown its source, and that is why we are now in a swamp, and why Algeria is up to its neck in mud.

Those eight days I spent wandering around that vast French province were brilliant, dazzling, and full of bitterness. I am not surprised that even men like Nasser and Chou-en-Lai admired what was left of French efforts after the pompous and incompetent government of Algeria had taken over. A certain French *ambiance* remained in Algeria in spite of everything.

The principle of integration, like so many other principles, was first called sacred and later called an act of treason. My feelings for integration were that the inhabitants of Algeria would only become truly French if they were integrated and had the same rights, the same customs and the same education as all other French people everywhere.

When Algerian stamps were replaced by French stamps, I genuinely believed that this was the beginning of Algeria's total integration into the French community. The fact that the *ultras* wanted the Moslem community to be totally integrated within the French state was later called a crime by the very same newspapers

236   RESISTANCE

that made such a fuss about segregation in the United States. They
had called Governor Faubus a reactionary because he wanted to
enforce segregation in Little Rock, Arkansas, yet they wanted to
do the same thing in Algeria. I don't understand why they felt that
in the name of progress there had to be integration in the US and
segregation in Algeria, yet those who called themselves 'objective',
realistic and 'advanced' all said the same thing.

On my return to Paris, I let it be known that I would be willing
to write a report of my visit to Algeria. I was not asked to do so.
I can get along perfectly well without an audience and I have
never tried to impose myself unless I felt that it was absolutely
vital; but I began to have serious doubts about the direction which
the new régime was taking.

The Rebellion

I saw de Gaulle on only two more occasions after that. The first
time was at Saint-Etienne, where he said to me, 'You disagree
with me over Algeria,' and I answered, 'Yes, General, you can
read about it every week.'

The second time was when I was asked to go to the Elysée to
receive the Liberation Cross which I had unofficially possessed
ever since August 1944. Some people in de Gaulle's entourage had
insisted, for his sake rather than for mine, that the cross should be
given to me in a formal ceremony. I was a bit surprised and not
particularly pleased when I received the invitation; but I finally
decided that I could not refuse any meeting which might be the
beginning of a reconciliation. General de Gaulle gave me the cross
according to the customary ritual and then explained to me that he
had not done so earlier because I had always been a minister until
that time (members of the cabinet are not eligible). I had not been
in the cabinet for five years; but great minds never bother about
trivial details like these. De Gaulle, who was the founder of the
order, has always had a strong sense of protocol, so that he had to
say those words.

A few days later, I understood why I had received the cross.
On 16 September 1959, it was announced that Algeria would be
given self-determination – in other words, that it would be handed
over to the Algerian rebels. With my recently-awarded medal for

the role I had played in the Resistance, I did what any honourable ex-member of the Resistance had to do. Without hesitation, I 'purely and simply rejected' the principle of self-determination, speaking in the name of the French Algerian Union which had just been founded. Self-determination broke all the existing laws, all the promises that had been made, and went against all my own feelings which could not change in the space of the presentation of a cross. I never saw General de Gaulle again, and I refused the formal invitations that were sent to some members of Parliament, many of whom were extremely proud of being chosen to go and hear the general's sermons.

I do not have the space to give a detailed account of all the painful and tragic events which eventually led to the final catastrophe in Algeria. There were moments of hope; but the process would start up again inexorably, as soon as soothing words had reassured those who were still reluctant to play the general's game. The entire nation was very gradually converted by clever propaganda and distorted information. The French people who had cheered the army on 13 May eventually became the general's accomplices. Prosperity and brainwashing made most Frenchmen agree to everything, so that they too have a share of the guilt. When the time came, a vast majority of French voters accepted the amputation of national territory. Unlike Alsace-Lorraine, they did not even lose Algeria; they were made to give it away and forbidden to mourn for it as well.

The speeches of de Gaulle and his followers show that the ideal of a French Algeria was neither stupid nor a conspiracy, as some have dared to call it, nor even a colonialistic invention. In the end, integration was called a conspiracy, just as the events of 13 May were called a coup d'état – even de Gaulle had the gall to say that. Without condescending to remember his own words, and naturally without feeling any gratitude towards those who had brought him back to power, de Gaulle finally condemned his own return to power, by contradicting the very events which had made him head of state. He obviously decided that the highly irregular way in which the Fifth Republic had begun did not fit in with his private theories on legitimacy. I don't care what he says about them, as I never had anything to do with the 'thirteen plots of 13 May'. I have no personal reasons for defending the events of May 1958, and I no longer have even any patriotic reasons for doing so, now

R.—9

that all the aims of the plotters of 13 May have been destroyed. But if there was any usurpation of power, then de Gaulle was the principal usurper.

After the referendum of 30 October 1958, de Gaulle said that the meaning of the Algerian vote was 'as clear as daylight' adding that the election results were tremendously significant because 'they link the destiny of Algeria and France for ever'. We all know what he meant by 'for ever'. His 'for evers' are like those of Mendès-France and Edgar Faure, who were both frequent and uninvited visitors at Colombey during the general's retirement. They converted de Gaulle to their point of view, and taught him how to use words like 'for ever' and 'never' until he learned that they were just useful tags to add to promises that were not meant to be kept. When an honest man says 'always' he means always, or at least as long as he is able or as long as he lives. And if he cannot keep his promise, he will explain why. When great minds like de Gaulle, Mendès-France and Edgar Faure say 'always', they mean until tomorrow, or until they change their minds, or until they decide to say the opposite of what they are now saying.

De Gaulle at first delighted the French nation, which grew trusting, then became hypnotized, then submissive. Finally, it gave in to him on every point. Three weeks before making the announcement that Algeria would have self-determination, which was the beginning of the end, de Gaulle had said to Colonel Bigeard, 'While I am alive, the FLN flag will never fly over Algiers.' De Gaulle is still alive; but the FLN flag is flying over Algiers and he calls this solution 'satisfactory', 'honourable', 'beyond our hopes'. He welcomes his long-lost brother Ben Bella to the Château de Champs and gives more money in return for every snub he receives. As for Colonel Bigeard, he may be promoted if he keeps his mouth shut.

Anyone who bothers to look up the facts knows that the present régime is fraudulent. Why bother to quote the words of lackeys when you can listen to the master speak? Michel Debré, who will not tolerate traitors and who stops at nothing to get rid of one, has made several attempts to reconcile his past and present roles. For two whole years, although he must have known he would eventually be forced to take a different line, he seized every opportunity to reassure the partisans of French Algeria. His speeches, declarations, articles and promises on Algeria would fill a trunk. After the

election of 1958, all the UNR members who had been elected
signed a declaration in which they pledged to 'keep Algeria within
the French Republic'. But how can we expect 'realists' to feel
bound by their word?

While I was at General Salan's house in Algiers, I met Lucien
Neuwirth, a colleague and a deputy for the Loire department.
Neuwirth belonged to the committee created by the men who had
participated in the events of 13 May. I admitted to this brilliant
man that I had doubts about de Gaulle's real feelings on French
Algeria and he answered, 'If I have to choose between my loyalty
to General de Gaulle and French Algeria, I will choose French
Algeria.' But in spite of this solemn declaration, Neuwirth finally
chose de Gaulle. There were quite a few like him who jumped on
to de Gaulle's band-wagon; however hard they try now to disavow
their past words, those words are never quite forgotten. Men of
this sort are always plaguing the government with their requests
for posts which have not been offered to them. They don't mind
what they are given as long as it's something. They'll take posts in
Tourism, Town and Country Planning, Technical Education,
Birth Control, anything to prove their loyalty to the régime if it is
ever questioned.

This group of men has provided the nucleus of those followers
known as 'unconditional' supporters of the new régime. But what
does 'unconditional' mean? Everyone knows that it does not mean
loyalty. A lot of 'unconditional' Gaullists were once 'unconditional'
Pétainists, and they will be anything each new régime asks them to
be just as unconditionally. Their only condition is an unwritten
one, but the régimes always know what it is: to let them have a
little bit of power and to make them feel a little bit important for
as long as possible. That explains how de Gaulle managed to keep
a following which cheered him every time he changed directions,
even when he made a complete *volte face*. Apart from a few exceptions, the majority chose to repudiate everything and to continue
following the Guide down whatever path he chose to go. A lot of
men who were not 'rotten to the core' tore up their oaths and
turned against everything they had once lived for, because their
leader changed in mid-course. As soon as they realized that it was
in their interest to do as they were told, they shouted first 'Long
live French Algeria', then 'Long live Algerian Algeria', and finally,
'Long live the Republic of Algeria'. The only thing that these three

slogans had in common was 'Long live de Gaulle'. Long live
whatever he likes. The weather-cocks turn with the direction of
the wind.

Meanwhile, the army was being gradually but drastically purged.
Those who had innocently helped de Gaulle back to power were
replaced in the higher and even the lower ranks by men who were
more flexible, and who did not mind obeying without understanding orders or thinking things out for themselves. A Socialist
minister had put Ben Bella in gaol, the man who had been asked
to help keep France great freed the Arab leader and handed over
Algeria to him and to chaos. Those who had fathered the régime,
who had placed the crown on de Gaulle's head with their own
hands, were finally sacrificed in favour of the rebels who massacred
2,000 Moslems in France alone and sixty policemen in the Paris
area. This sacrifice was carefully concealed by trickery, secret talks
and conferences to which negotiators (the first of whom was
M. Pompidou) were sent with only one instruction: to get it over
with as quickly as possible.

De Gaulle used to sneer at those who just wanted to get things
over with, whatever the cost. He called them cowards and vain
fools, but things have changed a great deal. Now the password is to
get somewhere, to settle everything as quickly as possible. Usually
the negotiators don't know where they are or where they are going.
They at least have that in common with Christopher Columbus
who discovered America when he thought he was heading for the
river Ganges. We are told that we have achieved greatness; but
everyone knows, although almost no one admits it, that the present
régime always mistakes its friends for its enemies and *vice versa*,
and that it doesn't even know what century it is.

During those years of change, de Gaulle had full control of
National Defence, as indeed he has now that we have nothing left
to defend. The army still believed in him and was waiting for the
day of victory, although it was receiving instructions not to exert
itself trying to win any battles as victory was such a certainty. Yet
our eventual withdrawal from Algeria was becoming more certain
every day. The French soldiers accepted everything, even the fact
that the government's attitude was making the war drag on need-
lessly. The army obeyed because the Gaullists were the legal
authorities and had a parliamentary majority as well as a constitution which had been accepted by the people. The army took a long

time to realize what in fact the government was planning to do
about Algeria.

The Army had not been enthusiastic about de Gaulle's return;
but it had been relieved because it knew his reputation for strength.
The fact is that this strength was used not for, but against the army.
Of course, illusions die hard, and it was a very long time before the
French soldiers realized that they would have to choose between
passive acceptance and their concept of military honour. All the
foreign officers who have had the opportunity to compare the
quality of the French professional army before and after de Gaulle's
purges have been struck by the difference between the old French
army and the new one. The new army is very inferior intellectually
and morally. It has lost its freedom of speech and has become
silent under de Gaulle; that is its one merit as far as the government is concerned.

And yet, when de Gaulle was a Captain, he did not keep silent.
He questioned all the military doctrines of the General Staff. He
was admired and supported by over two dozen politicians, among
them Paul-Boncour and Paul Reynaud. Men who have a strong
character find it terribly hard to keep their mouths shut when they
come across injustice, stupidity or lawlessness. It's easy to keep
silent when you have nothing to say. Today Pierre Messmer cheerfully agrees with everything he is told; but he ought to worry
about those men who say nothing, and keep their thoughts to
themselves.

The top-ranking officers, who escaped the purges and who still
have some dignity, have learned from bitter experience that in this
day and age words are mostly used for dishonest aims, and that if
they want to keep their integrity they had better say nothing. They
remember the speeches I have quoted only too well.

A military court decided that certain officers had been wrong to
disobey the order to withdraw from Algeria, even though they had
been made to promise that they would never allow this to happen.
But the officers were only following the example of another officer
who made history by disobeying an order on 18 June 1940. They
believed that de Gaulle had performed a great and noble deed by
refusing to accept defeat and this was their justification for refusing
to accept another unnecessary defeat. Army cadets celebrated the
anniversary of 18 June every year and held special lectures on those
days. What the army did not realize was that when great men go

RESISTANCE

into politics they have one rule and one alone: admire me, but don't try to do what I did.

At first glance, the army *coup* seemed far more likely to succeed than the desperate gesture of 18 June. It failed, but not for the reasons mentioned in court. The various attempts to overthrow de Gaulle did not succeed because they were not sufficiently well coordinated, so that each one was less effective than the previous one. Those who had not joined in the first effort found that they had fewer supporters, since many had gone to gaol by the time a second attempt was tried. This made every attempt that much less likely to succeed than the one before. As Clemenceau once said, if you are going to rebel, 'the first day is the best day'.

The French army failed because it was too divided and because it tried too hard to please everyone and to get the support of men who had already suffered in the past and who did not want to compromise themselves once again. The army wanted to include everyone, even those who were too weak to want to take any risks. One of the outstanding characteristics of the 'Fascist' officers, the 'activists' and the 'ultras' was their extreme conscientiousness. They did not follow the advice of the old Republican Clemenceau who was haunted by the ghost of the Commune. They believed that the best time to strike would be right at the end, when everyone's cup of bitterness had overflowed.

Nearly every French military leader of any worth or talent for war (and not just war on paper) was eliminated from the army and sent to gaol or disgraced or forced to retire. This did not just happen accidentally. The French army has never been very vocal and the law courts and the newspapers did their best to prevent our officers from explaining their intentions. But in fact, the French officers only wanted to save French unity when it was threatened by the régime which they had helped to install. Traditionally, the army has always remained in the service of the State, even when it did not approve of what the State was doing. The army served the Republic, even when its officers were Royalists. General de Gaulle should know all about the way Royalist officers once had to come to terms with their consciences before they could decide in favour of Republican legality.

There has never been quite such a rift before between the best elements in the army and the established government. The only explanation for the split is, of course, the promises which were made and not kept and the orders contradicting the promises. There is a great moral difference between men who agree to go back on their word and men who do not, between men who cheerfully carry out orders which they were told they would never have to carry out, and men who prefer to eat bread in a prison cell rather than feast with all the other servants of the State.

There is certainly no doubt that if a political leader had made it clear to the army when the time came that the solution of French Algeria would not work, and if he had stopped proclaiming his absolute determination to keep Algeria French, he would have run into a great many difficulties. He would have been extremely unpopular and would have had a hard time convincing those who were actually 'winning on the battlefields', as even de Gaulle admitted they were doing. But if he had turned out to be right, no one would have hated or despised him after the event. After all, political leaders have to make unpopular decisions and sometimes it is their duty to do so. If politics were to be only a matter of personal popularity and politicians always pandered to the public's wishes, sidestepping all unpopular issues, then we might as well choose the government and the assembly by lottery. Besides, when a leader spends all his time catering to the whims of all the people, he ends up by ruining his reputation and discrediting his régime. Two Republics have already fallen in that way: the Fourth Republic fell from power and the Fifth Republic fell into disgrace. I hope no one takes offence at the word 'disgrace' because I used it during a speech at the National Assembly and not a single member protested.

De Gaulle revealed his intentions only very gradually and always accompanied each change in his policy with speeches intended to reassure those who did not want to forget 130 years of French history. At the same time, he was beginning to court the interest and sympathy of those who call themselves 'progressives', although they are doing all they can to turn back the clock of Western civilization. De Gaulle had once reviled them; but later he welcomed them to Colombey and finally he adopted their ideas and their prejudices, their likes and their dislikes. He thought that he would have more 'political sex-appeal', if he turned against the Frenchmen of Algeria whom he had never liked anyway. It had all begun during the war when the French Algerians had preferred Giraud to him and had even kept a soft spot in their hearts for Marshal Pétain.

RESISTANCE

Not only did his antipathy for the French Algerians increase with the years; but he also wanted to appear up to date by adopting fashionable ideas. Jaded old men often turn against all they once preached and believed to adopt a more current ideology. Today, even old prelates do this too, particularly those who were complete conformists in their youth and had the most stereotyped convictions.

De Gaulle believes that today the wind of history is an East wind. He has not yet noticed that political winds are just as unpredictable as real ones, although he ought to have learned this from his own past experience. Almost nothing is 'irreversible' in human affairs, even though Hitler and Stalin always used to say that situations were 'irreversible'. When a talented man uses that expression, I know that he is ambitious, that he believes in nothing, and that he is making use of the concept to further his own career. And when a mediocre man says it, I know that he is just an ass, dutifully repeating whatever he reads in *Le Monde* or in his favourite newspaper. For if anything can ever be proved in history, it is that the 'wind of history' changes direction all the time.

I was officially prevented from returning to Algeria by some administrative measure. I went back only once, for a very short time. When I got there, I saw immediately that the good old days were definitely over. People were uneasy and the army's spirit was flagging. The army was under orders not to interfere, but to sit back and watch everything it had achieved being undone. The army was told to reassure the friendly Arabs and to keep them on our side as long as possible, but not to encourage them to make any definite plans for the future. There was no need to be an expert in Arab psychology to realize where this would lead.

There was already a very strong 'wait and see' attitude, and that was exactly what the government wanted. When a leader begins to sound more evasive and to speak in riddles which no one can understand (for the simple reason that they are meaningless), those who have been on his side until then soon begin looking in the opposite direction. The Arabs were subtle enough to understand that these vague, rather hesitant, words meant that the French were getting ready to leave. The younger officers and the civil servants who tried to counteract this effect with repeated assurances that the French would stay got nowhere, although they at least were in good faith. They would make simple but moving short speeches,

'We will stay. I promise you that we will not go away.' Some of
them were shrewd enough to see that France was playing a double
game and they were only following orders when they made those
speeches, however much their consciences bothered them. But a
great many others spoke with their hearts and genuinely believed
that they were saying the truth, when in fact they were only being
used by the government. The government wanted the loyal
Moslems of Algeria to trust France as long as possible. The
Arab soldiers, who did not believe that a French officer could tell
a lie, continued to risk their lives for France. These false promises
were of great help to the French government, and many poor men
died because they had believed them.

All this is very well known. But the facts which really matter
and which affected the lives of a million people as well as the future,
the honour and the security of an entire nation, must not be remembered whatever happens. Don't talk about them, don't write
them down. It all happened recently and many lies were written;
but the truth must not be known.

I am not qualified to give any precise information about the
heroic deeds of the OAS. I was forbidden to go to Algeria, and no
one ever asked me to go there illegally. Besides, I would not have
been very useful there, and so I never became involved in that
desperate and legitimate attempt of self-defence.

I did, however, have a lot to do with the Vincennes Committee
which was arbitrarily suppressed by the government after one brilliant meeting. It was indeed a seditious organization, for it was
trying to save France's heritage, to respect the constitution, and
to keep the promises that the State had made.

In April 1961, four generals tried to overthrow the government,
in what was wrongly called a *putsch*. This enraged the government
and also threw it into a panic. General de Gaulle made a speech on
television; his face was distorted with anger and he announced that
he would use 'every means' at his disposal to crush the generals
who only wanted to hand over a pacified Algeria to him without
any bloodshed. He used much the same expression as Maurras,
whom he had once admired, to talk about the defence of the Republic. As for Michel Debré, he completely lost his head when he
saw that others were following his advice to revolt. The tough ex-
ultra and old reactionary frantically begged his life-long enemies,
the workers and the Trade Unions, to help him. His terms were so

ridiculous that he supplied the one burlesque note during those sad days. He asked the staunch Republicans of the CGT and the FLN to rush to the airports of Paris, 'on foot, on horseback and by car', to prevent the landing of the paratroopers whom he had so often said would save France. In spite of this desperate plea, arms were not distributed and the Prime Minister merely added another comic touch by ordering military boots to be distributed. Those who now make fun of 'the men in the hobnailed boots' must not forget that it was they who wore them that evening.

When General Salan tried to save Algeria, which he had once sworn to hold and to defend, he was only acting in the tradition of the spirit of 18 June and following the advice of Michel Debré in person. Salan tried everything else before resorting to this final step. French soldiers had given their lives for Algeria ever since 1830. About one and a half per cent of all Frenchmen (including quite a few French and Arab Algerians) had died in the First World War to help France win back its lost provinces. One and a half million Frenchmen who came from both sides of the Mediterranean died for the sad little *Alsacienne* with the big black bow and the French flag which was once again to fly over the Cathedral of Strasbourg.

I once said to the National Assembly, 'French soldiers could not shoot at the French flag. If they did, I would have to see it to believe it.' Well, I did not see it, but hundreds of thousands of Frenchmen in Algeria did, and I had to admit at last that it had happened.

Of course, anyone can drape a flag over a barricade and yet fight for a cause which goes against the principles that flag stands for; but this was not the case. For the first time since the Armagnacs and the Burgundians, or since Charles VI, Frenchmen were ordered to shoot at men who were trying to hold on to one of France's provinces. A lot has happened in our long history; we have been defeated and betrayed; we have had to surrender; but, unlike today, we did not call those surrenders victories. Yet what we had never done before was to use the cannons, the machine-guns and the rifles we had been given to defend our country in order to cut off our own territory.

Quite apart from the tragedy in Algeria, this has created a sinister precedent. For just as 18 June had disciples, so the anti-June spirit, which is so much less risky, can also have disciples. Now that we

can no longer cheerfully abandon a whole nation which we watered
with our blood, sweat and tears, we have only French soil left; God
knows what we may be asked to do with it in the name of greatness. The precedent created in Algeria has revealed that no one
is completely safe. Anyway, we can still get rid of our precious
Antilles or our Pacific islands. When you've given away the sheep,
you might as well give away the lamb too.

I know exactly what it is like to fight against an army and a
powerful police force simultaneously. In Algeria around this time,
there were not only several police forces, but two enemies. As soon
as the OAS was created, the regular forces of law and order came
to an unofficial understanding with the Algerian rebels. The French
army probably won against the *fellaghas*, for de Gaulle never stopped talking about the French army's superiority 'in operation'; but
Paris wanted to lose at all costs.

The French army was determined to win in Algeria long before
13 May 1958. In those days, the succession of governments in
Paris were merely trying not to lose. They did not want and could
not afford to lose everything. At the very worst, they would not
have gone further than a compromise. And they would very
probably have been overthrown anyway, if they had tried to come
to any sort of agreement with the FLN. De Gaulle had been
brought back to power by Salan and the men in Algiers, who more
or less forced the French Assembly to accept him, and that was the
beginning of the end; as soon as he was firmly in control and
everyone trusted him sufficiently, de Gaulle began doing what no
other government had dared to do before.

From the moment he promised to 'get it all over with', he began
scheming to get rid of Algeria and to surrender. Anyone who dares
to claim that we did not surrender after our ignoble rout during the
'disengagement' is completely forgetting recent events, is refusing
to face the facts, and is indifferent to the fate of over a million
Frenchmen, whether Moslems or Christians or Jews. As the self-
appointed 'Guide of the Nation' once said about the French
Algerians, making himself much clearer than he usually does,
'Well, let them suffer!' That phrase gives him away: the loss was
not de Gaulle's, it was France's.

During the *'semaine des barricades'* when some French Algerian
patriots rebelled against the government in January 1960, General
Challe helped Paul Delouvrier to suppress the revolt. Challe still

genuinely believed at the time that de Gaulle would keep Algeria French by making some unspecified reforms to improve the Arabs' political and economic lot. When Challe realized that he had been completely deceived and that he had been used for opposite aims, he too rebelled against the central government with Salan, Jouhaud and Zeller in April 1961.

Salan did not create the OAS until after this revolt by the four generals failed. It was too late to try and save Algeria by threatening insurrection or by actually revolting, for the central government was now very stable, and Algeria was far less influential than it had been. Alone and exiled, Salan decided that even if there was not much hope, he could still try, and even if he failed, that was no reason not to continue fighting to the last. All the great men who have failed thought this way, but so did those who succeeded. The OAS was a risky enough venture; but the man who began that venture was great and noble and ready to fight against the misfortune which overtook him and others.

Salan refused to give up hope until the last. He defended the cause which he had received orders to defend before de Gaulle had returned to power. Both the Constitution and the Head of State had given him those orders. I know that I am repeating myself; but these things must be repeated over and over again. I will never tire of repeating that the French flag is the French flag, that a promise is a promise, and that King Midas has ass's ears. Salan was later found guilty of rebellion; but the court which sentenced him was illegal according to natural and constitutional law. Basically, we must determine whether a man is guilty when he refuses to obey orders given by a higher authority which are against the law, or whether he is more guilty if he carries them out. The soldiers who were ordered to massacre all the inhabitants of Oradour were punished for not rebelling, and one thousand Frenchmen died because those men unwisely obeyed their officers.

In fact, it is asking a lot from a simple soldier – or trooper, as de Gaulle calls them – to set himself up as the judge of his superiors and to go against a military order because his conscience tells him to do so. But when a man reaches a high military rank, it means that the General Staff has recognized his powers of judgement, his intelligence and his authority, and that he is considered fit to make the hardest choice of all: sending men to their deaths. Now when one of these leaders realizes that he has been given an order which is clearly against the written law of the State and the unwritten law of the national interest, he has the right, and in certain cases the duty, to disobey the order which he knows beyond a doubt to be harmful. If he does not have this right, then the verdicts of the Nuremberg trial were much too harsh and the soldiers of Oradour were not guilty.

What did de Gaulle's action on 18 June 1940 amount to, after all? A young and insubordinate officer who had only just been promoted set himself up as judge of a perfectly legal government. That young officer said 'No', proclaimed, 'I, General de Gaulle . . .' and now we celebrate his disobedience every year. I have certainly never blamed de Gaulle for his gesture; in fact, I thanked him for it in writing and by risking my own life. But no man in his right mind can approve of what one person does at his own risk and perils, knowing exactly what he is in for, and deny another person the same right in similar circumstances. The government which was set up in 1958 was just as dubious legally as the one of 1940. Why should de Gaulle have turned against his disciples and blamed them for continuing in his footsteps, unless he himself had turned against the tradition of disobedience for honour's sake? The hero of 18 June 1940 must think that he has a monopoly on such actions, and that he is the only one qualified to judge when they are justified and when they are not. The men who were his spiritual heirs were thrown into gaol or killed, when they tried to imitate his example.

General Salan had the reputation of being a good Republican general, who believed in the Republic and in discipline, and who always identified honour with military obedience. An attempt was made on his life and he escaped by a miracle; but his close associate, Commander Rodier, was killed. The FLN wanted to get rid of him precisely because he was so loyal to France.

I will not repeat all the accusations which were made against the men who fought in the OAS. Anyone who has had a taste of public life knows pretty well who is above reproach and who is not. As everyone knows, the Gaullists have the reputation of not being above reproach from the legal point of view; over the years, they have also acquired the reputation of not being financially above reproach either. I know that this is true; otherwise, I would not say it.

Although the court which tried Salan had been specially selected, it did not give Salan the death penalty as de Gaulle had wanted.

During the trial, documents written by the OAS leader were produced to prove his guilt. These documents, taken in their most
literal sense, could be considered a technical proof of guilt, although
they had been written in the heat of the moment and were just as
legal as the Constitution. The State may always seem to have
legality on its side; but there are times when it acts against the
interests of the nation, against the people it is meant to govern, and
against the achievements of that people. When this happened
during the Middle Ages, Joan of Arc invoked a higher law against
the established order, as Antigone did in antiquity.

A man who has risked everything without calculating the costs
to himself deserves to be heard. General Salan forfeited his long-
standing reputation for being the sort of man who would never set
off on any wild adventure. Salan, sixty years old, general in the
army, covered with medals and glory, deliberately gave up the
comforts of his home, the luxury, the flattery and the honours
which surrounded him, and the prospect of an honourable retirement. He set off into the wilderness, finding shelter where he could,
always fearing arrest by the army and the police to whom he had
once given orders, and not even possessing the proper weapons
with which to fight effectively. The man who can do that deserves
to be believed. A man like that, who has risked and lost everything
he has earned in his lifetime, does not deserve the abuse and the
slander of servile conformists who risk nothing. Salan's gesture was
far more difficult, more dangerous and more full of trials than
de Gaulle's was in 1940. He needed far more courage and had to
be far less calculating to set off on foot towards an unknown
destiny than de Gaulle, who left in General Spears' aeroplane, and
who knew that London and the BBC awaited him.

12

Algeria in Ruins /
The Return to the
Catacombs /
The Slaughter

I may be far away but the French newspapers I do receive cannot
completely hide the truth about Algeria. Through them I find out
what has happened there. Nasser and Chou-En-Lai cannot be
considered biased in favour of colonialism, yet they both agreed
that the French had left Algeria in perfect condition. The 'scorched
earth' was not scorched at all. A certain amount of destruction was
done right at the end by those who were fighting back in legitimate
defence; but it was nothing compared to the damage which has
been done since then by expropriation, carelessness and the total
incompetence of the pretentious Ben Bella régime. The new
régime is responsible for what happened to the ports, the railways,
the roads, the telephones and the buildings of Algeria, which was
once, except for South Africa, the most modern country in the
continent.

It is useless trying to claim that all these things were built with
Arab slave labour. There were only two million Arab 'slaves'
when we arrived in 1830. When we left, there were ten million.
There would never have been any complications if we had kept
the Arab population down to the number there was in Bugeaud's
time. French 'colonialism' increased the 'native' population, unlike many other colonial systems which either eliminated the local
inhabitants or else assimilated them by force. Bugeaud's Algeria,
Jules Ferry's Tunisia and Lyautey's Morocco could have been
preserved indefinitely, if the Arabs had been kept in a state of

economic and social stagnation. Anyway, even if Algeria had the right to take back all that French money and French efforts had achieved, the fact remains that Ben Bella and his followers have been totally unable to preserve Algeria's wealth. The situation there is growing worse all the time. The OAS did not ruin Algeria. Algeria run by Algerians ruined itself.

A general called Gardy in Oran had fought for the French flag and for the promises he had been asked to make by the central government. When he refused to give up his flag or to go back on his word, the government took away his stars and his medals. I only hope that Gardy, who is now an outlaw and in exile, has found asylum somewhere while he waits for his suffering to end.

In the same city, another officer, General Katz, was called a paragon of law and order by the French newspapers, which were enslaved by the government and lived in terror of the authorities. I suppose that Katz acquired this reputation by firing with cannon and heavy machine-guns at balconies draped in French flags, when the red and white and blue of the tricolour became illegal in the French province of Algeria. Later Katz was promoted and even received a special mention praising his humanity and his moderation. The French took a very long time to realize that they were being made to see everything upside down: they were being told that the hero was a murderer and that the murderer was a hero. General Gardy is not to blame for the fact that Oran is now a ghost town. President Ben Bella is the one to blame, and recently he saw the crowds which used to cheer him turn into demonstrations against unemployment. People shouted 'Long live France' on those days as they had always done; but these things are not mentioned in Paris any more.

Another symbol of the tragic end of French Algeria was the shooting incident in the rue d'Isly in Algiers. An unarmed and non-violent crowd, which was silent except for a few cries of 'Vive la France', was mowed down at close range by regular French army troops. Those troops had suddenly become uncontrollable; they were seized with a kind of blood lust at the prospect of an imminent FLN victory, and they killed between sixty and eighty people, which is three times more than the number who died on 6 February 1934, in the shooting which horrified all Paris, even the Communists. The slaughter at the rue d'Isly was so horrible that the 'great' and 'generous' French régime did not allow a detailed report to be published. After the shooting on 6 February, a full enquiry was made and endless debates and eye-witness accounts were published. But the witnesses at the rue d'Isly massacre were not allowed to speak. No enquiry was made about it or about the whole Algerian tragedy. The details were kept a secret, while cowards approved of everything that the men at the top said or did. While the Frenchmen of Algeria desperately tried to fight against the concerted efforts of the French army and the Arab rebels, not one liberal, not one progressive, humanist or fervent believer in human rights and human dignity ever raised his voice to defend those who had trusted not only de Gaulle but Mendès-France, Mitterand and Guy Mollet as well. The liberals spoke only on one subject: tortures and atrocities, which I will also discuss.

Obviously, all tortures and all atrocities are equally wrong, whichever side practises them. Yet the men who have had the courage to say this can be counted on the fingers of one hand.

Perhaps it is against the interest of the 'wind of history' and the spiritual progress of mankind to go over all these events. Our ideologists no longer have any principles; but one simple fact remains which no one can deny: Algeria did *not* win its independence. The French army, under General de Gaulle's orders, snatched Algeria out of the hands of the French Algerians.

Now Algeria flirts with Cuba, Peking and Moscow. It has its own diplomats, ambassadors, congresses and UN delegation, and France pays for it all. But apart from this window-dressing, Algeria has nothing to show. The majority goes hungry, the minor civil servants have very little, and the men at the summit live in luxury for all their affectations of austerity. It won't be the first time that a government pretends to be very frugal, hiding behind a military uniform. The Algerian government has been a failure at home and it makes up for this by giving advice abroad. It passes the time with border quarrels or disputes over protocol. It argues with its neighbours who gave shelter to the FLN soldiers during Algeria's war for independence and follows de Gaulle's example of showing total ingratitude towards those who were its supporters once. France cannot complain about ingratitude since it was the French leader who taught the Arabs to act in this way.

A million Frenchmen have left Algeria or rather have been chased away. They were deported by their own government which did not hesitate to turn a million people out of their homes. After

two years of independence, who will dare to say that if the Frenchmen of Algeria had not obeyed the OAS, they would have been
able to go on living in Algeria by giving up their French nationality? Not all those million Frenchmen went back to France to be
badly received by a suspicious government. Some preferred to go
elsewhere and to wait until the day that justice will be done.

As for those who went back to France (it must never be forgotten
that a million people were involved in the exodus), you can still
read a regular column in *Aurore* of French Algerians who are looking for missing relatives. In July 1962, one minister who shall
remain nameless dared to call this list a normal lost-and-found
column for 'holiday makers'. This noble euphemism is indeed
worthy of the French government and it should go down in the
history of falsehoods.

The French tax-payers who pay for Ben Bella's frequent journeys
to Moscow and elsewhere must remember that France's loyal,
honest and advantageous Algerian policies have had only one
result: we now subsidize an ex-convict who won the Lenin prize
and is a hero in the Soviet Union.

Only fifty thousand Frenchmen, at the most, remain in Algeria.
Every day more leave in spite of all the efforts that France makes
to find new recruits to go over there. They are trying to send
French teachers to Algeria now, although the Teachers' Unions
did not want their teachers to be forced to go and teach there when
Algeria was still French. But whatever anybody does, the people
who have stayed behind and the newcomers as well soon want to
get away. The French government pays a handsome salary to anyone willing to live in Algeria; but it still finds that people are very
reluctant to make the move, even professional anti-colonialists who
are all for decolonization as long as they can stay in Paris and don't
have to go and encourage the underdeveloped people personally.
Besides, even if they actually go there, they find it hard to stay.
They are constantly insulted; all their possessions are appropriated
both in the city and in the country. Life is continually frustrating
for those who work there. To make things worse, the Algerian
government insists that all salaries be payed in dinars and not in
francs. However determined a man may be to love Algeria, which
must be marvellous *a priori* since it is no longer French, he just
cannot put up with the conditions. Even those who thoroughly
approved of forcing the *colons* to choose between a coffin and a

suitcase now pack their own cases to avoid the coffin and quickly lose all their illusions.

Nothing, or practically nothing, is left of the absurd and infamous Evian agreements. The only link that is left between France and Algeria was not mentioned in the Evian agreements; that link is the almost limitless funds which France pours into Algerian Algeria. We are not even helping an underdeveloped country, we are only helping a country to grow more underdeveloped. But the cost does not matter and we put up with the snubs too, just so long as we can go on pretending that the French government's policy did not ruin Algeria. Even a really humiliating failure does not matter as long as you refuse to admit the fact. But you cannot go on hiding it for ever, and eventually people must find out that it was a disaster for France, that even those who benefited got practically nothing and actually lost in some cases, and that the Free World has suffered yet another blow.

But the awful thing is that there were other people besides the French, who were at least able to flee back to their ungrateful country. There were other people besides those who are leaving now, after waiting until the very last minute before finally admitting that life in Algeria has become impossible. There were the people who just disappeared. It would be ridiculous to believe the false figures supplied by the Prince de Broglie. The truth is that there are still Frenchmen and Frenchwomen in Algeria today, who have never been traced except in a few cases. The men are in prisons doing the most exhausting sort of hard labour. The women are in special brothels for *fellaghas*. And if any have got away from those prisons or those brothels, it is only because they are dead, as no one ever went to their help.

Yes, these things do happen. One can appreciate the true worth of a régime which thinks only of its citizens and its friends, and which would never even dream of practising the motto *civis romanus sum*. But only pedants these days invoke Rome or even French kings like Charles x. Just before he was overthrown, Charles x gave us a vast province, a 'New African France', which was the 'last conquest of the White Flag'. Before they decided to stop teaching history in schools and to teach only economic and social affairs, French children all learned how the conquest of Algeria began when the Bey of Algiers hit the French Consul with a fly-swatter. We all know how, under the great Gaullist régime, the French Consul was treated by a mob in the streets of Algiers. This time the blow with the fly-swatter was effective, for the Consul left. He went back to some minor post in France, and no one protested indignantly, no one wrote anything about the incident, no one fired a shot. In fact, there was no outcry of any sort; we simply went on paying Ben Bella's hordes, as we will go on doing until the régime changes.

We give money to those hordes not out of generosity or philanthropy, not even as a long-term investment. We are told that our gifts are in the noble spirit of French generosity, that we are helping the Algerian veterans who fought at Verdun and Cassino (they never get any of the money), and that we are giving a helping hand to our ex-Empire. We are even told that it is in our interest not to allow Africa 'to sink into chaos', and are reminded of Lenin's prophecy, 'Africa will bring about the downfall of Europe.' The advocates of the present French régime repeat this nonsense *ad nauseam* to make us forget that it is the régime which deliberately created all the ills that it is now doing everything it can to cure with money. The French, who have such a reputation for shrewdness, must remember that the Gaullists have gone back on their word twice; the first time when they promised to keep Algeria French, the second time when they said that France would pull out of Algeria completely and stop giving it foreign aid.

France is only paying to conceal the total failure of de Gaulle's Algerian policy. It is becoming harder and harder to do this because others are beginning to compete with us for the privilege; not because giving money is a good investment under Ben Bella's government, but because Algeria is a vital strategic point. So that we have to pay more and more all the time, while it becomes less and less profitable all the time. That, of course, is what always happens when you leave a government in the hands of blackmailers and give them every opportunity to practise their trade.

Ben Bella comes on visits to the Château des Champs and makes France pay for his entire budget: since our departure, Algeria has had no source of income whatsoever, except for the oil wells which we discovered, and the loans by other countries (including England) which the Algerians take to show de Gaulle that he is loved for himself alone and not just for his money: the general always likes to hear that. But this does not stop the Algerian leader from being absolutely determined to eliminate all traces of France from his country and to worship at the altars of Communism. He may be de Gaulle's favourite, but to him, de Gaulle is nothing but a rich backer who has to go on giving or else admit failure. Huge sums are thrown away, although France never hears about them; but the Algerians do not feel any gratitude or sense of obligation. It can even be rather pleasant to double-cross a benefactor when you are completely sure of him. But your heart belongs to another, perhaps Fidel Castro, whom Ben Bella claims to love 'unconditionally' (an expression he borrowed from de Gaulle), or Nikita Khrushchev when the Algerian head of state went to Moscow, or Chou-En-Lai when the latter comes on a visit to Algiers. This does not stop Ben Bella from feeling very friendly towards France, and the French government has decided that this is exactly how it should be. Pompidou may declare in Paris that 'everyone's patience has its limits', but as everyone knows, the Prime Minister's only function is to make speeches to which no one pays any attention. Nothing has ever come of Pompidou's firm words.

Besides, when our 'brother' Ben Bella courts Moscow and Peking, he basically agrees with de Gaulle, although his way of doing things may be different and his speeches can be a trifle embarrassing.

The Algerian government occasionally drops hints about crisp American dollar-bills, when it wants the French to give more francs. Our American allies were as delighted when Algeria got its independence as they were back in 1830 when Algeria was placed under French domination. How long will they take to realize that Ben Bella is the most dangerous of all the African imitators of Fidel Castro, and that he is a threat to the Mediterranean nations just as Cuba is a threat to the nations of Latin America? Because of the Sahara, Algeria is potentially twenty or even fifty times as powerful as Cuba, and the only difference between these two countries is that Algeria is not as close to Florida. General de Gaulle suddenly stopped noticing that Algeria was very close to Marseilles, and he made the danger of having such a neighbour even worse by giving up Bizerta recently as well as Mers-el-Kébir.

The Return to the Catacombs

Algerian Algeria became a Communist bridgehead as soon as it was made into a People's Republic; but even that is not so bad. There are already plenty of Communist bridgeheads on the African continent, without counting all the countries which are still in the process of changing over. The Moscow-Peking quarrel has not prevented them from multiplying; they merely receive aid from both Communist rivals at the same time. The United Nations must think that there aren't enough bridgeheads as it is and that Communism in Africa is not progressing fast enough. Maybe that is why it is doing all it can to create yet another Communist stronghold in Angola.

But Algeria is much more than a bridgehead, it is already an empire which hesitates between Moscow, Peking and anarchy. And this empire is a threat to black Africa towards the South and to the Arab world 'from the Atlantic to the Persian Gulf'. The vast territory of Algeria which used to be securely controlled by the French, who were then fervent adherents of the Atlantic Pact, is now a tremendous potential threat; it is large enough both in size and in population to take any risks it chooses. The subaltern officer who now rules Algeria pretends to be a faithful disciple of Mohammed; but I suspect him of being far more a disciple of Lenin. His Russian or Chinese advisers, who may soon be his masters, will always be on hand to help him in his ambitions. The white-skinned Russians may quarrel with the yellow-skinned Chinese; but they are all reds under the skin.

The Algerians themselves realize perfectly well what is happening to their country. In spite of its independence – not won by heroic efforts, but received from the hands of a few irresponsible Frenchmen – Algeria has remained French, far more French than even we ourselves could have imagined. About a thousand Algerians leave Algeria every day to find work and to get medical treatment in the capitalist and imperialist country of France. All the aeroplane and boat tickets are booked three weeks in advance, and the steady stream of would-be emigrants is not diminishing; if the seats on aeroplanes were free, there would soon be no one left in Algeria except for the old men, the glorious army of liberation (which fought safely from within Tunisia), and the government.

That is the 'honourable' and 'advantageous' settlement, so 'worthy of France' and 'unexpected', admired by the entire world and looked upon as a unique achievement which could only have been brought about by de Gaulle. At a congress of FLN veterans in Algiers, during the spring of 1964, the true situation was shown up during one of the 'themes' that were discussed *in camera*, when someone said: 'The colonial system has given the Algerian people consumer habits which bear no relation to the actual potential of the country.' A régime which has failed so ignominiously cannot survive long for all its posturing, however indulgently it is treated by everyone.

Nearly everything connected with France and Christianity has been eliminated in North Africa. This proves to anyone who believes in past greatness and noble memories that Frenchmen (or at least those who speak in France's name) must be very corrupt to tolerate the defiling of all these relics without protest. The statues were first mutilated and then removed. The Algerians finally realized that the French soldiers who were still stationed in North Africa might object to such mutilations, and so they decided to knock down all the statues to which the *fellaghas* had taken offence.

Bugeaud's statue was unceremoniously taken down and tucked away somewhere in a corner of France without any reinauguration; de Gaulle had constantly invoked Bugeaud's name during the war, but still the government preferred to re-erect the statue without any fuss, as though there were something rather nasty about the whole thing. Not long ago, there were still four statues of Joan of Arc in Algeria waiting in a warehouse to be sent back to France. Obviously, France does not need any more statues of a 'seditious' saint like Joan of Arc. The French government made it quite clear that it did not want to pay for the cost of bringing the statues of Joan back to France, or any other statues for that matter. Of course, no one said anything about the billions France sends to Ben Bella to pay for his trips to Moscow. If a shipping company wants to ship the statues back to France discreetly and free of charge, the government will be kind enough not to refuse to accept them.

The Christian cemeteries have been ploughed under. This has the dual advantage of eradicating all traces of Christianity and of making any sort of enquiry into the fate of people who have disappeared much more difficult. It will be almost impossible to trace their tombs, or even their bones, and time will soon erase all compromising clues.

The cathedrals have been turned into mosques. The 'defeat of Saint Augustine' advocated by a Tunisian weekly (the editor,

Robert Barrat, was a Christian Progressive) is becoming more and more certain every day. Why keep the cathedrals, now that there aren't any Christians left to attend mass, and now that the Algerian state is officially a Moslem and Marxist 'People's Republic'? This question was raised by Hervé Bourges, the ex-editor of *Témoignage Chrétien*, who is now one of Ben Bella's leading collaborators. But the distinguished position of collaborator is always precarious, as another ex-editor of *Témoignage Chrétien* could tell M. Bourges: he was always a fervent partisan of the FLN, but even so he was thrown out of his job as rector of Algiers University and then fired from his teaching post altogether.

I feel no sympathy for those honorary *fellaghas*, any more than I feel sorry for any of the traitors whom France did not put in prison (France preferred to keep its gaols for French patriots). But I do feel sorry for the country of Algeria which has been wrecked and ruined; I suddenly remember a curious episode which took place on 14 July 1940, at the POW camp of Mecklenburg, during the saddest, most hopeless hours of the war. A mass was celebrated in camp and a huge crowd attended the ceremony, for, as everyone knows, churches fill up when times are hard. I remember noticing two negro soldiers praying not far from me, and also a group of about fifty Algerians. They behaved neither well nor badly; but I was extremely surprised to see them there. Afterwards I went over to their leader to ask why they had attended the mass, and he simply answered, 'We're Frenchmen just like you.' Now the Algerians no longer go to mass, and they have changed flags. They have been told that they aren't Frenchmen any more, yet many of them feel a secret nostalgia for France and all of them are suffering from the consequences of our withdrawal.

In the old days of French anti-clericalism, some administrators thought that they were showing a spirit of independence when they claimed that the Moslem religion was a good antidote to Communist infiltration in the Arab world. The Catholic Church itself has always been reticent and even timid on the subject of Islamic expansion. This expansion is due to the fact that the Moslem faith is not very demanding, and that it is really more a party than a religion. And indeed, it was very difficult to explain to the Arabs, whose holy book makes no distinction between religion and the state, that in Western countries, the state decrees that religion and the law must be completely separated. Recently, the Catholic Church has become so diffident that many Christians are just as bewildered as the Moslems.

A French cardinal once said to me at the beginning of the Algerian rebellion, 'Whatever you do, don't proselytize.' There were some Moslem workers in his diocese. I still find this attitude extremely shocking, especially when I remember the words of the Gospel: 'Go forth throughout the world and preach the Gospel to every living thing' (Mark, XVI, 15). The successors of the apostles think that they will seem over-zealous if they spread the Gospel, although this is the essence of their mission; therefore I am not surprised that there are still so many infidels left. Some of today's theologians claim that the Church must be modernized and brought up to date. If that is so, they had better ban the Gospel which teaches us that the Church must not adapt itself to the times, but that the times must adapt themselves to the Church.

The reason I have brought this up is that the Archbishop of Algiers, Mgr Duval, overlooked the fact that the decision to separate Church and State would mean a state take-over of all ecclesiastical functions. Thus it was his duty to denounce this take-over of purely religious matters by civil law. Instead Mgr Duval anticipated the government by offering to make an outright gift of the cathedral of Algiers to the Islamic faith. In spite of the ecumenical spirit which pervades the Vatican today, the attitude that all religions are the same and equal in the eyes of God is not compatible with the thousand-year-old doctrine of the Catholic Church: *unam, sanctam, catholicam, apostolicam, Ecclesiam.*

One of the sequels to this surrender got very little publicity, because, I suppose, nothing must be allowed to harm the noble and lofty cause of progress. When the cathedral was hastily converted into a mosque, the coffins of the first bishop and the first archbishop of Algiers were left behind. The two coffins were present when prayers were sent up to Islam proclaiming the 'victory of Mohammed over Saint Augustine', as those two scoundrels, Ben Bella and Bourguiba, would say. Of course some people may say that the spirit of the Crusaders is an anachronism, but that is no excuse for leaving the bones of two successors of the first apostles as hostages to a Moslem Republic. They were finally remembered and men took away the corpses during the night like body-snatchers.

The Slaughter

Apart from the French money which has been paid not to the people of Algeria, but to the military caste and to the training camps which send out guerrillas to Angola and Israel and Morocco, and possibly Europe, France no longer plays any role in Algerian national life. Of course, it did leave the Algerians roads, railways, ports, buildings and an irrigation network, and good riddance to the lot! Including the oil reserves these assets are worth between 100 and 160 billion dollars, which is five to eight times France's annual budget. The only signs of French occupation left are what France spent there once and what it continues to spend there without any limit or control. All traces of France have been stamped out, so that the régime no longer even tolerates bad Frenchmen, those traitors who wholeheartedly endorsed the cause of those who wanted to destroy freedom and civilization. I must admit that the one consolation for all the tragedy and stupidity of Algeria has been the way those blind fanatics have been thrown out by the FLN. Those backward apostles of progress gave their services to the most sordid rackets, including prostitution; but now that there are several thousand Algerian pimps in Paris alone, no one needs them any more. These traitors now live quite comfortably in France; none of them have been exiled or imprisoned. They are not even worthy of persecution, and the FLN, which is not a racist but merely a nationalist and Communist party, soon realized that traitors can never be trusted and that the safest thing is to get rid of them once they have outlived their use.

The Algerians got rid of all things French, even when they were profitable. When Ben Bella was in the Crimea on his way to Moscow, he had the names of 213 streets in Algiers changed to wipe out the last traces of colonialism. Just for good measure, he also got rid of a few Roman and Turkish names. Algerian history began on 1 November 1954, when a schoolteacher called Monnerot was assassinated. The streets which have lost their names will all be named after heroes of the rebellion, so let us hope that the murderer of Monnerot will not be forgotten and that the murderers of the 320 men and women and children at Melouza will also have their street names.

The saddest thing of all was the murder of the *harkis* after

Algeria received its independence. The *harkis* were veterans and young soldiers who had fought on the side of France and had remained loyal to the French flag. By doing so they ran many risks; the long list of those who died during the revolt (most were killed in ambush) shows that they were always the chief targets of resentment and hatred. In Algiers, and in Paris too, the deeds of the FLN terrorists are still celebrated, and only the OAS is ever called a terrorist organization. The terrorist acts of the FLN are always called heroic feats.

People will say that the truth is always complex, and I agree. But there are certain facts which are clear and simple and undeniable. It is those facts which the French press has always refused to discuss and which it avoids mentioning today just as it always did. For example, a very active and influential leader of the FLN, Belkacem Krim, once said in public that every man who wanted to belong to the FLN had to have committed at least one terrorist act. In other words, every member of the FLN had to be a criminal by definition. But that fact was never publicized, and the FLN guerrillas were given a hearty welcome everywhere they went in Western Europe and in the United States. Of course, Belkacem Krim has since been disgraced, which is one of the occupational hazards of working for that sort of régime; but that does not alter anything, for he created a precedent which has flourished.

De Gaulle's Algerian policy subtly changed by degrees. At first, people spoke only of 'a brave man's peace', and said, 'de Gaulle will never tolerate anything else.' Then there was 'the white flag', then 'the knives in the lobby', and the 'tour round the Army canteens'. Then came the 'tour of Algerian Algeria'. Although the whole affair was hushed up, it became known that some genuine delegates from the Algerian *maquis* had come to Paris to ask for an armistice; they were weary of the fighting and had been ordered to make overtures by those Algerian rebels who remained at a safe distance. They were turned away at the Elysée, as they were getting in the way of de Gaulle's plans to abandon Algeria totally. When they returned to Algeria, they were all killed. Someone must have denounced them; I wonder who?

Finally, we reached the stage of 'disengagement', in other words, de Gaulle was ready to pull out altogether. As soon as the French abandoned everything, they began cooperating with their 'friends', in other words, their former enemies. When the French government decided to leave Algeria, the terrible problem of the *harkis* came up. These men had hopelessly compromised themselves by working for us until the very end, even after we had lost hope. There were more than one hundred thousand special delegates, civil servants, employees, and native troops who were all in danger if the rebels against whom they had fought came to power. They had fought on our side, under our orders, and the new régime would never forgive them for that. They should have all been taken back to France; but instead of doing this, the French government specifically forbade anyone to help them. In certain areas, the French took away their weapons, promising to give them better ones, and then sneaking away in the middle of the night without giving or saying anything.

As soon as de Gaulle had presented Algeria with its sovereignty, the French were ordered not to interfere in the affairs of an independent state. There were still 200,000 French soldiers in Algeria and those soldiers were armed. But their arms were to be used only on parade; the soldiers were forbidden to use them to defend their ex-companions-in-arms or even to help them to defend themselves. In some cases, the shutters had to be closed so that the French soldiers would not hear the screams of the *harkis* who were being massacred outside the barrack windows. The order was to let them scream, to let them be tortured and mutilated and plunged in boiling water, to let them be sawn in half or burned alive. These 'episodes' were unimportant and the soldiers would have to put up with them so that the French government could carry out its grand design on behalf of an Algerian Algeria, Ben Bella, decolonization, the third world, Mao and so forth.

The government had made up its mind. One day, an Algerian deputy who had believed in de Gaulle told him that many Algerians would suffer if the government gave up the struggle. De Gaulle replied, 'Well, let them suffer!' And so they suffered: over one hundred thousand Moslems were murdered after Algeria had got its independence.

If you look through the French and even the international newspapers, you will not find a single reference to this slaughter. All our outstanding thinkers have grown silent. I am still waiting for them to pretend that they have only just noticed the bloodshed which their propaganda helped to unleash. The cries of the tortured *harkis* fell on deaf ears. Men who were supposedly against all violence closed their eyes and blocked their ears. Those who dared to *say* something to excuse their silence in print, only said, 'I don't want to hear about it, it isn't true.' After all, the head of the French government, the French people, and particularly the French press, enthusiastically agreed that everything was for the best, so why should anyone have had any scruples? This was what our brave and sensitive intellectuals told themselves; one of the saddest things about this day and age is that there are so many hypocrites.

The newspaper correspondents who made such vicious attacks on the OAS and who sang the praises of the heroic FLN soon lost their passion for publicity. After Algerian independence had been declared, they kept a cautious silence, so as not to offend the 'guide of the nation'. They stayed at the Aletti bar, which was not yet nationalized, and avoided travelling around the country. The roads were dangerous and the sights they would see along the way far from appetizing. They were much better off staying in Algiers and writing articles about Ben Bella's great social revolution. They all wrote about the happiness of the Algerian people who were free at last. They preferred to wait until another nation began fighting for its independence before they set off again on new flights of rhetoric.

The international press in both the Free World and the Iron Curtain countries (they are becoming more alike every day), systematically distorted these events. The distortion of news is an art and even a science. You can alter opinions by using certain headlines, by setting type a certain way, by giving more space to some events than to others, by carefully selecting which version of the same event to print, by making insinuations and by the way you comment on the facts. You can give one item disproportionate importance and magnify what is completely insignificant. You can leave out vital details or be even more subtle and falsify everything by putting down as an incontestable fact something which is actually very debatable. You can put down what your enemies say in quotes and take out the quotes when you are setting down what your friends have said. You can use flattering adjectives for those you want to show up in a favourable light and use unflattering ones for those you want to seem evil. That is the way you change the public's opinion, particularly that of the better educated classes, the public who proudly claim that no one can pull the wool over

their eyes. All this can be done to further the interests of a particular ideology without ever defining what it is. It is quite easy
and much more effective to put across a concept of the world and
of the future without actually calling it by its real name. All you
have to do is to criticize the actions and the doctrines of which you
disapprove without referring to any political system; that will be
enough to influence public opinion which will go on believing that
you are completely impartial and objective, that you are impervious
to outside pressure, and that you are not in the pay of any party
or creed.

The end product may seem extremely well informed; but in fact
it is nothing but a tissue of ignorant lies. The truth can be distorted
indefinitely until it becomes too obvious to be denied. Unless this
happens, the public continues to believe that it is extremely well-
informed and everything it reads only confirms what it has been
led to believe is true. In the old days, a man had to read at least a
few pages of the *Littré* or the *Encyclopedia Britannica* to seem well-
read. Today, the pace is too fast; all a man has to do is to read *Le
Monde*, and, an hour later, he can parade his knowledge to his circle
of friends.

When it became obvious that the decolonization of Algeria only
meant a change of masters for the Algerians, and that the new
masters were harsher than the previous ones, the press of the Free
World deliberately applied all the methods I have just described to
conceal the truth. The press in the Iron Curtain countries never
said a word of course. The massacre of the *harkis* was hushed up
just as the massacres during the 'partition' of India and the 'liberation' of China had been. No one ever bothered to distinguish the
good victims from the bad ones, as they might have done at least in
the name of their 'wind of history'. No one even had the courage
(for, given the circumstances, it would have taken courage) to ask
like Barnave, 'Was the blood which they shed pure?' But no one
said a word, not even to claim that those who died because they had
fought for France were merely victims to progress, freedom and the
Resistance. We hear so many lies these days that this would not
have surprised me particularly.

But everyone kept silent, for weeks and months afterwards.
No one has said a word now for two years, and this alone shows
that the crimes committed in Algeria were monstrous and that
the results have been disastrous. Otherwise, there would have

been enough people around to explain and to justify de Gaulle's behaviour. None of the journalists, who would have been so indignant if the victims had been on their side and who never missed an opportunity to sing Ben Bella's praises, have mentioned the fate of the *harkis* because it was too hideous to try and justify. For once, the journalists showed their fanaticism and their lack of principles, not by what they wrote but by what they did not write.

They find it much safer to pretend ignorance. No one spoke about Hitler's gas chambers or about Stalin's concentration camps and massive purges while Hitler and Stalin were still alive. No one talks about the *harkis* today because, as in the other two cases, those who are responsible for such terrible crimes know very well that it is far safer to keep silent. Later on, when the truth comes out, as it must in spite of the concerted efforts of so many, I know very well that people will make the usual excuse, the excuse of all cowards and accomplices and criminals, 'I didn't know. I didn't want it to happen like that.'

13

Exile /
The Second CNR

I had reluctantly left France several weeks before General Salan was arrested. I was still a deputy for the Loire department, as I had been without interruption since 1945, in spite of all the national and political changes and all the alterations in the methods of election. As a deputy, I had done my best to defend the causes I felt really strongly about: social justice, the Atlantic Community, the reconstruction of Europe and French Algeria. At the beginning of 1959, I had made a speech before the Assembly recommending Algeria's total integration into the French community and a two-thirds majority had approved it. But the majority followed the government which had got its representatives elected to the Assembly and not the actual promises of that government.

Besides, the Assembly was made powerless long before it became the accomplice of the government. At first, the deputies had approved of the principles and the solutions I advocated. But later they became more and more debased, as I told them myself, and they grew hostile to what they had once praised, until they were booing what they had once cheered. Finally, I met a solid wall of organized indifference; those decadent and unscrupulous men deliberately chose to forget whatever was inconvenient. The French press was even more servile. A conspiracy of silence muffled the voices of the opposition. Cowards, conformists, defeatists and Communists joined hands, while French and Arab money bought articles in favour of the rebellion.

The Vincennes Committee was created to fight the influence of the Frenchmen who collaborated with the FLN. This organization tried to remind France of the promises it had made, of its national interest and its honour. In November 1961 this Committee held a

very successful meeting which was also its last. Jean Dides was
arrested afterwards and the Vincennes Committee had to be dissolved. Of course, the Communist party was not dissolved. The
Communists who had taken sides with Ho-Chi-Minh against
France during the Indo-Chinese war were never prosecuted. Anyway, they did not deserve to be in the same prisons as the heroes
who later fought against the régime. The government hunted down
the patriots but left the 'separatists' alone.

It was becoming more and more difficult to protest on a national
scale, and soon it became useless. I spent my time trying to
organize an effective opposition to the policies of the régime, but it
was in vain. I wanted to continue fighting in France; but my means
were growing limited. Some of my friends were losing courage
and were already thinking of seeking a compromise with the
government and with their conscience. These compromises were
completely illusory; but they made life much easier. It was also
becoming harder to find any money, for backers are not usually
idealists.

The police followed me wherever I went; but it was less interested in protecting than in watching me. I was able to throw my
guardian angels off my tracks a few times, after being warned on
the best authority that my escorts would look upon any attempt to
assassinate me quite favourably. The Issy-les-Moulineaux affair
and the kidnapping of Colonel Argoud have since shown the world
how the *barbouzes* operate (the members of de Gaulle's secret
police, many of whom are ex-criminals, have become known to the
public as *barbouzes* although their existence has been hotly denied
by some people). My little house was watched by two policemen
night and day. At night they stayed in their van warming themselves with a small heater I had lent them. They spent their entire
time taking surreptitious photographs of all my visitors, and giving
directions to passers-by who had lost their way. Well-informed
friends had warned me not to stand near my windows, to keep
away from rooms that were exposed to the street, and to wrap my
telephone in tight wads of material. I did all this, knowing very
well that the government did not have the best of intentions
towards me.

I am not the sort of man who gets frightened easily; but I knew
of the existence and methods of the *barbouzes*. Some top civil
servants and officers later swore in court that there was no such

organization, although today no one actually dares to deny their existence or their importance or their protected status under the government, not only in France but in other countries as well. Although the unmentionable has now been mentioned and recognized and acknowledged, the perjurers who swore in court that the *barbouzes* did not exist have never been prosecuted for perjury. In some cases, perjury is a crime, and it must be remembered that the French régime not only tracks down its enemies, but also influences the decisions of its friends. Therefore an impartial observer must admit that the Fifth Republic tolerates perjury when it is useful to the State. A régime is only as moral as its servants and its legislators.

I had been warned to expect some sort of action by the *barbouzes* very shortly, and so I decided to leave France. My journey abroad was perfectly legal. The Declaration of the Rights of Man stipulates that every citizen has the right to leave his country (Article 13, §2). But of course, these rights, which received so much attention recently on the fifteenth anniversary of the Declaration, are violated everywhere. Everyone knows that whenever societies feel the need to make declarations of rights, as they did after the French Revolution and the Second World War, this only means that all citizens have rights on paper that protect only the consciences of their rulers.

And so, I was making use of the rights I possessed on paper. But according to the French police, which is far more important than the Rights of Man, my papers were not in order. According to it, a duly elected representative of the people did not have the right to leave his country. The Czar or the Sultan a hundred years ago and modern totalitarian régimes in the East have always acted in this fashion. Now the Restorer of the French Republic is using the same tactics.

I went to Switzerland in March that year, and, on arriving at a hotel, I signed the register by my real name. Soon afterwards, I was amazed to discover that, although Switzerland has such a long tradition of hospitality and liberalism, the French authorities had immediately been warned of my whereabouts. After this incident, I was careful enough not to give my real name anywhere. The European nations under de Gaulle's orders would have to look for me.

Around this period I began to lead the life of a wanderer all over

EXILE   271

Europe. This existence, which was both nomadic and confined, went on for about a year; it was full of sad, painful and dangerous adventures. There were some very happy moments when I had meetings with the handful of brave men who gave me back my faith in France; but there were also many incidents which were extremely trying, both physically and morally. There were many annoyances and problems that bore little relation to the 'ushers, telephones and gilded mouldings', which were once meant to be my masters.

I am not a vengeful man and I do not wish this sort of existence on any of the men who are now in power. Most of them are not made for a life which is so insecure, so unrewarding and so lacking in pomp. But I do want those men to know that I am certain that their hour of reckoning will come and I find it oddly gratifying to watch their satisfaction and security from afar, while I am leading a miserable and hunted existence. I am not exceptionally stoical and I might not have started out on so many adventures if I had really believed that the cause I fought for was irretrievably lost. But I know that the present régime will soon be overthrown and that is why I find it amusing to watch de Gaulle's men from a distance, acting so smugly and confidently. I regret nothing and I would do it all over again if I had my life to relive. And I enjoy seeing the complacency of those in power, when I know that any of them can end up as I did, living a hard and sad life in exile.

I did not go to England in a British government plane, and when I did reach England there was no reception for the author of the Treaty of Dunkirk which Bevin had signed with me and for which Churchill had thanked me. I did not go to Spain in a sleeper with a passport issued to me by the government I intended to fight: Franco prefers Couve de Murville to me and probably even prefers André Malraux, although I never belonged to the international brigades which fought in Spain. Konrad Adenauer was a realist and so he sacrificed me to please General de Gaulle, which, according to the general, was a noble action and one which took the wind of history into account. For a second time, I was a street-corner fighter in the Resistance; I did not hide behind a microphone or in a monastery. I was banned everywhere, unlike de Gaulle, who was welcomed everywhere.

While I was hiding from the police, I visited the places where I had once been received officially and honoured. This experience is a great moral lesson which I recommend to those who revel in protocol and applause. I had obstinately defended the principle of a united Europe ever since the beginning; but I suppose it was inevitable that I should come to be treated as a public enemy in all the countries of Europe. For they were obeying the wishes of one who was the professional enemy of Europe until recently, and who, even today, systematically sabotages European unity. I had been a Resistance leader, the leader of the government and of the state, and yet my path all over Europe was strewn with stones on which I tripped three times. In this troubled age of ours, my disagreeable and dangerous fate must be considered the occupational hazard of any politician who has reached the summit of the Capitol. Only the geese are completely safe up there, which is why so many top politicians feel secure.

I was abroad when General de Gaulle asked the French people to vote in favour of his decision to abandon Algeria. We now see the disastrous results of that policy; but I would like to go over the events which led up to our final withdrawal. The French government, in other words, de Gaulle, had been having secret talks with the FLN ever since the beginning of 1961. The decision to pull out altogether had gradually taken shape, although the French government concealed this by telling endless lies and promising that France would 'never, never' consider taking such a step.

If a man does not mind contradicting himself all the time, and if he has decided to win personal fame at the expense of an entire nation and one million of his countrymen, he can make endless declarations, commit any errors, perform any ruthless tricks to achieve his ambition. He justifies himself by invoking Reason of State. Once de Gaulle had decided to give up Algeria, all he had to do was to convince the French nation that this capitulation would be a glorious and heroic feat. He broke down the resistance of the French people with endless reassuring speeches, until finally they shamelessly accepted the disaster and even learned to look upon it as an excellent solution. The French were actually grateful to de Gaulle for giving up a century of tradition, millions of their fellow-countrymen and France's honour. Because the French had no leaders worthy of the name, they accepted the peace offered to them by the president of the Fifth Republic. But it was not a 'brave men's peace' nor the peace of 'men of good will'; it was the peace of scoundrels and cowards.

De Gaulle made more and more speeches to win the confidence of the French public. He spoke on 20 March, 26 March, and 6 April. On 8 April, a large majority voted for giving up Algeria. Only 1,800,000 Frenchmen preserved their honour by voting No. Of course, the Communists all approved. If it had not been for the Communist votes, the number of those who voted Yes would have come to less than half the number of registered voters. As for the Frenchmen of Algeria, they were not allowed to vote and decide their own future.

When I reread the Evian agreements which were supposed to provide a justification for our humiliating defeat, I am amazed by the absurdity of this document. The French Constitution of 1958 is the only other document which has fallen so short of its promises. When I read the speeches of de Gaulle, Michel Debré, Louis Joxe, Christian Fouchet and even Pompidou, I am stunned by such an array of errors, of false assurances, of empty promises, and of solemn guarantees which were immediately forsaken. None of those speeches contains a word of sense. Some people say that government is the art of predicting the future well, but the present régime gives the lie to that maxim; every single one of its predictions has been false.

Once Michel Debré had accomplished his mission of going back on every single word he had ever said, he was discarded without further ado. He has nothing left to do now, except to have the occasional tantrum and parade the utter insignificance which did not prevent him from once bringing ruin to his country.

Georges Pompidou was 'summoned' by de Gaulle and made successor to Michel Debré. He took over his predecessor's task of explaining and justifying policies which he was not allowed to formulate or influence. Pompidou had had a curious career before he was appointed to the meaningless and frivolous post of being de Gaulle's prime minister. He always had a gift for adapting himself to every situation and to all the masters he happened to be serving. He had once been a Socialist and had gone almost directly from there to the Rothschild bank, from there to de Gaulle's cabinet, and finally to the post of Prime Minister. At least Pompidou has never pretended to have any principles and so he cannot be said to have betrayed them. His great talent for adapting himself to anything and to anyone makes him an ideal figurehead, particularly because he is shrewd and unscrupulous.

274 RESISTANCE

The Second CNR

I had naturally done my duty and opposed de Gaulle. The men
who now call themselves the official 'opposition' to de Gaulle are
in fact nothing but accomplices of his régime. From my exile I
sent out a message asking the people of France to vote against the
surrender of Algeria and declaring the creation of a second National
Council of the Resistance. I claim the honour of having created
the second CNR; but it was not I who sent out the orders which
accompanied my message; they had, in fact, probably been written
by General Salan. I did not approve of those orders and they
became poignantly ironic when Salan was arrested, as he was supposed to have ordered the arrest of all the ministers of the Fifth
Republic. I agreed with Salan's arguments and with his conclusion
that de Gaulle's government was illegal; but I also felt that
the document was not appropriately worded for that particular
crisis.

I was, and I still am, in complete agreement with Salan's theory
that a government which abandons an Empire and the French
Union and which tolerates the loss of an entire province, is an
illegal government because it is unworthy to rule. But everyone
has the right not to feel responsible for what he has not written,
signed or personally approved. I stress this point because later I
was accused of being the author of that document. Of course, I
don't care about unfounded accusations, and I am only emphas-
izing this point for the record. This does not mean that I dissociate
myself in any way from the authors of the documents attributed
to me in court. I am on the side of the Resistance, of all the
victims and the martyrs, alive or dead, who refused to abandon
hope.

I can obviously not describe everything in this book. Until the
situation in France changes and the special police departments
which serve the general everywhere are dissolved, until they stop
mercilessly hunting down anyone accused of subversion or merely
of hostility to the President, I cannot set down anything here which
might be added to the files of the police, which are thick enough
already as it is. I would make myself the accomplice of the police
if I gave any information which might lead to the persecution of
some of my friends. And, as everything I did as head of the second

CNR could be used against those who look upon the Resistance as the supreme authority, I will have to wait until better times to describe what my friends and I were able to do together.

Do not expect me to disown anybody, even if, as happened a few times, my CNR colleagues and I were held responsible for acts which we knew nothing about or which we may even have regretted. All I can say is that we never committed or advised others to commit any crimes. My conscience is clear on that issue. In spite of all the problems and difficulties I have never been more positive that I was doing my duty. It was not easy to give orders, as communications were slow and dangerous, and the orders were sometimes mixed up by the time they reached their destination. But given the means at our disposal and the ideals which we served, I am convinced that we acted as best we could, both in word and deed. My actions since 1962 will never give me the least pang of remorse; my comrades after the disaster were the purest and the noblest and the most disinterested that I have ever met. Those men faced exile, solitude and slander calmly and resolutely without bitterness.

This does not mean to say that the men who sacrificed themselves for a noble cause did not also commit a few mistakes and even a few excesses. We all know that this has always been the case, given human nature. During the war, the Resistance shed quite a lot of blood, some of it innocent. The most noble battles were marred by excesses; the Crusades cannot be called models of humanitarianism; Joan of Arc and Bayard were not able to eliminate all horrors from war, although they tried to limit them. Not to mention the wars of the Vendée and the Revolutionary Terror; not to mention the October Revolution and the great Lenin (who may be the hero of the intellectuals but who was just as inhuman as Stalin); not to mention the Commune which is celebrated every year by professional enemies of violence who enthusiastically justify the crimes which were committed during this supposedly Left-Wing uprising; not to mention the Spanish Civil War which was drowned 'in flames and blood' as Francisque Gay put it in his pamphlet on the atrocities committed in Albacete, Barcelona and elsewhere; yet I might add that the 'non-violent' tactics of Gandhi and Nehru were responsible for the deaths of several million people who were soon forgotten by 'world opinion'.

I have demonstrated that, although the desperate fight for

French Algeria may have been disorderly, it actually comes off far
better than most of the struggles which are so lovingly described
in the history books. In all my personal experience and in my
historical research, I have never come across such a record of
sacrifices in the face of such odds. And the sacrifices were made
by those who fought for French Algeria; whereas most fighters
have sacrificed the enemy, these men only sacrificed themselves.
Algerian Algeria and the men of Evian were responsible for the
bloodshed, not us.

I knew perfectly well that the French government would react
when I created a National Council of Resistance. The first step
they took was to persuade the Assembly to lift my immunity as a
member of parliament. To do this, they relied mainly on the
evidence of a letter which Salan had written to me and which was
found in the possession of André Canal when the latter was
arrested. I have often wondered whether de Gaulle would feel
guilty if a letter from me addressed to him were found in the
pocket of a third person.

I knew very well that if I spoke in my own defence at the
Assembly, I would probably be arrested when I left the Palais-
Bourbon. I had no desire to go to prison, because I do not trust
the prisons of the present régime, and because a prisoner can no
longer do anything, not even write articles. My ex-colleague,
Pierre Mahias, a deputy for the Loir-et-Cher department, read my
defence to the Assembly. In it, I acknowledged certain actions
which had been attributed to me and denied others that I had not
committed. I tried, once again, to demonstrate to Parliament that
it was in a sorry shape and that the Constitution was being violated
every day. I explained that if the members of the Assembly voted
against me, this would mean that they accepted governmental
purges. The Minister of Justice was unable to show by what
jurisdiction I should lose my parliamentary immunity and what
the government would do to me if this happened. He merely said
that steps would be taken against me.

On 15 July 1962, my parliamentary immunity was lifted by 241
votes to 72. At the time, the Assembly had 480 members, which
means that, although 241 members voted against me, 239 voted for
me or abstained. During the previous decade, I had always lost by
one or two votes in this fashion; in 1953, when René Mayer's government was overthrown, I received 313 votes when I needed 314

to become head of government. In April 1958, the MRP followed
the example of Pierre Pflimlin, Pierre-Henri Teitgen, Robert
Buron and Maurice Schumann and refused to support the government of its 'honorary president and founder' by twenty-eight votes
to twenty-five with two members abstaining, thus preventing me
from getting the parliamentary majority I needed. This particular
vote precipitated the events which led to the *putsch* of 13 May, and
three of the four men I have just mentioned eventually joined de
Gaulle's government. At the beginning of July 1962, 102 Algerian
office-holders including sixty-eight deputies had been eliminated
from the government. Although they were duly elected, General de
Gaulle arbitrarily put an end to their mandate. It was therefore a
rump parliament which sat in judgement on me.

The majority of those who voted against me were Communists,
Socialists and members of the UNR. Those same UNR members
had once given me a standing ovation; I suppose they were trying
to make de Gaulle forgive them for this by voting against me. The
Communists had always voted against me, and as for the Socialists,
they are consistently inconsistent; they called de Gaulle a Fascist
in May 1958, but, two weeks later, Guy Mollet joined the government. Therefore I don't see why I should take their votes too
seriously, since they never do. There were a few men in the UNR
and in the SFIO who obeyed their conscience and did not vote
against me; the members of the MRP all abstained, including
Pierre Mahias.

I was interested to see that a certain number of those who voted
against me were men who had been on friendly terms with me in
the past. But this did not sadden me, as I had expected it anyway.
Some were men with whom I had had to keep in touch, and I was
delighted when their vote put an end to any obligations I might
once have felt. I am grateful to those who voted for me and had the
courage not to bend in the direction of the wind of change; but I
am also grateful to those who severed all past ties. They did me a
favour; now, I don't ever have to think about them again. *Nec
nominentur inter nos.* (René Pleven and Claudius-Petit pretend not
to understand Latin.)

I finally learned through an article in *L'Express* that General
Salan had appointed me his successor as head of the OAS.
L'Express must be on good terms with the police; it accused the
Minister of the Interior, Roger Frey, of personally ordering the

arrest of Colonel Argoud, but soon retracted; although there were rumours that the police would prosecute the magazine this never occurred, doubtless because of its good connections. I never received the letter which appointed me head of the OAS and I therefore never gave orders in the OAS's name. Later, leaflets with the heading OAS-CNR were printed; but I have always regretted that this was done and I gave instructions for it to be stopped which were never followed.

Even so, I have always preferred men of action to men who do nothing. I hope no one will accuse me of ever having disowned a man whose heart was in the right place, even when he committed clumsy actions or just because he was unlucky. As for funds of one hundred million francs which I received according to *L'Express*, I never got them. It seems an enormous sum to a man as poor as myself. De Gaulle must be more naïve than I supposed if he really believes that the National Council of the Resistance received all that money. I am certainly not living on the 'billions' and the 'loot' of the OAS, and all my companions in exile are just as poor. The dry bread I eat in exile is buttered only by my friends.

I accept the full responsibility for the second National Council of the Resistance which I created in the spirit of the first.

I admit that this did not delight everybody, particularly those pseudo-members of the first Resistance who had done nothing during the war. These had decided retrospectively that they too had been members, solely because the real Resistance members, including myself, had treated them quite kindly after the war. These men spoke boldly of the 'pseudo-CNR' in newspapers like the *Barbier* and thought they were being very clever because they were slinging mud at a man they had once worshipped. They were busy worshipping elsewhere, so that they needed a scapegoat. Jackals like to howl along with the wolves.

But, leaving that breed aside, there were also some genuine ex-Resistance members who had really fought in the war and who were displeased when I resurrected the Resistance, although the aims of the second CNR were identical to those of the first. Let's admit it; a lot of old fighters had retired. Some of them had joined the régime, others were so-called liberals or Socialists who were in favour of any backward nationalism as long as it called itself anti-colonialism, and especially when it was hostile to France. These old fighters' opposition to Marshal Pétain had given them the habit of being against traditional values. They still felt the urge to fight against something and so they turned against France, forgetting the aims of their first struggle. They had become enemies of French Algeria because this was their idea of progress. Time, cowardice and outside pressure had turned them into the allies of the government and they now fought not for but against the interests of their country.

There were also many who felt that the struggle could not and ought not to be fought again. Their memories of the Resistance were too glorious and too special for them to start again. They wanted the Resistance to remain a museum piece at the Invalides, and what they loved about it was its uniqueness. They were getting older, and this made them reluctant to add an Odyssey to their Iliad. They could not bear to compromise or even, as some said, to tarnish the memory of their war exploits by repeating them. Besides, they felt that, wherever they were, they would always represent the Resistance and the interests of France. To them, the Resistance now meant avoiding complications and not disturbing the conscience of those Resistance members who had been assimilated once and for all.

The members of the Resistance who did not do anything when the French nation was amputated, who even praised this amputation and protested against those who protested, acted against the spirit which they believed they represented. I did not usurp that spirit, I merely kept it alive with the help of new companions, after the old companions had forsaken the spirit of the first Resistance, stopped fighting and surrendered.

What were the ideals of the first Resistance? I could not take the archives of the first CNR with me into exile; but I do have them somewhere, as I want to remind a few people who boasted about being members a bit too loudly during its twentieth anniversary celebration. Yet I have kept the remarkable document which was the gospel of the Resistance during the war, and which was written by no less an authority than de Gaulle himself. In fact, what the general said then is what I say today, and it is only he who has changed his opinions. For the Gaullists have sold out, and if the Resistance has not entirely sold out, they owe it to me and to those who have continued the struggle. This book, *Discours et Messages*, *1940–1946*, is a collection of the speeches which de Gaulle made during the war. It goes up to 1946 to include de Gaulle's speeches at Bayeux and Epinal, in which he already attacked those he considered unworthy of being his successors. This volume contains 747 pages in the French version, and most of them revolve around one great theme: the French Empire. The subject of the Empire comes up over and over again like a sort of Greek chorus; it is never far away from de Gaulle's thoughts.

I may add that this work, which was the handbook for the Resistance, is out of print and almost impossible to find. The collection of speeches which de Gaulle later made to the RPF is also out of print and unavailable, as it too contains declarations particularly about Algeria and all North Africa, which are just as categorical and dogmatic as the ones he made during the war. No wonder these monuments to the spirit of the Resistance have been withdrawn from circulation; they are a clear-cut condemnation of everything de Gaulle has done since then, and they clearly predict the results of policies which de Gaulle would one day carry out. And so, once the Empire had been liquidated, it was better to get rid of all that incriminating evidence.

I have only to quote a few passages out of those speeches to show the damning nature of the evidence.

On 19 June 1940, General de Gaulle said:

'All men of honour in the Africa of Clauzel, Bugeaud, Lyautey and Noguès have the strict duty to refuse to obey enemy conditions.'

During the Fifth Republic, the students of Saint-Cyr wanted to call one of their graduating classes the 'Bugeaud' class. De Gaulle did everything he could to persuade them to change it to the 'Reggane' class. His advice was not followed, and he showed his disapproval by not going to the Saint-Cyr ceremony even though it was held in the Louvre that year. The statues of Bugeaud have been torn down and shipped back to France. As for Lyautey, his coffin has also been brought back to France, although this was against his express orders in his will.

On 2 July 1940, General de Gaulle said:

'Would Dupleix, Montcalm, Bugeaud and Marshal Lyautey ever have agreed to evacuate the strategic points of the empire without a fight?'

No, they would never have agreed. But someone else agreed to surrender without a fight. Everyone knows his name.

On 30th July 1940, in London:

Frenchmen! Today I want to speak to you about our Empire. We are losing it because of the abominable armistices of June.

These abominable armistices might have been justified if they had been limited to a military agreement concerning the French mainland.

But they are totally unjustifiable and inexcusable as far as the Empire is concerned. The Empire was intact. The enemy has not even tried to attack it. But the armistices now deliver the Empire into the hands of the enemy. Our colonies are to be disarmed, our strategic points evacuated. German and Italian committees are to go there and to take over control of whatever they want. After that, without making any effort, because the French will do nothing to save their honour, their enemies will be able to take over the territories which were originally given to France by her explorers, her soldiers, her missionaries and her *colons*.

I may add that the native populations, those populations which were faithful to France, which believed in France, and which respected France, are outraged by this capitulation without a struggle for the Empire. One of the first likely consequences of these abominable armistices will be the alienation and probably the revolt of the native populations of the Empire.

I insist, in the name of France, that the French Empire must, in spite of them, remain in the possession of France.

Chief Commissioners! Governors General! Governors! Administrators! Inhabitants of our colonies and our protectorates, your duty towards France, your duty towards our colonies, your duty towards those whose interests, honour and life depend on you, consists of rejecting those abominable armistices. You are entrusted with the sovereignty of France which is at present being forsaken. . . . If necessary, I shall call upon the native populations.

Frenchmen of the new France, of Overseas France! You are free men, young men, courageous men. Be worthy of the new, free, young and courageous France which will emerge after the victory!

This was what de Gaulle asked of the new Frenchmen. This was the ideal for which the first members of the Resistance were to fight. No wonder the book cannot be found anywhere today.

On 27th August 1940, de Gaulle said:

Today, 27 August, 1940, the 360th day of the World War, I wish to single out the territory of Chad in the name of the Empire for the following reason:

Thanks to its leaders, Governor Eboué and Colonel Marchand, military commander of the territory, Chad has shown that it would remain, first and foremost, a land of brave Frenchmen.

Today, President Tombalbaye's Chad continuously seesaws between disorder and repression. It commemorates its independence with festivities that last for months and is now demanding the withdrawal of the French troops which are still quartered there according to a defence agreement between Chad and France. Tombalbaye now denounces this agreement and protests against the presence of French residents, experts and technicians. By doing this, he is talking and acting against the interests of his country; but nothing will stop the decolonizer, not even the prospect of total poverty or anarchy. De Gaulle's most poignant and personal war memories did not prevent him from sacrificing the Chad of Eboué and Leclerc to the wind of history. Things go from bad to worse in this manner when you have a leader who only remembers grudges and who changes his beliefs from day to day.

In October 1940, de Gaulle went to Léopoldville, the capital of the Congo which would still be the Belgian Congo, if it had not been contaminated by the disastrous Gaullist theories of decolonization. The speech made in Léopoldville on 27 October 1940 was full of references to *our* North Africa, *our* Syria and *our* West Africa. . . .

De Gaulle did not say *our* Equatorial Africa, because he was already in control of that territory; but he did say *our* Indo-China on 9 May 1945.

On 22 February 1941, he solemnly proclaimed the integrity of the French Empire:

General de Gaulle and the Council for the Defence of the French Empire wish to make the following statement:

(1) The temporary disaster which has overtaken France can in no way justify an attack by any foreign power on the integrity of the territories of the Empire or on the rights of France anywhere in the world.

(2) Any surrender to which the government of Vichy or its representatives may consent will be considered null and void by the Council for the Defence of the French Empire.

(3) This declaration and this resolution apply to the particular case of Indo-China.

This document specified *null and void*; that is what I call the spirit of the Resistance.

In those days, no one considered the Moslems unworthy of the name Frenchmen. On 18 January 1942, de Gaulle called on 'Moslem France, from Nigeria to Casablanca', and ended his speech with the words, 'French Moslems, on our side!'

He voiced the same feelings in a speech which he read over the London radio on 18 March 1943:

The festival of Mouloud ushers in a hopeful year.

This holy festival opens the way for the union of all Frenchmen, regardless of race or creed. The Moslems of French Africa have a great role to play in our progress towards victory. Their consistent and friendly attachment to France is the surest guarantee that the Moslem populations of French Africa will be ready to do their duty towards their great motherland, the France of yesterday and for ever.

The great motherland . . . the France of yesterday and for ever. How poignantly those words ring today! If 'for ever' meant 'as long as I have to talk in this fashion', he would have done far better to keep silent.

De Gaulle made a significant speech at a meeting of Frenchmen living in Great Britain at the Albert Hall in London on 18 June 1942. He made the following statement:

During these dreadful times, France has discovered one vital element which is essential to her future and necessary to her greatness – her Empire. . . . That is why the French nation has become aware of her achievements and of the profound solidarity which links her to her Empire. . . . In fact, any attack on France's sovereignty over her Empire would be odious. . . . For France's sake, we vindicate her rights to have the integrity of her Empire respected.

This speech was published in the appendix of de Gaulle's first volume of memoirs, published in 1954. In those days, *Discours et Messages* was still mentioned in the list of the general's previous works. Copies of those speeches were still available and were even recommended reading for Gaullists. Even as late as 1959, *Discours et Messages* was mentioned in the third volume of de Gaulle's memoirs. It was also in that volume that de Gaulle described how he had reminded Roosevelt that Algiers was 'a city of France'.

I could continue quoting de Gaulle *ad infinitum*; but I think that I have put down enough of his words to prove that it was my duty to start up the Resistance again in order to defend '*our* Algeria!'

At the end of the second volume of his war memoirs, de Gaulle said, referring to the Normandy Landing, 'We are bringing France back her independence, her Empire and her sword.'

Where is the Empire now? Who gave it up without so much as a word of justification? As for the sword, it lies broken now. The so-called *force de frappe* and the various police systems have taken over the traditional role of the army. And as for independence, the only ones left who possess it have had to leave France and to go wandering all over the world.

When I created the second National Council for the Resistance, I did not worry about whether I would be understood right away by many, whether I would shock everybody, and whether I would not be risking terrible difficulties and wild adventures. There are enough professional politicians around to worry about things like that, but I never assumed that one's sole aim in life should be to achieve security by conformity. I have never been popular with those who worship anyone who is in power, and I have often been misunderstood by those who hypocritically pretend to see no evil, hear no evil and speak no evil of the men at the summit. It is a good way to get along in life, but even Mauriac would admit that I could never be accused of being over-accommodating.

People who have always led an easy life and who know nothing about the way a secret police force operates may wonder why we did not continue our struggle openly in France instead of going underground. I have already explained that this would have been technically impossible, even outside France. Colonel Argoud was kidnapped in a foreign country, and the incident was immediately buried under an avalanche of lies and denials by top members of the various French ministries. Argoud had been kidnapped in a foreign country, and the whole story was soon hushed up, even though it went before the highest and most respectable of courts. Surely, after that, only the most sceptical and ill-disposed of men could have refused to understand why we could not work openly in France. There were too many officials who kept busy getting rid of those who made a nuisance of themselves, and, indeed, sometimes getting rid of them for good.

Anyway, fighting in the open presupposes a certain choice of weapons. But where were we to find those weapons? The newspapers were all for the régime and they gave us no coverage except to mention briefly that M. So-and-So had 'aired his usual grievances'. The National Assembly had become a sort of circus where a very small and silent audience watched the deputies go through their paces like dogs leaping through paper hoops, while M. Loyal cracked his whip. This was why I eventually had to do what my comrades had done before me; go into hiding somewhere in Europe.

I had been carried away on the wave of the Resistance twice. Both times, I had been irresistibly drawn into it and both times I had refused to calculate my chances of success, unlike those who chose a prudent 'wait and see' attitude. Some men do their duty only when they think success is certain and they join the Resistance just before the last minute and sometimes after that. Any man who goes into the Resistance to forge a career for himself or as an investment does not deserve the name of Resistance fighter. He deserves the name only if he joins the Resistance because he thinks of it as an obligation he owes to himself, whatever the outcome of the fight. The first time I felt this way, I was forty years old. After the victory, I told my comrades that one spell in the Resistance was enough for any man, but that if we ever had to do it again we would not hesitate.

Well, I did do it again. I was sixty years old the second time. And it is pretty tiring, but it also makes you feel younger in spirit. I hope that I will be through after this time and that I won't have to set off again for the *maquis* at the age of eighty. But if I am alive then and if it is necessary for any reason, I only hope that I will still have the strength to fight for what I believe to be right. I am no braver than the next man; but I hope to remain inflexible on this one point, whatever my age.

I have already explained why I will be discreet even if it makes my tale seem less exciting. After all, I do not want to give any names or details about the men I met, about the places where I stayed and the meetings I attended, or about anything else which might turn this book into a police dossier. The accusations made against us are preposterous and false; but they are still very dangerous. Therefore I will only try to give you an idea of my life as an outlaw during this period, when I was being hunted all over Europe. I had many sad moments and disappointments; but at least I always had the satisfaction of fighting for a just cause.

I wandered through nearly every country in Europe like the proverbial wandering Jew; I was also just as poor. An outlaw finds everything he sees on his travels far more moving than if he were only a tourist. I saw the spot where Goethe was arrested and also the one where William Tell made his vow. I saw the place where Wagner had composed his music, as well as the place where de Gaulle had spoken to his enslaved countrymen. Yet I was not on any romantic quest after the past and I did not make the round of famous historic spots deliberately. I needed no literary associations and I did not have to recall that I had once made official speeches in many of the places which I saw again as an exile. Even during the worst days, I found that I did not need historical or personal memories to revive the flame of indignation in my heart and to feel that my cause was both noble and right, in spite of the insults which were heaped upon me by nearly all the world.

I went back to a district in Italy where I had spent my youth. When I had gone back there once before, busloads of journalists had followed me along the mountain paths. My one problem was that my face was no longer unknown. I went all over Europe from the Italian to the Austrian lakes, from the Apennines to the Black Forest, from the snowy Alps to the foggy Thames, from the most easterly countries to the great rivers of Western Europe. But I crossed the frontiers more often than I crossed the streets of the cities where I stayed. Occasionally I was extremely careless; for example, I spent a whole day in a large Munich hotel being interviewed on television. I was told that the programme was in colour; but I don't know whether I shall ever find out as it has never been released. But a few days later one of the French weekly magazines which follow the Gaullist line printed a speech supposedly by me, although a lot of it was forged.

One snowy and windy night, we set off for some uncertain destination in a plane called Pluto. Another time, the plane I was supposed to take left early and I found myself stranded in a busy airport. The next day a stranger said to me without any malice that I looked like Bidault. I replied that there might indeed be a vague resemblance, but that I thought Bidault 'must be younger'. That day I was recognized by two different people.

One day while I was aboard a plane, my neighbour suddenly announced that he had had 'the honour' of meeting me once at the United Nations. On yet another occasion, I was in a large foreign city for the first and last time, when a Frenchman greeted me by my real name. And then there was the time when, somewhere in central Europe, we had a car accident and the other driver

demanded to see our papers; I then discovered that I had none on
me, not even false ones, and that the driver of our car did not have
any papers for the car. This all took place at one o'clock in the
morning. Luckily, the police decided they did not want to be
disturbed over such a minor incident, so that there is at least one
country which did not expel me.

I could go on and on with anecdotes of this sort; but I am not
at all sure that others will be amused by them. I do not want anyone to think that I led a very exciting life. I certainly had to take
risks every day, but more in an atmosphere of Simenon than
of the Three Musketeers. We lived in the shadows and by night,
moving in the unknown climate of adventure. But there were also
the grey days, the appointments that we had to miss, the letters
which arrived too late, the bad news, the time which dragged on,
and the feeling of helplessness since we were not able to do anything to prevent France from committing a suicidal blunder while
the whole world applauded.

At least we persevered. We stubbornly clung to our convictions
in spite of our bad fortunes. We spoke up for our beliefs. I remained firmly convinced that all our hidden sacrifices, our daily
humiliations and all our hopes would not be in vain. In the end
our beliefs will prevail in spite of the public opinion polls and the
electronic computers which have replaced political courage and
foresight.

I admit that we had counted on the hope that Europe was still a
collection of free states, which cared about the rights of individuals,
and which could even tell a friend from an enemy. But that was
not the Europe I found. Even if Europe had its memories this did
not prevent it from being extremely well-disposed towards its
powerful enemy, and extremely harsh towards its powerless friends.
Once again we learned the brutal fact that the weak have no
friends and that gratitude counts for nothing in politics.

Europe, in fact the whole world, says to those who fight for
what is right and for truth and for justice: 'Be strong and win first.
After that you can do what you like. Before that, down with you
all!' I had come to know this mixture of hypocrisy and cynicism
before, and yet I decided to try again when I went into exile. But
I soon saw that I had been right the first time; just as there is no
such thing as a 'noble savage', there is no such thing as a civilized
nation which actually practises the moral virtues which it preaches.

Men are all about equal as far as the progress of civilization is concerned. Whether they wear a ring in their nose or carry a dossier under their arm, they are both right at the bottom of the evolutionary ladder.

And yet, I am not quite certain that even this is true. There was a time in Europe when men spoke less about the future, but more about respecting certain rules and international standards. We claim to live in a great age of enlightenment and fraternity, yet our governments use more methods of repression and control than the old nations of Europe ever did, in spite of their many secret agents. There was a time when anyone could go anywhere in Europe, as long as he could pay for his transport. He did not have to have a passport except in the last few absolutist Empires. Everywhere else he could go where he liked as there were no restrictions on travel, on foreign currency, or on the rights of communication.

Today, fifteen years after the idea of a united Europe was born, the only issue which does not provoke a controversy during stormy international debates is the presence of the secret policemen who have overrun the new Europe. The irregular police forces which are used specially for political purposes are largely composed of riff-raff. If Jupiter so much as frowns from his Mount Olympus, they get to work and force other nations to act as their accomplices, as I know from personal experience. This experience is far from agreeable and it is even rather dangerous; but it is interesting as well. The fear of punishment is not what makes a man feel guilty; the nature of his crime does. The noble victims of the recent holocaust know this and so do the governments who let French *barbouzes* operate in their countries. The *barbouzes* can do anything they please. Eighteen months have elapsed since Colonel Argoud was kidnapped; but the powerful country where this crime took place has not yet received an explanation from France. Germany took long enough to ask for an apology, and by this time it has stopped asking for one.

Things were different once. In England, for example, constitutional law used to be very strict on this point. When foreigners were thought to be a menace to English security, they were dealt with harshly, but they were never persecuted just to please another country. Foreign governments could not give England orders on the way it ought to treat political refugees. England did not hand over Cadoudal after the peace of Amiens or send him off to the

New World. The Bourbon princes were not asked to go to Warsaw in spite of the First Consul's request, and there were many other refusals of this sort.

A hundred years ago, Erskine May wrote a treatise on the subject of political refugees in England. After describing England's battles with Bonaparte, he added:

The English government has stuck to its guns. The fact that a foreigner's presence or actions displease a foreign power does not suffice, because if that were the case, what would become of the right of asylum? The refugee could be pursued by the government of his own country and chased away from the shelter he had found in a free country. The English are very chivalrous on this point. Once they undertake to protect a foreigner, they look upon any threats to his security as a personal insult. The refugee is naturally opposed to the government of his nation; the very fact that he has been banished is sufficient proof of this. The Poles loathed the Russians; the Hungarians and the Italians were hostile to Austria; the French Royalists despised the Republic and the Empire; Charles x and Louis-Napoléon hated Louis-Philippe, King of the French; the Legitimists and the Orleanists disliked the French Republic of 1848 as much as the Second Empire of 1852. But all of them were protected in turn by the large shield of England. No political opinion or public speech which is not actually libellous has ever been suppressed. Every act which was not forbidden by law, however much it may have displeased other nations, has been protected. Indeed a large number of refugees who continued to be distrusted by their own governments were given protection under the liberal English law.

In 1858 while he was in England, Orsini plotted to assassinate Napoleon III. He threw a bomb which had been made in Birmingham. The French government complained that England was giving shelter to a murderer, and the English ministers decided to satisfy the French government and to prove that they did not shelter conspirators. They proposed measures to Parliament which would try and prevent the commission of certain acts on British soil by foreigners against the members of their native governments. The House of Commons decided that Napoleon III had influenced the cabinet; Palmerston, who had represented the great British Empire for fifty years (he had been War Minister in 1809), was overthrown. It seems incredible now that, one hundred years ago, a government could be overthrown for proposing a measure which

290

290 RESISTANCE

would protect the members of a foreign government, especially right after Orsini had tried to kill Napoleon III; but things were then very different. Today there is no room left for political differences.

The case of Victor Hugo is also instructive and very much to England's credit. When Napoleon III came to power in France, Victor Hugo was forced to go into exile. He went to Jersey first, then to Guernsey, so that he was protected by English law throughout. He wrote a book about these years called *Pendant l'exil*, in which he described what he did and how he was treated. I had only glanced through the book until I went to Brazil, but there I read it avidly. This fascinating collection of speeches, manifestoes, declarations, letters and messages is written with characteristic vigour and intensity. As my readers may not be familiar with the work, I would like to quote some of the more relevant passages. The introduction, which is entitled 'On the nature of exile', is full of amazingly shrewd observations. For example:

Anything can happen when you go into exile. You may have been thrown out of your country, but you have not been forgotten by its rulers. They are still very interested in you, and many eyes will continue to spy on you. They will call on you in a host of ingenious disguises. A respectable minister will pay you a visit, and then put his visit to good use. A distinguished professor will come to your house and you will find him reading your private papers. Anything can be done to you because you are an outlaw. You are outside the bounds of equity, reason, respect and truth. People will pretend that you gave them permission to publish a conversation they had with you, and they will make sure that you sound like a fool in print. They will put words in your mouth which you never uttered, they will quote from letters that you never wrote, they will discuss actions which you never performed. . . . Being in exile is like living behind an open-work screen . . . you are isolated and at the same time observed.

Do not write to your friends in France; it is permitted by law to open your letters. . . . If an honest man comes to see you, he will find himself in trouble as soon as he goes back. . . .

Things have not changed. Isn't it odd that progressives care so little about progress in this field?

A suspect stranger comes to whisper in your ear that he will assassinate the Emperor if you like. Bonaparte is proposing to get rid of Bonaparte for you.

That is the real explanation of all the ridiculous 'plots' which the newspapers write about in such detail and which are actually started by the police.

You might as well grow used to distortions, outright lies and smears. Whatever you do, don't try and complain. They will jeer at you and then continue exactly as before without even bothering to change their tactics.

They will grind you down as remorsely as a turning wheel. They never tire, they are imperturbable and their conscience is at rest. Because they know that they will not be punished, they will slander you to their hearts' content. Their accusations will be so vile and so stupid that you will grow tired of defending yourself before they grow tired of attacking you, and you will prefer to suffer in silence.

You don't have to be Victor Hugo and your enemies don't have to be the secret police of the Second Empire to know that all this is true. I can guarantee that it is just as he says and that his advice is sound.

Demagogues will ask you, what is the use of upholding the law and what is right when everyone has turned against you? How ridiculous you are to be so stubborn, so persevering, so intransigent! Success is what is right, success becomes the law, so just be on the side of success and everyone will thank you for it. Everyone will praise you. Instead of going into exile, you will become a Senator and you won't seem like a fool then.

I am sure that a lot of the people who were once my 'friends' must be saying the same thing and that my conduct shocks and embarrasses them greatly.

Secret funds are used to commit public outrages. . . .

Victor Hugo was right about this too. But his conclusion is consoling:

When an upright man falls as low as it is possible to fall, his position becomes impregnable. I claim that if a man is in the right, then it is a good thing for him to be persecuted, ruined, reduced to nothing, expatriated, thwarted, insulted, disowned and slandered. It is only when he is utterly defeated and powerless that he becomes all-powerful. . . . When a man loses everything and has no obligations left, he is in an ideal position to fight. . . . When everything is taken from you, you have been given everything. . . . When you are forbidden everything, you can do anything: you are no longer restricted by parliamentary considerations.

RESISTANCE

... A political outlaw has two assets: one is the injustice of his fate, the other is the justice of his cause.

It is impossible to analyse the nature and meaning of exile more brilliantly or lucidly. I quoted these passages because I knew I could not put it better. Besides, I also wanted to compare the way Hugo was treated with the way political refugees are treated today. Of course, he did suffer; but he would have been far worse off now.

The Royalist newspapers in England sing the praises of English hospitality; but I ought to point out that this hospitality includes night raids and expulsions, as does Belgian hospitality. ...
When dealing with dangerous individuals, governments lend each other a helping hand. They persecute each other's enemies, throw them in gaol, force them to leave the country and sometimes turn them in. ...

This is still done today even in countries which consider themselves 'free'. Victor Hugo's complaints were justified but he was better off than political refugees today. He was allowed to stay in England and to go on writing and making speeches. The régime which persecuted him was more lenient than the one in France today; he was neither kidnapped nor tried *in absentia*. His books were read in France, in spite of the fact that he had written, referring to the emperor, 'You may kill that man with a clear conscience.'
While he was in Belgium, he wrote *Histoire d'un crime* and *Napoléon le Petit*. When a law was passed in Brussels forbidding attacks on heads of state, Hugo left Antwerp, after making an impassioned speech. The moment he stepped from the boat in Jersey, he made another, equally impassioned speech, calling on all French political refugees to unite. He remained politically active throughout his stay in Jersey, even during times when feelings were running high. The English government never ordered him to stop making their task more difficult. In his first speech on Saint-Hélier pier, he called out, 'Long live the Republic, citizens! Political Refugees, long live France!' In October 1852, he wrote *Déclaration à propos de l'Empire* which was addressed 'to the people', and in which he said:

Citizens, Louis Bonaparte is an outlaw. ...
Friends and brothers! We are at war against a government of infamy, a government which is an insult to morality and an obstacle to all forms of progress, a government which chokes the people, which assassinates the republic, which violates the laws; this government reached power by violence and it must perish by violence; this government is criminal. ...

These words were spoken on British territory, so near to France
that the French coastline is always in sight. Hugo finished his
speech with the cry, '. . . any citizen worthy of the name can and
must do only one thing: load his rifle and wait for the hour to
strike.' Yet in spite of all this, the poet was not kidnapped by secret
policemen; in fact, the French government never retaliated.

Some time later, Hugo presided over a banquet given in honour
of Polish independence. He was surrounded by Polish, Hungarian,
German and French political refugees; but neither the Russian
Czar nor the French Emperor paid any attention.

Hugo tried to interfere with British law when a man was sentenced to death in one of the Jersey Islands. He wrote a lengthy
statement on the subject which was addressed 'to the people of
Guernsey'. The sentence was carried out anyway, some say as
a result of a meeting between the French Ambassador and
Lord Palmerston. Afterwards, Hugo wrote a scathing letter to
Palmerston which ended with the words, 'I am, Sir, your humble
servant.'

France and England were allies during the Crimean war, and
Hugo made a speech to an audience of political refugees in which
he attacked the policy of both England and France. And when
Napoleon III came to London on an official visit to the Queen,
Hugo wrote an open letter to the Emperor which was posted over
all the walls of Dover. This vitriolic attack warned the Emperor
not to come to England and was full of menacing references to
criminal courts, gaol and eternal damnation.

Still the British government did nothing to Hugo. 'Someone
who shall remain nameless but who is well-known' (in fact Sir
Robert Peel), did ask the British government to take measures
against the French poet. In a speech to the House of Commons,
Peel brought up the subject of Hugo's actions and writings,
announcing that he would ask the Queen's ministers 'if there was
no way to put an end to it'. But nothing came of Peel's efforts until
the day Hugo published yet another attack on the French Emperor
('Will the accused please rise') which ended with the words, 'Now,
you can throw us out.'

And he was indeed thrown out, even though the English public
took his side. He was forced to leave Jersey and to move to Guernsey; no, not to South America, only as far as Guernsey. He did not
even have to move to another country, just to another English

island a few miles away. And once he got there, he continued to take an active interest in European and American politics. Four and a half years later, he went back to Jersey, still unrepentant, still as inflexible, sarcastic and prophetic as ever. Occasionally, he went on visits to Brussels and it was there that he presided over a great international banquet in 1862. The Burgomaster of Brussels sat on his right, and the President of the Belgian House of Commons sat on his left.

Everything Hugo wrote or did was immediately known in France. He continued to fight against the French government throughout his stay in exile, and England continued to give him shelter without forcing him to stop writing, and without even making him change his residence a second time.

I have spoken about Victor Hugo's years in exile at some length because most people do not know the story. What is significant is that it took place one hundred years ago and that, in those hundred years, fantastic progress has been made in nearly every field, including a Universal and a European declaration of the rights of man; but I know from bitter experience that those declarations are nothing but a waste of ink and paper, and that no one takes them into account.

All the countries of Europe, including England, adopted the Fifth Republic's black list without a murmur. But I must admit that the BBC in England acted in a remarkably courageous fashion. I spoke on a BBC programme for a few minutes and my identity was carefully concealed at the recording studios. This may not sound like much; but in these grim times, even a little thing like that seems remarkable. The programme created quite a stir and the President of the Fifth Republic made his disapproval extremely clear. I will not even mention the lies of the French press; but I was interested in what the English newspapers had to say about my talk. *The Times* dismissed the whole thing contemptuously – contempt has long been its hallmark; but in fact, so many other newspapers have tried to imitate that tone of lordly disdain that it has become rather common. The friendlier newspapers thought that they were showing great magnanimity by being condescending to me. But there was not a single English newspaper which wrote anything really vicious or underhand like the reports in the American and the Italian and particularly the French newspapers.

A debate was held in the House of Commons after my speech

had been broadcast by the BBC. One of the speakers asked whether Hitler would have been allowed to enter England in similar circumstances. He may not have seen the irony of such a comparison; but I need hardly remind him or anyone of the fact that Hitler was never a friend of mine. Another speaker, whose name I don't remember, but who, I think, belonged to the Conservative party, called me an 'indiscriminate murderer'. This remarkably unenlightened legislator had probably never heard of the Dunkirk Treaty, which had been entirely my own doing. But even in England today, propaganda is so widespread that people hear only the official version of the men in power. When I read what had been said about me in Parliament, I thought of all the Englishmen who had known me well and who could have come to my defence. Not one of them ever did. I will not give their names or the names of men in other countries who never said a word on my behalf. I have simply struck them from the list of my friends; besides, I have reached an age when I prefer not to have too many useless memories; they only clutter up one's thoughts and give one a false sense of obligation.

After reading the account of this parliamentary session, I realized that the English Parliament and Cabinet were uneasy about my presence because they thought that if I stayed in England their relations with de Gaulle would degenerate – as though they could have got any worse. Besides, timorousness of this sort has never been the way to handle de Gaulle. The English were also unhappy about my false passport. There, I agreed thoroughly with them; it is most annoying to have to take on a false name, but I had to do this, because otherwise no one would have allowed me to enter their country. After all, one hint from General de Gaulle was enough to make every country put me on its black list. I was known to be an undesirable visitor in every police station and at every frontier post. In these circumstances, I thought it no more dishonourable to use false papers than it had been during the war. In those days it had been considered a noble, generous and heroic action to use false names and to carry forged papers. I know this because I was told so during a ceremony in which I received a medal for my role in the Resistance by a country which has refused me shelter since.

14

Expulsion /
The Argoud Affair /
Brazil

'Welcome to all adventurers!' This used to be the traditional phrase of greeting to those men who were criminals in the eyes of their own governments. Unfortunately I no longer had the advantage of passing unnoticed as I had done twenty years before, and my face, although it looked older, was only too well known. But I have not lost hope and I still believe everything I said two years ago on the BBC, particularly when I said my chances were greater than Churchill's in 1940. I think I can persuade my reader that this is not an illusion.

There was a tremendous outcry when my short speech was broadcast all over the world and once again I came under a heavy barrage of insults. The Dutch government, for example, decided not to broadcast the programme on which I spoke, in order to avoid offending France, even though my speech was only a passionate appeal to France asking it to come to its senses and stop letting itself be ruined. Of course, the Dutch government had every right to prevent me from appearing on Dutch television and even to cut off any network which might try to disobey its orders. But certain things were said about me in the Dutch Parliament which made me think that the Dutch men and women I had known once had forgotten me. The only time I had ever used the right of veto on the Security Council of the UN was over Holland: I thus helped them to settle their difficulties over Insulinde. The motto of the House of Orange may well be 'I shall maintain', but the Dutch have not maintained their sense of gratitude.

Meanwhile the West continued to cling to a few cowardly and

trite convictions that it insisted on calling 'daring'. In fact this meant a total surrender of all Europe's traditional values and beliefs. I often wondered as I travelled around the countries of Europe whether the West had not finally become a place where the sun sets in every sense of the word.

Wherever I went, I heard either by chance or by an occasional letter that another frontier had been closed; country after unsolicited country announced that it would not allow me free entry. I wondered why they refused before I had even made a request, as I could see no reason for saying no in advance and for grovelling to the strong by cursing the weak. I already knew that Paris was sending out lists of undesirables to every country; these lists were accepted on the spot and I found this shocking from the political and personal point of view. An animal who is being hunted by every hunter and park ranger in the area wonders why so many have suddenly ganged up against him. Nations used to guard their sovereignty jealously and took violent offence when foreign countries tried to interfere in their affairs; this is not true any longer.

After my trip to England, everyone tried hard to wash their hands of me. Austria announced that I would not be admitted if I tried to go there. When I heard this, I recalled the day when I had pleaded with Molotov not to treat ex-Chancellor Figl, who was then Austrian Minister of Foreign Affairs, as though he were a Russian satellite. But politicians do not live near the Danube, the Thames or the Seine: they all live near the river Lethe, which is the river of forgetfulness.

I do not think that the French Ambassador to Switzerland asked the Swiss to take steps against me; yet that country soon decided to forbid me from entering its frontiers. I sometimes wondered whether they were not just making a verbal sacrifice to the French Minotaur; yet I was pretty sure that if I actually tried to enter Switzerland, the police would soon identify me by looking through its files, and that it would then hand me over to the French police. The French President seemed to have as much of a hold over Europe as any Napoleon, except that, unlike the First Consul, he had not achieved this position by winning any victories.

I reflected upon all this as I roamed near the frontiers of Switzerland, which is, after all, a traditional asylum for political refugees. I also recalled that other men, carrying forged papers and

proud of being called terrorists, had once filled the hotels of Geneva
and Lausanne. These men had secretaries, powerful connections
and large incomes derived from rackets in France; they received a
great many foreign visitors and no one meddled in their affairs
which they never bothered to keep secret. In the spring of 1956, I
had gone to Geneva to deliver a speech at a conference on the
Arab world. Before I was allowed to do this, I had to get permission
from the Swiss authorities. I was told by letter that a special exception would be made in my favour and that the historic town of
Geneva would, just for once, permit someone to speak on a political
subject, although this went against the Swiss tradition of neutrality.
When I made my speech, I saw that an entire row of seats had been
reserved for the Arab press; their main function was to further the
cause of the FLN. These Arab journalists and refugees remained
in Switzerland as long as they liked; some of them are still there
today. The only moral is that you have to be an Arab to be well-
received wherever you go.

Indeed, this favouritism did not go unnoticed by the great
French Algerian patriot, Michel Debré. When he saw the use the
FLN was making of traditional Swiss hospitality, he wrote:

Even our friend, Switzerland, will have to hear our reproaches some
day. We must chide that nation in a friendly, sad, yet firm tone. What
sight do we see every week? Military attachés from various Arab nations
take a train at the Gare de Lyons and go to Switzerland, where they
visit rebel delegates from Africa. They give them advice and orders and
fix dates for massacres. Then the military attachés go back to France
and join in Parisian social life once again. France is guilty of a crime if
she believes that social elegance is any excuse for betrayal. I also think
that it is not very noble on Switzerland's part to consider that its
neutrality, which is often admirable, provides an excuse for giving
hospitality to those who plot massacres.

When Michel Debré became Prime Minister, he did not chide
the Swiss in a 'sad and friendly' tone. Instead, he asked them to
house and to protect the FLN members who were negotiating the
surrender of Algeria, first at Les Rousses and later at Evian. But I
do not want to say another word about that court jester and I leave
him for good to the ingratitude of his master and to the contempt
of everyone else.

While I listened to the Swiss radio, I thought about the irony of
my position; Switzerland was a highly civilized country, and

traditionally France's friend. In that little country a Communist bank-robber would be given shelter, yet I was excluded as a terrorist, because France had decided to call me that, and the Swiss authorities did not want to contradict their French friends. And, speaking of Communism, we must not forget that Lenin lived in Switzerland for a long time and that he left it only to go and fight in the October Revolution. While he was in Switzerland, he asked Zimmerwald and Kienthal to come and lecture there and make defeatist propaganda which might result in the victory of the Central Powers. Besides, Switzerland was not the only country which welcomed Lenin; throughout his long years of exile, the Bolshevik leader lived in almost every country of Europe. Things were very different in those days. But in my case, the press looked up an article in the Swiss constitution which was supposed to prove that the Swiss were absolutely right to prevent me from entering their country. This particular article was never used against Lenin; either I am an exceedingly dangerous man or else we live in very odd times. . . .

Some time before the uproar over my BBC speech, I was expelled from Italy while I was staying in the South at the Villa Bonaparte. I had not been able to inform the owner of my presence at his famous villa; but I believe that he never disowned his enforced hospitality when he found it out. I was not denounced by anyone to the police either there or elsewhere; it is not true that people always have the governments they deserve. It may be true at some times, but only rarely, even in France. Many people of many nationalities have aided me, including Frenchmen of every class who helped me and who did not deny that they had done so afterwards.

One morning a dozen policemen and *carabiniere* came into my bedroom at the Villa Bonaparte; I was in bed, quietly reading a book on the Thirty Years War. Someone had acted imprudently, although I only found this out later, and this had brought the police to my door. It was the first time such a thing had ever happened to me and it was most disagreeable. I showed the policemen my passport; it was the same as the one I had used to go to Turin to tell the Italians in the name of the three great Western Powers that Trieste would be given back to them. The house was searched for weapons and one was indeed found, although I knew nothing about its existence. I was then told that the house would be searched as a weapon had been found. Innocently I asked how they could

have found a weapon before beginning the search; but I got no
reply. I packed my bag and was taken to the police commissioner
in Macerata. This man was enbarrassed rather than pleased, too
annoyed to be courteous. But he did make me one promise, which
I have serious reasons to suspect he did not keep.

I wondered whether I ought to telephone the Prime Minister,
Fanfani, or the Minister of the Interior, Taviani. But I was not
alone and I also knew that men in high places find outlaws a
nuisance. In those days Fanfani was practising his famous policy
of *appertura a sinistra*, so that he was probably in no position to
remember that he had once been a visitor at my house, where he
had asked me many questions about Pierre Pflimlin. I could not
think of anyone who would be ready to help me for old times' sake
and for the sake of all I had done for Italy. De Gasperi was dead;
before his death, he had had the feeling that he had become superfluous and that younger men were eager to replace him. After he
died, Christian Democracy began to step backwards, to bend in
the direction of the wind of history, and to dig its own grave.

Finally, I did nothing, however tempted I felt to try and get
help. I allowed the Italian police to take me on an endless journey
towards 'the frontier of my choice'. The trip lasted all evening and
all night. I felt that the country was in no way responsible for what
was being done to me in its name. The Italian police is the most
subtle and complex of all police forces and its committees sit up
deliberating night and day from the Alps to Sicily. Some years ago,
the country grew so tired of the abuses committed by the police
that it handed the government over to a leader who had only fifteen
members in parliament. That was how Mussolini became dictator.
Since then, some of his youthful admirers have taken off their
black shirts and turned to another demagogic philosophy. During
that long night journey I thought about these things, reflecting on
the difficulties encountered by all noble ideals. I had not been able
to prevent my own party from breaking down or my own country
from becoming totally corrupt.

Travelling in a police van is a disagreeable but interesting experience. My escorts behaved well, although neither they nor I
enjoyed each other's company. But they were only doing their job;
they had arrested me and now they were watching over me until
they could get rid of me. I might have been a dope peddler, a
crook, a prelate or anyone. And they knew that the best way to do

their job was not to worry too much about my identity, but just to obey their orders. Within their limitations I must admit that they behaved very decently, considering the fact that, to them, I was nothing more than a common criminal.

The Argoud Affair

Soon after changing countries, the National Council of the Resistance published a manifesto which was heavily criticized. In spite of this, I believe that everything we said in it still holds good, although I no longer have a copy of it handy. I signed it with Soustelle, Argoud, and Gardy. We often disagreed because our characters clashed, but we agreed on all fundamental issues. We may have argued over means, but our aims were identical. This was our last reunion, and, although I will admit that it is never easy to work in a committee, I want to make it quite clear that there was never any real rift between myself and Soustelle or Argoud, as some people said. There were, and there still may be, some points on which I disagree with those men; but nothing can make me say that we quarrelled on any basic premises. We are fighting on the same side and no amount of lies or distortions can make me forget that.

On this particular occasion, we met in Bavaria. The weather was freezing; there was a great deal of snow and it was well below zero outside. But it was warm enough in the room where we worked; for, in those climates, people know how to keep warm. It is only in hot climates that you are ever cold in winter; in cold climates, people have learned how to defend themselves against nature.

Colonel Argoud may well owe his life to the cold. The *barbouzes* who were on his trail took advantage of the noise one Carnival night to kidnap him when he came back from a trip to Italy. He lived very austerely; but he was rash and took many risks. He was so fervent, so impatient to help his country and so utterly devoted to his cause that he must have felt that he led a charmed life and that nothing would happen to him. Even during the worst days, he wholeheartedly believed that we would win. Secret policemen leaped on him one night, knocked him out and carried him off in a van. The men who did this have been identified: we have photographs of them and they have even admitted their guilt. But they were never prosecuted and they were soon sent off on other missions. They had been ordered to get Argoud by the highest authority in France. Specially appointed judges dismissed the case after witnesses from the various ministries had given evidence of doubtful value in court. I am certain that Argoud owes his life to the fact that all the rivers were frozen and that it would have been impossible to dig a hole for his body quickly near the road because there was so much ice on the ground. Instead, he was sentenced to life imprisonment, which is what special courts always do when they do not dare to acquit a prisoner. But the army men behind this *coup* will one day be found out and punished.

After this shocking incident took place, I wrote a short article on it which I tried to get printed. This was dangerous; but then our way of life and everything we wrote or did was dangerous. I am positive that none of what I wrote was ever published in France, at least not in its original form. That is why I want to set down here what I wrote on the spur of the moment. I am not ashamed of any of it and I abridge it slightly only for the convenience of my readers:

There are certain French police organizations in addition to the six or seven regular police forces which once seemed sufficient to ensure the progress of democracy in France. These organizations stretch out over all the Common Market countries, and probably beyond that. They masquerade not as counter-spies, but as wine merchants. They have money and they also have criminal records. Europe is on the right track: after imitations of Charlemagne, we now have imitations of Fouché.

Colonel Argoud was kidnapped in the centre of Munich on the eve of *Mardi Gras* by a whole gang of ex-convicts calling themselves Gaullist policemen. I am not claiming that this is what happened, I am stating a fact which I know and which the German police knows as well. So far, their degree of complicity has not yet been established, and, as far as I know, there has not yet even been an enquiry. Anyway, no one believes the ridiculous theory hastily concocted right after the scandalous incident, that Argoud was kidnapped because of rivalries within the CNR. The French, the Germans, the Parisians, the Bavarians and world opinion have quite rightly dismissed the odious rumour that Argoud was kidnapped by his own side, and they have immediately understood that this was nothing but a trumped-up lie.

The most servile radio networks and the most deferential newspapers have avoided making such an imputation. Everyone has understood that the whole business was plotted and carried out by legally-sanctioned criminals, who have fought against their fellow-countrymen before in Algeria, and who now reveal how seriously de Gaulle considers the question of the individual sovereignty of the nations in the future Europe of his dreams.

The only integration in this loudly-proclaimed sovereignty is the integration of the secret police forces. And if the secret police forces of the various nations are not working hand in hand, the French *barbouzes* have usurped the functions of the German police and have committed an act of aggression against a neighbouring country.

The facts are clear. There are only two alternatives: either an act of aggression has been committed, or else there has been complicity on the side of the German police. In either case, there is only one solution: de Gaulle's right-hand men are responsible for the deed, and so they must once again intervene to undo their first deed. One side intervened, with or without complicity, and kidnapped a man; and that man might easily have disappeared or have been murdered. Therefore the criminal action must be cancelled out in the name of individual rights. The only acceptable solution between the two countries which so recently became allies, the only solution which will preserve whatever remains of European unity after such a blow, is the following one: Colonel Argoud must be taken back to the spot where he was kidnapped and apologies must be made both to him and to the country where it took place.

The whole world knows that:

(1) It was certainly a kidnapping.

(2) That an irregular French police force was responsible for this kidnapping.

(3) That this kidnapping took place in Bavaria, which is in the German Federal Republic, and that therefore the act was an insult to Germany, to Europe and to the honour of France.

The reason these things are now known everywhere is not because the foreign press, any more than the French press, has shown sympathy for the organization which the French Government continues to call the OAS. No one knows anything except what the French government chooses to say about this Algerian organization or about the Resistance organization which we created after the Algerian disaster deliberately engineered by the French government. But no one, however prejudiced against us, can dismiss the recent circumstances of Argoud's kidnapping, whatever they think of us on moral grounds. The only way to explain this mystery is to examine the facts. Recently, Munich was infiltrated by gangsters who believed they could get away with anything because their master has always got away with everything.

The *barbouzes* do exist, and they are many. Most people have realized this for the first time only recently. We have known about it all along; but nobody would believe that gangsterism was sanctioned by the

State. Most people waited until they could no longer suppress their suspicions before they began vaguely wondering whether the man they had taken for an angel might not perhaps be a devil. After all, Lucifer was the proudest and the most brilliant of the angels.

But let us forget about angels and even devils, and let us return to the *barbouzes* who roam all over Europe, doing far more than the official police and the spy network. *Barbouzes* do not work for the country – they are not worthy of belonging to any country – but for the government which pays them. I also want to point out that top civil servants, ministers and the head of the French General Staff have all sworn during recent trials that the *barbouzes* do not exist. They did not take a religious oath, as de Gaulle has not seen fit to put the name of God back on to the witness-stand; but they did swear on whatever honour they had left. They were committing perjury, for they knew that they were lying. Shall I again be accused of terrorism when I say that those perjurers must and will be tried and sentenced for their crimes?

And now, fellow Europeans (and fellow Frenchmen, of course), perhaps you will begin to understand our attitude, which does not correspond to the image that the French government has given of us; the government has monopolized free speech and it has never allowed us to answer any of its accusations. We have told you, time and time again, that nearly every article of the Constitution drawn up by the present government has been violated by the government. You did not believe us before: you did not even listen to us. Well, now that you see how much de Gaulle respects the sovereignty of individual nations, which he has called the only obstacle to a united Europe, you can understand that his words bear no relation to his acts. If he violates this sacred sovereignty, what makes you believe that he will not also violate the sacred Constitution? Everything has been violated: first the promises, then the printed words, and now the frontiers.

Perhaps people will begin to realize now that there is no longer such a thing as *habeas corpus* in France, that any man can be kept in prison for two weeks without trial, and that the Gaullist 'law' places no restrictions on the conditions or the duration of interrogations or on the quantity of sleep or food or anything else that a prisoner is allowed. The only thing guaranteed is that the prisoner will not be allowed to see a lawyer. The Senate has recently been able to establish certain judicial controls; but even so it is not the police who have to hand over the prisoner to the judges, but the judges who have to go and visit the police. I think it will be a bit harder now to accuse us of being 'terrorists' (I have already been accused of that in 1942, 1943 and 1944) and to call de Gaulle the defender of Republic legitimacy.

All this has taken place because power has gone to the head of the man we thought was so calm and collected. It has also taken place because Colonel Argoud was brave to the point of rashness, so that he fell into the hands of the *barbouzes*. I do not know what charges they will bring against Argoud; but I suppose they will accuse him of being a murderer, of being a Fascist, and of stealing the towers of Notre Dame besides. There are enough gangsters, forgers, *agents provocateurs* and narks at work to get him on some charge.

I too, if I remember correctly, am wanted for 'plotting against the security of the state'. At the beginning, I was accused of 'questioning the authority of the state', and I don't quite know what else besides. When I think of the present miners' strike, when I think how for the first time in the social history of France the engineers have declared their solidarity with the miners and have contributed two days' pay to the miners' cause, I wonder what 'questioning the authority of the state' means by now. The state's authority has never been so questioned as it is today.

Twenty years ago I risked my life every day for de Gaulle's cause; he has turned against that cause, but I hope that today free men will hear what I have to say about Colonel Argoud. I have met him on many different occasions, although not in the places mentioned by the press. I did indeed meet him in Munich. The only argument I ever had with him was over his safety. Recently, General de Gaulle has shaken so many bloodstained hands that he ought to be the last man to call Argoud an outlaw. The police will obviously have no trouble finding some witnesses to swear that Argoud gave them orders to assassinate so-and-so; accusations of this nature can always be produced at the right moment. There are also always enough radios around to repeat whatever they are told, ignoring the fact that such information is meant to be kept secret until a trial, although, of course, the government considers itself above such restrictions.

Colonel Argoud is a hot-blooded and determined man. His two great loves are France and the French Army. His only hobbies, which he had to give up, were horseback riding and mountain climbing. I know him well. He lives only for his cause, for our cause. He is for the principle of a united Europe and despises cowardliness and half-heartedness. He is a strict man, particularly for himself; but he is the opposite of a *desperado*. He believes in the greatness of his country and does not want revenge, but reconciliation. Of course he believes that those who are responsible for the misfortunes which have overtaken our country and for the surrender which came after such great hopes will have to be punished. But this will be done in a just and equitable fashion, without any painful delays and without any miscarriages of justice.

I wrote most of the CNR manifesto which was issued recently; but Colonel Argoud, along with all the members of the CNR, actively participated in the composition of this manifesto which was not published because it was banned. People prefer to believe what the press and the police say about us; they would rather listen to their accusations than to our defence.

It is my sad duty to speak up for Colonel Argoud who is now far away. I ask Churchill, Macmillan, de Gasperi and Adenauer, whether this Europe, overrun with French secret policemen, was the Europe which we hoped to build when de Gaulle was so hostile to our dreams of unity.

I have set down what I know and what I want to happen. Germany has just been the stage and the victim of a tragedy: I hope and I believe that you will not keep silent and that something will be done.

Even if this appeal had reached its destination, it would have fallen on deaf ears. Men in power do not usually want to be reminded about the rights of the people. They do not like to remember what they prefer to forget. They choose the present and the future rather than the past, although their concept of the future may be reactionary; you could certainly not accuse them of taking a gamble, let alone a gamble on defeated men. I was once told this point-blank by an Anglo-Saxon diplomat; but I won't further his career by giving his name.

I was staying in a very pleasant hotel near a lake in upper Bavaria, not far from one of those mad Wagnerian castles built by Ludwig II, and working very hard on the first draft of this book and of the one which is to follow. In this way, I grew to know the curious breed of people called literary agents. To be honest, I was writing not because I was driven by an inner necessity to express my feelings, but because I desperately needed some money for our cause. This just shows how badly we needed the famous loot we were supposed to possess. Writing a book of memoirs to earn a little money is a strange occupation. I knew no German, except for the few words I had learned while I was a prisoner of war; in those days, I used to be the camp interpreter, helping myself along with all sorts of comic gestures. The inhabitants of the little village where I lived were busy preparing for *Mardi Gras* and they did not seem particularly interested in me. I have always had a rather reassuring appearance: someone once said that I looked like a shy little bourgeois who hates the cold.

Yet because we were French, we were immediately told about the capture of Colonel Argoud. Events began to catch up with my writing. One day, we realized that the Bavarian police was beginning to suspect us. I was not surprised; after all, there was something odd about two Frenchmen spending a winter holiday in a tiny village without bringing any skis and without ever looking for distractions, without knowing anything about the country or its language, and apparently owning only a typewriter and reams of paper.

We left this particular village and went to another one in the same district. It would have been safer to leave Bavaria altogether after the uproar over Argoud's disappearance; but we could not move a great distance away because we had neither the time nor the money. We realized that the police might pay us a visit any day, so I decided to gamble on all or nothing and to send a letter to Dr Adenauer. I wrote him the following letter:

My dear Chancellor Adenauer,

I realize after listening to the radio that the kidnapping of Colonel Argoud has led to all sorts of enquiries and searches. These searches are being directed against those who belong to what the present French government calls the OAS, an active and subversive organization.

I feel that it is my duty to tell you that the OAS existed in Algeria when the French Army received the order to liquidate the partisans of French Algeria by any means, including that of reaching an agreement with the Algerian rebels.

I never went to Algeria during this time as I had arbitrarily been forbidden to go there by my government. As long as I could, I fought against the French government's policy, in my capacity as a member of the National Assembly, and as a free-lance writer. When this was no longer possible, I created the National Council of the Resistance. There were several of de Gaulle's ex-collaborators in this Council; these men had broken off with de Gaulle only because of the general's present policies.

The National Council of the Resistance, which the French government prefers to call by initials that have quite unjustly become dishonourable, has never given orders to execute anybody.

The present French government continues to call the clandestine opposition – it is clandestine because we can have no other possible opposition – the OAS, although that organization no longer exists. A man like yourself, who has also suffered from tyranny, will understand.

Excesses may have been committed by the OAS and other crimes have been falsely attributed to the OAS after the French government deliberately forced the French Algerians to accept the surrender of

Algeria. The government has exploited isolated individual acts which could not be prevented because communications were made so difficult and so slow. No one seems surprised when they hear that 'uncontrolled groups' have killed thousands of people in Algeria since independence.

Millions of East German refugees have poured into Germany; but at least in their case they could not blame their own government for their misfortunes. But when a million European and Moslem Frenchmen were suddenly deported from one side of the Mediterranean to the other, in spite of many oaths to the contrary, it was inevitable that they would commit certain acts of despair.

I may be a hunted man and I will perhaps be caught; but that will not prevent my saying that Colonel Argoud was abducted in disgraceful circumstances. If anything happens to me, things will not improve in France; in fact they may get worse.

I have not suddenly gone mad. At my age, men prefer meditation to wild adventures. Vulgar ambition did not dictate my conduct; I have had all the worldly honours this life has to offer. I could not act otherwise, and I still cannot act otherwise.

My dear Konrad Adenauer, you, de Gasperi, Spaak, myself and many others once tried to build Europe. The treaty of Franco-German reconciliation would have been signed more than ten years ago if General de Gaulle had not been violently opposed to such a measure. You know this and you cannot have forgotten it.

Not very long ago, a German court was asked to come to an impartial decision concerning the funds which had belonged to the Russian social democrats and which had been deposited in Germany. This took place during the reign of William II, and Lenin won the case.

Men of my sort have never been treated by European countries in this way; it goes against the rights of the public, against precedent and Germany's relations with France. Every country in the European Economic Community – which, as you know better than the rest, I tried harder than anyone to make a defence community too – has in the past considered it an honourable action to give shelter to outlaws who were not all like the man you knew so well in the days when we met often.

Therefore, Mr Chancellor, I have the honour to draw your attention to the fact that it might be better not to chase the oldest advocate of an entente between France and Germany like a hunted animal. The German Federal Government naturally wishes to sign a treaty of reconciliation with the man who once refused to do such a thing. A treaty of reconciliation is worth something and I would be the last, as you know, to disapprove of such a project, whoever may sign it in France's name.

Should you feel like looking up my past reputation, I hope you will allow me to remind you of the transcripts of the Berlin Conference on Germany, where I spoke in the name of the whole West. In this document you will find much to interest the respected leader of the Federal Republic as well as any regular court, to which these papers might be submitted.

I, Mr Chancellor, have feelings that have not altered since we met; I remain, in hiding as in power, a man who wishes to stay your friend,

Georges Bidault

8 March 1963

I soon got my reply. Two days later, the police came for me. At dawn, the town was encircled by dozens of armed men with dogs; the operation was obviously important as well as dangerous. They made so much noise that, of course, by the time they arrived, I was ready and waiting for them. I gave them the only weapon in my possession, a small penknife which I still keep as a souvenir. Later, some higher officials came to see me. I was guarded against any potential abduction by a whole army of night watchmen, dogs and searchlights; I must say they certainly went to a lot of trouble for me and they were extremely polite. But they obviously found my presence a great nuisance, as they had to watch over my safety and at the same time protect the German people from me. They set conditions for me which were decent, but extremely strict; these they obviously meant to enforce. I soon decided under these conditions that I would be happier to go to Timbuctoo, and I finally went even farther.

My letter to Chancellor Adenauer was returned with the reply that the Chancellor had refused to read it. The letter was sealed; but it had obviously been opened and read, and I am absolutely certain that it hastened the events which led to my discovery.

I left Germany by 'the frontier of my choice', and while I changed planes in Zurich I was recognized. The news immediately leaked out and I was pursued by hordes of journalists. Journalists are a very strange lot; they invoke professional secrecy to protect murderers or spies; they publish the letters of mad killers; they publish detailed reports about the activity of any idiot, and they especially love to hound political refugees to death. Sometimes, it is very hard to tell police informers from journalists; in any case, the police came for me two days after I reached Portugal, sick with 'flu. I was not surprised, for I had received the usual warning signals.

I may scandalize anti-colonialists and the few sincere democrats who are left, when I admit that I do not bear Portugal a grudge for refusing me shelter and freedom of speech. It would have been illogical to expect an authoritarian government to tolerate the presence of a man who opposed the established government of another country. The Portuguese government's principles were totally incompatible with my presence in the country, once I had been identified and once it knew my intentions. Besides, Portugal was fighting a difficult battle over its foreign territories and it was being slandered by nearly everyone: it could not afford to antagonize the last few countries which were not yet openly hostile and baying at its heels. It could not risk losing whatever lukewarm support it got in the United Nations where it was constantly attacked by a collection of irresponsible nations, which work on the cowardice and the complicity of other countries to give Portugal the reputation of being the only threat to peace left on the planet.

In Lisbon, I asked permission to go to the United States. I knew many people there, all the ex-Presidents and several ministers. I had friends there, or at least people I had thought were friends. I sent a letter to the American ambassador in Lisbon and got the following reply:

Dear Sir,

I received the letter which you sent yesterday, and I immediately sent on your request for permission to enter the United States to the competent authorities in Washington.

I have now got a reply from Washington, and I regret to inform you that they have decided to reject your application for an entry visa to the United States, on the basis of Section 212 (a) (28) F of the *Immigration and Nationality Act of 1952*. In view of this, the Embassy will not be able to grant your request for a visa.

The ambassador did not bother to explain the content of Section 212(a) (28)F of the *Immigration and Nationality Act*. He just hoped that I would go and look somewhere else, as did the other countries which were afraid I might cause them complications.

In my letter to the American ambassador to Lisbon I had enclosed a letter addressed to an ex-ambassador to France whom I had known very well and who called me by my first name; I had even placed a very fine government building at his disposal. But he never answered my letter.

I never received an answer from him; but I prefer it that way. I would rather not owe anything to anyone. I will always like the American people, in spite of the fact that I did not find a single man from that country to help me when I needed it, or to remember past friendships. But the very fact that I do not owe the Americans any gratitude makes my friendship for the American people disinterested, especially now that it has had to survive the despicable behaviour of several Americans who were afraid to compromise themselves for me.

Yet I ought perhaps to remind my readers that the United States agreed to follow certain rules like the rest of the world and that they do not follow them any more than the rest of the world. The International Declaration of the Rights of Man (which was signed by the United States and by France) contains the following articles:

Article 13. (1) Everyone has the right to freedom of movement and residence within the borders of each state.

(2) Everyone has the right to leave any country, including his own, and to return to his country.

Article 14. (1) Everyone has the right to seek and enjoy in other countries asylum from persecution.

(2) This right may not be invoked in the case of prosecutions genuinely arising from non-political crimes or from acts contrary to the purposes and principles of the United Nations.

Article 19. Everyone has the right to freedom of opinion and expression; this right includes freedom to hold opinions without interference and to seek, receive and impart information and ideas through any media and regardless of frontiers.

All this is just another piece of paper that the US has torn up, like many other states but with less excuse. I have no idea what the connection is between this Declaration, which in international law takes precedence over any country's internal laws, and the obscure conditions the American ambassador quoted at me. But because it should be known what they have made of the rights of man, I would like to point out that the US President was called Kennedy, and that his attorney general bore the same name. The first died courageously, as he had lived. The second seems to have forgotten that law is above success.

I hold no grudge against Portugal for acting in its own interest and according to its own principles. My two previous expulsions were in contravention of the officially proclaimed principles of the states that kept me off their soil, and besides that, there were people involved for whom memories and obligations had counted for nothing. Salazar did not owe me anything. Even so, it was in his country that I met with the greatest courtesy from officials who had to carry out an unpleasant duty.

Brazil

It was from Lisbon that I flew to Brazil with my companion in misfortune and adventure. Certain pointers indicated that the régime that is still in power in France was not sorry to have me on the other side of the world. De Gaulle had not then decided on his prima donna tour of South America. The aircraft made a detour around Senegal, a precaution that I thought unnecessary at that time. Subsequent experience taught me otherwise. Léopold Senghor has come a long way since the days when he and I were friends and he voted for me in the elections for President of the French Republic.

I arrived during the southern hemisphere's autumn, though on the Tropic of Capricorn it is hard for a man from a country where snow falls to tell one season from another. From the top of Corvocado, at the feet of the great Christ with outstretched arms, I looked for the first time over the mountains, the forests, the ocean dotted with islands and the immense metropolis that make up the astonishing beauty of Rio de Janeiro. I had never been there before, though successive Brazilian ambassadors to Paris had extended invitations. And now here I was, uninvited.

This did not prevent my reception being dignified and considerate. I had expected some difficulty in entering the country, but justice and gratitude compel me to say that once the door was open, conditions and controls were kept to a minimum. I was not hounded about, my movements were not restricted, and nobody pestered me. The conditions fixed when I entered the country were interpreted in the most liberal way. If I acted with discretion, I might do as I wished. President Goulart's government welcomed me and left me in peace, in spite of the fact that I could hardly be said to have much in common with its political viewpoint. After the fall of the régime on 31 March/1 April, I feel obliged to speak

out for a man who now, in his turn, is an exile. However marked
the difference between his fate and mine, I can only feel towards
him as he acted towards me.

After a few days in Rio, we sought asylum in one of those
secluded places 'where one is free to be a man of honour'. My
terms of entry forbade a long stay in Rio, and it was not advisable
in any case. There was a French embassy there, though somewhat
inactive since the business of the 'Lobster War'.*

We let ourselves be persuaded to act on what at the time seemed
to be a stroke of good luck. I say we, because as before my misfortunes and everything else that happened to me were shared by
Guy Ribeaud, the companion whom hope and exile had given me.
At the time of writing, we have been inseparable for over two
years. I owe him almost everything, from ordinary everyday
assistance to the most outspoken advice on questions of great
importance. Between two companions on a long and arduous
journey, the most profound contact is also the most difficult to put
into words. But it is my duty to state that my comrade has never
failed me in lucid judgement, loyalty in combat, and in that
superior form of loyalty that consists of always being frank. He has
shown me friendship and uncompromising allegiance. I could not
have been more fortunate than to meet this man whose arm and
heart have never failed me. As for spirit, he has more than enough
to sell to those who believe it can be bought. I thank him for his
support, so longstanding and so constant.

So we left 'for the interior' as they say in Brazil, for Brasilia
notwithstanding, Brazil is essentially its Atlantic seaboard. With
time, and with the accelerating race to develop the virgin territories
of the world, the Atlantic regions of Brazil have expanded inland,
but the interior is still a pioneers' land. We wanted to go there,
although communications with Europe would become even more
difficult, because we had been told about a place which sounded
ideal for us.

We were told that if we went to the distant capital of Minas
Geraes, the second largest state in Brazil after Sao Paulo, we would
find a businessman there whose hobby was giving shelter on his
estate to politicians in exile. The gold and diamond prospectors

* A fishing dispute between Brazil and France early in 1963. It was finally
taken to the Arbitration Court at The Hague, but not before both France and
Brazil had sent warships into the disputed area.—*Translator*.

who worked on his lands were all friends of his and would defend us if necessary. We were also told that this businessman had been the host of Bernanos, although when I had arranged for Bernanos and his family to be repatriated I had not heard of this estate. Yet I was tempted to look for the place where Bernanos had perhaps lived out his time of exile. Several Presidents of Latin American countries were also supposed to have gone and lived there after fleeing from their own countries. And so, with the encouragement of the Brazilian authorities and of friends who assured us that it would be the ideal place for two French political refugees, we decided to try.

Diamantina is a delightful town; it is famous but unpretentious; world affairs seem very remote there, although books and newspapers are available. You have to adapt yourself to the quiet rhythm of life there, which comes as a shock to outsiders. We left for that city accompanied by some officers who were to escort us. The road was sometimes excellent, sometimes terrifyingly bad. After a rather hazardous journey, we reached the old city at nightfall. Diamantina had once been the centre of all Portugal's gold and diamond trade, and the Portuguese crown had depended on its wealth.

At nightfall, we got to a hotel built by Niemeyer, the architect who built Brasilia with Costa. This hotel was startling amongst those quiet plateaux at an hour when the city was falling asleep. We got a warm welcome there; but, at first, everyone seemed extremely surprised to see us. It turned out that the *fazenda* of the generous businessman was not there and that no one had announced our arrival. Those who had escorted us on the journey were kind enough to worry about us and to try and arrange something. They made investigations and discovered that neither the businessman nor his estate existed. We had travelled six hundred miles away from Rio, only to come to the end of the night and to find nothing there but wind on the lonely plateau.

Our escorts were most embarrassed by this turn of events, and they decided to go and find the Mayor of Diamantina. They left us in his care, and from that moment we began to discover what the Brazilians are really like. We might well have been disillusioned with the people of that country after our latest adventure, which had happened because of a Brazilian's naïve boast. But the mayor welcomed us into his house like two old friends, although he had never seen us before and had not been expecting us. During a whole week he looked after us, as though he had nothing else to do and invited us for dinner at his house or in the best *churrascarias* of the town. We were officially received at the town hall, in that simple and dignified manner which I had almost forgotten. I met the archbishop of the province; his powerful personality exerts a strong influence over all Brazil, and I hear that, at the Vatican councils, he makes no concessions to the 'wind of history'. He probably believes – as I once put it in a speech I made at Sao Paulo to the pupils of a large religious school – that the Church should not try to adapt itself to its century, but that the century should try to adapt itself to the Church.

We finally left Diamantina by plane, thanks to the mayor's help, and went back to the capital of one of the Brazilian states, Belo Horizonte, and finally back to the Atlantic coastline. But I wish I could describe in detail the friendliness which I found wherever I went, from Minas to Rio de Janeiro, and from Rio to Sao Paulo. I cannot put everything down here, although I am pretty sure that the Frenchmen who keep an eye on me already know everything about me. But I do realize better than even those Brazilians who love France, what has happened to our country, so I prefer not to give any names. I will speak about all of them some day and describe in greater detail the incredible kindness of the Brazilians, who behaved so well towards a political refugee with a reputation blackened by the newspapers and by the police and with a forgotten role in the Resistance against Hitler and in the top posts of the French government. All I can say is that I have felt highly honoured by my welcome everywhere.

There was one newspaper in Brazil which I read with pleasure; it was so intelligent, so well informed and fair that it deserves a place on the list of the dozen or so newspapers which ought to be read. If things get any worse, we will soon be able to count the newspapers which deserve to be read on the fingers of one hand. But this particular paper, *O Estado de Sao Paulo*, was excellent, and, although I disagreed with much of what it said, particularly with their French correspondent's opinions on Algeria, I have never lost my admiration for its objectivity. For this reason, I agreed to write a few articles on political philosophy for *Estado*; the director of this paper was immediately criticized for printing my articles, but he did not allow this to worry him for a moment.

During the political events of March 1964, which led to the overthrow of the Left-Wing President Joao Goulart, a press campaign was started against me, although I had long been left in peace. Joao Doria, a deputy from Bahia who called himself a Christian Democrat, made a speech in the Chamber against me, asking the Minister of Justice (who also acts as Minister of the Interior) to expel me from Brazil. Doria claimed that my presence 'constituted an act of aggression against France, where he has been condemned to death for an attempt to assassinate the President of the French Republic, and he provides a stimulus here for the savage terrorist activities which started only after his arrival'. This well-informed man proceeded to denounce my 'close connections with the avowed enemies of Brazil', and enquired about my sources of income.

Apart from his notorious talents for making erudite speeches, this man was particularly well known for being extremely fat. Today, he is no longer a deputy; his mandate was ended and he was sent off into exile when the government changed. I respect the rights of exile, even for men so utterly unworthy of any rights; therefore I do not hope that the country where he found shelter – Yugoslavia, I think, and before that, France – questions his sources of income or his reputation, which was never of the best.

A Communist newspaper, which did not even bother to disguise its affiliation with the CP, published a long editorial about me containing several columns of headlines. I think I ought to quote from that article just to prove that public opinion is being manipulated. Some maestros in the journalistic world use the pen like a musical instrument to produce certain definite sounds. The so-called liberal world is being brain-washed; but it does not realize this and actually spends its whole time praising the objectivity and the open-mindedness of those who are fooling and corrupting the public:

It has been announced that the authorities are looking for a French terrorist in Mexico . . . who is there for the purpose of trying to assassinate General de Gaulle.

What interests us about this piece of information is that the terrorist left from Brazil. We did not know that Brazil was being used as a headquarters for the OAS, which is notorious for its plastic bombs and the many atrocities it has committed. But we have given shelter to Georges Bidault (see photograph), self-admitted leader of French terrorism. Georges Bidault occasionally writes articles for the newspaper *O Estado de Sao Paulo*, because he is the friend and guest of Julio de Mesquita, owner of that newspaper. We begin to understand. Bidault is also protected by the right-wing adventurer, Adhemar de Barros. He has been identified as the author of the plan for a 'Defence of Democracy', which was attributed to Adhemar de Barros. This plan divided the capital of our state into 'hostile districts' and appointed military instructors and even chaplains for each of them. In his spare time M. Bidault may well still be trying to find a way to kill General de Gaulle. Perhaps he is waiting for the French President to come on his announced visit to Brazil.

Considering what we know about the man, the deportation of Georges Bidault would only be a security measure. Our country is known for its hospitality and it has never hesitated to receive refugees of every political shade. We must continue to do this because it provides a guarantee for our own democratic freedoms; but when one of our guests behaves like Georges Bidault, the logical solution is to deport him. . . . This is perfectly in keeping with our democratic traditions.

Probably the finest example of loyalty, honesty and intelligence was an attack on me printed the same week in a newspaper called *Brasil Urgente*. This Sao Paulo newspaper, which calls itself Christian progressive, was started by a Dominican. I let the reader judge the following extract:

We have a man here in Brazil who is wanted by the French police. His name is Georges Bidault. He has been sentenced to death in France and declared responsible for crimes committed by a terrorist organization which served as model to the one we presently have in Brazil.

As far as his crimes are concerned, Bidault is absolutely unforgiveable. Nothing can be said in his defence. Like other Fascists, he defended the colonialist policy which reduced Algeria to slavery. Not only that, but he ordered his Hitlerian hordes to kill Algerians in Paris who were fighting for national liberation and who were defending human dignity. But Bidault is responsible for far greater crimes than that.

He is the intellectual author of the terrorist group to which he belonged and still belongs; it has committed the worst crimes in the history of France. Betrayals, shooting of patriots, murder of women and children, derailing of trains, sabotage of planes and boats. Torture of political prisoners. . . .

Readers who followed the terrible events in France will remember that, every single day, the newspapers were full of crimes committed by Bidault's gangsters. At times their crimes were so hideous and perverted that they almost rivalled the Nazis for cruelty.

The man who has been sentenced now lives in Brazil and has made it

R.—12

his 'fatherland in exile'. The whole world has closed its doors on this criminal, but he has found shelter with us. He does not deserve this shelter because – and all the independent newspapers of Brazil have confirmed this – he has become involved in Brazilian politics.

He has helped subversion on the Right. He has drawn up plans for local Fascists. He has created a secret organization of terrorist guerrillas. . . .

The Federal government must expel this intruder. We must get rid of our unworthy guest. Let Bidault go and ask Salazar for protection, or let him go and keep Franco company, or let him go to the Devil! But he should be sent away from the country which he has not respected.

This decision is particularly important and urgent at the present time, when Brazil is developing closer ties with France, and now that our country is full of admiration for de Gaulle's policy of French and European independence from the bondage of the American dollar.

I have quoted this ridiculous attack because I want to point out a few things: (1) these attacks came at the same time, and they were almost identical; (2) they contained the same lies and the same demands to have me prosecuted; (3) a so-called Christian-Democratic newspaper and deputy were following the Communist line except that their attacks were even filthier than the Communist ones; (4) this campaign against me in Brazil was started at exactly the same time as the one that was launched in France by the well-paid journalists who serve the régime although they have neither talent nor scruples.

This last attack is a striking proof – it is unfortunately not the only one I have had – that a certain form of 'Christian Progressivism' is at the service of Communism, and that it does not hesitate to lie and to slander in the stupidest fashion possible.

When I was made the victim of this scurrilous attack in *Brasil Urgente* (at a very dangerous time for me), someone came to my defence and refused to keep a cautious silence. I had appealed to Cardinal Motta, who was then archbishop of Sao Paulo, but I got no reply from him. On the other hand, Professor Paulo Duarte, who had once been an exile like myself, wrote from Toledo to defend me in a letter to one of the directors of *Brasil Urgente*, whom he knew to be honest. Professor Duarte is a Socialist and an atheist; we disagree on some vital subjects and on a horde of minor ones. Yet he did not feel forced to keep silent just because he happened to have more in common with those who attacked me than with me. I will not quote his letter, as it is too flattering, but at least I found a courageous and friendly man where I had not expected to find one. As for the other door on which I had knocked, there was no answer.

So far, this incident has had no unpleasant repercussions. But when I heard about the celebration of the twentieth anniversary of the Liberation recently, I felt very strongly that my position was vindicated and that the condemnations which I have made in this book were fully justified. I am waiting calmly for the present régime in France to collapse, as I know it will.

A great actor has been touring around a world he used to ignore, looking for applause at the end of his career, but I know that the curtain is about to fall. It will put an end to the dramatics which all began because he can never forget a grudge.

People may flock to him and cheer his performance but I see my country in bondage, and I know the work which will have to be done there sooner or later, the changes that will have to be made. And I repeat what I said at the very beginning of this book concerning the spirit of the Resistance.

But before I leave this great country which has given me shelter when I was an outlaw, I thank Brazil and its generous inhabitants, and I salute the flag which flies over the country where I lived in exile, and whose colours symbolize that country: green for its forests, gold for its sun and blue for its sky.

Appendices

I

Self-Determination

Self-determination is the fashionable slogan of today. Everyone talks about it as though it were a noble concept which had just been discovered but which was now obvious. In fact, it is merely another version of an old idea which evolved during the nineteenth century: the right of countries to self-rule. For one hundred and fifty years, this right was ardently debated. The French Revolution, which began by helping to liberate other countries but soon tried to annex the liberated countries, the Revolutions of 1830 and 1848, and one of Wilson's Fourteen Points, all represented efforts to establish the right of nations to choose their own form of government. At least this notion had one advantage over the one of today; it stated more or less explicitly that only those countries which already possessed a national conscience had the right to be independent.

If you look at the world today, you will soon see that the idea of self-determination, which most people think of as very simple, is in fact extremely vague. It is also arbitrarily applied; some people are given it although they have not asked for it while others demand it and are refused. A few men from various countries insist that certain territories must have self-determination and then refuse it to others which have a similar if not a better claim to independence. We live in an age of hypocrisy equal to if not worse than preceding ones, using vague and ambiguous terms to mask extremely precise designs.

The terms nation, people, state and even territory are employed at random as though they were interchangeable. Anyone who is not a complete fool will realize that independence is meaningless in countries like Oubagui-Chari or Nyasaland, as they used to be called, or in British Guiana. We have reached the point where nationalism is condemned if it applies to nations that have existed for thousands of years while territories that are not and never have been nations are encouraged to be as nationalistic as they please

The so-called Left Wing rants against nationalism in Europe and at the same time waves the flag of nationalism over every nomadic tent and every patch of coconut palm.

Christian progressives have tried not only to 'renovate' the Church but also to transform it into something more pleasing to modern taste. Perhaps I ought to remind them that the Church has always looked upon the proliferation of states as a threat to Christianity. For this reason, the Catholic Church has consistently refused to approve of new states created exclusively in the interest of nationalism. It disapproved in cases like those of Italy and Germany, where nationalism was responsible for the fusion of states which had previously had a separate existence. It also disapproved in cases like that of Austro-Hungary, where nationalism led to the break-up of one large state into many smaller ones. The Church has always felt so strongly on this subject that the Pope never gave his support to the Polish uprisings against Czarist Russia even though Roman Catholics were being persecuted by members of the Orthodox faith.

The Vatican has always been reluctant to endorse any attack on the established order whether in the name of Revolution or Nationalism, even when the established order was of questionable merit. From a historical point of view this attitude may be debatable; but it is sound as dogma. Only the vainest and most ignorant can go on maintaining that the multiplication of new countries at the United Nations will automatically usher in a new era of peace, equality and dignity.

In fact, anyone who keeps his eyes open must admit that countries are given their independence not for altruistic reasons but because of interests that have nothing to do with a set of principles based on fairness and objectivity. The policy of great powers is entirely pragmatic; they praise or attack independence according to what suits them. The fact that Algeria was given its independence but not Turkestan or Tibet has nothing to do with fairness.

There is only one state in the Soviet Union. Theoretically of course, Russia is made up of many states. The Ukraine and White Russia are even represented at the United Nations as separate members in their own right; but everyone knows that this is strictly for show and that there is only one centralized control. The fact remains that the Russian Empire contains many different peoples and that some of them have a strong sense of national identity. The existence of these separate nations is proved by Stalin's appointment as Commissar of Nationalities. Of course, his task was to turn these separate nationalities into one homogeneous Russian state made up of true Communists; but it certainly shows that the problem existed and that the Bolsheviks recognized this.

The Russian Empire is the largest in the world; yet it is set on furthering the principle of self-determination everywhere, except at home of course. The French had been in Algeria for sixty years, with the Pope's blessing and the official approval of the United States, before the Russians took over Turkestan. And yet, although it was decreed that Algeria had to have self-rule, no one mentioned independence for Turkestan.

For the first time in history, there is such a thing as the State of Algeria. A great deal was said about Algeria's independence in 1962, but for some reason much less has been said about the results. There may be an Algerian state, but there is no Algerian nation yet. When the FLN was given power, its leader spoke of the 'Arab Nation'; in fact, Algeria is nothing but a state which rules over several nationalities and countless tribes. And the harshest colonialism of all is that which denounces other people's colonies until it can take these over.

It was UN pressure which forced the Belgian Congo to remain a single state, although that country boasts two hundred and seventy-five different tribes and can hardly be called a nation or a people. Yet Ambassador Stevenson declared without hesitation that the secession of Katanga was as unthinkable as the secession of an American state. It really is impossible to understand why people felt so strongly on this point. After all, Katanga could easily have been made Portuguese by Serpa Pinto or English by Cecil Rhodes. It so happened that Leopold II and Stanley took it over and made it Belgian; but it is no more Congolese than Rhodesian or Angolese. And how could the UN approve of Algeria's secession when it condemned Elizabethville's? Perhaps I ought not to repeat one explanation: that there was too much petrol and copper on the world market and that the best way to check Katanga's copper production was to refuse to allow Elizabethville to go independent while the best way to slow down the Sahara's oil output was to give Algeria its independence. But I really ought not to repeat this slanderous accusation; I am positive those who made it forgot what a fraternal and disinterested world we live in.

I will not accept the argument that Katanga was refused independence because this would have harmed the Congolese economy; after all, the partition of Ireland never hurt the Irish economy. And the fact that the Papuans of New Guinea were not given independence and were placed under the leadership of Sukarno in no way improved the economy of Papua. The splintering of Africa into so many small countries has certainly not furthered the economic development of that continent. This fascinating question ought to be gone into thoroughly; but it is more convenient to mouth the slogans of today. And new slogans will be found to replace the old when the present ones become too preposterous.

If Algeria could not remain French because it was five hundred miles away from Marseilles, then how can Hawaii, which is so much farther from San Francisco, become an American state? And if Algeria could not remain French because the majority of its inhabitants were Arabs or Berbers, then how could Hawaii become American when its population is nine-tenths Japanese?

The answer is obvious. The aim of self-determination is to destroy multiracial communities that group together countries from different continents; the great powers think that it is in their interest to break up such communities and to do this they invoke vague principles which they often make up for the occasion. This noble enterprise rests on the assumption that countries must be liberated from the yoke of colonialism and imperialism. But they make one exception which explains all these paradoxes: it is absolutely forbidden to touch the colonies of the anti-colonialists or to criticize the imperialism of the anti-imperialists. In France, our great Resistance hero of 18 June, helped by some 'enlightened' Frenchmen, perpetuated this myth, and the people he was supposedly liberating are paying the price today.

II

Violence

Several volumes could be written on the subject of violence, and historical documents on it would fill a library. I have no such ambition of course; but I would be satisfied if a few really honest persons read these pages and, after thinking matters over, decided that they would not let themselves be taken in by propaganda in the future.

The whole of history throughout the ages has been a succession of bloodbaths. Names like that of Attila still make us shudder although we have seen far worse atrocities during the last fifty years. Every wise and charitable man, every leader worthy of the name, has tried to limit the harm caused by violence, even when legitimately used.

The advocates of non-violence today may mean well, but they are in fact playing into the hands of people with violent aims. The concept of non-violence today is no different than it was at the time of Munich, when André Delmas said, 'Better slavery than war.' In the end, we not only had slavery but war as well, and the war was drawn out by this form of non-violence. Besides, those who wanted to make us slaves were just as harsh with us as they would have been if we had fought them to the bitter end.

The philosopher-scientist Blaise Pascal once said, 'Justice without strength is powerless; strength without justice is tyrannical . . . therefore, we must seek to combine strength and justice in such a manner that strength may be just and that justice may be strong.'

This moderate statement, although not made by a warrior, shows that Pascal had few illusions on the nature of strength and justice. But we don't have to go back as far as Pascal; the Constitution of 1793 proclaimed the right, and even at times the duty, to revolt. It was this right which we invoked during the years of the Resistance.

Some men like Clemenceau have claimed that true revolutionaries must accept the revolution *in toto*. In other words, they cannot disown the September massacres, the drownings at Nantes, the shootings at the Place Bellecour and the Terror (no appeal, no lawyer, execution on the same day) if they accept the principle which underlies these atrocities.

The Christian faith has never made a similar assertion about the Crusades, which is significant; but then no one is interested in the Crusades any more. People are far too busy studying the French Revolution and reading even falser accounts of the Russian one.

The fact is that no historical event or series of events ought to be judged *in toto*, neither the last war, nor the Resistance, nor the Algerian tragedy. Today, the OAS, the 'ultras', the 'dissidents' or the 'subversives' are blamed for everything which happened in Algeria; biased or merely servile individuals find this attitude most convenient. According to them, one side consisted of nothing but liberals who always acted humanely and charitably, while the other side consisted entirely of brutes who spent their time murdering and looting. This is all wrong of course; everyone knows that good and evil are to be found on both sides.

Every year, on 28 May, the Communists, the Socialists, the CGT and other Left-Wing groups go to the Père-Lachaise cemetery to commemorate the execution of the *Communards*. The Commune was indeed brutally and arbitrarily suppressed, and it is an excellent thing to honour the dead. But, although speeches have been made and red banners waved over the tombs of the *Communards* for seventy-five years, not a word has ever been said about the first victims of the Commune, the four hundred and sixty hostages who were shot without trial by the *Communards*. These hostages included the Archbishop of Paris, the First President of the Law Courts, as well as many Jesuits and Dominican friars. The Jesuits and the Dominicans used to commemorate their dead as well, but they have discontinued this practice, and today, only the dead *Communards* are remembered. No one mentions the burning of the Tuileries, the Cour des Comptes and the Hôtel de Ville, nor the attempt to set fire to the Louvre. If the members of the Left Wing, including the Christian 'Progressives', accept everything which was done by the Commune, then how can they have the audacity to put on airs of virtuous indignation whenever the other side does anything which displeases them? I prefer the

VIOLENCE

complete cynicism of someone like Jean-Paul Sartre to this form of hypocrisy. At least, Sartre admits frankly that, on the good side, all things are good, while on the bad side, all things are bad. He makes no bones about putting all his heroes into one category: Carrier, Fouquier-Tinville, Robespierre, Babeuf, Blanqui, the Commune, Ferrer, Sacco and Vanzetti, Lenin, Stalin, Mao, Fidel, Ben Bella and Lumumba.

People will say that I exaggerate; but the following example proves the utter hypocrisy of those who condemn violence only when the other side practises it. On 21 October 1916, the Austrian Prime Minister, Count Stürgkh, was assassinated. He had a very small share in the responsibility for starting the war, compared to men like Francis-Joseph, William II, Berchtold and Bethmann-Hollweg. The murderer, Friedrich Adler, was the son of a political leader who, along with Engels, Kautsky and Liebknecht, had founded the German Socialist Party, and had then helped to establish Marxism in Austria. The assassin was sentenced to death but not executed; he was released in 1918, at the time of the Armistice. One might think that this ruthless act of terrorism and gratuitous violence would have disgusted Adler's companions; but not at all. Far from being disowned by the Left-Wing, Adler played a leading role in the founding of the Austrian Republic and he was later made secretary of the Socialist Internationale at Zurich. Of course, this was in 1923; in those days, innocent men were not denounced as terrorists at Zurich airport while real terrorists led a carefree existence in the same city, openly pursuing their activities.

Besides, Adler had killed a man, which seems to have made things easier for him; whereas Bastien-Thiry was shot for his part in an incident in which no one was hurt; even *France-Observateur* had to protest against the execution of a man who had neither killed nor wounded anyone.

In 1963, no less an authority than Bertrand Russell himself announced that the use of violence was sometimes justified. When *The Times* criticized the Aldermaston marchers for acts of rowdyism, Lord Russell retorted that nothing in history had ever been accomplished without some acts of violence. This is false, actually, and I would be the last person to make such an inexact and dangerous statement; but of course, Lord Russell is always right. He is Bertrand Russell, so he has to be right. As for those who were driven to rebellion by injustice and false promises, they were all criminals and their cause was criminal too. The whole of Marxist doctrine rests on the theory that everything which helps Communism is right, in other words, that the end justifies the means. How can anyone doubt that Marxists of every shade believe this axiom, when there is so much evidence both in word and in deed? But the guardians of society prefer to ignore this; they choose to court the enemy rather than fight him, and sometimes even hand over everything to him.

I have never approved of violence and I have always felt that it could only be used in very exceptional cases where it was obviously justified; as, for example, when a country was threatened with extinction, or when it had to safeguard its rights. I also want to mention the fact that General de Gaulle used to be far more lenient on the subject of violence than he is today. He once wrote:

Individual attacks on the German forces began in September, 1941. The garrison commander at Nantes, an officer at Bordeaux, two soldiers in the rue Championnet in Paris, were among the first to be killed. The enemy retaliated by shooting hundreds of hostages, by throwing thousands of patriots in gaol only to deport them later on, and by imposing heavy fines and penalties on the towns where Germans had been killed. When we heard about these acts carried out against the occupying forces by individuals at such tremendous risks to themselves, we felt a sort of sombre pride.

When Darlan was killed, de Gaulle accused the military tribunal of reaching a verdict too hastily. 'It was a kind of act of defiance in the face of circumstances. These circumstances may not have justified this tragedy, but they did explain it and, to a certain extent, excuse it.' It is also in this passage that de Gaulle makes an extremely equivocal and half-hearted criticism of terrorism. 'Of course, no individual has the right to kill outside the battlefield. Besides, Darlan was a major political figure and as such he ought to have been tried by the nation, not by a group of individuals, or by one individual. And yet, it is so easy to understand the intention. . . .'

We can see that de Gaulle chose to be non-committal on the subject of violence in many important cases, always expressing himself in very cautious terms. I will not quote from a letter which

he later wrote to Colette, who wounded Laval and Déat very
seriously, and who was pardoned by Laval; but even in the carefully written *Mémoires de Guerre*, we find sentences like, 'the
assassination of Georges Mandel, Jean Zay and Maurice Sarraut
by Darnand's militia, the *execution* of Philippe Henriot by a group
of Resistance fighters . . .'

Now I cannot pretend that my friends and I were sorry to hear
about Philippe Henriot's death; he was killed by certain individuals within the Resistance, but not on an official order from the
Resistance. Emmanuel d'Astier de La Vigerie recently claimed
that he had meant to kidnap Henriot, not to kill him, although how
he could have done this with the Gestapo, the German Army and
the French Militia at his heels is a mystery to me; besides, there
were others who admitted at the time that their intention had been
to kill Henriot. Still, if we accept the theory that they only wanted
to kidnap him, then maybe we ought to suppose that this was
exactly what Bastien-Thiry wanted to do to de Gaulle. It is no use
answering that the *barbouzes* would obviously have made this impossible when de La Vigerie was not afraid of the Gestapo. The
significant difference between these two incidents is that, in the
first case, the man they meant to kidnap got killed, whereas in the
second case, he is very much alive.

The other significant difference is that the man who was
responsible for the 'abduction' of Henriot is still alive, unlike
Bastien-Thiry, who is dead.

None of us have ever pretended that the Resistance always acted
blamelessly. I myself denied this during a speech I made at the
National Assembly when we were debating a law on amnesty. It
would be impossible to approve of everything the Resistance did
during the war, even while acknowledging that, on the whole, it
was a magnificent and courageous effort which helped us to win
victory. But it committed some excesses, and no honest man
ought to deny this.

Of those Frenchmen who, by murder or delation, had caused the
death of the resistance fighters, 10,842 were killed without due process
of law, 6,675 during the *maquis* struggles before the Liberation, the rest
afterwards, during the course of reprisal actions.

This is certainly a fair estimate and not an exaggeration. Everyone who has a sense of honour will feel sorry for those who were

not guilty among this number and even for those who were guilty but who were killed without receiving a fair trial.

I do not know how many people were killed by those who were trying to keep Algeria French. Some of the victims had committed murder, others had been torturers, and some were doubtless innocent. We must mourn for those who were innocent, without forgetting that the principles at stake were the same as those of the Resistance, as I have tried to prove in this book.

But what about torture? Legal 'experts' in the service of Communism have said a great deal on the subject of torture in Algeria, never anywhere else of course. Well, my answer to them is always the same. I only repeat what I said when Guy Mollet was Prime Minister, and anyone can look up my exact words in the *Journal Officiel*: even worthy ends cannot justify unworthy means, whatever anyone says to the contrary. Many have tried to get around the fact, including one top political leader who used to say to someone I know, 'I only use experts for torturing.' Anyway, one thing is certain: those who backed Stalin and Vishinsky ought to keep quiet on the subject of torture, at least until the day that they decide to make a long overdue admission of their own past errors.

Torture is evil even when used for good reasons; it is a barbaric practice which must not be tolerated under any circumstance. My mind is irrevocably made up on the subject. For this reason, I feel bound to repeat something a friend of mine told me, even though I swore to keep it a secret. But the situation in Algeria and everywhere else has degenerated so much, and those who are to blame have acted so irresponsibly that, after thinking it over for a long time, I decided that it was not only my right but my duty to break my promise to this friend. And if I was wrong, I want everyone to know in advance that I accept the full responsibility.

My friend was a genuine law expert, even though he never belonged to the much publicized 'Safety Committee' (which was really only out to protect its own safety). He had been in charge of many vital legal matters concerning the State, and when he went to Algeria, he had a long talk with a most distinguished and qualified person on the subject of torture. He explained to this person that some conscientious individuals were worried about the use of torture in Algeria, and were wondering whether the use of 'every method' short of death or mutilation, was justified in cases when a man refused to divulge the whereabouts of a hidden bomb which might go off at any moment.

'Well,' the Archbishop of Algiers, Mgr Duval, replied, 'the Church has never actually disowned the Inquisition.'

The other side amnestied a Vice-Minister of the Interior before trying him, just to make sure that he would not get a sentence, yet they had consistently refused a general amnesty. Their conduct has shown that it is not our side which is set on revenge but theirs.

As Lord Acton once put it, 'Power corrupts, absolute power corrupts absolutely.' How prophetic his words were! I have no desire for revenge; all I want is to see justice being done. France has known too much bloodshed, too much hatred, too many divisions and quarrels and purges. What our country needs is a great pacifier like Saint-Louis or Henri IV. We thought that we had found such a man, but how wrong we were! And yet we need a man of that calibre today more than at any other time in our history.

Curriculum Vitae of Georges Bidault

Georges Bidault, born on 5 October 1899 at Moulins (Allier), France.

Came first in the *agrégation* examination in history and geography at the Sorbonne in 1925, and received a degree from the university. Was editor-in-chief of the Christian Democratic newspaper *l'Aube* between 1934 and 1940; wrote numerous editorials for *l'Aube* and campaigned against Nazism and Fascism, for freedom of opinion and Democracy.

Was president of the 'Society of the Friends of the French Republic', known as the AARF (*Association des Amis de la République Française*).

Volunteered to go to the Front in May 1940, was taken prisoner but released in 1941.

Founder of the Resistance movement called COMBAT in 1941.

President of the National Council of the Resistance (CNR), an amalgamation of all the Home Resistance groups which recognized the authority of General de Gaulle who had fled to London in 1940.

Received General de Gaulle in the name of the CNR at the Hôtel de Ville after the liberation of Paris in August 1944.

Founder of the *Mouvement Républicain Populaire* (MRP), a Christian Democratic party.

Was Minister of Foreign Affairs under de Gaulle from September 1944 to November 1945, and under Félix Gouin from January to June 1946.

Signed the UN Charter for France on 26 June 1945. Was member of the two Constituent Assemblies (1945–6).

Head of State and President of the French provisional Government from June to November 1946.

Minister of Foreign Affairs from January 1947 to July 1948.

Was appointed head of the French Delegation at the Third General Assembly of UNESCO at Beirut in 1948.

French delegate at the European Consultative Assembly and president of the General Political Committee in August 1949.

President of the Council of Ministers from September 1949 to July 1950.

Vice-President of the Council from July 1950 to July 1951.

Vice-President of the Council and Minister of National Defence from August 1951 to February 1952.

President of the *Comité d'Action de la Résistance*, an organization of ex-Resistance Movements in 1952.

Was active president of the MRP from 1949 to 1952.

Minister of Foreign Affairs from January 1953 to June 1954.

Was the founder and president of the party called *Démocratie Chrétienne de France* in 1958.

Was the founder and president of the *Conseil National de la Résistance* in March 1962. This second CNR opposed the French government's unconstitutional policies and demanded the re-establishment of freedoms guaranteed under the Constitution; campaigned for the preservation of the integrity of the territory of the French Republic.

Wrote editorials for various newspapers and magazines until, in 1961, this was forbidden by the French government, thus violating the Declaration of the Rights of Man and the French Constitution which guarantee freedom of opinion.

Index

All organizations are listed under their initials only. Full titles are given on pages vii–viii. Conferences are listed under the place at which they were held.

Illus. refers to illustrations
GB refers to Georges Bidault

340

RESISTANCE

Duval, Mgr, 261, 333

Echo de Paris, 133

Eden, Anthony, 62, 129, 191, 196, 215; and Indo-China, 200–1; *illus.*

Ehrenburg, Ilya, 65

Eisenhower, Dwight D., xix, 42, 185; and Indo-China, 192, 193, 195–6, 197, 206; *Mandate for Change*, 193–4, 201–2

Ely, General, 204

England; and World War II, 8–9; and de Gaulle, 21; and Middle East, 97, 99, 101, 140; and France, 142; and Germany, 148–9, 175; and Algeria, 256; *1945* change of Govt., 128–9, 141; English law, 119; political refugees in, 288–95; GB in exile in, 271, 294–5; *see also* Allies, British House of Commons *and* London

Erhard, Ludwig, 109

Estado de Sao Paulo, O, 315–16, 316–17

Europe, x, 156, 158, 174, and Russia, 4; and UN, 103; and Marshall Plan, 150; split, 82; unity of, 157, 161, 164–5, 175–6, 178–9, 181, 205, 304; in *1963*, 306; Free, 149; Western, 156–7; Eastern Govts., 151, 156, 265, 266; GB in exile in, 270–2, 285–8, 294, 296–302, 306–12

'European Army', 182, 190

European Common Market, 165

European Consultative Assembly, 165

European Council, 165, *illus.*

European Customs Union, 157–8, 165

European Defence Community, 170, 179, 182, 190, 194, 204, 205; *1953* conf.; *illus.*

European Economic Community, 308

European Iron and Steel Com-

munity, 174; *see also* Schuman Plan

Evatt, Herbert Vere, 130–1

Evian agreements, 205, 222, 255, 273, 276, 298

exile, xvi–xvii, xx, 290–2, 294; GB in, *see under* Bidault, Georges

Express, L', 277–8

FLN, 216, 238, 246, 247, 249, 252, 253, 262, 263, 272; in Switzerland, 298; *1964* veterans' congress, 298

Fabien, Col., 43

Fallières, Armand, 108

Fanfani, Amintore, 158, 300

Farouk, King of Egypt, 169

Fascism, 4, 6, 88, 130, 133, 157

Faure, Edgar, 182, 204; and Morocco, 186, 187, 188, 189; head of Govt., *1955*, 214–15; and de Gaulle, 238

Favre, Jules, 206

Ferry, Jules, 251

Figuères, Léo, 192

Finland, 125, 151

Flouret, Marcel, 49, 50, 52

Fontainebleau conference, 192–3

Fouchet, Christian, 199, 273

Frachon, Benoît, 5

France; and World War II, 8–9, 14; occupied, 16–18, 22, 45; after war, 58, 64, 111; frontiers, 76–7; and Russia, 65–70, 151; and USA, 76–9; and Germany, 83–91, 143, 147–9, 156, 158–9, 166, 176, 177, 181–2, 190, 308; and UN, 92–3; and Middle East, 97–101; and Spain, 132–9; and England, 140–2; and NATO, 169–70; and Marshall Plan, 151–2, 164; and Morocco, 182–9; and Indo-China, 191–206; admission to conferences, 80, 125–6, 145–9; in *1949*, 169–73; in *19th century*, 290, 292–4; and Algeria, 209–48, 251–2, 268–9, 274, 276; on

Munich; GB TV interview in, 286;
Argoud arrested in, 301-3, 305
Munich Pact, the, 7-9, 14, 28, 155,
327
Murphy, Robert, 216-17
Murville, Couve de, 128, 130, 162,
271
Mussolini, Benito, 300

NATO, 169, 177, 185
Napoleon III, 289-90, 292, 293
Nasser, Gamal Abdul, 235, 251
nationalism, 183, 324; see also self-
determination
Navarre, General, 191
Nehru, 275
Nepal, S. Asia, 137
Neuwirth, Lucien, 218, 239
Noguès, General, 183
Normandy, 47
Normandy-Niémen, 127
Nyasaland, 323

OAS, 245, 247, 248, 249-50, 252,
263, 265, 307, 316, 328; and GB,
277-8; and CNR, 278
OCM, 38
Order-Neisse line, the, 67
Oradour, 248, 249
Oran, Algeria, 229, 235, 252
Orania, 134
Orsini, Felice, 289-90

PSU, 42
Pacific Islands, French, 247
Paget, General, 101
Palewski, General, 103
Palmerston, Lord, 289, 293
Papua, New Guinea, 326
Paris, France; 1934 shooting in,
252-3; in 1941, 14-15; occupied,
16, 17, 38-40; CNR meeting in,
26; Fabien métro station, 42-3;
uprising, 47-54; de Gaulle
enters, 54-7; Govt. set up in, 58,
59-61, 71; Churchill in, 62; 1945
parades in, 85-6; 1946 peace

conf., 124-32; 1947 conf., 150-1;
press, 64, 69; Czech. Embassy,
155; Entente Cordiale Celebra-
tions, 202; in Algerian rebellion,
240; see also Quai d'Orsay
Parodi, Alexandre, 36-7, 51, 52, 53
party political system, 170-1
Pascal, Blaise, 327
Pasha, Nokrachi, 169
Paul-Boncour, Joseph, 91-2, 241
Peel, Sir Robert, 293
Peking, China, 4, 137, 253, 257
Peron, Jaun Domingo, 93
Pétain, Marshal Henri P., 20, 22,
55, 123, 219, 243
Petsche, Maurice, 172, 179, 181
Pflimlin, Pierre, 172, 219, 277, 300;
his cabinet, 209-10, 217, 218, 226
Picasso Museum, Antibes, 167-8
Pinay, Antoine, 188
Pius XI, Pope, 134
Pius XII, Pope, 183
Pleven, René, 160, 178, 277;
his Govt., 181, 182
Poland, 68, 69, 143, 148; Polish
Govt. in London, 68; rising v.
Russia, 324
Police, French; in war, 30, 39-40;
Vichy, 22; at Paris uprising, 49;
under de Gaulle, 7, 277-8, 302-3;
see also barbouzes; secret, 284,
291; German, 302-3, 307, 309
see also Gestapo; Italian, 299-301
politicians, pressures, on, xvii-xx
Pompidou, Georges, 233, 240, 257,
273
Popular Front, 113, 188
Portugal, 136, 309-12
Potsdam conference, xii, 80, 86,
128, 141
press, the, xvii-xviii, 30, 303, 315,
316-18; distortion by, 265-6; on
Algerian independence, 264-5,
266-7, 268; in 1963, 294; see
also individual papers
Prague, Czechoslovakia, 4; Govt.,
154-5; coup, 155, 156
Prussia, 162